CONTENTS

PREFACE

April is the cruelest month.   —T. S. ELIOT

THE seeds for this book were planted in 1989, when the senior class at Swarthmore College honored me with an invitation to address it at graduation. Preparing a graduation speech is a most unenviable task. I wanted to say something that wasn't trite, that would have meaning not only for the graduating seniors but also for their parents and grandparents, and that hadn't been said a thousand times before. I wanted to say something that was an honest reflection of my somber expectations about what awaited these students in the outside world, but was not so pessimistic that it cast a pall on what should have been, after all, a moment of great joy and celebration.

As I struggled to find a way to meet these challenging objectives, I started to think about these graduating seniors the way I thought about my own children. My two daughters were only slightly younger than the students who had asked me to speak. What would I tell my children if they gave me an hour in which to offer them the most important advice I could about how to live their lives?

Thought about in these terms—as a dinner table conversation with my children—the task suddenly became more manageable. For I did have something to tell my children, something about the paradoxical, bittersweet character of freedom. My children, and the Swarthmore graduates, were living at a time and in a place in which freedom of choice about every aspect of life seemed almost lim-

9

itless—a time without parallel in the history of human society. Everything seemed possible. Young people were free to choose where to live, how to live, whom to live with, what work to do and how hard to do it, what friends to make and how committed to be to these friends, what religion to practice and how seriously to practice it, whether to have children and when to have them. They were free to make up the rules of the game of life as they went along. They were constrained in pursuing their unique goals only by their own energy and enthusiasm as individuals. What made all this freedom possible was a social structure based more and more on the model of the free market, in which individuals made their own decisions about what to buy and sell, and about how to spend their time, and the "invisible hand" of competition ensured an ever growing measure of efficiency, prosperity, and satisfaction.

What could possibly be wrong with this much freedom? Where was the bitter that went with the sweet? Where was the paradox? Answering these questions was the content of my talk, and is the subject of this book. What this book tries to show is that there can be too much freedom in life, and that too much freedom has a serious moral, social, and emotional price. There is a price for freedom—danger; a price for individualism—loneliness; a price for autonomy—vulnerability. By embracing the "freedom" of the marketplace in all aspects of our lives, we find that many of the things we value most deeply—meaningful, satisfying work; intimate, compassionate friends, family, and community; real education; significant spiritual and ethical commitment; political involvement; and even, ultimately, material well-being—are increasingly difficult to achieve. As a marketplace orientation penetrates the noneconomic domains of our lives, these domains become less and less worthwhile. This book argues that the market should be restrained, not encouraged—that the things we really value should be protected from it, not provided by it.

This is a personal book, emphasizing the features of modern life that are especially important to me and to many of the people with whom I spend most of my time. I have written as a psychologist, trained to think and ask questions about fundamental aspects of human nature. I have written as a person who is "forty-something" and who grew up with the unbridled optimism of the postwar (World

War II, that is) middle class. I have written as a person who was taught that, with hard work, discipline, and determination, it was possible to do and have everything, who was brought up believing that there could never be too much freedom. And I have written as a person who has come to see, in my own life, in the lives of my friends, and in the lives of my children and the students I teach, that none of the things I was brought up believing are quite true.

Rather than presume to be able to speak to and for the needs of people whose experience is very, very different from mine, I have written principally to people like me—to Yuppies, to Muppies (middle-aged urban professionals), and to Puppies (potential urban professionals). I have written about education because I am an educator. I have written about business because I grew up in a family that ran a small business and felt degraded by what they had to do to earn a living and worked hard so that their children could be professionals and do better. I have written about the professions—like medicine and law—because when my family's children did grow up, they discovered that the professions could be just as degrading, in just the same ways, as the businesses from which their parents had spared them. I have written about sports because I have always been a devoted sports fan, and found many of my heroes on various playing fields and in various arenas. And I have written about efforts to build a new kind of religious community that makes sense of spiritual commitments in the modern, secular, materialistic world because I myself am trying to make sense of religious commitment in the modern, secular, materialistic world.

I have written about these topics because they are central to my life, and it is most unlikely that precisely the issues that grab and trouble me will be the ones that grab and trouble others. And yet, everyone is touched by education, whether or not she worries about it. Everyone must deal with businesspeople and professionals, even if she doesn't aspire to escape from the life of the former into the life of the latter. And everyone has some religious influence lurking in her background. So I have some hope that many of the issues that are of central importance to me personally will have substantial resonance for most readers.

In addition, there are some issues I discuss that are central to my life that I know are central to everyone's. I have written about what people are, and what people value, and how they come to be what they are and value what they value. I have written about love, about friendship, and about family. I have written about democratic political culture. Everyone cares, or should care, about these matters.

I have both institutions and individuals to thank for the support, enthusiasm, and critical advice they have given me as my ideas made their way from a commencement address into a book. Swarthmore College has always been a place where ideas matter and where faculty are encouraged to escape the bounds of their disciplinary training both in their research and in their teaching. I have taken extraordinary advantage of this flexibility—talking, teaching, and writing with colleagues in several different disciplines. I have learned much more from my fellow faculty than they know. And my colleagues within the Psychology Department are also to be thanked for tolerating—even encouraging—my forays into other disciplines though it sometimes strained our own curriculum a little, making our departmental course offerings look a bit peculiar. In addition, a Brand Blanshard Faculty Fellowship that supported a sabbatical leave is what made the first draft of this book possible.

Among individuals, both colleagues and friends, Jeff Bell, Joe Bernheim, Andrea Bierstein, John Brodsky, Karen Broitman, Rick Eldridge, Marty Fleisher, Natalie and Harold Gorvine, Eve and Ken Klothen, Hugh Lacey, Rich Schuldenfrei, Marty Seligman, and Brian Walt read parts of the manuscript with eyes that were at once critical and sympathetic. Paul Rozin read all of it—as a friend, an adviser, and an indomitable enthusiast. And I owe special thanks to Ken Sharpe, a colleague in political science. Together we designed and taught a course that became the outline for this book, and I learned a great deal from discussions with Ken and with our students about what needed to be said and how to say it.

At W.W. Norton and Company, I thank Don Lamm for agreeing to publish this book, and for fostering the (increasingly rare) commitment to publish serious books and keep them in print. And I must especially thank Don Fusting, my longtime editor, for staunchly advocating that Norton publish the book, and then for reading through several drafts and helping turn a manuscript that might have been a year-long project for readers into a proper book. Through my fifteen years working with Don Fusting, on more than a half dozen projects, he has always behaved with honor, respect, sympathy, and critical insight. It was only as a result of an early misadventure on this book with another publisher—one that exemplified in its behavior most of the problems this book is about—that I came to appreciate how rare it is for an author to be treated the way Fusting and Norton have treated me, and how lucky I am. I also want to thank Fusting's assistant, Bonnie Hall, for providing perceptive comments from the perspective of a member of a younger generation on much of the manuscript, and for helping me with many of the details that are a part of turning a manuscript into a book. Also from the publishing world, I thank my agent, Richard Pine, whose confidence in me and support and enthusiasm for the book kept me going as I encountered the slings and arrows of the outrageous book business.

Closer to home, Allie Schwartz read a substantial portion of an early draft of the book and stopped. She stopped because she couldn't bring herself to tell her father that she disagreed with a lot that he had to say. Her kind reticence forced me to realize that I was putting too much emphasis on the negative aspects of individual freedom of choice, and neglecting the domination, injustice, and sometimes arbitrary constraint that characterized ways of life governed by tradition. The final draft of the book has corrected this imbalance to some degree—enough, I hope, to suit her. Conversations with Becca Schwartz, a young woman with an extraordinary and precocious sensitivity to the dangers of a society that forces individuals to make it on their own, influenced much of my thinking. An especially significant conversation with her helped me to see what penguins and leopard seals have to teach human beings about the courage that is required and displayed by those individuals willing to risk the first, lonely steps in a profoundly new social direction. As both of my daughters educated me while I was trying to educate them, our discussions, though often heated, were full of love, kindness, mutual respect, and admiration. They provided a wonderful example that it is possible to be critically sharp and intellectually demanding without being inhumane, or inhuman. Annette Berson, Allison and Becca's aunt, read the book with the eyes of a nonacademic, made many wonderful suggestions that helped sharpen and simplify my ideas, and became my biggest fan, promoter, and cheerleader. Her enthusiasm for the book convinced me of the project's importance at many times along the way when I got discouraged. And finally, Annette's sister, Myrna Schwartz, my devoted and loving wife, helped me by being a model, every day, of how people should live their lives. In addition, Myrna twice read through drafts of the book extremely carefully and critically, and on long walks on deserted beaches showed me the holes, the contradictions, and the excesses in my arguments, and helped me to fix them. It is to these four extraordinary women—Allie, Becca, Annette, and Myrna—that this book is dedicated.

THE COSTS OF LIVING

1

THE IRON CAGE

The care for external goods should only lie on the shoulders of the saint like a light cloak, which can be thrown aside at any moment. But fate decreed that the cloak should become an iron cage. —MAX WEBER

About five years ago, I was visited by a former student (let's call him Allen), one of my favorites, who was back in town for his tenth college reunion. He came to my office looking healthy and prosperous. He was doing well at his (large, New York) law firm, and expected to make partner in another year or two. While he worked very hard, and didn't like all the clients he had to work for, his work was often interesting, and he knew that he was good at it. His wife, Nancy, was embarked on a successful career in marketing. The marriage was good. He and Nancy enjoyed the same things, liked the same people, had fun together, and rarely argued. They had more friends than they had time for. They owned a nice, though small, condo on Third Avenue in Manhattan, and a spot for their car in a garage just two blocks away. In the summer, they had a share in a rental in Southhampton, a quarter mile from one of Long Island's more beautiful beaches.

It all sounded good to me, but there was a dullness in his eyes and a weariness in his voice that made me wonder. I asked him if he and Nancy were planning on having children, and he told me how much they loved spending time with his sister's kids, and how they definitely wanted to have kids of their own. It was just that, right now, they both worked so hard, and their careers were so important, that it wasn't clear how they could manage it. And besides, if they had kids, they'd have to find a larger apartment, and before long they'd have to find schools and the money to pay huge tuitions. If not that, they'd have to move to the suburbs and take up even more time struggling with commuting. And neither his boss nor Nancy's was especially sympathetic to stories about sick kids or irresponsible baby-sitters. They worked for old-fashioned, division-of-labor types who thought that being serious about your work and your family at the same time was not possible. Having kids would transform their lives, and it just wasn't clear that they were ready to have their lives transformed. At least not now.

So I told Allen that it sounded to me as though he and Nancy both must really love their work if they were thinking seriously about not having a family, in order to preserve the lives they were currently living. And he said to me that he wouldn't use the word "love" to describe his feelings about his work. It was challenging, it was often interesting, it paid very well, and he was good at it. But he didn't love it. He wasn't sure that he was really doing anything especially worthwhile. Mostly he just helped rich people get richer or large corporations get larger. He rarely felt, at the end of a day, that he had spent his time making the world a better place, and he had thought, when he started law school, that he would sometimes get to do that. And Nancy felt pretty much the same way. Her task was to get people to want things that they didn't need and couldn't quite afford. She was very good at it, but aside from advancing her own career, she didn't see much point. So she met the daily challenges, took satisfaction from her individual successes, and didn't think too much about the big picture. It was hard to love finding tax shelters or selling bluejeans.

I said to Allen that even if he didn't love his work, at least he must love being able to live the "good life" with his friends—that his friendships must be providing a substitute for a family or for total satisfaction in work. But he said no, his relations with his friends were not that *close*. Everyone was too busy. There was just no time for casual get-togethers. He thought twice about burdening friends with his life and its problems because he knew how consumed they were with their own, and what a sacrifice it would entail for them to spend the time required to listen to him and to help him out.

Friends were mostly for having good times, not for sharing burdens. For unloading burdens, he had his psychotherapist once a week. His psychotherapist got paid to listen to him whine, so he didn't feel guilty about doing it.

When I said to Allen that at least it must be great to be living in the middle of such an exciting city, to be at the center of the world, he told me that actually, to tell the truth, the city was no bargain. The key to survival was insulation. You needed to make enough money to do the things you wanted to do without having to mix it up with the poor, the crazy, the dispossessed, or the angry. It was threatening and unpleasant to be a part of the city. It was okay to live in it, but only if you could stay apart from it. Besides, after you've done it enough times, even eating in great restaurants or going to clubs or to the theater stops being such a thrill. And anyway, he got home so late from the office most days that all he had the energy to do was get something to eat sent up, open a beer, and watch the tube.

So I told Allen that I was confused—that he didn't feel at home where he lived, he didn't feel comfortable and secure with his friends, he didn't love or respect his work, he didn't get a kick out of the things he spent his money on, when he had the time to spend his money on them. He said he wanted a family, but he was reluctant to have one, because it would force him to give up all these things that he didn't much like. What was I missing?

And he told me that I was right, but what else was there? He said he was doing all the things he thought he was supposed to do, and he was doing them well. He was succeeding. Yes, he was doing something wrong—very wrong—but what was it? What was the alternative? And how did you get there from here?

I had been thinking seriously about these questions for several years before my visit with Allen. His experience was hardly unique; I had encountered something like it in other former students and in several friends who were further along in their lives and careers than Allen was. This book attempts to explore these questions. It attempts to make sense of the growing number of people who play by the rules, do everything right, get everything they think they want, and end up profoundly dissatisfied and confused. And it attempts to sketch the kinds of changes that must be made in the lives of individuals and in society as a whole if people like Allen are to find the answers to their questions about what has gone wrong and what can be done to fix it. What I will suggest in this book is that the source of problems like Allen's lies right at the center of a feature of modern American society that most of us deeply value and respect—that it can be traced to the extraordinary opportunity and freedom provided to us by the economic marketplace.

A few years ago, I served as the moderator at a debate about the virtues and vices of the American economic system—the so-called free-market system that lies at the center of most of our lives. The debate began with a defense of the free market by an economist. He told the audience that all societies are faced with the problem of deciding how to distribute scarce resources—of deciding who gets what. There are basically two ways that a society like ours might make these decisions. We could let society as a whole decide what everyone should have in an organized, democratic fashion. Or we could let individual people decide for themselves, by making things available in a marketplace and allowing each member of society to pursue and purchase what is valuable to him or her.

Each of these systems for the allocation of goods has both virtues and drawbacks. The virtue of democratic decision making is that it gives everyone a voice. The drawback is that it is hard work. It requires education, coordination, debate, and election. Reaching democratic decisions often takes a long time. As a result, it is often extremely inefficient. And in the end, it always leaves some people (the losers in the democratic process) dissatisfied.

The virtue of the marketplace is that it takes much less work than democracy. By giving people the freedom to buy and sell what they want, it requires much less education and coordination. People don't have to be organized; elections don't have to be held. People can "vote" for what they want, as individuals, with their credit cards. There need be no dissatisfied minority, since the will of the majority is not imposed on everyone. The drawback of the marketplace is that there is no guarantee that society will produce what its people need, or that the needs of all members of society will be met. Thus a substantial amount of inequality and a fair amount of deprivation are virtually guaranteed.

Which of these systems, then, should we choose for deciding

who gets what? The position articulated by this economist was this: When the things that we are talking about are judged by society to be important—things like food, housing, education, health care, transportation, jobs—democratic decision making is worth the hard work. If society judges certain things to be important, then everyone should have them. The vagaries and inequalities of the market are unacceptable, and society must simply figure out, as a collective, how to provide for all its members. When, however, the things we are talking about are trivial—designer jeans, compact disks, deodorant soap, different types of breakfast cereal—then democratic decision making is a waste of effort. It just doesn't matter enough what color toothbrush people use for society to embark on a campaign of social coordination and decision that will result in society's "official" toothbrush color. For trivial things like this, the market is perfect. It's orderly, it's peaceful, and it's relatively effortless. And so, the economist concluded, democratic politics should be the system we use for the distribution of everything important, and economic markets should be the system we use for the distribution of everything trivial.

The choice between democratic politics and economic markets for distributing goods is not a mere abstract exercise dreamed up by intellectuals to give themselves something to do. Right now our society is engaged in a debate about this very matter, in connection with major issues like health care and education. Should we let the market govern access to health care, and live with the inequalities that result? Or should we find a way to provide universal access to health care, and live with the inefficiencies that result? Should we have a private school voucher system to engender competition in the education "market," or should we resolutely devote ourselves to making all public schools better? Proponents of a program of vouchers for private school tuition favor efficiency over equality, whereas supporters of public education favor equality over efficiency. With regard to both health care and education, the issues are complex, there are strong opinions and arguments on both sides, and the debate is likely to continue for some time. In part, the debate is over practical matters—over whether a system of universal access to health care or private school tuition vouchers can work, and over whether we can afford them. But in part the debate is also about whether, no matter what the cost, a society like ours can live with itself if health care and education are goods to which not all of our citizens have equal access.

When the economist at the debate suggested that the market should be reserved for the distribution of trivial things, I don't think he meant his position to be taken quite literally. He was an economist, after all, and surely he didn't want to relegate his discipline to an insignificant corner of the world stage. Nevertheless, he had things exactly right. For a variety of reasons, societies should not leave the distribution of important things to the market. The market system fails to ensure that important goods will be distributed in a way that is just. And even when the market system does a reasonably good job of producing and distributing goods, it does bad things to the goods that are distributed through it. And it does bad things to the people who depend on it. It costs them dearly—emotionally, ethically, socially, and even financially. Many of the best things in life—love, friendship, family, education, meaningful work, and political freedom—lose much of what makes them so good when the market gets too close to them. Showing how and why this is so is one reason for this book.

The second reason for this book is that in contrast to the idea that important goods should be kept off the market, the eighties were a time in American society in which public sentiment and government policy moved together on exactly the opposite path. The market-centered revolution, begun by President Ronald Reagan and continued with somewhat less missionary zeal by President George Bush, was to rely on the market for more and more, to privatize the provision of all kinds of goods and services, and to make the visible hand of government (democratic decision making) as insignificant as possible while making the "invisible hand" of the market as significant as possible.

At the time when I began working on this book—at the end of the "excessive eighties"—there was building a public outcry about what a decade of reliance on the market had brought. People were becoming increasingly concerned about grotesque and growing disparities between rich and poor. They were becoming outraged by the examples of unbridled greed, corruption, and fraud that they encountered almost daily on the financial pages (and often the front pages) of their newspapers. They were appalled by wealth produced in corporate boardrooms by the making of deals rather than things. They were embarrassed by rampant consumption, much of it fueled by irresponsibly easy credit. They were horrified as life imitated art and caricatures of acquisitiveness and greed like writer Tom Wolfe's novel *Bonfire of the Vanities* and filmmaker Oliver Stone's *Wall Street* were overtaken in excess by the realities they caricatured. Taken together, these social developments left some people desperately worried that the pursuit of wealth and the dedication to consumption were rapidly destroying the ethical values and moral commitments that had made the very idea of America possible and the nation great. Cries went out that ethics and morality could not be taken for granted—that explicit instruction in ethics should be part of the curriculum in business schools, medical schools, law schools—even elementary schools. Cries went out that greed and consumerism were not just immoral but socially destructive, and that unless America changed its ways, it would soon find itself economically subservient to other societies in which social and ethical commitments served to harness and control individual ambitions and channel them in productive directions.

As I worked on the book, and the eighties gave way to the nineties, the social landscape began to change. The decade of optimism and of plenty (if only for a chosen few) gave way to recession, unemployment, and poverty so widespread that it could not be ignored. Plants closed, throwing not just individual workers but whole communities into economic depression. Farms were foreclosed. Cities were so impoverished that the provision of essential services had to be dramatically curtailed. Bright, eager, and ambitious college graduates found themselves unable to get any jobs, let alone good ones. They shared unemployment lines with laid-off automobile workers, business executives, and even stockbrokers. Suddenly, many of the people who had embraced the excessive eighties with great enthusiasm found themselves worried about how they were going to be able to meet the mortgage and pay the doctor. The party was over. And because the party was over, public discussion about eroding ethics and values receded into the background. Who can worry about ethics and values when it takes every ounce of energy and attention to keep a roof over your head and food on the table?

The excessive eighties did not spring up, full-grown, all at once and out of nowhere. They marked the culmination of a process that began even before the United States as a nation was born. That process—some call it "modernity"—encouraged people, when faced with a choice between freedom and constraint, to opt for freedom; when faced with a choice between the individual and the collective, to opt for the individual; and when faced with a choice between innovation and tradition, to opt for innovation. As that process developed, the marketplace—a collection of free, independent individuals, choosing from among a wide array of competing alternatives whatever satisfied their individual interests best—became a model for the organization of social life in general.

We have all benefited in many ways from the choice of freedom, individualism, and innovation over constraint, collectivism, and tradition. The benefits are obvious. But we have all suffered as well. Our pursuit of unlimited economic (and social) freedom has paradoxically turned modern life into an iron cage. And unless we understand the nature of that iron cage and of the suffering it has produced—unless we understand what was wrong with the eighties, by paying attention to the values they threatened, undermined, or destroyed—the nineties may be with us for a long time to come.

And so I've written this book, which attempts to argue that the market should be restrained, not encouraged—that the things we really value should be protected from it, not provided by it. I have written as a person who grew up as a member of the privileged, white, middle-class. There are many people in American society who have not been a party to privilege. These people have always known what I have had to learn—that the American dream is not all that it seems, at least not for everybody. And their concerns are probably rather different from mine. While I worry about the impossibility of having everything, they worry about the difficulty of having anything. While I worry about the excessive involvement of people in the market, they worry about the market's inaccessibility. While I worry about too much freedom of choice, they worry about too little. While I worry about living a life as an isolated individual, detached from a caring community, they worry about being trapped in communities that are detached from social life as a whole. It is easy for me to imagine that people who read this book who have been left out of the American dream altogether will find themselves quite happy to trade their problems for mine. Nevertheless, I believe that the social forces that have created problems for people in my position have also created problems for people in their position, and I believe that social changes that are responsive to my problems will be responsive to theirs as well.

And what I will suggest in this book about all these social forces and the problems they create was powerfully put by historian R. H. Tawney some years ago:

> The burden of our civilization is not merely, as many suppose, that the product of industry is ill-distributed, or its conduct tyrannical, or its operation interrupted by embittered disagreements. It is that industry itself has come to hold a position of exclusive predominance among human interests, which no single interest, and least of all the provision of the material means of existence, is fit to occupy.

2

BUSINESS IS BUSINESS

This American system of ours, call it Americanism, call it capitalism, call it what you will, gives each and every one of us a great opportunity if we only seize it with both hands and make the most of it.

—AL CAPONE

I have this recurring fantasy. I go into a store that specializes in audio equipment to buy a new stereo system for my home. I want a good and relatively complete system: turntable, tuner, amplifier, tape player, CD player, and speakers. I've done my homework. I've read *Consumer Reports,* and I know what makes and models it recommends and what prices it regards as reasonable. So I go into the store with the magazine under my arm—and I'm blown away. I see displayed before me the most bewildering array of stuff I've ever encountered. There are dozens of models of every type of component, each with features that I can't begin to comprehend. The prices vary wildly, so I could spend anywhere from $1,000 to $10,000 before I'm through. And, of course, none of the specific models mentioned in the magazine are there.

I walk through the store, trying to look knowledgeable and confident, displaying my magazine prominently in order to let the salespeople know that I'm no sucker. I refuse several offers of assistance, acting as though I know what I want and how to find it. But it's hopeless. As I glance at price tags, push some buttons, and scrutinize manufacturers' specs, it becomes clear to me that I'll never be able to figure out what I should buy. I begin to grow despondent, even morose. I try to convince myself that the system I have, with a turntable that rumbles, a tape player that eats tapes, and speakers that cut in and out unpredictably, can last another few years. Thoroughly defeated, I am about to slip out of the store when a salesperson approaches me and says, "Confusing, isn't it? Why don't you sit down and tell me what you're looking for. Maybe I can help." Brandishing my *Consumer Reports* as a weapon, I tell her no. But she persists. "Listen," she says, "I know you're worried about being ripped off, but I'm here to help you. It's almost impossible to figure this stuff out for yourself. There's too much variety, too much to know. I'm the expert. I learn all about this equipment so that you don't have to. Just put yourself in my hands, tell me what kind of music you listen to, how carefully you listen, what your room is like, how much money you're prepared to spend, and together we'll put together a system that's just right for your needs and your wallet."

"Look," I say, "how can I trust you? I know you're here to make sales. You're going to talk to me for a while, figure out how little I know and how much I'm willing to spend, and then get me to buy whatever will earn you the biggest commission. You may even try to stick me with old merchandise that you get an extra bonus for unloading. I'm no fool. I've been around the block a few times." And I wave my *Consumer Reports* in the air, as though to underscore my sophisticated suspicion.

"No, no, you don't understand," she says. "I'm *not* here to make sales. I'm here to make *matches*. Between people and equipment. I take my work very seriously. My goal is to find just the right system for every customer. I'm your agent. If I sell you more or less than you need, I will have failed. That's why I spend so much time learning about all of the things we sell here. Think of me the way you think of your doctor, as someone who acts with your interests at heart. I don't even *get* commissions."

What can I do? Either I trust her, or I keep listening to my broken-down system. So I sit down and we talk. She asks me dozens of questions about my music listening habits, to find out what kinds of features are important to me and what kinds are unnecessary. She has me listen to different speakers. She tests to see whether I can hear a difference between expensive CD players and inexpensive ones. After an hour or so, she puts together a system, having talked me out of lots of options that the advertisements say no sophisticated audiophile should be without. She tells me openly what the system's strengths and limitations are. She urges me to take it home and listen to it in my own living room, with my own music, for a few weeks. And she tells me the price—several hundred dollars less than I was intending to spend. Now completely convinced of her honesty and integrity, I tell the salesperson that I was actually prepared to spend more, and I ask whether, for another $200, I can't do better. And she tells me no, that I would just be wasting my money. Then she tells me that I could probably get the same system for a little less at a nearby discount house, though of course I wouldn't get the service that she had just provided. But she thinks I should know that the cost of her time and attention is reflected in the price of the components that together we have chosen.

So I buy the system, bring it home, set it up—and love it. It works reliably and gives me years of pleasure. I send all my friends to shop in this store, with this salesperson, and they are similarly satisfied. When the time comes to buy a new TV, I call her up, expecting to buy it from her. But she tells me that she doesn't know much about TVs, and sends me to another store and another honest, knowledgeable salesperson. And then she tells me where to go to buy a new car, where to go to buy a washing machine, where to get good advice about life insurance, and who the best travel agent is. She tells me which restaurants really serve fresh fish and which serve frozen fish advertised as fresh. She tells me that she's part of an underground network of honest salespeople, and that she'll be happy to plug me into the network whenever I need to buy something. And then, alas, I return to reality.

Perhaps you've had this fantasy too. It's a fantasy that the people with whom we engage in commercial transactions regard their work not as a job but as a kind of calling. It's a reflection of a desire to be able to trust someone, to put yourself in someone else's hands and know that that person's principal objective is to do right by you. I really would like to have the same confidence in my stereo dealer that I do in my doctor, for somewhat similar reasons. There is a need for trust in both cases, stemming from the absolute impossibility of knowing enough to make fully informed and intelligent decisions on our own. While there is plenty we can do to make ourselves educated consumers—of stereos, medical services, or anything else—we can't make ourselves sufficiently well informed about everything that the need for trust goes away. Caveat emptor—let the buyer beware—has always been the rule of the marketplace. This rule may once have been adequate, when the kinds of things people bought in the marketplace lacked the complexity and seemingly infinite variety that they have now. But nowadays, being wary mostly succeeds in making life a nightmare. It makes each transaction a contest, a confrontation. It leaves us feeling all the time that we've probably been taken. It makes acquisition a full-time job.

Those who enthuse about the efficiency and productivity of the marketplace don't place much importance on trust. We can "economize" on trust; we don't need trust if we've got competition. Competition will drive the dishonest merchants out of the market, for no one will buy from them.

But we need more than competition to make trust unnecessary. We also need information. People need to know enough about the things they're buying to know when they're being cheated. When economists formulate their theoretical accounts of the operation of the market, they typically assume that people have the needed information. They assume that people know the differences between slightly different products and between different brands of the same product. They assume that people know about the prices at which the same product sells in different stores. It's only when people have all this information that they can take advantage of market competition to get the best products at the best prices, and drive the cheaters out. "Our best customer is an educated customer," store advertisements sometimes say, as a way of suggesting that if we really knew all there was to know about the products being sold, it would be clear to us that this store provided the best merchandise at the best prices. But what happens when people don't have all the information they need? Then market competition doesn't work. It does us no good that one product is better than another, or one brand is cheaper than another, unless we *know* it. And now, more than ever before, knowing it is impossible. Too much variety. Too much complexity. So now, more than ever before, the economists' assumption that people have complete information is suspect. Now, more than ever before, people must *rely* on trust instead of economizing on it. And now, perhaps more than ever before, such trust is unwarranted.

Business is business. This all-too-familiar expression gets trotted out whenever someone expresses outrage at one business practice or another that is ruthlessly competitive, dishonest, insensitive to human suffering, or downright illegal. It is a verbal shrug of the shoulders, meant to convey to the outraged party that it's naive to expect anything different. Snow is white, water is wet, the sun rises in the east, and business is business. It is simply part of the essential nature of business activity that people will use every device or strategy they think they can get away with in order to get ahead. Shady business practices require neither explanation nor justification. They are considered the way of the world. It is far wiser for us to defend ourselves against them than to waste time asking why they exist or whether they might be changed. This is one of the reasons why our economic system must "economize" on trust. But for how long, and in what situations, should we be willing to shrug that "business is business"?

THE PETTY LARCENIES OF EVERYDAY LIFE

Let's imagine an ordinary day in the life of an ordinary person—a lawyer, say, or a secretary, or an electrician. First, a friend drops him off, on his way to work, to pick up his car, which was being repaired. Then, after a morning on the job, he has lunch at the local sandwich shop. After work, he stops at a bar for a drink, goes to the market to pick up some fresh fish and vegetables for dinner, and fetches the prescription he's had filled at the pharmacy. After dinner, he and his wife go to the mall to take advantage of a big sale that the department store is running. Then they go to a restaurant for a late snack before calling it a night. It's a busy day, but not an unusual one.

The chances are pretty good that, in the course of this ordinary day, our lawyer, secretary, or electrician has been cheated or exploited about a half dozen times. The chances are pretty good that he had work done on his car that wasn't necessary, that the meat in his sandwich was long past its prime, that the premium scotch he asked for was actually a cheap substitute, that the "fresh" fish was frozen, that the "fresh" vegetables were days old, that there were actually only 96 pills in the 100-pill prescription he paid for, that the "sale" prices that were handwritten on the tickets in the department store were actually the original retail prices while the prices *printed* on the tickets were 20 percent higher than the store had ever charged, that the french fries on his plate were the ones that remained after assorted servers had taken samples from his order, and that, perhaps, the burger that accompanied the french fries had been dropped on the filthy kitchen floor, only to be returned to the grill to be "cleaned up." What a day! Living a day of ordinary life is like walking through a minefield.

Is this all made up? In his recent book *The Predatory Society*, sociologist Paul Blumberg documents that deceptions and abuses like these are everyday occurrences. Blumberg teaches at a university in New York City in which the majority of students work at part-time or even full-time jobs while they are attending school. Over a period of about fifteen years, Blumberg asked the students in his classes who held jobs to write about the nature of their jobs and their employers, with particular attention to company honesty. During that period, Blumberg collected over six hundred accounts, written right from the trenches, of common practices in supermarkets, department stores, restaurants, pharmacies, and a wide range of other retail establishments. And abuses like the ones I have just suggested were routine. Less than 30 percent of Blumberg's students reported no known deceptive or dishonest practices, and roughly an equal percentage indicated deceptive or dishonest practices that were systematic and serious.

Here are some of the grim examples, forming a kind of topographical map of the minefield that is retail commerce.

In department stores:

- Prices are marked up a week before a sale so that they can later be marked down with the original retail price now being touted as the sale price.
- Size tickets on garments are changed to move inventories of unpopular-sized items. Salespeople are instructed to tell customers who try the garments on that they're "cut big" (or small) if they seem suspicious.
- Left and right shoes of different sizes, whose mates have gone astray, are

made into pairs with sizes re-marked accordingly. Customers are told that almost everyone has one foot bigger than the other.

• Salespeople are instructed to tell their customers that they "look great" in whatever they try on, especially if it's expensive.

• Salespeople are taught to steer customers toward merchandise that is not selling by giving them "inside information" that makes more popular merchandise seem less attractive.

In supermarkets:

• Produce is prepackaged with the bad side down.

• Tap water is put in "spring water" bottles and sold as spring water.

• Frozen fish is defrosted and sold as fresh.

• Relatively inexpensive cuts of meat or fish fillets are packaged, labeled, and sold as more expensive cuts.

• Butchers scrape the mold off meat that is long past its prime, then wash it in salt water, repackage it, redate it, and offer it for sale as fresh.

• Packages of meat are short-weighted. (In New York City in 1982, 26 percent of the butcher shops that were inspected were caught short-weighting their meats.)

In restaurants:

• Less expensive types of fish are substituted for the more expensive ones when they are similar in appearance.

• Food that drops onto the floor en route from the kitchen to the dining room is picked up, brushed off, and served.

• Cooking and serving staff help themselves to bits of food off their customers' plates before they leave the kitchen.

• Restaurant food preparation areas are filthy. (In New York in 1984, more than five thousand restaurants failed health department inspections, including many in which the cost of a meal could feed a family of four for a week. And many of the restaurants that passed inspections did so not by keeping their kitchens clean but by keeping their inspectors' pockets lined.)

• Restaurants and bars pour low-grade whiskeys into premium-brand bottles and sell the drinks for premium prices. Some dilute the low-grade whiskeys with water as well.

In pharmacies:

• Pharmacists short-count prescriptions.

• Pharmacists fill prescriptions with generic drugs and charge for brand names.

• When customers come from their doctors with prescription blanks that include over-the-counter drugs as well as drugs requiring a prescription, pharmacists treat all the drugs on the blank as if they required prescriptions and charge accordingly.

In gas stations:

• Low-octane gasoline is sold as high octane.
• Unnecessary repairs are done. (In a random national test of the honesty of car repair establishments conducted in 1987, people disconnected a spark plug wire in an otherwise perfectly maintained car and brought the car in for repair. This very simple and easy-to-detect problem was correctly diagnosed and fixed in only 28 percent of all cases. Most commonly, other very costly but quite unnecessary repairs were suggested.)
• Sometimes repairs are not done but are nevertheless charged for. An old part is spray painted so that it looks new, and the customer is charged for the new part as well as the labor. As one service station proprietor said, "A mechanic's best tool is his paint can."

In television and stereo repair shops:

• Unnecessary repairs are done.
• Repairs are not done but are charged for.
• Charges are determined on the basis of an assessment of the customer's willingness to pay. A repair on an expensive piece of equipment may cost twice as much as the same repair on an inexpensive piece of equipment.

Feeling vulnerable and unprotected in everyday commercial transactions? Of course, this is not news to us. We all know that this kind of thing goes on, and many of us make efforts to defend ourselves, at least some of the time. When we are looking for big-ticket items, we comparison shop, get the advice of friends, consult consumer magazines, and the like. But none of us has either the time or the stomach for this kind of vigilance in all transactions. So we let many things slide, knowing or suspecting that we will be cheated out of nickels and dimes with some regularity. The alternative— vigilance in all domains—would essentially require us to give up eating in restaurants, buying processed foods, and doing many other things that we find pleasurable or convenient. But I suspect that when we decide to relax our vigilance in some domains, we believe that we won't be cheated every time, and that when we are cheated, it won't be for much. Finding out that unless we're careful, we'll get rotten or dirty food in restaurants and supermarkets makes it a little more difficult to relax our vigilance. Hearing that (as Blumberg reports) in one bakery there is a salesperson who licks the chocolate icing off the chocolate doughnuts and then sells them as glazed will change the way we look at glazed doughnuts in all bakeries. We can live in the minefield if we willfully keep our eyes closed and pretend that there aren't really very many mines, but once someone or something has forced our eyes open, our willful innocence and ignorance can't be recaptured.

Why does all this dishonesty, deception, and abuse occur? Do the people who do these things take pleasure from fooling and exploiting their unsuspecting customers? Do Blumberg's students relish the opportunity to take advantage of people? It doesn't seem so. The students almost invariably indicate that they are following the bosses' instructions when they engage in deceptive practices. They claim that when no one is looking, and they think they can get away with it, they treat their customers with honesty and respect. They give the impression that if they were running the business, the deceptive practices would stop.

But we know that this can't be true. We know that the bosses were students once themselves, and we can reasonably suspect that they were no less scrupulous and principled as students than their current student employees are. They may also have thought that if they were running the business, the deceptive practices would stop. But when that day actually came, the deceptive practices continued. Something or several things must have happened to deflect them from their honorable intentions, just as something or several things will probably happen to deflect their current student employees. What things?

Blumberg asked his student informants why the deceptive and dishonest practices in which they engaged occurred. In general, they reported that they were given explicit instructions from their bosses or supervisors. When they expressed doubts or reservations, they were typically told that these practices were standard, that everybody did these things. They were sometimes told that what they were being asked to do was actually quite benign in comparison to what went on in other places. The argument was not that since everybody did it, it was all right. The argument was that since everybody did it, you *had* to do it also, in self-defense. If other department stores ran "sales" that weren't really sales, and the public was deceived, then your department store had three choices. Either it ran a real sale, and sacrificed profits that its competitors didn't sacrifice. Or it didn't run a sale at all, and lost customers to its competitors' fake sales. Or it did what the competition was doing. If other restaurants were filthy, then again, you had three choices. You could employ staff to keep the kitchen clean, throw away food that had been tainted, and keep prices competitive, thus sacrificing profits. Or you could pass the costs of your cleanliness on to your customers, and thus have to charge more than your competition (for services that your customers wouldn't see and thus wouldn't appreciate). Or you could do what the competition was doing. In competitive situations like these, it seems inevitable that dishonest practices will drive out the honest ones; honesty becomes a luxury that few shopkeepers can afford.

On top of these competitive pressures faced by the bosses, the pay structure in many retail trades establishes incentives for salespeople to sell as much as they possibly can without concern for method. When the money a salesperson takes home consists largely of sales commissions and bonuses, honesty can have a substantial price. In situations like these, it frequently happens that base salaries are set so low that only a very productive salesperson can make a decent living. This puts salespeople in the position of having to choose between being honest and being able to pay the rent. It's great for the boss, because it encourages employees to work as hard as possible to sell as much as possible. And it's great for the hustling, unscrupulous salesperson, whose hard work and dishonest methods will be rewarded by sizable commissions. But it's not so great for salespeople who want to be honest or for customers who depend on honesty. The recent scandal involving the automobile repair division of one of the nation's largest retailers is an example of this problem. Its mechanics received a commission for the repair work they did. The idea, presumably, was to make sure no car left the shop in less than tip-top condition. But this incentive had another under-the-hood effect. Mechanics started recommending repairs that were completely unnecessary. Only after this scandal came to light did the company eliminate the incentive.

To emphasize what incentive conditions do to honesty, Blumberg asks why it is that the butcher puts his finger on the scale while the postal clerk does not. The answer is so obvious that the question doesn't really need to be asked. But the very obviousness of this question raises another: If the structure of the competitive-market system so plainly encourages people to be dishonest, why do we support the system so enthusiastically?

Here there are several possibilities. Perhaps we have so much confidence in the inherent integrity of people that we believe that abuse and deception will be infrequent even when the incentive structure of the system encourages them. Or perhaps we have confidence in the system of government regulation and inspection designed to protect us from abuse. Or perhaps we believe in our own ability as smart shoppers to detect potential abuses and protect ourselves from them. Or, finally, perhaps we think that occasional deception and abuse is a small, if inevitable, price to pay for the productivity, efficiency, and freedom of choice that the competitive market makes possible. Let's examine each of these possible explanations of our willingness to tolerate a system of commerce that encourages people to deceive us.

First, what about the possibility that most people are inherently honest? Without being unduly cynical, we can see this as a very slender reed on which to build consumer confidence. People can be taught to value honesty by a culture that values honesty. If the virtue of honesty is both preached and practiced in the family, the school, the church, and the government, then people will grow up believing that they should be honest. But when they enter the world of commerce, this belief will be sorely tested. It will be tested because, as we just saw, people will find themselves tempted to resort to dishonest practices in self-defense. As market practices render it increasingly difficult to make an "honest living," the cost of being honest will be substantial. And as more and more of the best things in life (decent housing, health care, education) become available for purchase on the market, the cost of being honest will increase. When we read every day about people cheating for financial gain in schools, in scientific laboratories, in athletics, in churches, and in government, where can we turn for models of honesty in practice? So counting on people to be honest won't do. People are neither inherently honest nor inherently dishonest. They *can* be either, and they *will* be what their social institutions demand.

What, then, about government regulation and inspection? In light of the antiregulatory sentiments that have dominated politics in the last decade, it seems odd now to appeal to government regulation as the way to protect consumers from deception. But even if political sentiments change, as no doubt they will, government regulation and inspection can't do the job. The reason is that if we assume that the *only* reason people will refrain from dishonest or deceptive practices is the fear that they will be caught and punished, the task of regulation and inspection becomes overwhelming. There are so many businesses, each with so many different opportunities to deceive their customers, that it would take an army of inspectors to police them. The task of regulation and inspection is a manageable one only if we can assume that the substantial majority of people will obey regulations not because they're afraid of getting caught but because it's the right thing to do. If everyone has larceny in his or her heart, we can give up: the bad guys have won.

And even if we could solve the numbers problem, we would have another one. If we set an army of inspectors loose on the retail trade, how could we be sure of the honesty of the inspectors themselves? Surely they would be vulnerable to corruption, willing to look the other way at dirty kitchens, dishonest scales, and the like in return for a regular income supplement. We would need a whole other army of inspectors to regulate and police the inspectors. And of course we would be faced with the problem of regulating and policing them.

A vivid example of just this difficulty, also discussed by Blumberg, comes from the efforts to keep restaurants clean in New York City. New York has thousands of restaurants, and each is supposed to be inspected once a year. Leaving aside whether a once-a-year inspection schedule is adequate, we see that in 1984, presumably a typical year, New York didn't even come close to meeting it. More than one-third of the city's restaurants went uninspected. Spot inspections of these restaurants by health department officials revealed that more than half would have failed inspections if they had had them. This is the numbers problem. In addition, auditors visited many restaurants just after they *had* passed inspection, and they found that 14 percent should have failed. This is not a numbers problem; it's a corruption problem. An FBI investigation in 1988 revealed that fully half of New York's restaurant inspectors were taking bribes.

Whenever corruption like this is exposed, and a scandal ensues, we can assume that for some time thereafter, performance will improve. But as long as the incentives—of both the inspectors and the inspected—don't change, we can be reasonably confident that, after a short while, practices will return to their previously unacceptable patterns.

There is a general lesson in this example. We can depend on regulation, inspection, and punishment to protect us only as long as we don't really need it, only as long as most people can be counted on to obey the law. The Internal Revenue Service can keep up with tax cheats so long as most people pay the taxes they owe. Restaurant inspectors can keep up with health violators so long as most proprietors live up to the regulations. Traffic cops can control unsafe drivers so long as most people obey the traffic laws.

If we can't count on inherent honesty or government protection, perhaps we can count on ourselves. We can shop carefully, read consumer magazines, inspect our purchases, and demand satisfaction from the merchants with whom we deal. We can take caveat emptor seriously and be very, very wary consumers.

Or can we? Just how feasible is it for individuals to protect themselves in all their market transactions? How can we be wary consumers in restaurants? We can insist on seeing a certificate of inspection, but we've just seen that sometimes these certificates aren't worth the paper they're printed on. Can we demand a tour of the kitchen as well? Can we insist that we watch as the meal is being prepared? Even if we were permitted to do these things, it would certainly take most of the pleasure out of eating in restaurants.

And more generally, as my recurring fantasy about the stereo salesperson was meant to illustrate, for many of the things we purchase and consume, there is simply too much to know. Stereos, televisions, computers, dishwashers, automobiles, wristwatches, diamond rings, microwave ovens, VCRs, and pharmaceuticals are all so complex and varied that no one can be a watchdog in all things, and few people can be watchdogs in any. Caveat emptor might work when buyers and sellers have roughly equal information about the quality and price of goods and services offered in the market. And there may have been a time before our technological era when buyers and sellers did have approximately equal information. But that time is long gone. Just as we don't expect to have to be fully knowledgeable consumers of medical services in order to be treated properly by our doctors, we can't expect to be fully knowledgeable consumers of anything else. Whether we like it or not, we are at the mercy of the experts—those who try to sell us things, and those who write magazine articles to help us buy those things.

There are two ways that salespeople might respond to the enormous informational advantage they have over their customers. They could see it as a wonderful opportunity to be a part of communal interdependence and solidarity. In a complex, specialized world, everyone needs everyone else. No person is an island. The stereo salesperson may be a master in the stereo showroom, but she is vulnerable in the automobile showroom. The car dealer may know all about cars, but he is helpless in the computer store. In a society built on trust, in which salespeople with informational advantages take the opportunity to educate their customers and protect them from harm or exploitation, being a seller takes on meaning and significance above and beyond the earning of a living. The seller has an important social role to play. Like the social worker who negotiates the overwhelming government bureaucracy on behalf of her clients, the seller looks after the welfare of her customers. And the seller derives satisfaction from successfully meeting her customers' needs.

And this is true not just of the sellers of things but of the makers of them. Knowing that the people who will eventually buy the things you make are depending on you to produce stereos, cars, refrigerators, or clothing of quality and reliability can induce you, as a producer, to see yourself as a guardian of the public trust, not to mention the public health and safety.

Alternatively, salespeople and producers can regard their informational advantages as a wonderful opportunity for something else—not education and protection, but exploitation and predation.

The more you know that your customer doesn't know, the greater your opportunity to get your customer to buy what you want him to buy; the more you can entice him with superfluous but expensive options, the more you can charge, and the more you can profit. The more you know that the eventual customer doesn't, the more careless and effortless can be your time on the production line. With profit or an easy workday as your primary aim, informational advantages are to be cultivated and nurtured, not overcome. Education is the enemy.

Given the choice between education and exploitation—between protection and predation—what does the typical salesperson do? Blumberg's students provide an answer. The market does nothing to encourage protection and everything to encourage predation. The pursuit and exploitation of individual advantage in the service of profit is built into the ideology of the market. Those who fail to capitalize on their advantages will earn less money, or be fired by their bosses, or be driven out of business by their competitors. If profit is the point, and the sole point, of commercial activity, then giving your knowledge advantage away would be like telling your opponents in a football game what play you are about to run, or showing your hole cards to the other players in your poker game. If you don't play these games to win—football, or poker, or commerce—what's the point of playing them at all?

You might respond that commerce isn't like football or poker. Those games are "zero-sum games"; you can win only if someone else loses. Commerce isn't a zero-sum game; everyone can win. You enter into an exchange, and you get what you want (some good or service) while the salesperson gets what she wants (a sale and a fair profit). But what's a fair profit? What standards set limits on the profits people should be able to make? Why isn't a fair profit whatever profit you can manage to extract from each exchange? It's true that commerce *could* be a game in which everyone comes out a winner, but it certainly doesn't have to be. For it to become a game in which everybody wins, the rules and the objectives have to change. The objectives have to be expanded to include the satisfaction customers feel when they are well taken care of. And the game of commerce as currently practiced leaves no room for objectives other than sales and profits.

So we can't count on people's inherent honesty, government protection, or consumer education to solve the problems of deception and abuse that face us in the marketplace. The final alternative response is to grin and bear it, to resign ourselves to occasional dishonesty and exploitation, and regard them as the price we have to pay for an economic system that is amazingly productive, impressively efficient, and able to cater to all the idiosyncratic desires of millions of individual participants. While it is true that we may not always get what we pay for, or what we want, or even what we need, on balance the system serves us very well.

This response won't do either, and here's why. The price we pay for the free market—in deception, abuse, and dishonesty—is neither occasional nor modest even now, and it will only get worse. In the absence of either a sense of responsibility toward customers or a set of enforceable government regulations and sanctions, abuse and dishonesty can only escalate. Every day, someone will come up with a new way to wring extra profit out of each sale by misleading the people who buy. Others will follow suit, either to get some of a good thing themselves or merely to keep up with the competition. Petty deception is not stable. It will stay petty only if forces that countervail the forces of the market are a strong and sustained presence. If one of those forces must be government regulation and inspection, then the market will become much less efficient and productive. It costs money—lots of money—to police the marketplace, and, as abuses proliferate, the costs of policing rise. And these costs don't buy us any products. We don't usually factor them into the cost of buying and consuming, but that's because we don't pay for them in the restaurant or the department store. We pay for them in our taxes. If we could figure out what we have to pay as a society to keep our merchants behaving honestly (recent estimates are that fraud and abuse in retail trade costs us over one trillion dollars a year, excluding the cost of enforcement of regulations), and add these costs to the costs of the products we buy, the market might not look so efficient after all.

And if instead of relying on the government to keep abuses petty, we rely on our own self-education and vigilant consumption, we again introduce a very substantial, though largely hidden, cost. It takes time—lots of time—to be a knowledgeable, vigilant consumer.

It is time we would rather spend doing other things. It is time that can't be replaced. There is no really good way to quantify the value of time, but just for the sake of the exercise, imagine someone shopping for a stereo. If she earns $50,000 per year, her salary for a working day amounts to about $200. Suppose she spends two full days consulting audio consumer magazines and a third day comparison shopping. By the time she gets her stereo, she will have spent $600 worth of her time on the purchase. She would have to get quite a bargain to justify this magnitude of expenditure on "research."

I know that this is a very crude analysis. It ignores the possibility that the shopper enjoys learning about stereos and values being sufficiently empowered to make intelligent purchasing decisions on her own. It ignores the fact that she is almost certainly doing all this research in her spare time, during which she wouldn't be earning anything at all. But if she's doing *this* in her spare time, then she can't be doing other things. She can't be reading, listening to music, socializing with friends, playing tennis, performing public service, and so on. And even if she'd rather be learning about stereos in her spare time than doing anything else, she simply doesn't have enough spare time to learn about all the things she will be buying in the course of a life. So no matter how you think about it—whether crudely or subtly—the cost of being your own policeman is steep.

And there is still another subtle, hidden cost—the cost of deception and dishonesty to the seller (or producer). Because people don't enter the world of business eager to get rich at the expense of their customers, discovering that the system impels them to be deceptive deprives them of significant sources of meaning and satisfaction in their work. If they are unable truly to serve people's needs, all that remains for them to get out of their jobs is a healthy paycheck. The cost—in self-respect and job satisfaction—may be impossible to measure, but it's also very steep.

Indeed, when we put all these hidden costs together, they are too steep for any of us to afford. When we cannot depend on trust, government regulation, or our own vigilance to keep market practices in line, the costs stop being measurable in dollars or hours. They escalate and escalate until they have to be measured in lost jobs, destroyed industries and communities, ruined lives, and preventable injuries, illnesses, and deaths. For when captains of industry are free to engage in the same kind of deceptive, dishonest, and abusive practices that we've seen in shopkeepers and car mechanics, the stakes become much, much higher. Let us turn, then, to the corporation, to examine abuse on a larger scale.

THE GRAND LARCENIES OF CORPORATE LIFE

Deception, dishonesty, and abuse by corporations or their chief executives make front-page news regularly these days. Attempts to estimate the frequency of corporate crime suggest that in the last decade, more than half of the five hundred largest corporations in the United States have been brought up on federal charges at least once, and half of them have actually been convicted—in several instances, more than once.

The most eye-popping current examples of crime and abuse come from the world of finance. The Wall Street insider-trading story began to emerge about ten years ago. It began with the case of Dennis Levine, a stockbroker who had made more than $12 million trading secretly on stocks that he knew, from inside information, would soon be the target of takeover bids. What was so striking to me about this case was that Levine had been making more than $1 million a year legally. Yet he felt the need to make more, even if it meant breaking the law.

How naive I was! For soon, with Levine's help, the trail led to Ivan Boesky, who made more than ten times what Levine made. And from there, it led to Michael Milken, who made ten (and in a good year fifty) times what Boesky made. Why does an individual who already makes several million dollars a year still feel compelled to cheat? Boesky was fined an amount that could support a small town for a decade—and he was able to pay it! Milken paid a fine that could support a small town for a century. Milken's firm, Drexel Burnham Lambert, pleaded guilty to charges of fraud, paid fines of $650 million, and had to cease operations. But even these astronomical numbers, we soon discovered, were only the tip of the iceberg. As these big-money players in the financial world started making deals that earned them and their companies tens or even hundreds of millions of dollars, smaller players, who had previously been content with their half-million-dollar-a-year salaries, wanted to get in on the action. The result was a major breakdown of American banking. As the banking industry began to unravel, Americans learned that people who played the same games that Levine, Boesky, and Milken played had taken several hundred billion dollars out of the economy. In the process of doing this, they had left behind countless unfinished real estate projects, ruined businesses, and emptied nest eggs. Many of the things these bankers did to enrich themselves at the expense of their customers were illegal. But many of them were not. For the most part, the bankers operated within the law. They cleverly exploited a system that encourages people to do whatever they can to promote their own interests. And all of us will be paying for their successes for decades to come.

Enough has been written, and will continue to be written, about the details of the various Wall Street scandals and the savings and loan collapse that there is no need to discuss them at length here. They are the complex product of greed, inadequate or bad government regulations, insufficient, incompetent, or corrupt regulators, and complicit elected politicians. But these excesses simply illustrate vividly a fundamental and pervasive change that has occurred in the character of big business in America. This change threatens all of us.

"The business of America is business," it used to be said. And "What's good for General Motors is good for America." What slogans like these asserted or implied was that when businesses prospered, we all prospered with them. Businesses prospered by making the things that Americans needed and wanted, and they especially prospered if they could find ways to make these things more cheaply and efficiently than they had ever been made before. Not only would we be provided with the things we wanted at prices that we could afford, but we would also be provided with employment, so that we could earn the money with which to buy these things. And in our employment, we would be provided with opportunities to use our intelligence and ingenuity to get ahead, enriching ourselves and our society in the process. Furthermore, as large companies prospered, and the people they employed prospered with them, the communities and towns in which these companies were located would prosper as well. The success of the GMs and U.S. Steels of America meant the success of countless towns and cities as places to live and raise families.

How much of this was ever actually true is hard to know. But it is clear that, whether or not these slogans were true in the past, they are not true in the present. They are not true, because the orientation to economic activity that has come to dominate corporate life in the last decade or so identifies the maximization of profit as the exclusive goal of all economic activity, elevating it above all other possible goals, like productivity, efficiency, or quality. This profit-maximization goal has the managers of companies oriented almost exclusively to short-term profitability, often at the expense of company development as well as loyalty to employees and communities.

Before I am misunderstood to be suggesting that in the "good old days" people engaged in economic activity out of an altruistic regard for their fellows, let me clarify. Where previously the pursuit of profit was linked to the particular activities of production or commerce that individuals were engaged in, it is now detached from any particular activities, and floats freely above them all. Where previously a company might define itself as a manufacturer of cloth that endeavored to make cloth manufacturing profitable, now that company would define itself as a pursuer of profit that happens to manufacture cloth. It's just a difference in emphasis, but sometimes emphasis can make all the difference.

Think, for example, about a hypothetical steel company that might have operated in, say, 1950. The goal of that company was presumably to make money. Well, no, not quite. The goal of that company was to make money making steel. Activities in pursuit of that goal might have included research and development of technological advances that improved production efficiency and perhaps created new products. They might have included development of employee management policies that maintained a highly skilled, highly motivated workforce. They might have included development of marketing strategies that would increase sales. And they might have included the raising of capital for expansion. Each of these activities could be understood as efforts to improve and extend the practice of manufacturing and distributing steel. Steelmaking and steel selling were what this company did; they were a part of the company's essence.

Now think about a hypothetical steel company operating in 1990. The goal of this company is to make money. Period. Activities in pursuit of this goal might include the ones I just mentioned, but they might also include closing down or selling U.S. plants and building new ones in foreign countries where labor is cheaper. They might include buying stock in IBM or in a Korean steel company. They might include investing in real estate or opening gambling casinos or fast-food restaurants. For this modern steel company, steelmaking and steel selling are simply a means, a contingency, a historical accident. They have nothing to do with the company's essence. Profit making, not steelmaking, is what defines this modern company.

The difference between these two hypothetical companies is reflected in the organization of many real ones. Over the last several years, control of many major corporations has shifted from people in the organization who are involved with production to people in the organization who are involved with finance. This shift in leadership reflects a shift in organizational goals. Production people know and worry about making things. Financial people know and worry about making money. Production people move assets around so that the product can be made more efficiently. Financial people move assets around so that money can be made more efficiently.

This shift in emphasis has many consequences, several of which have economists worried about the long-term well-being of the U.S. economy. There is enormous concern about how the single-minded pursuit of short-term profit leads chief executive officers of large corporations to sell the company's future for a profitable quarter. There is enormous concern about what is called me-first management, where corporate executives, knowing or suspecting how precarious their own positions are in an age in which "loyalty" is not in the corporate lexicon, pay themselves unbelievably high salaries and bonuses that are essentially unrelated to their or the company's performance. In addition, there is the merger and acquisition mania, less rampant now than a few years ago, but still looming over many CEO's shoulders. Often in mergers and acquisitions, the buyer has no expertise in running the business of the seller. On this issue, an illuminating, large-scale study of corporate mergers by David J. Ravenscraft and F. M. Scherer, *Mergers, Sell-offs, and Economic*

Efficiency, indicated that, in general, these mergers resulted in increased efficiency and profit only when they were "vertical" mergers, that is, when the acquiring company was already in the business that it was acquiring. "Horizontal" mergers, in which companies acquired new and unrelated businesses, tended to be unprofitable. Indeed, almost half of such acquisitions lost money and were eventually sold off. Perhaps more telling, in a study of companies acquired in the mid 1980s, money spent on research and development decreased by almost 13 percent after the acquisition. This contrasts with an increase of more than 5 percent in spending on research and development by similar companies, at the same time, that had not been acquired.

In a recent review of different historical and cultural patterns of industrial organization, *Scale and Scope: The Dynamics of Industrial Capitalism*, Alfred D. Chandler summarized some of these trends, which incidentally, while dominant in the United States, are largely absent in Japan and Germany. Where previously in U.S. industrial history, corporate expansion and diversification came by extending into new domains production processes that the company already controlled, twenty years ago U.S. corporate managers began to invest in facilities and enterprises in which they had absolutely no expertise. Along with this came a breakdown in communication between top-level and middle-level management, largely because the top-level managers knew about managing money but not about managing any of the specific activities with which the midlevel managers were concerned. These two developments, together with practices of asset allocation and assessment that made the most profitable arm of a corporation the standard of comparison against which all other arms of the corporation were judged, led to the development of a new business—the buying and selling of companies. All of a sudden, the people with controlling interests in companies had no interest in the activities of the companies they held, and manipulated and exchanged them, without losing any sleep over the long-term consequences of their transactions. These are some of the consequences, vividly illustrated a few years ago in the movie *Wall Street*, of the shift in emphasis from making steel for a profit to making a profit with steel.

The Wall Street scandals, the banking failures, and the merger and acquisition mania in pursuit of the greatest profits are interrelated. One thing that unites them is the "junk bond," a debt instrument essentially invented by Michael Milken. Junk bonds are used to finance risky ventures, ventures that have a reasonably high chance of failing. In return for taking a big risk, investors in junk bonds are paid very high rates of interest, much higher than the going rates on government bonds, certificates of deposit, or blue-chip corporate bonds. These high rates of interest are paid by the people who borrow the money raised by the bonds for whatever ventures they are starting.

The junk bond radically changed the standards and expectations by which the world of finance operated. The prospect of high returns enticed many to invest in the bonds. And the resulting availability of easy money made it possible for groups with little capital to get financing. The normal cautions that once prevailed in the making of loans went out the window. Small companies could raise huge sums of money with which to take over big ones. Managers of companies could raise similar sums with which to "take the company private," that is, to buy it back from the shareholders. Bankers put their depositors' funds into these kinds of instruments; brokers packaged and sold them, earning huge commissions; and entrepreneurs used them to buy companies the way the rest of us buy suits.

In theory, finding new ways to raise money for investment in new ventures could be a wonderful thing. It could give people with great ideas but no money a chance to put their ideas into practice. It could give successful businesses the opportunity to expand. Each of these developments would mean economic expansion: new products, new jobs, heightened productivity. Indeed, this is what the whole business of selling stock in companies had originally been for. The owners of a company "went public" and sold stock, not because they wanted to share their good thing with the rest of the world, but because they wanted to raise money for expansion or diversification, and selling stock was a good way to raise money. Junk bonds, risky though they may have been, could have been used as a new source of investment in technological change and economic growth.

But they weren't. Instead, when companies were taken private, or were bought by other companies, there followed not expansion and innovation but contraction. Assets were sold off for cash, either to help pay the huge debt that the junk bonds created or to enrich the principals in the transaction, or both. Instead of jobs being created, they were eliminated. Instead of new products being developed, old products were no longer being made. The long-term well-being of the company and its employees was sacrificed for the short-term enrichment of the entrepreneurs and their financiers. And of course many of these ventures failed altogether, contributing to the multibillion-dollar bank bailout bill that we are now all paying.

There is nothing illegal in the shift of corporate concern from making things to making money. To the contrary, corporate executives often suggest that their fiduciary responsibility to the company's shareholders impels them to act in a way that will maximize the return on their investor's dollar. They are responsible not to their employees, not to their communities, not even to their customers, but to their shareholders. And shareholders aren't interested in continuing to own stock in a steel company because it makes good steel, or treats its workers well, or contributes to the life of its community. Shareholders are interested only in a steel company that makes them money. This is especially true nowadays, with the bulk of shares in the hands of institutional investors whose funds are managed by investment advisers whose considerable management fees can be justified only if the portfolios of their institutional clients outperform the securities market as a whole. If the steel company stops making its investors money, or even if it makes them less money than they could make by putting their money elsewhere, the shareholders will be gone.

Loyalty is neither to be expected nor to be encouraged in the world of business. Indeed, it is the very absense of loyalty—on the part of shareholders, executives, and even salaried employees—that some applaud as the constant goad that keeps companies "lean and mean." If you're only as good as the balance sheet for your last quarter, you will be eternally vigilant, striving to take advantage of every opportunity and to cut every unnecessary cost. The result, it is claimed, is an extremely efficient and responsive economy. The cost—in lost jobs, disrupted lives, and depressed communities—is small in comparison to the gain in economic efficiency. Or so the champions of the "new corporation" say. I doubt whether the many skilled and conscientious workers whose jobs were casualties of this pursuit of "efficiency" and profit would agree.

The Grandest Larcenies of All

It is hard to look at corporate and financial practices that have cost society billions of dollars, thousands of jobs, and dozens of communities and still come away with respect for the efficiency and productivity of the market. And yet, modern corporate practices have an even meaner dimension. Modern corporate practices encourage the adoption of profit-seeking policies that sometimes result in injury and death.

In Arthur Miller's powerful play *All My Sons*, much of the drama centers on the belated discovery by a son that his father knowingly shipped defective airplane parts to fulfill a government contract during World War II. The parts were installed, some of the planes crashed, and pilots and their crews were killed. The man responsible, the father, is a good man, a kind man, a man who cares deeply about his family and would do anything to protect them and provide for them. Indeed, one reason why it takes so long for the truth to come out is that the son simply can't imagine that a man like his father is capable of such an act. But he is. As he explains, he was under enormous pressure to deliver the goods. The military needed the parts right away, and failure to deliver would have destroyed his business. He had a responsibility to take care of his family. And anyway, there was no certainty that the parts would not hold up when in use. As the truth slowly comes out, the audience shares the son's incredulity. How could it be? If a man like that could do a thing like that, then anyone is capable of doing anything.

This, of course, is one of the play's major points. Almost anyone is capable of almost anything. A monstrous system can make a monster of anyone or, perhaps more accurately, can make almost anyone do monstrous things. We see this as dramas like Miller's get played out in real life, with horrifyingly tragic consequences.

Each time we hear about an example of corporate irresponsibility, neglect, or willful disregard for human health and safety, we are no doubt outraged and eager to see that the guilty parties are punished. What we miss when we encounter these examples one at a time is a sense of how widespread and systemic the potential for catastrophe is.

Some efforts have been made in the last few years to accumulate examples of corporate practices that have led to illness, injury, and death. Paul Blumberg discusses many in *The Predatory Society*, and Russell Mokhiber discusses others in *Corporate Crime and Violence*. Among the more striking examples are these:

- All too close to the story of *All My Sons*, military contractors have been caught knowingly making and selling defective brake systems for U.S. jet fighters, defective machine-gun parts that cause the guns to jam when used, and defective fire-fighting equipment for navy ships.
- An automobile manufacturer knowingly made and sold a dangerous car, whose gas tank was alarmingly likely to explode in rear-end collisions. This defect could have been corrected at a cost of a few dollars per car.
- An aerospace contractor allowed a space shuttle flight to be launched under conditions that made some of the critical components of the shuttle unsafe. The shuttle exploded, killing all the astronauts and their civilian passengers.
- A chemicals company continued operating a chemicals plant in Bhopal, India, long after it knew the plant was unsafe. A gas leak killed more than 2,000 people and seriously injured more than 30,000. The $5 billion company responded to this tragedy by sending $1 million in disaster relief and a shipment of medicines sufficient for about 400 people.
- Other drug and chemicals manufacturers make and sell to the Third World products known to be sufficiently dangerous that their sale is banned in the United States.
- The tobacco industry targets much of its marketing of cigarettes to young adolescents, notwithstanding the fact that the sale of cigarettes to minors is illegal.
- The asbestos industry knowingly concealed the hazardous nature of its products for years from workers who were exposed to carcinogens on a daily basis.
- Trucking companies put on the road trucks more than 30 percent of which would fail safety inspections and are thus hazards to their drivers as well as to other motorists.
- A medical equipment company sold hundreds of millions of dollars worth of cardiac pacemakers that it knew to be defective. Many of them

had to be surgically removed from their recipients and replacements installed.

- A tire company made and marketed a line of tires that it knew did not approach the company's minimum standard of lasting 15,000 miles. Repeated blowouts, often within a few thousand miles of installation, caused thousands of accidents, hundreds of injuries, and at least thirty fatalities. The company continued to sell these tires until the results of a government study showing how dangerous they were were made public. At this point, rather than destroying the tires, the company dumped them on the market at deeply discounted prices.

- The chief economist at the World Bank argued in a memo that it makes sense for First World manufacturers to "export" their pollution-generating, health-endangering activities to the Third World because the "cost" of pollution in the Third World (in lifetime earnings loss brought on by premature illness and death to workers) is much lower than this cost in the First World.

What happens to the people responsible for these tragedies? Typically, nothing. Most commonly, there are fines so meager that they constitute only a tiny fraction of the amount of money the companies spend just on advertising their harmful products. The economic consequences to the companies of these instances of willful disregard of public safety are virtually never significant enough to make such behavior unprofitable and to deter the company from doing similar things in the future. Significant punishment is almost always left up to the initiative of the victims. If they secure lawyers and sue, they may get the company to make substantial reparation—usually several years and many court battles after the harmful event at issue.

The people within the company who seem to suffer most from such scandalous events are the ones who try to prevent them or, failing that, make their knowledge of danger and irresponsibility public. Whistle-blowers, as they are called, don't get promoted; instead, they get ostracized or even fired (or, in the case of Karen Silkwood, an employee at a plant that refined plutonium who blew the whistle that workers were being contaminated, killed; the movie *Silkwood* is a dramatization of her story). The engineers and chemists, who should and frequently do know better, are subservient to the marketers and the accountants. They are required to submerge their professional standards and behave in a way that is good for the company. Those who feel obliged to speak out pay a very heavy price, unless they can garner enough publicity to be protected by public opinion from dismissal. The vulnerability of whistle-blowers is so pronounced that the U.S. Congress has devoted substantial attention in recent years to finding ways to protect them.

Contrast the lack of punishment of responsible corporate executives for acts that kill or maim hundreds and thousands with a case that occurred about five years ago. It was a case of drug tampering. An individual put small amounts of rat poison into various different over-the-counter drugs marketed by a large drug company. He then tipped off government officials anonymously to the contamination, requiring the company to withdraw the affected products from the market and then reintroduce them in more tamper-resistant form. Estimates were that this act of "economic terrorism" cost the company about $40 million. No one, however, was killed or injured. The drug tamperer did his evil deed because he wanted to make a killing on the stock market. He had bought stock options in the company that would have made him extremely rich if the price of the company's stock had plummeted. He hoped that a highly publicized tampering incident would have that effect. It did not. The man's punishment for his crime was a twenty-seven-year prison sentence.

Why does a man get twenty-seven years in prison for an admittedly horrendous act that in fact harms no one while corporate executives go unscathed (or, if punished, serve prison terms that on the average are less than two years) after far more horrendous acts that kill dozens or hundreds or thousands? The answer, in part, is that corporate executives are protected by a network of corporate laws that treats corporations as if they were people under the law and thus holds them, and not their leaders, liable. You can't put a corporation in jail. But why do we allow such laws to stand? Why do we tolerate the insulation of responsible corporate leaders from the consequences of their evil decisions? Is it because we believe that "business is business"?

And just as important, how do these corporate leaders allow such things to happen? Why do they do it? What can they be thinking? Are they unaware of the misery they are producing? Are they monsters, on a par with the people who sell crack and heroin to teenagers? Are they caught up in a system over which they have no control? Or do they simply accept that "business is business"?

Consider today's talented, ambitious, enthusiastic students. Many of them aspire to a future in which they will take a major part in the production of cars, drugs, chemicals, foods, military supplies, and so on. But do they aspire to jobs that will require them to do things that will imperil the lives of thousands of people as they pursue their goals? They are good, decent people, as far removed from those who seek to turn human weakness into profit as anyone could be. And yet, some of these students surely will accept such positions, just as some of their predecessors already have. They will also marry, have families, and raise wonderful children who won't believe their parents could ever do such things. Surely there is an urgent need to figure out what it is that makes good people do such bad things, and stop it.

A few years ago U.S. Catholic bishops drafted a position paper, a pastoral letter, on the economy. In it they said, "Every perspective on economic life that is human, moral, and Christian must be shaped by two questions: What does the economy do *for* people? What does the economy do *to* people?" I have been suggesting that our economy does terrible things to people, even to those people who succeed. It makes them into people that they shouldn't and don't want to be, and it encourages them to do things that they shouldn't and don't want to do. No matter what an economy does *for* these people, it can't be justified if it does these things *to* them. Where, then, can we look, for the first steps toward reshaping and redirecting the business of business?

3

AND PROFESSIONS ARE BUSINESS TOO

Most of us believe we are parties to a social contract, not a business contract. We are not vendors, and we are not merely free economic agents in a free market. —ARNOLD S. RELMAN, M.D.

That any sane nation, having observed that you could provide for the supply of bread by giving bakers a pecuniary interest in baking for you, should go on to give a surgeon a pecuniary interest in cutting off your leg, is enough to make one despair of political humanity. But that is precisely what we have done. And the more appalling the mutilation, the more the mutilator is paid. —GEORGE BERNARD SHAW

The seemingly empty statement "Business is business" carries powerful implications about how little we can expect or hope for from people who are engaged in the pursuit of profit. "They're out to get us. They'll stop at nothing. We had better defend ourselves." Or so the story goes. But while this story *may* be true, it doesn't *have* to be. People *can* enter business with the aim of serving society while making a living rather than exploiting it in doing so.

Is there someplace we can turn for models of work life in which goals other than profit motivate and organize the activities of participants? An obvious candidate is the professions. Doctors, nurses, lawyers, accountants, architects, engineers, research scientists, teachers, social workers, journalists, and the like receive sometimes adequate and sometimes generous compensation for their work. But, beyond this, they are governed by a set of objectives and standards that demand honesty, integrity, and commitment to excellence. In seeking to meet such standards, people engaged in these professions can take pride in achievement, exercise their intelligence and creativity, and serve society at the same time that they are providing a good income for themselves and their families. Perhaps by examining the professions we can develop a model for work life governed by considerations other than the bottom line.

WHAT IS A PROFESSION?

What makes something a profession? The attributes we tend to think of when we think of professions include these:

- specialized knowledge
- long and intensive preparation, including instruction in skills and methods as well as scientific, historical, or scholarly principles
- maintenance of high standards of achievement and conduct, usually by a professional organization
- commitment of its members to continued study
- commitment of its members to a kind of work that has as its main purpose the rendering of a public service

When people undertake the arduous training required to become doctors or lawyers, we expect that along with the development of special skills and expertise will come a commitment to pursuing and upholding the goals and standards of the profession, goals and standards that have to do with the provision of a public service and not with the accumulation of wealth. We expect that there will be professional organizations that certify the competence of their members, lay down codes of professional conduct, enforce those codes, and discipline people who violate them. We also expect that professionals will continue to educate themselves, keeping up with the latest developments in their fields. For these commitments—to service and to excellence—we hold professionals in high esteem. And we don't begrudge them the opportunity they have to earn substantial incomes, for we know that it's the service, and not the income, that draws them to their professions.

Historically, there is a deep connection between the word "profession" and the rendering of a public service. "Profession" was originally used in a specifically religious sense, to describe the act of taking vows to consecrate oneself to special religious service. At least in the past, just as central to the notion of profession as the ideas of training, skill, and high standards was the idea that the work of the professional was valuable, was in a sense holy work.

When we think of professionals, we tend to think of doctors, lawyers, engineers, or accountants—white-collar workers who are educated first in colleges and then in professional schools. But there is nothing in the definition of a profession that is restrictive in this way. Plumbers, electricians, carpenters, and general contractors could easily be viewed as professionals. Their work requires substantial skill and, usually, substantial training. They render a valued public service. They must keep up with technological developments in their fields. They may lack professional organizations that establish and maintain rigorous standards of achievement and conduct, but such organizations, and such standards, could certainly be developed. By force of cultural habit, we may see vascular surgeons or psychotherapists as people whose commitment to the standards of their professions and to the well-being of their patients is unquestioned, while we see the plumber as someone whose commitment is to charge as much money as possible for as little work as possible. But there is nothing inherent or unalterable about this. There is nothing about what plumbers do that makes it less amenable to the application of high professional standards of achievement and conduct.

We can see how easily a culture can change what it thinks of as professions by looking at the history of professionalization in our own culture. Until the latter part of the nineteenth century, very few occupations were regarded as professions. There were very few professional schools, and there were almost no professional organizations. Medicine, for example, was quite a low-status occupation. University professors complained about the waste of talent when one of their gifted students chose to go into medicine rather than, say, business or the ministry. And many people who practiced medicine did it alongside other activities, like farming, that actually earned them their livelihood. Newspaper accounts from this period speak of doctors who "besides drugs, sold tea, sugar, olives, grapes, anchovies, raisins and prunes," of surgeons who were also wigmakers, and of midwives who also sold dresses. With little in the way of special training, and nothing in the way of professional standards of performance to distinguish them, there was little reason to regard "professionals" as different from any other tradespeople.

All this changed rapidly and dramatically in the late nineteenth century. The change was spearheaded by a major upgrading of university education. Prior to the 1850s, education in universities was uneven at best. There were virtually no entrance requirements, so almost anyone who could pay the fees (and who was white, male, and Christian) was welcome. And there were no written examinations, so what students did while in the university was completely unmonitored. As a result, the possession of a university degree said little or nothing about an individual's knowledge or character. Reform efforts by several university presidents in the mid-nineteenth century began to change the character of a university education. Entrance and graduation requirements, as well as written examinations in courses, were instituted. Various domains of rigorous professional training grew up. Whereas in 1850 there were seven law schools in the United States, by 1900 there were fifty. Whereas in 1850 there were twenty medical schools, in 1900 there were eighty-five. In 1850, two dental schools; in 1900, fifty. In 1850, four schools of pharmacy; in 1900, forty.

The possession of a university degree began to mean something, to certify a level of expertise and training. With this kind of training available, it began to make sense to develop professional standards of knowledge and performance. And along with the development of standards came professional organizations to oversee and enforce those standards. In the period 1860–90, professional organizations grew up in chemistry, engineering, forestry, biology, geology, physics, various branches of mathematics, economics, history, political science, modern languages, and more than a dozen different medical specialties. The professional training, along with the professional organizations, insisted on the mastery of a certain body of knowledge, attained at an accredited institution. It also insisted on a commitment to an ethic of service, which taught that dedication to a client's interest took precedence over dedication to the pursuit of personal profit.

The professionalization of various occupations brought with it an enormous improvement in the quality of the services that practitioners of these occupations provided. This change was of obvious social value. But it also brought with it something that was, and is, more problematic. As training programs succeeded in making practitioners more and more expert at their professions, they also made the people who employed the services of professionals less and less able to evaluate the quality of what they received. If the practice of professions required expertise, the evaluation of the practice also required expertise. Aside from occasional crude but dramatic evidence of success or failure (did the patient live or die?), clients were at a loss when it came to judging how well they were being cared for. They had no recourse but to trust in the integrity of the trained professional, as well as in the institution that did the training and the organization that set the professional standards. The procedures followed by professionals must have seemed mystifying, if not downright mystical, to the untutored amateur. As a speaker addressing a public health association meeting in the 1870s said, "Once, the priests were physicians. Now, the physicians are becoming . . . priests, and giving laws not only to their own patients, but to society." Trust—not only in a person's skill but in his or her character— was absolutely essential.

Today our reliance on expertise and the need for trust in character is no longer restricted to doctors, lawyers, and engineers. As the technological complexity of the goods and services we want continues to increase, we become less and less able to evaluate them for ourselves. The technological complexity of modern life calls for the professionalization of more and more occupations, so that we can rely on high standards of training, performance, and character to ensure that we get what we are looking for. Such professionalization would also allow the people who engage in these occupations to derive the satisfactions that come from performing an important public service in a way that meets high standards. So professional organizing is a way to enable both producers and consumers of goods and services to get more satisfaction out of what they produce and consume—as long as professional organizations have as their principal mission the assurance of high-quality service to customers, patients, and clients.

But, of course, professional organizations have another mission. In addition to seeing that society is well served by their members, these organizations try to ensure that their members are well served by society. By developing high standards of training and procedures of certification, professional organizations ensure quality of service. But they also keep people out of the profession and thus help guarantee that members of the profession will be needed, valued, and well compensated. By insisting on expertise that is so arcane that only insiders can evaluate it, professional organizations help ensure that only people up on the latest and best techniques can practice the profession. But they also help protect practitioners from public scrutiny. Thus professionalization is a two-edged sword. It has the potential to establish and maintain public service of the highest quality and integrity. And it has the potential to establish and maintain a monopoly that protects insiders and exploits vulnerable outsiders. Even in the 1850s, when professionalization was just beginning, both edges of this sword were apparent. At the same time that the medical profession was establishing and monitoring high standards of performance, it was establishing codes of professional training and conduct that restricted access to the profession, ensured high fees, and vigorously discouraged public criticism of one physician by another. Indeed, physicians could lose their licenses for criticizing one another in public. So, in order for professionalization and professional organizations to serve the public good, they must keep the public-service side of their sword sharp and the self-serving side dull. Have they?

MODERN MEDICINE

For almost everyone, what comes to mind as the best and clearest example of a profession is medicine. The practice of medicine requires extensive training, highly specialized knowledge, and continuing education. Doctors perform an invaluable public service. They save lives, ease suffering, prevent disease, and help bring new life into the world. And the performance of doctors is held to very high technical standards, standards that are developed and enforced by professional organizations. And it is held to high ethical standards as well. For example, the International Code of the World Medical Organization states that "a doctor must practice his profession uninfluenced by motives of profit." And the American Medical Association (AMA) has laid out a set of ethical principles meant to govern the conduct of all doctors that include the following:

- Doctors should show compassion and respect for human dignity.
- Doctors should deal with patients and colleagues honestly.
- Doctors should expose incompetence or dishonesty in their colleagues.
- Doctors should respect the rights, including the right to confidentiality, of their patients.
- Doctors should continue to study, and to make relevant information available to patients and to colleagues.
- Doctors should recognize a responsibility to participate in activities that contribute to improving the community.

It is because doctors provide such a valuable service and have such high standards that we respect them. And it is largely because medicine *is* a profession with high standards and commitment to public service that so many talented young people choose to enter it.

At the same time that the professionalization of medicine created people of skill and dedication, and certified them, it was having another effect. It was setting itself up as a kind of gatekeeper, regulating public access to the profession and its products and services. At the same time that state licensing requirements ensured a certain standard of expertise, they gave the medical profession the power to determine who became a doctor and how many doctors there would be. At the same time that the use of prescriptions regulated the distribution and use of powerful drugs, they ensured that even the treatment of the most mundane diseases would require mediation by the doctor who would have to issue the prescription. And as the health insurance industry grew up, the fact that insurance companies would provide reimbursement only for authorized procedures provided by authorized personnel, while it protected people from quacks, also forced them to get all medical care through professional medical channels. While each of these gatekeeping functions helped ensure a high quality of medical care, it also offered the potential for abuse in the service of the doctors' economic interests.

That there was a tension between professional standards and commitments and economic incentives was recognized very early by medical organizations. Medical organizations understood that professionalization violated the rules of the marketplace. People were not free to enter medicine as they pleased, or to offer whatever kind of medical service they wanted for whatever price they wanted. It was not left up to consumers to judge between various "brands" of care by choosing freely in an open market. The medical community judged that people lacked the specialized knowledge to make intelligent choices. Left on their own, they could easily be deceived and exploited by unprincipled charlatans. So the profession of medicine protected consumers by imposing and policing standards. This gave the profession a monopoly on medical care; it protected the profession from the discipline imposed by a competitive market. In asking for and getting monopoly power over their profession, doctors were in effect asking their patients for trust—trust that they would adhere to professional standards, that they would judge one another, that they would never let their monopoly position allow them to become either greedy or careless.

In return for this trust, organizations like the American Medical Association developed all kinds of guidelines to keep medicine professional—to prevent it from becoming a business. As the AMA put it, "Where physicians become employees and permit their services to be peddled as commodities, the medical services usually deteriorate, and the public which purchases such services is injured." These organizations also adopted strict ethical codes, to ensure that the patient's interests always came first. And so a person entering the medical profession through most of this century could be confident that his hard work and commitment would lead to a calling in which he served humanity with dedication and compassion, and was rewarded with both the successes of his ministry and the respect, admiration, and even love of his community.

But nothing lasts forever. The tension between commercial and professional interests is persistent, and the balance is unstable. As health care needs and expectations change, along with the costs of providing for those needs and meeting those expectations, new pressures develop, for which the old professional protections against commercialization may be inadequate. We are now in the midst of a dramatic change in the practice of medicine, a change that has threatened to turn the profession of medicine into a business. People who became doctors in the 1960s and 1970s entered the profession under one set of rules and expectations and have watched those rules change right before their eyes. Trust has been replaced by suspicion, and respect replaced by disdain, as modern doctors have come increasingly to be seen as unprincipled hucksters in relentless pursuit of wealth. To see why this has happened, we must examine some of the economic and social pressures faced by modern doctors that were not faced by their predecessors. Many, though not all, of these pressures are pressures of the profession's own making. They are seriously threatening the character of medicine as a profession, as well as the quality of medical care available to society.

The principal source of these pressures is cost. Partly because modern medicine is expected to provide more and better services than were expected in the past, and partly because the cost of even ordinary services has been rising much faster than people's incomes, medical bills have become much more salient and significant in recent years than they ever were previously. Medical bills take a big chunk out of individual paychecks, and they take a big chunk out of the collective, national paycheck (health care is currently estimated to take up about 14 percent of the gross national product). The chunk has become big enough that, both as individuals and as a nation, we have serious doubts about our ability to continue to afford to keep ourselves healthy. When costs begin to escalate out of control, the entire profession comes under careful scrutiny. The ethic of providing needed care without worrying about the bill becomes difficult to sustain. And as doctors are challenged to reduce costs, they feel pressured to defend their practices and their incomes from assault.

There is no simple story to tell about why medical costs have skyrocketed. Partly, it's the result of technological advance that has made possible vastly improved, though extremely costly, services (dialysis, bypass surgery, transplants, computerized imaging techniques). Partly, it's the result of ways having been found to keep people alive long enough that they can contract chronic illnesses that require long-term management and care. Partly, it's the result of a national commitment to subsidizing the medical care of old people (Medicare) and poor people (Medicaid). Partly, it's the result of years and years of operation of a health care system in which service was emphasized and cost ignored, so that there were no incentives leading people involved in the system to try to save money. And partly, it's the result of doctors' having taken advantage of their monopoly, and of the people's trust, and dramatically increased their incomes. For some or all of these reasons, the national per capita health bill increased from $142 a year in 1960 to $336 in 1970 and to about $2,500 in 1990.

The existence of government-financed programs to subsidize the health care costs of the aged and the poor was in effect a license for some doctors to print money. These programs ran on a fee-for-service basis, which meant that the more services a doctor or a hospital performed, the more he or it earned. In addition, these government-financed health plans paid doctors not on a fixed fee-for-service basis but on the basis of "customary fees," which were set on a regional basis. Within limits (reimbursement was pegged to "usual, customary, and *reasonable*" fees), doctors who normally charged very high fees got more from the government than doctors who charged much lower fees for the same service. Since the patients were rarely paying any of these fees themselves, they had little reason to argue about them, or even to examine their bills to see that all the services for which they had been charged had actually been performed. The urge was apparently just too much for many doctors to resist. Professional ethics or not, more and more doctors succumbed to the temptation to charge exorbitant fees and do unnecessary tests. Doctors, together with widely publicized advances in medical technology, contributed to the development in people of expectations about the level of care they should receive that were unrealistic and excessive and that led to the provision of services that were grotesquely expensive.

To illustrate just how dramatic the increase in medical costs has been, consider that at the turn of the century, when medical insurance programs were just getting started, the principal aim of insurance was to make up for lost wages. The costs of the hospital and the doctor were insignificant in comparison to the cost of losing two weeks' pay. By the 1920s, this was beginning to change; hospital bills amounted to somewhat more than lost wages. By 1990, it wasn't even close. Today a two-week stay in the hospital, along with bills for tests and doctors' consultations, can cost $50,000, much more than the average American earns in a year. Medical insurance nowadays really is *insurance*. People (or their employers) pay several thousand dollars a year in return for protection from the total financial ruin that would result if they actually got sick and had to pay their hospital bills out of their own pockets.

In the 1970s, concern started to surface that the United States and its citizens could not continue to pay health care bills that rose every year by substantially more than the rate of inflation. Reports started to appear about doctors who were abusing or defrauding the system, billing hundreds of thousands of dollars a year for services that, at best, were unnecessary and, at worst, were not even performed. Private health insurers started losing money and found themselves having to increase rates by 10, 15, or 20 percent a year. The bulk of these increases was borne by employers, who saw the cost of their fringe-benefit packages go out of control (in 1987, employer health care spending was equivalent to 94 percent of after-tax profits, up from 14 percent in 1965), necessitating either cost sharing by employees or lower pay increases to make up for exploding fringe-benefit costs. All of a sudden, everyone was complaining about the high cost of medical care. The public attitude toward doctors changed. Instead of being viewed as dedicated professionals, they were being viewed as greedy businessmen.

This change in attitude spilled over from the financial side of medical practice to the evaluation of the quality of medical care itself. If we couldn't trust doctors to adhere to professional standards and resist the temptation to be greedy, perhaps we couldn't trust them to practice good medicine either. After all, if doctors charged like greedy businessmen, perhaps they practiced like greedy businessmen as well, always trying to get the most and do the least. People started to think of themselves as "consumers" of medical services and to approach their doctors with the same wariness with which they approached car dealers or stereo salespeople. They sought second or third opinions (sometimes encouraged, or even required, by their cost-conscious and suspicious insurance companies). And when things went wrong, patients sued. Large court judgments dramatically increased the cost of malpractice insurance, which in turn increased the cost of medical services. The threat of malpractice actions also pushed doctors to practice defensive medicine, ordering every test under the sun, no matter how unlikely the tests were to be revealing. This also dramatically increased the costs of medical care.

Something had to give. Something had to be done. And that something was the coming to medicine of the health maintenance organization (HMO). Dedicated physicians—appalled at the cost of medical care, distressed that even routine health care (like annual checkups, which were not covered by insurance) was pricing itself out of the reach of many people, concerned that the existing system focused on costly cure rather than on inexpensive prevention, and upset at the pressure doctors were feeling to see as many patients as possible in the course of a day—developed HMOs in the hope that they would alleviate each of these problems. People would pay annual fees to the HMO, a nonprofit organization, in return for which they would receive all the care they needed, including the routine physical examinations that might spot problems in advance and prevent them from becoming serious and expensive. The doctors themselves worked for fixed annual salaries. In general, they earned less than they could have if they had been in independent practice. But they also avoided the costs and headaches of maintaining an office, paying malpractice premiums, and having to hassle with insurance companies. The HMO seemed like the perfect solution to the health cost problem. It provided quality care that was coordinated and comprehensive at much lower cost than the old, independent-practitioner system made possible.

In setting their annual fees, HMOs had to guess about how many expensive diagnostic services, visits to specialists, and corrective procedures the average patient would need in a year. If they overestimated, they would be left with a surplus at year's end. If they underestimated, they would suffer a loss. Because HMOs could not afford to sustain losses year after year, there were substantial incentives against the routine recommendation of unnecessary or questionable procedures. The less doctors did for (to?) people that was not essential, the lower they could keep the annual fees. But keeping fees low, and thus succeeding in one of its principal missions, was the only incentive that HMOs had for not recommending follow-up procedures. There was no point to operating at a profit per se, since the HMO wasn't in existence to make profits.

However, before very long, profit-making HMOs entered the scene, and they were joined by private, for-profit hospital chains (right now, it is estimated that two-thirds of the nation's HMOs and 30 percent of its hospitals are for-profit organizations). With this development, the discipline of the marketplace entered the profession of medicine. Entrepreneurs who themselves might not be doctors hired doctors to staff practices or hospitals. The salaried doctors were encouraged, if not pressured, to be efficient, seeing many patients per hour so that a small medical staff could handle a large practice. Profit was also increased by ordering as few follow-up tests and consultations with specialists as possible. In the hospital, profit lay in keeping beds full, and keeping them full with patients whose insurance companies reimbursed generously. The autonomy doctors had previously enjoyed to practice medicine as they saw fit was seriously compromised. So was their commitment to treat the sick, no matter what their ability to pay. The for-profit hospitals became adept at performing what sociologist Paul Starr calls "wallet biopsies." They would treat all emergency cases, but if intake assessment (the "wallet biopsy") revealed that a person had no medical insurance, he was transferred to a public facility. As one for-profit hospital official noted, in commenting on the death of a patient who was transferred to a public facility one day after suffering a heart attack, "These freebies cost $2,000 or $3,000 a day. Who's going to pay for them?"

This behavior of profit-making medical institutions had spillover effects on nonprofit institutions. These institutions were required to take in all the nonpaying, noninsured patients that the profit-making institutions turned away. The result was a constant struggle on the part of nonprofit institutions to maintain financial viability while still delivering adequate care. Nonprofit hospitals had to start competing with the profit-making ones for patients who had generous insurance plans, and thus began promoting the quality of their services in advertisements. Without an appropriate patient "mix" that included patients whose insurance provided generous reimbursement, the nonprofit hospitals would have gone broke or found themselves forced to diminish the quality of the services they provided to such an extent that no one who could choose between profit-making and nonprofit institutions would ever elect the latter.

The result of the growth of profit-making medical institutions, whether hospitals or HMOs, is that many physicians who joined HMOs precisely in the hope that they could practice better medicine, with less financial pressure on them than in independent practice, have found themselves locked into a system that is even more commercial than the system they left. Profit-making hospitals, clinics, and HMOs are turning out to be much more aggressively bottom-line oriented than independent practitioners. In addition, these profit-making organizations charge more, and are no more efficient, than their nonprofit counterparts.

Doctors don't like these changes in the nature of medical practice. They don't like being evaluated by superiors on the basis of the number of patients they see per hour. They don't like having their bathroom breaks scheduled. They don't like being discouraged from ordering tests and specialist consultations that they think appropriate, because they cut into company profits. They don't like being thought of as greedy and untrustworthy.

They don't like any of these things, but they seem to be stuck with all of them. More than half of all physicians practicing today are salaried employees. Among physicians under the age of thirty-five, more than 60 percent are salaried. The independent practitioner seems to be on a rapid road to extinction. Why have so many doctors given in to the pressure to work under conditions in which the practice of medicine is a profit-making business?

To gain some insight into this question, let's look at some of the problems that a newly graduated doctor faces. Medical school education, though heavily subsidized by various types of federal granting agencies, typically costs students more than $20,000 a year. The average medical school graduate begins practice with a debt of almost $50,000. If she decides to set up in private practice, the cost of outfitting even a simple office can be another $50,000. If she practices a specialty, the cost can be twice that. The annual cost of malpractice insurance can exceed $30,000. Once in practice, she will discover that negotiating the maze of health insurance forms and procedures can be a full-time job, so if she wants to get paid for the services she performs, she will need a staff person just to handle insurance claims. Medical associations estimate that in order to meet debt payments and various overhead expenses, a doctor will have to be earning more than $100,000 a year within five years of beginning to practice. This stunning fact leaves doctors with two choices: either they go into private practice and do everything they can to make as much money as possible as quickly as possible, or they avoid the headaches and financial pressures and go to work for a (frequently profit-making) HMO. Either choice often forces doctors to compromise their professional commitments and standards.

In the worst cases, it leads not to a *compromise* between commerce and profession but to the wholehearted embrace of commerce. When private hospitals refuse Medicaid patients because the reimbursement rate provided by Medicaid is too low to make the treatment of these patients profitable, commerce has won. And when studies report that uninsured patients lucky enough to be admitted to private hospitals receive worse care than insured patients (largely because of staff choices not to perform tests and procedures that are not absolutely mandated by the patient's condition, since these tests will not be paid for), commerce has won. When doctors are discovered involved in kickback schemes, admitting patients to particular hospitals in return for referral fees ($70 a head, or dinner for two plus a round of golf at the local country club), commerce has won. When specialists start selling shares in their practices to nonparticipating, but potentially referring, primary-care physicians, commerce has won.

A particularly significant (significant because it is growing more and more common) recent example of the triumph of commerce over profession concerns what is known as physician "self-referral." Physicians refer their patients to diagnostic or treatment facilities in which they—the physicians—have an ownership stake, though they play no role in the management of these facilities. Some recent studies comparing rates of referral and costs between physician-owned and non-physician-owned facilities have found that when the facilities are physician owned, physicians order many more tests, at much higher cost, than they do in non-physician-owned facilities, with no evidence of better diagnostic or treatment outcomes (indeed, with some evidence that more cases of inappropriate use of diagnostic and treatment procedures occur in physician-owned than in non-physician-owned facilities). While a body of delegates of the AMA officially disapproved of this practice of self-referral at the end of 1991, except under a small set of unusual circumstances, it reversed itself only a few months later—a reflection, I think, of the growing confusion and conflict physicians feel between professional obligations and commercial opportunities.

As examples like these accumulate and get reported, as these were, in daily newspapers and popular magazines, the public attitude toward the medical profession deteriorates. It becomes more and more difficult to show the doctor the respect and admiration he may once have received, and deserved. The doctor, in turn, may decide that if he's going to be treated like an ordinary businessman, he may as well act like one. It may not gain him respect, but at least he can console himself with wealth. The AMA, which previously tried to prevent the commercialization of medical practice, has apparently given up. Whereas once it regarded advertising and entrepreneurial activities by physicians as unethical, it now officially sanctions both, presumably in acknowledgment of the cold economic realities of modern medical practice. Indeed, it may even have given in to the temptation to make a *virtue* of its failure to prevent the penetration of commercial concerns into professional practice when it recently said, "Ethical medical practice thrives best under free market conditions, when prospective patients have adequate information and opportunity to choose freely among competing physicians and alternative systems of medical care." This (resigned?) acknowledgment of the role of the market in the provision of health care may help explain the great enthusiasm that exists in some quarters for a "managed competition" approach to health care reform. This approach is a key component of President Clinton's recent proposals regarding health care.

The commercialization of medicine is having profound effects, both on doctors and on patients. In a series of articles in the *New York Times* about three years ago, the attitudes of doctors and their patients were surveyed. Even though the average doctor at that time was earning almost $150,000 a year, only 25 percent of the practicing doctors surveyed said they would definitely go to medical school now if they had the choice to make over again. More than 40 percent said they would definitely or probably not go. This disappointment that doctors are experiencing with their profession is reflected in the career decisions being made by current college graduates. In 1985, 36,000 people applied to medical school; in 1990, the number was down to 27,000 (though in the last two years applications have increased). Almost three-quarters of the doctors polled said that the public has less respect for the profession now than it had a decade ago. And a quarter of the consumers of medical services polled confirmed that assessment. Two-thirds of the people polled thought doctors were too interested in making money, and 60 percent thought they didn't care as much about their patients as they had in the past.

A moving, personal account of how financial pressure is changing the character of medical practice was offered in a newspaper article a few years ago by Dr. David Hilfiker. He had recently left a rural medical practice to practice among the urban poor in Washington, D.C. Again and again he was told stories by patients about how they were refused care by physicians in private practice all over the city. These stories led him to do an informal telephone survey, which revealed that less than 10 percent of the doctors in Washington had sliding fee schedules and that more than half of them turned down Medicaid patients. Private hospital emergency rooms all over the city routinely shipped indigent patients to the city's only public hospital. For this deplorable abandonment of the poor, Hilfiker blamed not the individual physician but the system that pressures physicians to become businesspeople. He put it this way (and I quote extensively because he said it so well):

> The structure of day-to-day medical practice alters one's perspectives. In 10 years, I have become aware of the pressures which have subtly encouraged me to measure my work according to its economic productivity and have thus distorted the physician-patient relationship. . . . The increasing technical intensity and busyness of medical practice has led to a preoccupation with better "management" of the office. This has generally led to the hiring of additional nurses, technicians and assistants: the physician suddenly finds himself the administrator of a large staff, a task he may never have expected and for which he was probably never prepared. . . . So the physician scurries around from patient to patient, trying to do enough to pay for the office and the staff. Very

soon, a business approach seems necessary just to keep afloat, and the physician has already become an entrepreneur. . . .

The entrance of corporate medicine into health care has exacerbated all these tendencies. . . . Efficiency is now not only important but mandated from above. If the physicians, as healers, do not want to measure their work by its economic production, their employers certainly do, and the attitude filters inevitably down. . . .

The realities of medical economics encourage doctors to do less and less listening to, thinking about, sympathizing with and counseling of patients. . . . Instead, the doctor is encouraged to *act*, to employ procedures. . . . Charges for procedures . . . are universally higher than fees for talking with the patient. . . .

Over the years, I found myself valuing brief interviews over real listening, aspiration of a joint over taking a good history, removal of an appendix over counseling a distraught teen-ager. . . .

There is no code in the fee book for comforting the grieving family of a patient who has just died; it is difficult to charge a panicked parent for middle-of-the-night telephone reassurance. The very fact that money has become the basis of physician-patient interaction often inhibits a patient from raising "extraneous" issues which may be vitally important to health; it may even inhibit a patient from coming to see a doctor in the first place. . . .

At some deep level, I think, we physicians know that something is wrong. We are invested with enormous trust and confidence predicated ultimately upon our role as healers who place the patient above our own personal needs. The monetization of medicine strikes at the heart of this trust. As patients gradually realize that their physician is getting rich from the services rendered, the very core of the relationship is shattered. We physicians must recognize that there is a contradiction between a vocation of service and the inordinate earnings we now command. Though we physicians may deny it even to ourselves, we know it is true.

These sentiments were echoed by Arnold S. Relman, a physician, former editor of the *New England Journal of Medicine*, and one of the most persistent contemporary critics of the commercialization of modern medicine:

Society has given us a licensed monopoly to practice our profession. . . . We enjoy independence and the authority to regulate ourselves and set our own standards. Much of our professional training is subsidized.

. . . Most of all, we have the priceless privilege of enjoying the trust of our patients and playing a critical part in their lives when they most need help.

All this we are given in exchange for the commitment to serve our patients' interests first of all and to do the very best we can. In my view, that means we should not only be competent and compassionate practitioners but also avoid ties with the health care market, in order to guide our patients through it in the most medically responsible . . . way possible. If the present organization and incentives of our health care system make it difficult or impossible for us to practice in this way (and I believe they do), then we must join with others in examining ways of reforming the system.

Given the direction that modern medicine has taken, we can hardly look to it as a model of professionalization from which other occupations can learn. Rather than being part of the solution, it seems to be part of the problem. We had better look elsewhere.

MODERN LAW

If we depend on doctors to keep us alive, we depend on lawyers to show us how to live. The law and lawyers are absolutely central to American democratic culture. We are, it is said, "a nation of laws, not men." The laws are many and complex, and our relation to all of them is mediated by lawyers. We are helpless before the legal system without lawyers. Lawyers mediate in our relations with the government and its formal, legal apparatus, and they mediate in our relations with other people. Whether we are entering into contracts, writing wills, paying taxes, seeking redress for grievances, starting businesses, or ending marriages, we depend on lawyers. We depend on them to help us interpret the laws, to live within them, and to seek the protection they provide. As a nation of laws, we require a nation of lawyers.

The premise that lawyers and the law are central to our national character suggests that a healthy and respected legal profession is as central to our national well-being as a healthy and respected medical profession is to our personal well-being. It is thus both significant and distressing that if the public sees the modern doctor as perched precariously at the edge of a precipice, clinging to the high ground of the professional, but on the verge of falling to the low ground of the commercial, then it sees the modern lawyer as already having fallen—or jumped. The dominant modern attitude toward lawyers is cynical and suspicious at best, and downright contemptuous at worst. What has gone wrong? About sixty-five years ago, the distinguished jurist, and later Supreme Court justice, Felix Frankfurter said this about the law:

> The great, big fact about American national life which differentiates it from that of all Western countries . . . is the part played in our affairs by lawyers. . . . Ours is a *legal* society. . . . We must have law and lawyers . . . that are sensitive to the feelings and needs of the various ingredients that make the sum total of the American Nation, lawyers that are hard-headed without being hard, lawyers that are wise rather than smart. . . . In the last analysis, the law is what the lawyers are. And the law and lawyers are what the law schools make them.

So what kind of law and lawyers are the law schools making?

When I ask college seniors who have chosen to go to law school why they have decided to become lawyers, I get a variety of different answers. For some, it's a kind of holding action; they're not sure that they actually want to practice law, but they believe that a law degree will serve them in whatever they decide to do when they "grow up." (That they believe this is an indication of how central a part of American life the law has become.) For some, it's the route to a lucrative career. For some, it's a way to earn a living that will provide interesting intellectual challenges. For most, though, it's a kind of public service, a way to contribute to the making and preserving of a just society. The law is a tool for the pursuit of justice. In our society, it is the principal tool. The complexity of modern law has made it virtually impossible for ordinary, untrained citizens to work within the system without a guide. And so the majority of students with whom I speak want to serve the public by becoming guides.

I don't mean to suggest here that all my students imagine themselves as crusaders, protecting indigent people from being turned out on the street by heartless landlords, or protecting First Amendment rights of war protesters or avant-garde artists before the Supreme Court. They expect, many of them, to do detailed and often complicated work for ordinary people, and to be well compensated. They expect to write wills, draw up contracts, set up corporations, execute real estate deals, and find ways to mediate and resolve disputes between people. But what underwrites their commitment to the ordinary is the belief that participation in the legal system is in itself a contribution to the democratic political culture that they value— that what the practice of law is about is the pursuit of justice.

Then they go to law school. And what most of them learn in law school is that the law is not primarily about the pursuit of justice; it's about the pursuit of capital. Several different accounts, some of them firsthand, have recently been written about legal education. While they differ from one another in detail, they converge on the view that law school changes people in fundamental ways; it creates a new person. Best-selling novelist and U.S. attorney Scott Turow describes his professors as "brain thieves." "They're turning me into someone else," one of his classmates observes. "They're making me different. . . . It's someone I don't *want* to be." Another law student notes, "When you enter law school, they tell you that you won't be the same person when you leave, and you think it's a crock of shit. But it's true. . . . It's some very wicked form of brainwashing."

What students learn in law school is to value doing well more than they value doing good. They learn to abandon their naive belief that law exists to serve the public good, and replace it with the realistic view that law is a business and that it serves other businesses. They learn this from the law school curriculum itself, which serves the needs of corporations with courses on finance, taxation, business transactions, securities, and so on. They learn it from their experience as very well-paid summer associates with corporate firms. And they learn it from the intense recruiting efforts of these firms. The budding lawyers are taught to see themselves as commodities, as "hired guns," obliged to serve the (typically financial) interests of their clients. As one writer notes, "It should come as no surprise that law students, trained during their legal education to see themselves as commodities, begin to see law itself as a commodity, and end up selling themselves to the highest bidder."

Many of their professors, who may be hostile to the aims of the practice of corporate law, are nevertheless extremely enthusiastic about the intellectual challenges that corporate law provides. There are puzzles to be solved in a corporate context that public-interest law, for example, can't match. And those students who are not seduced by the financial incentives of corporate law are frequently attracted by the intellectual challenge:

> Before I took [a course on corporations], I thought it would probably be dull, but when I started taking the course I realized it was very intricate, that there was a lot to deal with and it was a challenge.

> I think that my original choice of jobs was based on sort of a "helping the other people" attitude, and that was like the prime thing. And now it's more—I think I'm more interested in getting something that's intellectually stimulating for myself.

What students are exposed to, both by their professors and by their lucrative summer jobs with corporate firms, is a legal hierarchy that places corporate law near the top and public service near the bottom. And if this indoctrination isn't sufficient, law students, like medical students, incur huge debts in the course of their very expensive law school training that push them out the door in pursuit of jobs that will pay well enough for them to pay off their student loans. Twenty years ago, the salary for beginning lawyers in corporate firms was about the same as the salary for beginning lawyers in legal-aid organizations. Now corporate jobs pay about four times as much as legal-aid jobs pay. Between the content of the curriculum, the summer contact with the corporate profession, and the debt, the result is overdetermined.

But there is another aspect of legal training that I think has an even greater role in creating "new people"—"hired guns." It is the professional commitment to what Rand Jack and Dana Crowley Jack call an ethic of "neutrality and partisanship." These two words seem explicitly contradictory, yet in the training of lawyers, they are combined. Lawyers are supposed to be neutral in regard to clients. They are supposed to take on "whoever walks through the door." Our legal system depends in part on everyone's right to representation. The lawyer's personal values are not supposed to intrude on her selection of cases and clients. Of course, the system doesn't actually work this way; many lawyers in fact exercise discretion in choosing clients. Indeed, there are some practitioners who argue that "a lawyer is not a bus; she doesn't have to take everybody." But this selectivity by individuals can be tolerated only so long as there is always someone out there willing to represent everyone. In principle, that someone could be—and might have to be—you. Thus the ethic of neutrality. And the "ethic" of neutrality is reinforced in the corporate firm, where the only criterion for accepting clients is their ability to pay, and young associates have little or nothing to say about whose interests they are assigned to represent.

Having adopted the stance of neutrality (either out of principle or out of corporate compulsion) in the selection of clients, the lawyer must then abandon this stance once the client has been selected. Now the lawyer must act as a partisan. She must make her client's interests her own. No matter what she may think of her client, during the time in which she represents him, she must act as though pursuing his interests were the most important and the noblest thing in the world. She must, in effect, *become* her client.

This combination of neutrality and partisanship may be unique to the practice of law. Doctors, ministers, and teachers are also supposed to be neutral in regard to whom they will heal, comfort, or teach. But they are not required to take on the values and interests of their patients, their supplicants, or their pupils. Lawyers do precisely this. The Jacks put it this way:

> In a service-oriented society, many pay for services, but few consumers make so comprehensive a claim on the total person as a client does on an attorney. A lawyer becomes the voice and presence of a client, perhaps advocating things the lawyer regards with distaste. . . . In a sense, the client has purchased more than a hired gun. The client has also acquired a piece of the attorney's integrity, credibility, mind, and soul. The lawyer stands in the client's shoes, thinks the client's thoughts, speaks the client's words, advocates the client's position. The attorney is the client's mouthpiece, the client's alter ego.

It takes a lot of practice to become, even temporarily, another person. And lawyers get this practice:

> A practicing lawyer will soon detect in himself a perfectly astonishing amount of sincerity. By the time that he has even sketched out his brief,

however skeptically he started, he finds himself believing more and more in what he says, until he has to hark back to his original opinion in order to orient himself. And later, when he starts arguing the case before the court, his belief is total, and he is quite sincere about it. You cannot very well keep your tongue in your cheek while you are talking. . . .

A lawyer is required to be disingenuous. He is required to make statements as well as arguments which he does not believe in. . . . And he must never lose the reputation of lacking veracity, because his freedom from the strict bonds of veracity and of the law are the two chief assets of the profession.

The lawyer, in short, takes other people's ends and makes them his own. He is free to choose the means to achieving those ends. Indeed, his professional training and his skill reside principally in the ability to discover or invent clever means. But the lawyer must allow others to determine his goals. The lawyer is required, in the pursuit of his profession, to suspend a significant part of his *self*— his moral compass, his identity. In the short run, as he pursues the interests of his clients, he may be able simultaneously to hold on to his own values. But as the years of eighty-hour weeks in the service of other people's interests accumulate—as the years of saying things he doesn't believe, in the service of ends he doesn't believe in, pile up—the lawyer is hard-pressed to keep what is his. It is ever so much easier to abandon the schizoid tensions of this sort of life and allow his clients' values to become his own.

For giving up his self, for acting as if another person's goals were his own, the lawyer demands and receives substantial compensation.

Extrinsic rewards (pay, career, advancement, working conditions), which are often lavish, displace intrinsic satisfaction, which is limited to the exercise of technical skill. . . . The strongest evidence that professionals have relinquished control over the ends for which they work may be their inability to perceive the loss.

And increasingly, lawyers who work for corporate firms are even being asked to give up the intrinsic satisfaction that comes from exercising technical skills to serve a client's interests. Increasingly, corporate firms are demanding that their lawyers be loyal and dedicated not to the clients but to the firm itself. The aim of the firm is to extract the greatest possible fee from its clients. Lawyers are encouraged—even required—to take as much time (and thus as many billable hours) as they think they can get away with in handling each matter that comes before them. They are required, in other words, to charge what the traffic will bear. They are required to act *as if* they were dedicated to pursuing their clients' interests, when in fact they are dedicated to pursuing the interests of their own firm.

This point was bought home to me by a former student of mine who works for a large corporate firm. At his annual performance review, he was told by a senior partner that he had been providing his clients with expert legal advice extremely efficiently. My former student thought he was receiving high praise for a job well done until his boss added "*too* efficiently."

Recent surveys of lawyers indicate that very few of them give their profession up; they have among the lowest attrition rates of any of the professions. Alongside this, however, is survey evidence that they are the most dissatisfied. The material rewards of their work may keep them at it, but they don't seem to compensate for the loss of self that the work demands.

There are other "professions" that demand that a significant part of the self be submerged or sacrificed. Airline attendants, for example, are required to "be nice" for a living, to act as if every passenger request were reasonable and nothing were more important than passenger comfort and satisfaction. Arlie Hochschild documents the toll that this professional niceness exacts on genuine emotion, in her book *The Managed Heart.* Therapists are often required to treat their clients as if their problems were the most challenging and important things in the world, no matter how banal and commonplace they may be. As practitioners of "the oldest profession," prostitutes must act as if their current client were the only one, as if their passion were genuine and unbounded. And I once heard a very popular disc jockey say, when asked about the secret of his success, "The key to success in this business is sincerity; if you can fake that, you've got it made." But none of these other professions demands a sacrifice of self as profound or as significant as that of lawyers. Lawyers are selling more than passion, affection, and sincerity; they are selling their moral commitment, the very heart of what it means to be a person. They may have in their hearts a sense of what it means to serve truth. They may have in their hearts a sense of what it means to serve justice. But their profession requires that they suppress or abandon both truth and justice so that they may serve their client or their firm.

To some extent, this problem is inherent in the structure of the adversarial system of justice. Especially in the context of criminal law, the system demands that everyone get the best defense possible. But outside the criminal context and, more generally, outside the context of litigation, the system permits lawyers to exercise a fair amount of discretion in what they do—what matters they pursue and how they pursue them. They would not be so vulnerable to self-transformation if what they did when they were not trying cases were consistent with their own values and commitments to justice. But it is here—in the making of deals and contracts—that the commercialization of the legal profession takes its toll on the selves of its practitioners. The deals lawyers do can be no more principled than the businesspeople they do them for. And we saw in the last chapter what such deals are often like. It is hardly surprising that when lawyers serve as handmaidens to corporate profit seekers, they are turned into profit seekers themselves.

Having been trained to detach their own moral standards and commitments from their professional activities, where do lawyers, acting as lawyers, turn for guidance as to what is appropriate conduct? The answer is that they turn to the institutions within which they work, the canons of their profession. As long as they perform appropriately in their appointed role, it is the responsibility of the system to see to it that justice is done. They owe the system vigorous representation of their client. But they also owe it other things. They must not knowingly present perjured testimony. They must not advise clients on how to evade legal processes, nor may they abuse legal processes by pursuing ends for which the processes are not intended. They must not knowingly file frivolous claims; they have a responsibility to determine that there is a basis in fact or in law for their claims before they pursue them. All these professional canons, and others, are designed to keep legal proceedings honest and just. If dishonesty and injustice occur, it's the fault of the system.

If the system is responsible, the people working within that system are not. If the system authoritatively determines right and wrong, the individuals working within that system are absolved. It is this orientation that makes it possible for lawyers to represent without qualms of conscience many of the scoundrels (individuals and corporations) I discussed in the last chapter. They are doing what they're supposed to do. If a corporation goes unpunished for polluting the air, or putting death traps on the road, or defrauding investors of their money, it's the system that has failed, the system that has lost its moral compass. For the lawyer, it's an indication of a job well done.

Lawyers tell themselves this, but they aren't very happy about it, and they aren't entirely convinced that it's true. This no doubt explains why so many are dissatisfied with their work. But unfortunate as it is for lawyers that they must often auction off their conscience to the highest bidder, it is even more unfortunate for society as a whole, for, unlike flight attendants, therapists, prostitutes, or disc jockeys, lawyers are at the very center of modern social and political life. They are everywhere. (The United States has 5 percent of the world's population and 65 percent of the world's lawyers; there are about 650,000 practicing lawyers in the United States and about 10,000 in Japan.) The law and lawyers touch almost every aspect of modern life. The law and lawyers provide us with an inescapable model of how one lives a life. And it's a model that tells us to submerge our moral concerns, pursue our interests, and trust that somehow the system will get things right. It's a model from which notions of justice and responsibility are conspicuously absent. It's a model that tells us to seek and press every advantage we can over potential adversaries, and to assume that they are doing the same. As a result, it's a model for the disintegration of the person and the social fabric, with clever advocates—hired guns—and an adversarial system to take their place.

As it turns out, the system to which lawyers abdicate responsibility and in which they place their trust is breaking down. In the criminal system, the jails are so full and the courts are so backed up that criminals are set free and the pursuit of justice has been replaced by the pursuit of speedy dispositions—of plea bargains. In the civil system, it can take years for cases to come to trial. And the cost of seeing things through to the end is so prohibitive that only the wealthy can stay the course. Frivolous lawsuits can be filed in the expectation that defendants will settle rather than endure the ordeal and the expense of a trial. The dominant strategy now seems to be to sue no matter how unlikely it is that a jury will find that your adversary has done anything wrong. Aside from interfering with any chance of obtaining just outcomes, this new strategy has dramatically increased the costs of legal fees to corporations as well as malpractice premiums paid by various professionals. None of these increased costs contribute to economic productivity or to the well-being of anyone except the lawyers. We all pay their fees, by paying higher doctor bills and higher prices for the products we buy, but we get nothing for it. This breakdown in the legal system is demoralizing those lawyers who have not been completely remade by their legal education. It frustrates and subverts those for whom the law continues to be a domain for public service and for the pursuit of justice.

There are two different ways to respond to the breakdown of the system. One way is to acknowledge it, accept it, and change your goals and expectations about what the system is for. This kind of response is exemplified by what has come to be known as the "law and economics" movement, spearheaded and developed by legal scholar and U.S. appeals court judge Richard A. Posner. Posner advocates a system of adjudication that essentially forgets about justice altogether or, more accurately, redefines justice in economic terms. What the system should be asking is not who's right and who's wrong but what the potential costs and benefits to each side are. And the system should be deciding in a way that minimizes costs and maximizes benefits for the disputing parties and, thus, for society as a whole. This point of view, in effect, makes the legal system an extension of the market, a device that uses the criteria of the market to settle the occasional disputes that the market can't take care of by itself. This strategy may not make lawyers any more satisfied with what they do, but it will make the system run more efficiently, at least by economic standards of efficiency.

Alternatively, you can refuse to accept the system as it is, refuse to be remade by law school, refuse to leave your moral compass at home when you go to the office each day. This response to the disintegration of the system and the disintegration of the self is becoming increasingly common among young lawyers. And it is becoming increasingly common, according to the Jacks, because more and more women are entering the legal profession. Whereas in 1963 only 4 percent of all law students were women, twenty years later 40 percent of law students were women. Though the reasons for it are unclear, on the average, women lawyers find it much more difficult, and much more unsatisfactory, to adopt the standards of neutrality and partisanship than their male counterparts. They are more reluctant than men to try to win at all costs. They are more reluctant than men to leave their moral center at home. They are concerned, many of them, with acting in a way that minimizes harm to all the parties concerned, even if this sometimes means settling for less for a client than they might be able to get. In child custody cases, they are interested in what's good for the child, in addition to what their client desires. In bankruptcy cases, they are interested in preventing both sides—creditors and debtors—from being destroyed. In general, they are interested in using their concern for all the parties involved, in addition to, not instead of, the rules of law, to resolve disputes in a way that is fair and compassionate. This difference between male and female lawyers may reflect the more general difference between men and women in their approach to matters of justice, fairness, care, and responsibility that psychologist Carol Gilligan documented in her book *In a Different Voice*.

Women who have these concerns find that their (mostly) male employers are unsympathetic. They regard the concerns of women as a sign of lack of commitment, of unwillingness to do what it takes to be a successful lawyer. Thus many women find themselves having to make a difficult choice: "Forsake the self or forsake the law," as Rand and Dana Jack put it. And many women faced with this choice, far more than men, are choosing to give up the law. Their superiors say, ironically, "If you can't stand the heat, get out of the kitchen." A sensible reply to this, say the Jacks, "would be to ask what is wrong with the kitchen that there is so much heat? Why do so many bright, competent people find it difficult to work there? What happens if people work all day in a kitchen that is too hot?"

The kitchen is not just too hot for women; it's too hot for everyone—women and men, lawyers and clients. Dissatisfied women "can take the lead in helping to restore sanity, balance, and respect to the profession." But they need help. They need help from their male colleagues, who work in the same, oppressive kitchen. And they need help from their clients. Pressure from the people who hire lawyers, as well as from the lawyers themselves, can reestablish law as a profession that serves the public, and reestablish lawyers as people who do good at the same time that they do well. They may do less well, but they'll do more good, and they'll derive more satisfaction from their work as a result.

•   •

The professions, in their modern form, hardly offer an alternative to the "business is business" attitude that dominates the commercial world. Having been unable to beat the commercial world, the professions are moving to join it. But at least in some of the professions—in medicine and in law—the move is creating a backlash. There is growing dissatisfaction, both from within and from without, regarding the directions that law and medicine have taken. They are failing to complete their mission, and they are failing to maintain the commitments of their practitioners. Society is demanding that they change, and it remains for us to determine the direction that the change will take. In my view, the direction of the change must be toward easing the commercial pressure, and the resulting commercial orientation, of these professions. Doing this may require that we devote social and economic resources to making the training of these professionals and the provision of their services less costly. Doing this may require that fewer of the services that doctors and lawyers provide be available for sale on the market. And doing this may provide a model from which other professions, and even commerce itself, can learn.

4

AND GAMES ARE BUSINESS TOO

*[H]ow a society takes its leisure is as important a social index of its
health as how it does its work. . . . [L]eisure time and the values
informing that time have been understood to be more reflective of a society's aspirations and goals than its work—for while labor ennobled . . .
leisure perfected.* —A. BARTLETT GIAMATTI

Where have you gone, Joe DiMaggio?
A nation turns its lonely eyes to you.

—PAUL SIMON

In the fall of 1992, the Toronto Blue Jays made history by becoming
the first team from a non-American city to win baseball's World
Series. They did it in what has become the modern style—they
bought it. Four of their stars—their most important players—were
new to the team. One had come from a team he had helped win
the World Series only a year before and to which he had sworn his
undying loyalty. Another had come in a midseason trade, only to
sell his services to yet a different team while the taste of celebratory
champagne was still fresh on the tongues of Toronto fans. If business
is business, and professions are business, then games are business
too. Organized athletics, whether professional or amateur, are so
inextricably bound to commerce that the sports pages of our daily
newspapers look more and more like its financial pages. Any attempt
to distinguish the sports "industry" from other modern industries
seems artificial and arbitrary.

We all know that games are business, and this is nothing new.

Games have always been business. Teams have always had owners, owners who were usually rich and who tried pretty hard to get richer. And teams have always had players who tried to make a good living out of their athletic ability. Nevertheless, the commercial side of our games has changed dramatically in character in the last two decades. The business of sports was once conducted backstage, as though the people making money were embarrassed to let the public in on their dirty little secret. Even if people made money by playing games, or by owning the teams that played them, making money was not what the games were *for*, and the less said about it the better. At present, what once went on behind the curtain has moved in front of it, and what previously was a cause for embarrassment has become a cause for celebration. The commercial side of sports has moved from the periphery of its conduct and of public awareness to the very center. And sports have been significantly changed as a result.

This change is captured well by an anecdote related in the *New York Times* a few years ago by Suzanne Stout. The experience is so poignant that I quote it almost in full:

> Baseball is our little boy's passion and Gregg Jefferies, the rookie second-baseman for the Mets, is his first, and beloved, hero. A photograph plaque of Gregg Jefferies hangs in a position of honor, alone on the wall over his bed. On his seventh birthday, my son solemnly placed a Gregg Jefferies baseball card in the center of his birthday cake.
>
> So, when we heard that Mr. Jefferies would be signing autographs in a toy shop in New Jersey, it was not a question of would we go, but of how?
>
> However, as we investigated, we realized that Mr. Jefferies would not simply be visiting with kids and signing autographs. No, he would be *selling* his autograph, which required buying a $10 ticket, advance purchase advised.
>
> I called the toy shop to ask if we really needed to buy a ticket in advance. The owner said that 800 had already been sold and they were expecting to sell 2,000. I was stunned. . . . I bought three.
>
> Expectation kept our son in a state of frenzy. The night before the event, he couldn't sleep. He greeted us at dawn in his Mets uniform, ready to go.

When we arrived at the toy shop . . . hundreds of families were there, with many mini-Mets in uniforms just like our son. The toy shop had taken over the adjacent vacant store for the day, and sold Gregg Jefferies photographs, baseball cards and other items for him to sign. The line moved fast, and before we knew it, we were standing in front of Gregg Jefferies.

He sat with his cute girl friend at a table, signing his name as fast as he could. Gregg did not look up when he signed our son's picture. He never saw our son's face go white, his eyes pleading to make contact. This was an assembly-line operation. Ninety seconds after we had entered the shop, we stood outside, autographs in hand.

As we drove back, our son sat staring sadly at the autograph. Exasperated by his misery, I snapped: "What's wrong? You got to see Gregg Jefferies and you got his autograph. . . ."

"But Mom, he didn't even look at me."

"Well," I said, "the format wasn't right for a visit or eye contact."

"Yeah, but Mom, he's my guy. My all time top guy. You don't understand, Mom. He's my hero."

My husband and I slumped in our seats. Now we all felt terrible. But what had we expected? I suppose we had hoped to meet a hero: a symbol of possibility for our son, a whole-hearted man who excels at playing his part on a team in a game with rules. And more: A man with enough respect for his craft, the game and his role not to merchandise his signature.

After a bit, our son's mood lifted. "Mom, if there were 2,000 people out there, that means Gregg Jefferies made $20,000. And he made it in three hours. Does the toy shop get some? How's Gregg spending that money, Mom? Is he helping the homeless?" I told him I didn't know. My son begged me to find out.

"Because," he continued, "if I know how much money he needs to make for three hours work, maybe I can save up enough to pay him to come to our house for dinner."

"Hold it," I wailed. "We are not paying anybody anything to come to our house for dinner."

"But Mom, that's what Gregg Jefferies wants: *money*."

We've had this same conversation many times since that day. . . .

I did call the toy shop on behalf of my son. The owner's wife would not disclose the finances, but she offered some advice: "In today's world, it's never good to get too close to your heroes. Better to view them from afar." But I don't want today's world to be like that. And I wish Gregg Jefferies would take his signature off the market.

I tell this story not to single out Gregg Jefferies. There is nothing unusual about his willingness to spend an afternoon selling his auto-graph, and many of the other professional athletes who do it have salaries more than ten times what Jefferies was earning in his rookie season with the Mets. Nor do I tell this story to pick on professional athletes generally. While it is true that athletes demand and receive extraordinary salaries, and are willing to endorse almost anything, their commercialism is merely the most visible and most dramatic part of a thoroughly commercial system. The athletes are no more and no less greedy than the owners of their teams.

No, I tell this story because it exemplifies so well the changes that have occurred in sports over the last few decades. I still remember quite vividly my own attachment to baseball when I was about the age of Suzanne Stout's son. My heroes were Mickey Mantle and Whitey Ford, star players for the New York Yankees. I rushed home from school every day in the hopes of catching the last few innings of the game on the radio. When the team played at night, I begged my mother to let me stay up late and listen or watch, especially when Whitey was pitching. I developed the habit of reading the newspaper out of my intense desire to read every word that was writ-ten about my heroes. I developed a facility for arithmetic computa-tion during Mickey's greatest year, as I spent my time recomputing his batting average after each of his turns at bat. I played imaginary baseball games, against the stoop of my apartment house or against the wall of my school in the schoolyard, pretending to be Mickey or Whitey (or both) as I murmured a running play-by-play account under my breath of the game I was playing. I learned to enjoy vis-iting the library because it was in the library that I discovered the *Baseball Encyclopedia*, the repository of every baseball statistic a fan could ever want to know. When I went to games (always in a Yankee cap and sometimes, before the pseudo-sophistication of early adoles-cence hit, in a Yankee uniform), I got to the stadium early and stayed late, hoping to catch a glimpse of my men, to tell them how great they were, and perhaps to get a smile, a word, an autograph in return. I chose my seat in the ballpark so as to maximize the chances that I would catch a home run off Mickey's bat (left-field bleachers when he was batting right-handed; right-field bleachers otherwise).

In a word, I worshiped these players. I worshiped them because they played the game I loved for the team I loved, because they played it hard, and better than anybody else. Of course, they played the game for money. But however important the money may have been to them, it was always, or almost always, kept in the background. You don't have to be a sports fanatic to know that times have changed. And this chapter is about how they've changed.

THE VALUE OF SPORTS

Many people think of sports, at any level, to be rather frivolous. Whether we watch them or play them, sports are just one diversion among many, a form of entertainment that distracts us temporarily from the real business of life. I think that this view is mistaken and that sports provide us with several significant moral lessons.

The practice of sports is guided and defined by the pursuit of excellence. Each sport has unique and fairly explicit standards for what constitutes excellence, and a highly articulated set of constraints (the rules of the game) within which excellence is to be pursued and achieved. The pursuit of excellence in sports requires discipline, dedication, commitment, and, in many cases, loyalty to the team and a willingness to sacrifice the interests of the individual participant for the good of the team. The pursuit of excellence in sports also requires honor, a willingness to play by the rules. Those who bend the rules, or cheat, may win individual contests, but they will not be achieving excellence, since, for it to count, excellence must be achieved within the rules, not outside them.

The significance of sports lies partly in the way they develop in their participants virtues of character like dedication, discipline, and loyalty. It lies partly in the way sports hold these virtues up for all of us to see, admire, and try to emulate. And it lies partly in the way the achievement of excellence in sports exemplifies for us some of the extraordinary things of which human beings are capable if they put their minds, and bodies, fully into it. The achievement of excellence, even in a purely recreational domain, points us toward excellence in more important domains. In this respect, sports represent a kind of training for life, ideal in a way just because we can develop the virtues of character we will need for important matters in a domain in which nothing of much concrete significance rides on success or failure. While it is true that other aspects of society can provide similar lessons, the fact that so many members of American society take sports so seriously, especially when they are young, may make sports as significant a source of developing values as any institution we have. Our children may learn as much about how to live from observing their sports heroes as they do from observing their teachers, their political leaders, their ministers, or their parents. Philosopher George Santayana had this to say about excellence in sports about a century ago: "The value of talent, the beauty and dignity of positive achievements depend on the height reached, and not on the number that reach it. Only the supreme is interesting: the rest has value only as leading to it or reflecting it."

And when we see people capable of producing the supreme—whether Gregg Jefferies, Mickey Mantle, Michael Jordan, Jack Nicklaus, or Martina Navratilova—we make them heroes. When we're young, we aspire to be like them, maybe even to *be* them. We make their triumphs and failures our own. Almost all of us, as we get older, learn that our excellence will have to come in another domain of life. But still we take these athletes as examples of what dedication and commitment can do. "I'm no role model," says one basketball star in an athletic-shoe commercial that is currently running on television. But he is. Whether he wants to be or not—whether he *should* be or not—he is.

There are many people who criticize the worship of athletes and the fanatical involvement with sports that characterizes our culture. They see it as a commitment of time, of energy, of talent, and of money that is wholly out of proportion to the significance of the activities themselves. For millions of Americans, the world essentially vanishes in the weeks leading up to football's Super Bowl. For other millions around the world, the same thing happens during the competition for soccer's World Cup. It's bad enough, critics say, that so many people start their reading of newspapers every day with the sports page; what's even worse is that some of these people never leave it. Critics see people willing to talk endlessly about the pros and cons of this or that trade, or about whether a different strategy would have produced a different outcome in a championship game, and complain about the unwillingness of these same people to talk and think about who should be the next president, or what strategy might effectively deal with urban poverty. Furthermore, the critics of sports see them as encouraging an attitude of competitiveness, of win-at-all-costs aggressiveness, and of almost jingoistic team loyalty that encourages a destructive kind of belligerence when it is imported into the boardroom, the courtroom, the negotiating table, or even the battlefield.

My own view is just the opposite of this critical view. We have not taken sports seriously enough to protect them from the rest of life. We have listened to people who say that sport is just a business, just another form of entertainment, competing for our leisure dollar. In listening to these people, we have allowed sport more and more to become just a business. This in turn has threatened or compromised much that makes sports distinctive and valuable.

Historian Christopher Lasch has argued as follows:

> Play has always, by its very nature, set itself off from workaday life; yet it retains an organic connection with the life of the community, by virtue of its capacity to dramatize reality and to offer a convincing representation of the community's values. . . . Games and athletic contests offer a dramatic commentary on reality rather than an escape from it—a heightened reenactment of communal traditions, not a repudiation of them.

It is precisely because of the capacity of sports to "dramatize reality and to offer a convincing representation of the community's values" that the modern degradation and commercialization of sports is important and distressing. Like the doctor and the lawyer, the athlete provides an example for us of how to live a life, a model of what is valuable and what is virtuous, a model that offers an alternative to the model of business. But like medicine and law, instead of holding up an ideal for us, sport has become just like business. This not only undermines what makes sports distinctive and valuable, but it also tarnishes a model we might use as we try to reconstruct our other important cultural institutions.

AMATEURISM, PROFESSIONALISM, AND COMMERCIALISM

There is nothing wrong with the professionalization of sports. The opportunity to earn a living at sports opens participation up to people whose financial circumstances would otherwise make it impossible. "Amateurism" is a form of class-based elitism. The very notion of an "amateur" arose in Victorian England, in the late nineteenth century, and it was intended to keep "gentlemen" and riffraff separated. Only an English gentleman could afford to be an amateur, to live on inherited wealth and devote time and effort to the perfection of his athletic skills. By and large, the line between amateur and professional was a line between the unpaid members of a privileged class and the paid members of an underprivileged class.

So professionalization actually opens sports up to people who without pay could not afford to devote themselves to the pursuit of excellence. The result is a much larger group of participants in athletics. This leads to greater athletic achievement both because the world of athletics is open to people with talent but no money and because people can devote themselves fully to developing their skills. If you have any doubt about how professionalization provides access to people who would otherwise be excluded, the fact that the majority of those who participate in major sports today come from working-class or poorer families should eliminate it.

In the last chapter, I suggested that a "profession" is a domain of activity that requires extensive training, highly specialized skills, high standards, an organization to monitor those standards, and a commitment to public service. I think it will be useful if we think about the "professionalization" of sports in this sense. In the modern world, there are virtually no world-class athletes, no matter what the sport, who don't earn their livelihood at their sport. Being able to earn their livelihood allows them to work at their sport all the time. Even during the off-season, they engage in rigorous conditioning programs designed to keep them fit for the next season. The issue for us is not whether athletes are professional in the sense that they earn their living at their sport but whether they are professional in the sense that they are committed to the high standards of excellence and achievement that we expect the profession to uphold. The issue for us is whether athletes and, more important, the organizations that support them remain true to the "goods" of the games in which they participate, or whether they are willing to compromise those goods in the pursuit of money. We can ask about athletes and their employers, just as we asked about doctors and lawyers, whether they are true to their professional ideals. But asking this question requires that we distinguish between professional and commercial, not between professional and amateur.

THE COMMERCIALIZATION OF PROFESSIONAL SPORTS

Back in the "good old days," professional sports were very different from what they are now. First, teams belonged to cities. Though not all cities supported their teams with equal enthusiasm, it was virtually unthinkable that a team might scout out greener pastures and move. The Yankees, the New York Giants, and the Brooklyn Dodgers were no less a part of New York than the Empire State Building or the Metropolitan Museum of Art was. Second, players belonged to teams. Though trades of players between teams were common enough, they were usually "supporting players," either veterans past the peak of their abilities, or young players who hadn't yet reached the peak. The core of each team, its stars, was (unlike that of the world champion Toronto Blue Jays) solidly a part of the team and the city. The team and its personnel were something a fan could count on. Each new season was resonant with memories of past seasons. The team and its particular players had a history, one that could be integrated into the life history of the people who supported the team. Teams had histories that spanned generations, so parents (mostly fathers) and their children (mostly sons) could find in their shared enthusiasm a common discourse, a common loyalty, and a common set of standards for evaluating and appreciating excellence. Fathers and sons could revel in the disagreements they had about whether *this* generation of players was better or worse than previous generations. They could revel in these disagreements because they occurred in the context of deep agreements about what made the game, the team, and the players exciting and valuable. It was not nearly so easy to take pleasure from other intergenerational disagreements—about things like career choices, living arrangements, decisions to move out of town, and the like, where deep agreements about what made life exciting and valuable may not have been present.

So in the good old days, teams and players were community resources. Teams were expected to be loyal and committed to their communities, players were expected to be loyal and committed to their teams, and fans were expected to be loyal and committed to both. But, even more important, in the good old days, most of every fan's attention was directed to what went on *on* the field. The point of the game was the game itself. The game was what you talked about. And the game was what the sportswriters wrote about. The sports fan's universe was encapsulated by the sidelines. What went on on the other side of those lines was insignificant. Sure, the players had lives off the field, but, by and large, they were of little interest. And certainly the teams had owners, and the owners were businessmen, but the business side of the game usually sat quietly in the background. Only rarely did sportswriters trouble themselves to write about player contracts, gate receipts, TV deals, and the like. If it is true that sport has always been a business, it is also true that the business side of it was not allowed to intrude on what was important—the games and the athletic performances.

Before I am accused of romanticizing the past, let me make it clear that there was plenty about the "good old days" that wasn't good. Most owners exploited their players, mistreating them, underpaying them, and regarding any public complaint from the players as a violation of the very loyalty to team and community that I just celebrated. And because each owner retained exclusive rights to his players' services in perpetuity, the players were essentially chattel, with absolutely nothing to say about where they played. They may have been well-paid and admired chattel, but they were chattel nonetheless. As for the players, many of them led private lives that were hardly exemplary, with the details kept out of the newspapers largely to save the players and their families from embarrassment. Many players squandered their quite considerable talents, abusing their bodies with postgame carousing during the season and neglecting their bodies altogether between seasons. It was a very rare athlete who was the "consummate professional," taking care always to be at his best, devoting himself in the off-season to correcting whatever weaknesses in his abilities might remain, driven to being the best there ever was at what he did.

In the eyes of people like me—the fans—it mattered little *how* the job got done, as long as it got done. Whether our heroes' brilliant performances derived from natural talent or from hard off-season work was unimportant. As long as they played as hard as they could during the games, and produced the many performances that took our breath away, they remained our heroes. Everything else was irrelevant. We took what they did on the field much too seriously to be distracted by details of their private lives. What we demanded of our professional athletes was that they do everything possible to help the team win and to bring glory to themselves, their teams, and their fans. If they transgressed as human beings, we could easily forgive them. If they transgressed as athletes, forgiveness was not so simple.

I remember quite vividly the attitude that fans would have when backstage issues concerning the business side of the game occasionally sneaked to the other side of the curtain. There would once in a while be serious contract squabbles, typically involving star players who "held out," or refused to play, without a higher salary. When a contract disagreement first came to light, the public was invariably on the side of the player, hardly a surprise since the player was someone fans worshiped, whereas the owner was largely invisible. As the disagreement continued into the period of preseason practice, and the player in question refused to appear at practice without a signed contract, concerns would start to be raised. What these concerns reflected, I think, was the belief that a player, whether his position was just or not, should never let money stand in the way of what was important—the prospect of a successful season. Of course, the owner shouldn't either, but what, after all, could we expect of owners. They were just businessmen; they didn't know any better. The player knew better, and maybe his priorities were out of whack. On those rare occasions when the contract problems persisted into the season, and the player refused to play in games that actually counted, he usually lost most of his public support.

Holding out for more money was not a rare event. Every few years, some big star on some team would do it. It happened in *my* good old days, the fifties, and it happened in my father's good old days, the twenties and thirties. So issues involving money and sports have crept out from behind the curtain repeatedly over the years. They are not a late-twentieth-century invention. However, although these issues were not unheard of, they were infrequent enough to command attention and disapproval. People sat up and took notice. They took notice that something was going wrong. The athletes and their employers were worrying about the wrong things, the sportswriters were writing about the wrong things, and the really important things—the games themselves—were getting overlooked. No one could possibly have this attitude today and continue to follow professional sports. For in the modern world of professional sports, what was unusual has become commonplace and what was exceptional has become the norm.

Hardly a day passes without at least one "business" story on the sports pages. Owing to changes in the legal structure of professional sports, teams can no longer own their players in perpetuity. Once players have achieved a certain level of seniority, they are free to negotiate with anyone; they become "free agents." This gives players a degree of leverage that they never had before. If their team won't meet their salary demands, they can simply sign with another team. Thus the world champion Blue Jays are a team that is unusual not in its purchasing of players but in its good judgment about which players to purchase. What this means is nonstop contract negotiation and player movement from team to team. When star players sign contracts, it's big news. Newspapers report the terms of the deals in fine detail. And there are details aplenty, from signing bonuses to performance incentives to deferred compensation to low-interest loans, as deals are structured by accountants and business managers with an eye toward tax laws, investment opportunities, and projected inflation rates. The player's contract gets the same kind of microscopic attention that his athletic performance does. Players are ranked not just by batting average or strikeouts but by average annual salary. Each year, lists are published reporting the salary bills of each of the professional teams. Business has gone from backstage to center stage.

The freeing up of players to move from team to team has had an enormous effect on players' salaries. For the 1991 baseball season, the average salary for a major league baseball player was over $1 million. More than one hundred players earned over $2 million, and more than forty earned over $3 million. And it should go without saying that if team owners are paying out salaries like this, they must be making plenty of money themselves. With such money at stake, it's not surprising that the deals are complex, requiring the services of lawyers, accountants, and business managers. Players have become corporations.

It's tempting for someone who finds the financial side of sports a distasteful encroachment on what's really important just to ignore it, regard it as irrelevant, and continue following the athletes and the teams on the field. It's tempting, but it's nearly impossible, at least if you really care about your team, for your team's fortunes are intimately bound up with the contractual terms it manages to negotiate with its players. There is no guarantee that anyone, even the brightest star, on this year's team will still be around on next year's. Only long-term contracts can lock players in. You can struggle with your team as it suffers through a string of losing seasons, nurturing a collection of talented young players to the verge of stardom. And then, just when it seems that it's finally going to be your year, one after another of these young stars signs contracts to play elsewhere. Being able to find and develop talent no longer guarantees your team's success. To be successful, the team must be able to get that talent to put its names on dotted lines. So the future of your team on the field depends on how well its management does its business off the field. This makes the business side of the game hard to ignore.

And as business news takes up more and more of the sports page, it's just a matter of time before sports fans get accustomed to it, and start incorporating it into their ongoing talk and reflection about their team. It's just a matter of time before salary becomes as interesting and significant a "stat" as batting average or runs batted in. I remember a few years ago overhearing a conversation involving my teenage nephew and a few of his friends. The discussion was heated and the disagreement intense. It involved comparisons among various baseball teams and their players, and it reminded me of many similar conversations I had had twenty years before—except that the focus of the discussion was on which teams had made smart deals with their players and which teams had made dumb ones, which players were being overpaid and which underpaid. Salary had entered the debate as a relevant dimension of comparison of the quality of different players and teams. It was a sports discussion all right, but very little of what was at issue concerned what goes on *on* the field.

All this could be taken as an attack on greedy ballplayers who are willing to forsake fan and teammate alike in search of the highest buck, but to the extent that the players behave in this way, they are only taking a page from the owners' book. Beginning in the 1950s, owners began to realize that there was no law requiring them to stay in their city of origin. As the development of airline transport made long-distance travel quick and convenient, new potential markets for professional sports opened up throughout the country. Where earlier virtually all professional teams had been located in the Northeast, possibilities now arose in California, in Texas, in Florida—in short, wherever there was a population center. Much of this nationwide desire to house professional teams was met by league expansion; new teams were created in all the major sports, and located in these previously deprived cities. But in addition to the creation of new teams, the possibility was open for already established teams to move. At first, teams relocated only in desperation. If the people in their hometown had stopped supporting them by coming out to games, if they were losing large sums of money, if all attempts to increase local support failed, a team would relocate in a new city that was full of people so eager for a team of their own that they would support virtually anything. But as owners got accustomed to the idea that teams could move, what counted as "desperation" began to shift. "Desperation" could be created instantly, simply with the opportunity for a better deal elsewhere. The notion that a team owed loyal fans loyalty in return quickly disappeared from the owners' minds. The owners saw balance sheets and profit margins, and little else.

The event that most dramatically signaled the end of the idea that teams belonged to cities was the move of the Brooklyn Dodgers baseball team to Los Angeles. The Dodgers were one of the two or three most successful teams in baseball, with a long history of great teams, great players, and tremendous fan support. Their rivalries with both the New York Yankees and the New York Giants gave baseball fans many of their finest memories, and owners some of their richest seasons. The Dodgers were doing just fine in Brooklyn in the 1950s. They were in no danger of going broke. Their teams were winning, and their fans were coming out in large numbers to watch them win. But Los Angeles beckoned, a virgin city with several million people and offers of land and a new stadium. The Dodgers left Brooklyn, making their owner countless millions, changing the nature of professional sports, and breaking the hearts of many thousands of people in the bargain.

The move of the Dodgers to Los Angeles ushered in a new era, an era of "have pro team, will travel." Teams that were making money relocated if they saw an opportunity to make more elsewhere. Or if they didn't relocate, they threatened to do so, extorting a host of concessions from their home city in return for staying. Concessions included tax abatements, land and money for the construction of new stadiums, and commitments by the city to upgrade the streets and highways that led to the stadium. All told, such concessions frequently cost the cities many millions of dollars. The cities, though probably strapped for money already, felt they had no choice but to give in to the demands of the teams. The teams were so central to the social and cultural life of the cities that watching them leave was too painful (and very likely too unpopular with the voters) to contemplate. Even with concessions, teams might still move, abandoning stadiums and arenas with a rich history of their own in the central city for new antiseptic facilities in the suburbs. As the various unique playing areas were replaced by new arenas stamped from a common mold, a bit of each team's particular history disappeared with them. And the lesson in all this—from the owners to the players, and from the players to the fans—was "follow the money; business is business."

So both players and owners are now out chasing the money. But where does all the money come from? How can professional teams afford to pay multimillion-dollar annual salaries? The money does *not* come from the sale of tickets, beer, hot dogs, and souvenirs. Or at least not the bulk of it. Although innovations like "luxury boxes," along with soaring ticket prices, have greatly enhanced the gate receipts available to owners, if professional teams had to count on the turnstiles as their main source of revenue, most of them would be essentially small-time operations, and most players would still be looking for jobs in the off-season just to make ends meet. The bulk of the money available to professional teams and athletes comes from television.

Forty years ago, sports teams had TV and radio contracts with local stations. Virtually all the games were broadcast on the radio, and some were also broadcast on TV. The money involved was not big. Indeed, it's not clear who should have been paying whom. Having the games available on radio and TV almost certainly raised the level of fan interest in the team and brought people out to the arena or the stadium. So broadcasting games was almost an advertisement for the team. For those under forty, it is helpful to keep in mind that TV was black and white, most sets had twelve-inch screens, reception wasn't great, there were only a couple of cameras at the game, and there was no instant replay or slow motion; in no sense was watching the game on TV as good as (or better than) being there; at best, it was a tease, an invitation to the real thing. In 1952, the total TV revenues for Major League Baseball were about $5 million. In 1970, TV revenues for the National Basketball Association were about $1 million.

Times have changed. The National Basketball Association got $70 million for its TV rights in 1986. Major League Baseball got over $1 *billion* just for *network* TV rights in 1990, and deals between individual teams and their local stations provided millions more. The National Football League gets enough money for TV rights to finance the annual budgets of many Third World countries. In general, more than half the money that major league teams receive comes from broadcast rights. This means that teams now have $20 or $30 or $40 million in the bank before they have sold their first ticket.

Because of these TV deals, professional teams can afford to pay the unbelievable salaries that they do. They can afford to be much more independent of local fan support than they were in the past ($40 million in the bank before the first ticket is sold). With TV deals, the market value of professional teams has grown to astronomical levels; teams now sell for tens or even hundreds of millions of dollars. It is hardly surprising, with such sums of money involved, that high-powered corporate financial people have taken control of the operations of many teams.

Why does TV throw this kind of money around? TV is in the money-making business, and if it signs big contracts with professional sports organizations, it expects to make a profit, by attracting many viewers and thus being able to sell advertising at very high rates. What this means, of course, is that TV has a very large stake in creating a "product" (the game) that lots of people will find exciting and attractive to watch. Because TV needs viewers, and professional sports need TV, much of the character of modern professional sports is now driven by the commercial interests of the TV networks that bankroll it. It is through the influence of TV that we can see how concerns about commercial interests can pull sports in directions that do not serve the good of the games.

TV is not about to spend a billion dollars to put something on the air that will appeal to only a handful of fanatics who live it and breathe it, who appreciate every nuance, every subtlety, who are steeped in the history of the game and alive to every strategic possibility. TV wants to appeal to as many people as possible, to the lowest common denominator. TV wants spectacle; it wants action and excitement. It wants games that move fast, with lots of scoring. It wants people watching games who don't care much about the games themselves, but are interested in the players in the way they are interested in entertainers. It wants the games to be available to viewers at times that are maximally convenient. It doesn't want people to have to stay up half the night, or leave work early. Of course, the fanatics will try to adjust their life schedules so that they can watch the games whenever they are on, but there aren't enough fanatics to generate a billion dollars a year in advertising revenue.

The demands of TV have an enormous impact on the character of the sports it televises. TV dictates rule changes that make a more attractive product. TV dictates schedules, so that games are played at times that are most convenient for the audience, no matter how inconvenient they may be for the players. The most dramatic example of this is baseball's World Series, which was traditionally played in the daytime, even long after most regular-season games were being played at night. There are some good reasons for playing the World Series in the daytime. Because visibility is better, the chances are that the quality of play will be better. Perhaps more important, because the World Series is played in October, when in many northeastern cities it gets quite cold at night, nighttime games might subject players to playing conditions that are far from optimal, that indeed might expose them to the risk of serious injury (especially the pitchers, whose throwing arms seem especially vulnerable in the cold weather). So day games in October meant better weather, better visibility, and, almost certainly, better play. But they also meant many fewer viewers. People work during the day. For a billion dollars, TV wants prime time. And for a billion dollars, TV gets what it wants.

I had thought that the shift of the World Series to prime time represented the culmination of TV-induced schedule and rule changes that had been going on for decades. But apparently I was wrong. The most recent network TV contract offer to Major League Baseball demands that it change fundamentally the way it determines its champion each year. For the good of the game? Perhaps, but that is highly debatable. For the good of prime-time TV audiences? Without a doubt.

As noteworthy as the schedule changes dictated by TV is the way in which TV covers the games. The broadcasters are charged with the task of doing whatever it takes to make the games exciting. Real enthusiasts don't need to have games *made* exciting; they simply are exciting, in themselves. And even when they're not, there's still plenty to watch and appreciate. Real enthusiasts want information and analysis, not fabricated excitement. But broadcasters aren't playing to the enthusiasts (who will be glued to the TV set anyway); they're playing to the dilettantes. So announcers talk personalities, create controversies, have the cameras pan over the crowd (attractive women in shorts and bare-chested men, especially when it's freezing cold, are current favorites), and keep discussion of the game itself and its intricacies to a minimum. The level of discourse maintained by the "play-by-play" man and his "expert" sidekick tends to be insultingly superficial to anyone who takes the game seriously. The fanatics are willing to tolerate these annoyances, for without them the games might not be broadcast at all. But they don't like them.

Both fans and players respond to the game as spectacle by participating in it. Fans do increasingly outlandish things to bring the cameras in their direction. And players develop "signature" moves and celebratory gestures that will make them stand out as "personalities." After all, it's just show biz. They're there to entertain the people. And achieving recognition as a personality may mean athletic-shoe endorsements, soft-drink commercials, autograph-signing sessions, and who knows what other ancillary sources of income. In keeping with this lowest common denominator, show-biz orientation, the arenas themselves surround the games with nonstop distraction— blasting music, hyperactive mascots, and bouncing cheerleaders— so that there is never a dull moment, never a moment of silence in which fans can actually think about the game and imagine all the things that might happen next. In the midst of all the entertainment and the hype, the game itself gets lost. An ever broadening array of ever less knowledgeable spectators gets what it wants, but what it wants has little to do with what makes sports valuable and makes players heroic.

Two decisive TV phenomena bear primary responsibility for turning sports into an entertainment and a spectacle. Both were the doing of the ABC television network. The first was the introduction of an "up close and personal" feature to many of ABC's sports telecasts. During a lull in the action, ABC would show a brief feature that introduced us to an athlete, showed us where he lived, how he trained, who he was married to, what his kids were like, and what he cared about in life. It was an attempt to get us to know, and care about, the whole person. It was an attempt to introduce "human interest" into sports. This feature was enormously popular. Viewers who had little interest in the sport itself, and little knowledge about it, could develop an interest in the people. And then they could root them on as people, exult with them in triumph, and suffer with them in defeat. "Up close and personal" worked. Ratings went way up, and the nature of sports broadcasting was permanently changed.

The second, and perhaps even more significant, ABC innovation was "Monday Night Football." This very bold move entailed quite a risk. It involved putting the most mysterious, least accessible of our major sports before the public in prime time. Until this point, network sports coverage was almost exclusively on weekend afternoons, when ratings expectations were much lower. It was targeted for the man of the house, who knew his sports. Prime time, in contrast, was family time; it was targeted for everybody. Having decided to risk putting football in front of people who didn't understand it very well, ABC had to get them to watch it. This it endeavored to do by making the game the background and the exploits of its broadcast team the foreground. A two-man broadcast team wasn't enough. So in addition to Frank Gifford, a former star player, who struggled, often in vain, to try to describe the game, audiences were treated to folksy, funny, down-home Don Meredith, another former star, and "tell it like it is," pull-no-punches Howard Cosell, a Brooklyn lawyer turned sports news commentator and, finally, broadcaster. Meredith told his funny stories, ridiculed Cosell, and, as much as possible, ignored the game. Cosell ridiculed Meredith (and the straight-laced, soft-spoken Gifford), invented controversy, and also ignored the game. Mostly, what the audience heard each week was three hours of Meredith and Cosell talking to and about each other, only occasionally distracted by Gifford's persistent efforts to remind them that there was a game going on on the field.

This venture into prime time also worked. "Monday Night Football" became hugely popular, attracting audiences of people who had little interest in or knowledge of football. They didn't need it. The broadcast wasn't about football; it was about the broadcasters. Another dose of personality. Another dose of entertainment. Another blow to sports. For the success of "Monday Night Football" also changed the character of sports broadcasting. If you could get people who didn't know much to watch on Monday night, maybe you could get them on the weekend too. And thus developed the modern celebrity broadcaster, determined to create a show for which a lack of knowledge of the sport was no barrier to entertainment. "Monday Night Football" set the standard for all subsequent attempts to lure viewers to the TV for sporting events.

By now, we've all grown used to these things. We've all grown used to business news on the sports pages, to players and teams coming and going like commuter trains, to broadcasters as stars, athletes as personalities, and broadcasts as entertainments. We've grown used to seeing our athletes perform under far from optimal circumstances, and to seeing them sell anything and everything—from shoes to drinks, to autographs, to underwear, to cars, to insurance, to earth-moving equipment. We've grown used to seeing athletes covered with patches endorsing different products, and tournaments renamed for their corporate sponsors instead of for the cities in which they are held. People my age remember, however dimly, that it once was different, and we believe that something has been lost. For people my children's age, the way it is now is the way it's always been.

Trickle Down: The Amateurs

Those of us who are disappointed with the commercialization of professional sports can perhaps turn to the amateurs. Amateur players don't earn multimillion-dollar salaries, and amateur teams have no profit-making owners. But if we do turn to the amateurs, we'll be disappointed again. The romantic image of an amateur athlete as someone who works hard all day studying at the university and then comes home to his dorm room and gets into his athletic clothes, to train and participate out of love for the sport, has always been a myth. But in recent years, the gap between the romantic image and reality has grown much wider. For various commercial reasons, the pressure to win in the amateur domain has intensified, forcing people to go to greater and greater lengths to recruit and secretly compensate star athletes. The pressure to win has pushed the athletes themselves to seek various illicit means to secure an edge on the competition—from performance-enhancing (and often dangerous) drugs to illegal equipment. It has simply become impossible to keep the corrupt, disingenuous practices of amateur athletics a secret. The result is a public cynicism about the athletes, their coaches, their sports, and the institutions that run the sports, as well as a more general cynicism about honesty, integrity, and respect for rules. Modern amateur athletics may make the pros look pure by contrast.

In the United States, the principal domain for high-level amateur athletics is the university. Universities compete in dozens of sports. At the universities whose teams we read about on the sports pages and see on TV, the romantic, "student-athlete" myth bears almost no relation to reality. Athletic participation at these schools is a very serious matter. Students are recruited specifically because of their athletic ability. They are expected to arrange their class schedules so that classes and assignments don't conflict with practices or games. They are expected to put their hearts and souls into training and competition. The sports in which they participate are often at the center of campus life, and the athletes themselves are certainly local celebrities and frequently national ones. They can attract more than 100,000 spectators to football games, more than 20,000 to basketball games, and millions of TV viewers and dollars.

Down through the years, universities have played a cat-and-mouse game with the National Collegiate Athletic Association (NCAA), the primary body that sets and enforces the rules for participation in intercollegiate athletics. The NCAA would issue regulations governing the recruitment of high school athletes, or the limits of scholarship aid athletes could get, or the academic standards athletes were required to meet in order to remain eligible to compete, and universities would do everything they could to subvert or circumvent those regulations. Thus, if *coaches* were allowed only a certain number of visits to high school recruits, alumni would be enlisted to visit them instead. if athletes were allowed only scholarship money to cover the cost of tuition, room, board, and books, coaches would see to it that their athletes got undemanding evening and summer jobs for which they were paid exorbitant wages. And if athletes had to maintain a certain course load and grade point average to remain eligible to compete, courses would appear in the curriculum ("Body Building," "Football Tactics," "Introduction to Coaching," "How to Give an Interview") that even the most indifferent student athlete would find a way to pass.

As the NCAA discovered these various ingenious devices for violating the spirit, if not the letter, of its regulations (though plenty of schools were violating the letter of the regulations as well), it would toughen them up, which in turn led to new and even more-ingenious ways to circumvent them. On and on the thrust and parry went, punctuated periodically by a public scandal whenever an especially egregious violation of the rules was uncovered. And so it has continued to the present. The rules are so many, so detailed, and so complex that coaches probably need full-time attorneys on staff to help them figure out what they can and can't do. They complain that these rules have so tied their hands that it has become impossible to recruit, train, and field excellent teams. Nevertheless, they do manage to continue to field such teams, and they manage to find loopholes in the rules big enough to let a supertanker through. And when the loopholes won't do, they break the rules, convinced that all their competitors are doing likewise. They just hope that by the time the NCAA catches up with them, if it ever does, they will be safely installed in some amateur athletic hall of fame somewhere, identified as brilliant coaches, teachers, and molders of character.

Universities were willing to bend and break NCAA regulations when only pride and reputation were at stake. Now the temptations have grown much greater, for in addition to pride and reputation, what's at stake is money—lots of money. TV now pays the NCAA millions and millions of dollars for the right to broadcast college football and basketball games (indeed, CBS just agreed to pay $1 *billion* for the right to televise college basketball for the next six years). Much of this money goes directly to the schools involved in the games. In football, individual schools receive as much as $4 million for appearing in one of the major end-of-the-season bowl games. In all, the various postseason football bowl games paid participating institutions $60 million in 1990. In basketball, during the national championship tournament, each victory might mean several hundred thousand dollars for the winning team. So successful teams mean significant revenue for their schools. And even the money that is shared among schools—winners and losers alike—depends upon their being able to provide a high-quality product. TV networks aren't going to pay $1 billion for the right to broadcast games involving teams of bumblers, out to have a good time and get some exercise. TV wants the best. Its viewers won't be interested in anything less.

On top of the TV money, many schools have huge football stadiums and very large basketball arenas to fill, and nothing fills the house like a winning team. Thus universities now have financial incentives that are not very different from the incentives of pro teams. They don't have to pay their athletes multimillion-dollar salaries, but the costs of running a high-powered athletic program are substantial, and revenues generated by the major sports meet those costs. The high-stakes finances of modern college athletics put everyone under enormous pressure to win.

The pressure on the coaches is especially dramatic. Their jobs depend on their ability to win. Coaches of major college football and basketball teams are not kept around because they are good physical education teachers, or even good teachers of football and basketball. They are not kept around because they build the character of their players, encouraging them to work hard in the classroom and prepare themselves for life after athletics. College coaches are expected to win. They are expected to get their teams into bowl games and championship tournaments. They are expected to generate publicity for their schools and financial support from alumni. They are expected to keep their players eligible. As for how they accomplish these objectives, the less said (and known) the better. College coaches are subjected to the same expectations, and the same pressures, that professional coaches are. And because of the premium that schools place on success, the successful coaches are very much in demand. They command salaries that far exceed the salaries paid to any other university employee, including the president. Alumni watch the appointment of new coaches like hawks. For university presidents, choosing the coach is often the single most important personnel decision they will make. Nobel Prize–winning physicists can come and go without anyone's batting an eye, but should the presidents lose a good coach to the competition, or hire a questionable one for themselves, their jobs are in jeopardy.

That the pressure on coaches to win has been intensified in recent years by the escalation in the financial stakes attached to winning is clear from the comments of the coaches themselves. A few examples from a few years ago will suffice to make the point. In college basketball, the pinnacle of the season is the championship tournament that comes each March. The best teams in the country compete against one another. A single loss eliminates a team, and after three weeks of competition, only one team, the champion, is left. This championship tournament has *always* been the pinnacle of the basketball season. But in the last decade, the financial stakes have escalated to a point where hundreds of thousands of dollars may ride on the outcome of each game. A few years ago, two games were decided by controversial decisions by officials as to whether a crucial shot had been taken before or after the buzzer ending the game had sounded. A coach involved in one of the games said this: "You've got an awful lot at stake here nowadays, for the players, for the schools, for the conferences. There should not be a mistake by the officials on whether a shot beat the buzzer or didn't beat the buzzer." A coach involved in the other game said this: "Yes, we need to go back to look at the replay. The game has become such big business, and I don't particularly like that. But there's too much at stake if a guy misses a call, if we let a clock determine a game. There's too much money that the conference or the school will lose. It's sad to say that, but it's a fact of life." What is important to realize is that so far as the games or the championship itself was concerned, there was no more at stake two years ago than there was thirty years ago. There is only one champion, and if you lose a game, the champion isn't you. But the sense of these coaches is that tournament games are much more important than they once were—that the (financial) stakes are too high for the mistakes of officials to be tolerated.

The principal task of a successful college coach is recruiting players. By and large, the teams that win are the ones that put the best players on the field, and the way to put the best players on the field is to persuade them to come to your school. Once a coach manages to get an athlete to come to his school, the next task is to keep that athlete eligible to play. Often this means finding either easy courses or friendly professors. But sometimes more is required. One coach was caught after having written three term papers for a star player; another was caught giving a player an A in a course (in basketball tactics) that the player never actually attended. The problem is that many of the very best of today's college athletes come from high schools where the level of preparation, even of the best students, is barely adequate for the demands of college. And frequently the athletes are far from the best students at their high schools. So these athletes hit the classrooms almost totally unprepared for what's expected of them. In many ways, putting them into a regular college classroom is analogous to taking one of their calculus classmates at random and installing him as the quarterback of the football team. Ordinarily, if a student whose preparation left him extremely disadvantaged entered the university, great care would be taken to make sure that there were no demands on his time and energy except for the demands of his classes, at least until he demonstrated, to himself and to school administrators, that he could handle the work. For star athletes, just the opposite is true. The football players are engaged in exhausting, day-long practices even before they've attended their first freshman class. Whether they play football or basketball, they must commit themselves to hours of practice each day, in addition to extended and frequent trips to games, during which they miss classes and assignments. They are, in effect, expected to be students while holding the equivalent of a full-time job. This would be pretty tough duty even for a well-prepared, highly motivated student. One recent football recruit put it this way: "It's not a game, it's a business. You put in eight-hour days . . . there's too much preparation, too much work, to call it a game. . . . And it's year round. Even in the off-season, you put in three or four hours a day lifting weights, running, trying to stay in condition and gain strength."

Given the academic background of many of the athletes, the task is just impossible. But the coach has to find a way to make it possible. If they can't pass their classes, the athletes can't play. And so coaches and their "academic assistants" find ways for the athletes to do the barest minimum required to maintain eligibility. The classes that the athletes take may not in fact be moving them any closer to meeting the various institutional requirements for a degree. But no matter. The NCAA doesn't demand progress toward a degree, just a certain number of academic credits.

Just how much of a mockery do athletic programs make of university education? Estimates are that about one-third of all participants in major college football and basketball actually earn their university degrees. One-third! A significant reason why the graduation rate is so low is that at many institutions, once the athletes have exhausted their four years of athletic eligibility, the scholarship aid stops. There is nothing in it for the school to continue paying an athlete's way when the athlete can no longer play for the school. So in the event that an athlete *is* making progress toward a degree, but doing it a little more slowly than his classmates, many of whom do finish in four years, he suddenly finds that if he wants to finish, he will have to find the tuition and fees himself. Even worse, the schools are obligated to an athlete only for one year at a time, so if he disappoints on the playing field, he can lose his scholarship, no matter how well he is doing in the classroom.

Just how much of a mockery do college athletic programs make of university education? Well, unbelievable as it may seem, several college athletes managed to have complete and successful athletic careers at college while remaining virtually illiterate, illiterate enough that they could not order from restaurant menus. Imagine what it says about at least some of the courses being offered in a university that it is possible to be a student in good standing for several years and not be able to read a menu!

WHY WE SHOULD CARE; WHAT WE MIGHT DO

I have presented a very negative picture of modern sports, both professional and amateur. It could be argued that this picture is distorted, that while it may reflect my own nostalgic wish to return to the past, it does not reflect the views of most people. After all, as I have said repeatedly, TV would not be shelling out the kind of money it does if people weren't watching. And the fact that so many people *are* watching (and attending in the flesh)—far more than in the "good old days"—is pretty good evidence that most people don't feel as I do.

This criticism is fair enough, but it might be shortsighted. Many people who are enthusiastic about sports are enthusiastic about features of the games we watch that are fast disappearing and that, in another generation, may be completely gone. What is disappearing is a certain attitude toward the game on the part of those who participate in it. A childlike love of the game itself, a sense that the athletes would be happy to be doing exactly what they're doing even if nobody paid them and nobody watched, is largely absent from the modern athlete. "It's a beautiful day for baseball; let's play two," former baseball star Ernie Banks would say—every day. A loyalty and devotion to the team, a willingness to sacrifice for the good of the team and do whatever it takes for the team to succeed, is largely disappearing from the modern athlete. Even when modern athletes play hard and achieve great things, and bring their teams championships, it's hard to interpret what they do as being any different from what mercenaries do when you know they did the same things for a different team last year, and may be doing the same things for yet another team next year. Yes, athletes are marvelously talented, and they play hard, but they play hard because of the rewards it will bring them—the lucrative contracts and product endorsements. The young child who participates in the modern world of sports from afar aspires not merely to match the athlete's performance but to live the athlete's life, replete with fancy cars, a big house, product endorsements, and celebrity status. For the child, as for the rest of us, increasingly it's the life that matters; and the performance is only a part of the life. As the shopkeeper's wife told Suzanne Stout after her son's disappointing encounter with Gregg Jefferies, "in today's world, it's never good to get too close to your heroes." Do we want this to be even more true in tomorrow's world than it is in today's?

We can't make the money that surrounds modern sports go away. But we can do some things. With the amateurs, we can use the money to support aspects of university life that have nothing to do with athletics. All universities can share equally in the revenues from sports. And they can be required to use those revenues for general educational expenses. Coaches can be treated as regular members of the faculty, with the salaries of regular faculty members, with outside income opportunities restricted, with responsibilities for teaching and serving on university committees, and with evaluations based on criteria similar to those used to evaluate other faculty members. Changes like these would eliminate any *economic* incentives for individual schools or athletic conferences to excel. No doubt, changes like these would reduce the quality of athletic performance somewhat. No doubt, they would encourage some players and coaches to pass up college all together for a shot at the pros. Should these kinds of changes occur, some of the money will undoubtedly dry up, since people will be less interested in watching as the quality of performance goes down. But the big money will seem much less important to institutions if their big athletic budgets that support these teams are scaled down to proportions that are appropriate to a sensible role for athletics in the life of the university.

With the professionals, various steps can be taken to reduce the financial incentives that have turned professional sports into a big business. Major progress would be made if we simply stopped allowing private individuals to own professional teams. If teams belonged to their cities, and if the revenues they earned were used to support general city services, many of the incentives that currently operate would go away. Owners could not extort special favors from their towns or move to cities where the deal is sweeter. Players could not demand, with justice, a piece of the wealth, since there wouldn't be any owners getting it either. Players would move around less, teams would belong to cities, and the focus of attention could return to the playing field rather than the boardroom. The "professional" athlete could again be someone dedicated to excellence and to the success of his team. Our kids could again have heroes worthy of the adulation they receive. There would be less reason to worry about their getting too close to their heroes. A new Joe DiMaggio might appear.

•   •

In these last two chapters—on the professions and on sports—I have suggested that influences from the world of commerce are making the activities of the doctor, the lawyer, and the athlete less worthy of value and respect than they can and should be. As these activities grow increasingly commercialized, we are deprived as a society of models of how to live and what to value that are different from the models we see in the marketplace. Economic success becomes the measure of all things, and even as our material lives become enriched, our social and moral lives become impoverished. Throughout my discussion, I have been suggesting that people are experiencing this commercialization of life with acute dissatisfaction as opportunities for other things they value are being foreclosed. Sure, we can learn to pursue economic success single-mindedly if that's the only game in town, but we will know that something important is missing. Or will we? Is it possible that, if we live under the conditions I've described for long enough, what just "happens to be," at this moment, the only game in town will come to be perceived as the only *possible* game in town, that the commercialized character of modern life will come to seem as natural and inevitable as the phases of the moon and seasons of the year? I explore this question in the next chapter, which asks what human nature is like—what we are.

5

WHAT WE ARE AND WHAT WE VALUE

"This is the best of all possible worlds," said the optimist.
"I know," said the pessimist.

Hatred, the mischievous delight in the misfortunes of others, the lust to
rob and dominate, and whatever else is called evil belongs to the most
amazing economy of the preservation of the species.

—FRIEDRICH NIETZSCHE

How do you feel about buying gasoline at a gas station that offers a
discount for paying in cash? How about a gas station that imposes a
surcharge for using a credit card? Does the first of these options seem
like a good deal while the second seems like a ripoff? Most people
see it this way, but in fact the two options are identical. A discount
for paying in cash *is* a surcharge for using credit. This is not obvious
to most of us. Imagine two gas stations at opposite corners of a busy
intersection. The one offering a discount for cash has a big sign
that says:

DISCOUNT FOR PAYING CASH!
CASH—$1.25 per GALLON
CREDIT—$1.35 per GALLON

The other, imposing a surcharge for credit, has a small sign, just
above the pumps, that says:

Cash—$1.25 per Gallon
Credit—$1.35 per Gallon

The sign is small, and doesn't call attention to itself, because people don't like surcharges.

What's the difference between these two gas stations and their price structure? There is no difference in the price structure, as is clear from the signs. What's different is that one gas station proprietor is shrewder than the other. He knows that people like discounts and dislike surcharges. Is this shrewd proprietor who is advertising the cash discount lying? Surely, the two gas station signs can't both be telling the truth, since they are giving such radically different representations to the same objective data. Or can they? What is going on?

THE FRAMING OF DECISIONS

What is going on is a powerful example of the effect of what psychologists Daniel Kahneman and Amos Tversky have called *framing*. Think about what determines whether a given price represents a discount or a surcharge. We certainly can't tell from the price itself. In addition to the current price, we need to know what the standard price, or reference price, is. If the reference price of gas is $1.35, then people who pay cash are getting a discount. If the reference price is $1.25, then people who use credit are paying a surcharge. So the two gas station proprietors differ in what they are implying is the reference price of gas. Each of them constructs a frame, or a context within which the current price is evaluated. Without the context, evaluation is impossible. If all we know is that the price of gas is $1.25, how can we judge whether the gas is cheap or expensive, discounted or inflated? We can't judge anything about it.

The lesson here is a little like the old joke about a man who wakes up after being in a coma for twenty years. He immediately goes to a pay phone and calls his stockbroker. As the broker rattles off the current prices of the securities in the man's portfolio, the man can hardly contain his excitement. Almost everything he owns has increased to ten, twenty, even fifty times its value of twenty years before. The broker is still going down the list when the operator cuts in to say, "Your three minutes has expired. Please deposit one hundred dollars for the next three minutes." The operator's announcement punctures this happy man's illusion that he has become rich, by establishing the frame within which increases in the value of stocks should be evaluated.

Economists tell us that we aren't supposed to be influenced by frames in this way. As rational people, assessing the costs and benefits of various possible actions, we should be able to see *through* the way in which various options are presented to us, and respond only to the net costs and benefits—the bottom line. If we were actually able to do this, we would not be attracted by nominal discounts or repelled by nominal surcharges. We would know that $1.25 a gallon is $1.25 a gallon no matter how it is packaged. Framing obscures net costs and bottom lines, and thus creates a kind of economic illusion, a smoke screen, a trick. It's a trick that advertisers and retailers spend lots of time and money perfecting. It's a trick that nearly everybody falls for.

Why talk at such length about the price of gasoline? The answer is that the frame effects that the discount / surcharge example illustrates are not rare or idiosyncratic. They are pervasive. An ingenious series of investigations by Kahneman and Tversky over the last twenty years has shown that most people are consistently and systematically affected by the way in which situations are framed. They fail to see past the superficial way in which alternatives are framed, to the underlying reality that the alternatives represent.

Consider being asked the following question:

> You are a physician working in an Asian village, and 600 people have come down with a life-threatening disease. Two possible treatments exist. If you choose treatment A, you will save exactly 200 people. If you choose treatment B, there is a $1/3$ chance that you will save all 600 people, and a $2/3$ chance that you will save no one. Which treatment do you choose, A or B?

The vast majority of people faced with this choice choose treatment A. They prefer saving a definite number of people for sure to the risk that they will save no one. But now consider this slightly different problem:

> You are a physician working in an Asian village, and 600 people have come down with a life-threatening disease. Two possible treat-

ments exist. If you choose treatment C, exactly 400 people will die. If you choose treatment D, there is a ¹/₃ chance that no one will die, and a ²/₃ chance that everyone will die. Which treatment do you choose, C or D?

Now the overwhelming majority of people choose treatment D. They would rather risk losing everyone than settle for the death of 400.

These two problems illustrate what seems to be a fairly general principle people use when they are making choices among alternatives that involve a certain amount of riskiness or uncertainty. When the possibilities involve gains, people seem to prefer a small, sure gain to a larger, uncertain one. Most people, for example, will choose a sure $10 over a coin flip (a fifty-fifty chance) that determines whether they win $20 or win nothing. People are said to be *risk averse* in situations involving prospective gains. When the possibilities involve losses, however, people will risk a large loss to avoid a smaller one. For example, they will choose a coin flip that determines whether they lose $20 or lose nothing over a sure loss of $10. People are said to be *risk seeking* in situations involving prospective losses.

So in the case of our serious disease, in the first problem, when the choice is between a sure "gain" of 200 lives and an uncertain gain of 600, most people make the risk-averse choice of treatment A. In contrast, in the second problem, when the choice is between a sure "loss" of 400 lives and an uncertain loss of 600, most people make the risk-seeking choice of treatment D. Your own choices may have fit this pattern.

What has this to do with framing? Well, in case you missed it in reading through the two problems, they are actually identical. If there are 600 sick people, saving 200 (choice A in the first problem) means losing 400 (choice C in the second problem). A ²/₃ chance of saving no one (choice B in the first problem) means a ²/₃ chance of losing everyone (choice D in the second problem). So if someone is the type of person who likes to take risks, she should choose B and D in the two problems, whereas if she's the type of person who likes sure things, she should choose A and C in the two problems. Either of these patterns of choice makes sense. What does not make sense is choosing certainty in one case and risk in the other, because the two cases are the same. And yet this is what most of us choose. Just as in the matter of discounts and surcharges, the framing of the choice affects our perception of it, and this in turn affects what we choose.

Consider now, another pair of questions:

> Imagine that you have decided to see a concert where admission is $20 a ticket. As you enter the concert hall, you discover that you have lost a $20 bill. Would you still pay $20 for a ticket to the concert?

Almost 90 percent of people asked this question say yes. In contrast:

> Imagine that you have decided to see a concert and already purchased a $20 ticket. As you enter the concert hall, you discover that you have lost the ticket. The seat was not marked, and the ticket cannot be recovered. Would you pay $20 for another ticket?

Now less than 50 percent of people say yes. What is the difference between these two cases? From one perspective, the perspective of "bottom lines," they seem the same; both involve a choice between seeing a concert and being $40 poorer or not seeing it and being $20 poorer. Yet people don't seem to see them as the same, since so many choose differently in the two cases. Kahneman and Tversky suggest that the difference between the two cases has to do with the way in which people frame their "psychological accounts." Suppose that in a person's psychological accounting frame there is a "cost of the concert" account. In the first case, the cost of the concert is $20; the lost $20 bill is not properly charged to that account. It's charged to some other account, perhaps a "miscellaneous" account. But in the second case, the cost of the concert is $40; the lost ticket *is* charged to that account. And for many people, $40 is too much to pay. Thus the difference in choice.

Suppose, in contrast, that a person's psychological accounting frame had a "cost of a day's outing" account. Now the two cases might well be judged as equivalent, in that the lost ticket and the lost $20 both add the same amount to the cost of the day. Some people may keep narrow, "cost of the concert" accounts, while others keep broader, "cost of the day" accounts. Which kind of account they keep will determine whether they respond in the same way or not to the two examples.

Which response is the correct one? What is the right way to keep accounts? It is possible that the right way to keep accounts is whatever way makes us feel best. If it makes someone feel better to keep the lost $20 in a separate account from the concert costs, then she should do it. If not, she shouldn't. If it makes someone feel better today, she should do it today. Tomorrow she can keep accounts differently. After all, it isn't things or money per se that people are after in their commerce with the world; it's the pleasure or satisfaction they get from things and money. And pleasure and satisfaction are subjective, individual affairs. Different people get different amounts of pleasure from the same objective circumstances. So if the way in which choices and situations are framed by and for people actually affects their subjective experience of the possibilities, it is hardly surprising that it also affects their choices. If our reactions to possibilities are mediated by the frames in which they are cast, then our experience of pleasure or satisfaction will also be mediated by these frames. To suggest that people should "see through" frames to the underlying objective reality of the situation is to deny that frames actually affect the way in which that reality is experienced and evaluated.

And the range of possible frames or accounting systems is enormous. For example, an evening at a concert could be just one entry in a much larger account, say a "meeting a potential mate" account. Someone might go to concerts, to the theater, to the ballet, and so on because she hopes to meet *her* type of person there. Or it could be part of a "getting culture" account, in which case it would be one entry among others that might include subscribing to public television, buying certain books and magazines, and the like. It could be part of a "ways to spend a Friday night" account, in which case it would join entries like hanging out at a bar, going to a basketball game, staying home and dozing in front of the television, and who knows what else. How much this night at a concert is "worth" will depend on what account it is a part of. Forty dollars may be a lot to spend for getting culture, compared with available alternatives, but not much to spend to find a mate or pass a Friday night. In sum, just how well this $40 night at the theater satisfies a person will depend on how that person does her accounting.

We often talk jokingly about how "creative" accountants can make a corporate balance sheet look as good or as bad as they want it to look. Well, the point here is that people are all creative accountants when it comes to keeping their own psychological accounts. This very creativity raises an important question. If there are no norms or standards by which to judge accounting systems, and if the number of possible accounting systems really is very large, what is it that determines which accounting systems people actually use?

In our approach to this question, a look at real accounting practices can be instructive. Real accountants can also organize accounts in indefinitely many ways. What constrains the way they operate? There are three sources of constraints. One source is legal. Tax laws impose a set of requirements on how the books must be kept. A second source is professional. The accounting profession establishes certain standards that guide how accounting is to be done. They maintain those standards in part by educating new accountants to do things in just that way. The final source is customary or habitual. Accountants keep accounts in certain ways because they have always kept them in those ways, or because the accountants who preceded them kept them in those ways. There is nothing especially privileged or rational about these constraints. Tax laws could be different, as could professional standards, and habits are accidents of history. So, in a sense, these constraints are arbitrary. Yet, arbitrary or not, they are there, and they serve to narrow and shape the way accountants do their work.

Precisely the same things could be said about the way people frame their psychological accounts. People are influenced by legal and social sanctions, by customs and traditions, and by old habits. These influences may also be arbitrary. Nevertheless, people inherit them and their effect on the keeping of accounts. People don't include their income tax, or the cost of supporting their children, in their "charitable giving" account, though they could if they understood charity to include all contributions to the support of people other than themselves. They don't keep food costs in a "medical expenses" account, though they could if they took seriously the role of proper diet in maintaining good health (and doing this, incidentally, might have a big impact on how people shopped; "health foods" that seem outrageously expensive when compared with other foods wouldn't seem so expensive when compared to prescription medicines or medical procedures). They don't keep the cost of vacations in a "psychotherapy account" (though I actually have a friend who does; he justifies his family's occasional extravagant vacations to himself by comparing them, and the psychological benefits they provide, to the costs and benefits of weekly psychotherapy). They don't keep college tuition and movie theater admissions in the same "educational costs" account, though they could if they thought seriously about the education that many movies provide. They don't treat school taxes as child care expenses. They don't treat the money they give to houses of worship as entertainment costs. People may have good reasons for not doing these things, but they are not *economic* reasons.. They stem from being influenced by their culture as to what categories to establish, and what items to put in each category. Psychological accounting practices in different cultures are probably quite different from ours, but just as reasonable.

The customs, habits, and legal constraints that influence how we keep our accounts are not fixed and unalterable. They change, and the boundaries or frames that separate different domains of life change with them. Frames are both permeable and fragile. They can be pushed around. For example, whether a doctor frames her work with a focus on ethics or on economics is very much up for grabs, and what kind of doctor she will be hangs in the balance. Indeed, my discussion of business, the professions, and sports in the last three chapters has suggested that we are all experiencing increasing pressure to locate all of our activities within a single, economic frame in which the goal is maximizing wealth and options are compared to one another in light of that one goal. The result of that pressure is that other important goals we might have—fairness and honesty in business, community service in the professions, excellence in sports—get threatened and perhaps crowded out.

I can illustrate the way in which the maximization of wealth can crowd out other goals with a study done by Kahneman, in collaboration with Jack Knetsch and Richard Thaler. The study concerned people's judgments of fairness over a range of different hypothetical economic situations. Each of the situations was described, and people were asked to assess whether the behavior in question in each situation was fair or unfair. Here was one situation:

> A hardware store has been selling snow shovels for $15. The morning after a large snowstorm, the store raises the price to $20. Is this fair?

Let's consider how a person might go about answering a question like this. From what perspective or frame is fairness to be assessed? Suppose we are operating from within a purely economic frame. What the economics of the market teaches us is that buyers and sellers alike are out to get as much as they can for as little as they can get away with. If the store owner can get $20 for a snowshovel, he's entitled to it. If the buyer can find a shovel for less in another store, he should buy at that store. What substitutes for fairness in the marketplace is competition. Store owners who price gouge will be punished by competitors who charge lower prices. Store owners who price gouge at a moment of high demand may so turn off previously loyal customers that they will lose future business. In any case, the store owner should be guided by the goal of maximizing his profit. If he is mistaken in charging $20, it is not because it's unfair but because he has misgauged either the competition or the reaction of his customers, or both. So the "economic" answer to this question is that yes, of course, it is fair to charge $20. More accurately, the economic answer might be that "fairness" has nothing to do with it. The real question is, Is it profitable? And this question will have different answers in different circumstances.

Now suppose we are operating from within a noneconomic, or not purely economic, frame. Suppose that fairness implies a certain responsibility to meet the needs of the community and to honor the loyalty of regular customers. Suppose that fairness appeals to some moral principle that says we are entitled to a reasonable profit, but not to whatever the traffic will bear. From within this frame, we might well decide that it is unfair to charge $20 for the shovel, even if we *can* get away with it.

So how did you answer the question? Eighty-two percent of the people in the study judged the $20 price to be unfair; this suggests that the majority of people do not make decisions of this kind from within a purely economic frame.

Several other, similar examples yielded similar results. People's responses to these examples point up that the average person seems to think it is perfectly appropriate to apply moral standards—standards of fairness—in evaluating economic transactions. The market is not an amoral playing field in which anything that is not illegal is acceptable. The market is not a place in which the naked and unrestrained pursuit of self-interest is condoned. People may have come to expect the worst in the market, but they have not yet come to accept it. Instead of allowing economic considerations to encroach on the moral domain, the respondents in this study seemed to insist that moral considerations should encroach on the economic domain.

We don't really know what exactly the concept "fairness" means to people. We don't know that what it means to people in general is what it means to people in the kinds of situations probed by this study. Fairness on the football field may be quite different from fairness in the market. Indeed, it would be quite surprising if this weren't the case. Surely almost everyone thinks it is fair for football teams to exploit their opponents' weaknesses as much as they possibly can, while they obviously don't think the same thing about sellers and buyers. Indeed, the very notion of what is fair may depend in part on what you think the particular institution or domain in question is *for*, on what its goals are. If football is for winning, then anything within the rules goes. If football is for exercise, then perhaps substantial restraint is needed. If the marketplace is a mechanism for producing and distributing the goods that meet people's material needs, then perhaps restraint on profit seeking is called for. If the marketplace is a playing field for the pursuit of wealth, then perhaps what is fair is what you can get away with.

If people are willing to impose standards of fairness in the marketplace, as the respondents in this study clearly were, then perhaps the concerns I raised in the last three chapters are idle. Perhaps I'm just crying wolf. Perhaps the growth of commercialization of life that we are witnessing is a temporary aberration that will soon correct itself. Perhaps, but I don't think so, and here's why. Many of these questions about fairness were put to a group of M.B.A. students at a prestigious business school. In general, their fairness judgments were quite different from the judgments of the respondents in the original study. In general, their judgments were that efforts to maximize profit were fair. All's fair—from increasing prices to decreasing wages—in the market. This should make clear to us that there is no reason to count on the concern for fairness as an ineluctable part of our approach to social life.

Standards of fairness must come from somewhere. Since there is no place for fairness within the frame of the market itself, these standards must be developed in other frames. It seems likely that they are developed, encouraged, and sustained in the various nonmarket institutions within which we all live—institutions like the family, the local community, the school, the athletic team, and the church. And then they are imported, at least by some people, into market situations.

As long as these nonmarket institutions retain their noneconomic character and purpose, concern for fairness can continue to be nurtured. But if they are invaded by economic considerations, the nurturing of concern for fairness will surely weaken. The fact that the respondents in the original study showed concern for fairness may show only that the nonmarket institutions that helped shape these people had not been deeply penetrated by economic considerations at the time that these people were being shaped. But this offers no guarantees for the future.

Had the students in the M.B.A. program, who responded differently from the rest of us, learned this in their programs, or did they seek M.B.A.'s because they already learned it elsewhere? Or is it possible that this attitude toward commerce doesn't really need to be learned—that it is a basic and fundamental part of our natures that just gets covered over when social institutions like the family, the school, and the church tell us not to be so greedy? Are the different frames we use to allow us to think about fairness *and* about profit, about honesty *and* about sales, about saving lives *and* about saving money, just an illusion that hides what we really are deep down? What exactly *are* we deep down?

WHAT IS HUMAN NATURE?

Should abortion be legal, or legal only under some circumstances, and, if the latter, who is to decide what the appropriate circumstances are? Do people have the right to refuse medical treatment, even if by doing so they will die? Do they have the right to smoke cigarettes, whenever and wherever they want to? Do women have the right to rent out their bodies, either for sexual service or to bear another woman's child? Do they have the right to smoke, or to consume alcohol, when they are pregnant?

And what do people owe to others? What do they owe to their families? To their friends? To their communities? To their nations? Is it acceptable for people to be concerned only about their own welfare? If not, at what point should concern for self stop and concern for others take over? And about which others should people be concerned?

These questions, and others like them, are hot items on many people's agendas these days. They are the subject of intense debate and disagreement, of controversial legislation, of lawsuits, and of Sunday sermons. They divide nations, communities, and families. And while stated in specific form, they seem utterly modern, stated more generally, they have concerned people for centuries. What is the extent of our responsibility to other human beings, and to the society to which we belong? What is the proper mode of human conduct, and how should it be instilled in people? How much should individual freedom be restricted, and in what ways?

Centuries of concern about questions like these have failed to provide any clear answers or, perhaps more accurately, have provided clear but different answers at different times. Within a frame of British tyranny, and optimism about human rationality, Thomas Jefferson and his colleagues focused on the freedom of individuals from governmental or traditional restraint, taking it for granted that individuals would use that freedom in ways that served the public welfare. Within the current frame of self-serving greed and excess, and "rationality" used to damage the earth and many of its inhabitants, modern thinkers focus more on restraint and social responsibility. Nevertheless, though people disagree—both across history and at a particular historical moment—about the answers to these kinds of questions, they seem to agree that these are all important questions to be asking. The questions all make sense, and they are significant enough to justify the anguish, frustration, sweat, and even sometimes bloodshed that attempts to answer them have caused. What the questions have in common is that they are all *moral* questions. They all involve figuring out how people *should* act. They are all concerned with spelling out right and wrong, good and bad. And people seem to agree, as they have agreed for millennia, that it is appropriate to assess human beings and human social relations from within a moral frame.

Making moral evaluations—calling some things good and some things bad—depends on our ideas about what people are like. Indeed, a good deal of how we decide what is or is not a moral issue depends on what we think we know about human nature. We can see how various kinds of knowledge about what people are and what it means to be a person might help resolve moral controversies. If we *knew* when a fetus becomes a person, it might help distinguish moral from immoral abortions. If we *knew* how harmful cigarette smoke is to passive recipients, it might help us decide where and when to prohibit smoking. If we *knew* when children attain the level of rational competence that allows them to make decisions for themselves, we might be able to decide at what point parents no longer have either the right to control their children's lives or the responsibility for what their children do.

In none of these cases is the moral issue simply and certainly settled by this knowledge. But in each of them possessing the relevant knowledge would help people see their way more clearly to a resolution of the moral debate. If nothing else, such knowledge would rule certain kinds of moral arguments out. Whatever one thinks of abortion, it couldn't be called murder if it were known, by an agreed-upon definition of what a person is, that the fetus is not a person until, say, the last trimester of pregnancy. So what we think people ought to be and do depends in part on what we think they are and can do. Resolution of moral debate depends on people's conceptions of human nature, on how they frame what it means to be a person. From where, then, do these conceptions of human nature come?

The answer is that they come from many of the same places that our "accounting" frames come from. They come from our habits—from our individual, everyday experience in the so-called school of hard knocks. As we interact with others, we discover regularities in the way others react to certain situations. From these discoveries, we build up a picture of what a typical person wants, does, and expects us to do.

But the teachings of personal experience have their limits. If they were all we had to go on in constructing a picture of human nature, we'd be in trouble. It takes time to accumulate experiences, it is not always easy to interpret them, and everyone has different ones. Personal experience must be supported by the social institutions into which people are born, institutions whose very shape is itself framed by an operative conception of human nature. There is first the family. By socializing children, by teaching them how to behave, parents are teaching what is expected of people and, by implication, what it means to be a person. Similarly, the church, the school, and the state all contribute to socialization by teaching people what they should and shouldn't do. In general, the dictates of our social institutions teach both about the noblest of human aspirations and about the basest of human frailties. And by absorbing these dictates, we absorb a conception of human nature that guides us in filtering and interpreting our own, particular, everyday experiences with other people. One of the consequences of living in the modern world, where social institutions are so varied and dynamic in character, is that a coherent picture of human nature is hard to come by. This has the virtue of freeing us from a set of expectations and preconceptions about people that may be inappropriate. But it also has the attendant drawback that it leaves us uncertain, with nothing to replace these expectations.

SCIENCE AND HUMAN NATURE

Increasingly in the modern world, everyday experience together with traditional social institutions have been supplanted as sources of our ideas about human nature by a third source—the institution of science. Experience doesn't tell us that our rock-solid desk is actually made up of tiny particles of matter moving around in empty space, but science does. The Bible doesn't tell us that sore throats are caused by microorganisms invading our bodies, but science does. When our experience or our traditional institutions tell us one thing, and science tells us another, we often go with science.

When science as we know it began to emerge, several centuries ago, it centered on understanding the natural world and left thinking about human nature to others. But as science has developed, the domains in which it has sought authority have expanded to include human beings. In the last hundred years or so, the disciplines of psychology, economics, sociology, anthropology, and biology have attempted to show that no aspect of human life can resist the power of scientific scrutiny.

We can see the influences of these sciences of human nature all around us. We can see them in the work of marriage counselors who help couples keep foundering relations together, and in the work of psychotherapists who help people come to terms with guilt and overcome depression. We can see them in the work of penologists who seek to treat criminals rather than punish them, and in the work of economists who try to forecast the future of the economy and suggest interventions that will help it to flourish. We can see them in the work of sociologists who help us understand how social class, race, and ethnicity affect human aims and aspirations, and in the work of educational psychologists who try to develop effective techniques for educating young children. We can see them in the work of sex therapists who try to help us achieve sexual satisfaction, in the work of family therapists who try to keep parents and their adolescent children from harming one another, and in the work of career counselors who give us batteries of tests in order to determine the kind of work we can do best and will like best. Again and again, in one domain of human life after another, we are taking our cues from science.

Though the various human sciences are quite diverse in the problems they tackle, as well as in the explanations they provide, most of them share a core of beliefs about the nature of human nature. It is a vision of human nature that originated at the dawn of modern science, in the writings of philosopher Thomas Hobbes. And it is a vision of human nature that frames many of the social developments

I discussed in the last three chapters and makes them seem all but inevitable.

Hobbes lived in the England of the seventeenth century, at a time when modern science was just taking root. He thought that human beings are driven by two persistent motives. People are, on the one hand, driven by fear of death and, more particularly, fear of other human beings and the evil they may do. They are, on the other hand, driven by the desire for pleasure and glory. Moreover, Hobbes thought that people never rest in these pursuits. People can never be secure enough, or have enough. People always want something, and what they want is conditioned on what others around them have. Value and worth are measured by comparison with others. To satisfy desire is to have more than the people around you do. But because satisfaction of desire means this to everyone, there is endless competition among people to outdo one another. And the competition can be ugly, for the best way for one person to outdo another is simply to take what the other person has. And the best way to do that is by being powerful. Thus there is in people a desire for power that ends only in death. It has to be perpetual, requiring eternal vigilance, for if one person lets down his guard, even for an instant, someone else will be there to dominate and exploit him.

What Hobbes meant when he said that it is human nature to pursue the satisfaction of unlimited desires is that you cannot be a person and act in any other way. People have no more control over their natures and actions than flowering plants or stinging bees have over theirs. People are machines, set in motion by external, causal forces. They can be influenced by influencing the forces acting on them. But they cannot influence themselves; they cannot exert self-restraint.

Hobbes's views about human nature may seem a little extreme, but there is a distinctly modern ring to them. Like Hobbes, we tend to regard people essentially as selfish individuals, each in pursuit of his or her own interests. Like Hobbes, we tend to believe that people are never satisfied, that they always want more, that they are desperately trying to keep up with the Joneses. We see luxuries turn into necessities before our eyes when everyone has them. We may believe that it is wrong for people to engage in ruthlessly aggressive competition and that many people, if not all, will think twice before doing what is wrong. Hobbes might agree that it is wrong to pursue ones selfish interests no matter what. But he would argue that good or bad, right or wrong, it is simply the way people are. Deceive yourself into thinking they are otherwise, and you will be swallowed up. And when we shrug our shoulders and say that "business is business," we are in essence agreeing with Hobbes.

During this century, scientists from several different disciplines have been embarked on the project of turning Hobbes's philosophical speculations into rigorous scientific formulations. At the heart of these developments is modern economics. In his famous book *The Wealth of Nations* (1776), Adam Smith put forth a conception of our economic nature—of what he called economic man—that has guided economics ever since. At the center of his ideas is the "market," a stage on which economic men play out their propensity to exchange. The actors on this stage, the economic men, are guided by a few simple principles. They are ruled by self-interest. And they are never satisfied; they always want something. Smith thought that if people are left alone to exchange in the market, the market's "invisible hand" will guide people to produce efficiently and trade fairly. What assures this result is competition. The invisible hand of competition is the same kind of hand that pushes the planets around the sun; it is the hand of nature. Ever since Smith formulated these ideas, most of the work done in the discipline of economics has been devoted to developing them. According to modern economists, the pursuit of self-interest is not a matter of discretion, moral evaluation, and choice; it's a matter of natural inevitability. People need justify their selfishness no more than planets need answer for their movement around the sun.

The modern economist has important intellectual allies from the discipline of evolutionary biology, whose foundations were established in the nineteenth century by Charles Darwin. Darwin's theory of evolution by natural selection argued that competition for scarce resources is what drives evolution. Organisms are born possessing highly varied characteristics. Because resources are scarce, however, not all organisms will survive. Natural competition in the face of scarcity leads to survival—natural selection—of the fittest. This Darwinian view of "nature red in tooth and claw," as Tennyson put it, is still very much a part of modern evolutionary biology. Modern biologists take it for granted that organisms are out to serve their own interests, either in the service of personal survival or in the service of reproductive success. As one modern Darwinian, Michael Ghiselin, says, "The economy of nature is competitive from beginning to end. . . . No hint of genuine charity ameliorates our vision of society once sentimentalism has been laid aside. What passes for cooperation turns out to be a mixture of opportunism and exploitation . . . Scratch an altruist and watch a hypocrite bleed."

To the picture of human nature developed by economists and evolutionary biologists, we can add the principles of a branch of psychology known as behavior theory, a discipline given its shape and direction by B. F. Skinner. The central principle of behavior theory is known as the law of effect. The law of effect says that behavior is controlled by its past consequences. If something we do is followed by a good outcome—a reward—we are likely to repeat it. If something we do is not followed by a good outcome, or is followed by a bad outcome—a punisher—we are unlikely to repeat it. Thus all of our behavior is to be understood in terms of our pursuit of reward, our pursuit of things that give us pleasure, satisfaction, utility. Armed with this simple principle, behavior theorists have developed a technology that is used to control behavior in classrooms, mental hospitals, and prisons. And there is hardly a workplace in modern America whose compensation practices do not embody and reflect this principle—that to get people to do what you want them to do, you have to pay them for it, to make it worth their while.

When taken together, economics, evolutionary biology, and behavior theory constitute a truly general theory of what it means to be a person. And it is a theory that is consistent with the views of Thomas Hobbes.

It is one of the great ironies of modernity that the enterprise of science, the very essence of which suggests an optimistic picture of the possibilities of human rationality and perfectibility, should give rise to a scientific picture of human beings as enslaved by both biology and psychology to pursue ruthlessly their selfish interests. This is hardly the sort of frame that would inspire anyone to let loose upon the world full human freedom. Indeed, it's the kind of frame that might lead one to seek to strengthen every traditional and governmental constraint on human freedom one could find. But ironic or not, this is the scientific picture of human nature that has become ascendant.

There has existed an alternative vision of human nature. Its most famous proponent is perhaps Jean-Jacques Rousseau. In *The Social Contract*, Rousseau argued as follows:

> The first man who, having enclosed a piece of ground, bethought himself of saying "this is mine," and found people simple enough to believe him, was the real founder of civil society. From how many crimes, wars and murders, from how many horrors and misfortunes might not anyone have saved mankind, by pulling up the stakes, or filling up the ditch, and crying to his fellows, "Beware of listening to this imposter; you are undone if you once forget that the fruits of the earth belong to us all, and the earth itself to nobody."

In Rousseau's view, human potential is indeed, by nature, limitless, and the kind of greedy, ruthless person we see walking around is the product of society, not of nature. It is a set of misdirected and misguided social institutions that poison human potential. And Rousseau's view was echoed, at least in part, by many others—by Voltaire, by Condorcet, by William Godwin, by John Stuart Mill, by Thomas Paine, and by Thomas Jefferson. Condorcet said of human beings that the "perfectibility of man is truly indefinite." Godwin said that human beings are "eminently capable of justice and virtue" and that efforts must be made to "wake the sleeping virtues of mankind." It is true that "men are capable, no doubt, of preferring an inferior interest of their own to a superior interest of others; but this preference arises from a combination of circumstances and is not the necessary and invariable law of our nature." Half a century later, Mill said that the real impediments to attaining general happiness among human beings are not any natural and ineradicable flaws in human nature but "present wretched education" and "wretched social arrangements." Indeed, if there is something natural about people, it is not their selfishness but their concern for the well-being of others, their concern for the general welfare. When Jefferson wrote, in the Declaration of Independence, about our "inalienable right to life, liberty, and the pursuit of happiness," he was celebrating freedom and individualism. But heavily influenced by philosophers like Thomas Reid and Robert Hutcheson, Jefferson believed that we possess deep and solid moral intuitions that naturally engender in us conscience and sympathy for others. We are naturally inclined to do what is right. We are naturally inclined to pursue our private happiness by achieving the public good. Given these essentially unshakable, benevolent moral impulses that we have, we will, by increasing individual freedom and encouraging the development of rationality and of science, greatly increase the efficiency with which our benevolent impulses are actually channeled to serve the common good.

A similar, if somewhat more guardedly optimistic, vision of human nature is contained in the writings of Karl Marx (is it another of modernity's ironies that Thomas Jefferson and Karl Marx could have had anything in common?). True human liberation, self-expression, creativity, and community are all possible, according to Marx, but they require the right material conditions. Only when society as a whole has attained a certain level of material wealth, so that basic human needs can be met, can human nature at its best reveal itself. As this material, economic development occurs (largely as a result of the applications of science), people will be forced to live through mean-spirited, unjust social arrangements in which the freedom of individuals is greatly restricted and the distribution of power, influence, and wealth is grossly unequal. But the march of history is progressive, and ultimately the full flowering of each individual as a member of an integrated, concerned, moral community will be possible. Thus, for Marx, as for many of his predecessors, the moral limitations of human beings are not the product of an essential human nature but instead the product of the social and material conditions in which people live.

Economist Thomas Sowell has written about many significant thinkers of the last three centuries who promoted one or another of these visions. Sowell calls the first vision—the dominant vision from Hobbes to Smith to modern mainstream economics, behavioral psychology, and biology—a *constrained* vision. It is constrained in two senses: first, in the sense that human nature is fixed, and thus social life must accommodate the reality of a fixed human nature; and second, in the sense that the actual nature of human nature is such that if people are left alone to do whatever they want, society will be mean-spirited and dangerous. The alternative vision Sowell calls *unconstrained*, and it is unconstrained also in two senses. First, human nature is variable, not fixed, and thus can be molded to meet the needs and expectations of society. And second, people possess plenty of potential for behaving with honesty, responsibility, care, and concern for the general welfare, so that they needn't be imprisoned by social institutions and government power. Sowell suggests persuasively that the positions people take on many of the controversial issues of our time—from abortion to drugs and crime to sexuality to gun control to affirmative action to government regulation and control of health care, education, and the economy—can be traced to whether people are operating from within a constrained or an unconstrained vision—or frame—of human nature.

MORALITY AND VISIONS OF HUMAN NATURE

It is not hard to see how a constrained vision of human nature based on the scientific conceptions shared by economics, evolutionary biology, and behavior theory poses a challenge to our traditional understanding of human beings as moral agents. Think for a moment about what makes someone a moral agent. Selfishness, honesty, competitiveness, aggressiveness, loyalty, fidelity, compassion, and the like are regarded as moral traits in part because people believe that they are all subject to human discretion and control. Thus we have arguments among ourselves about good and evil. But these arguments would lose much of their significance if we, like other animals, were only doing what our natures impelled us to do. After all, not all of our social activities in themselves are uniquely human. Other animals mate, raise offspring, allocate resources, and fight. It's just that most people believe that whereas these other animals can't help what they do, human beings can. But the "constrained," scientific vision of human nature suggests that just as it is inappropriate to blame a river for overflowing its banks and flooding a town, it may be inappropriate to blame husbands for cheating on their wives, to blame adolescents for behaving recklessly, to blame thieves for stealing, to blame businesspeople for lying, or to blame teachers for failing to educate. These people, like flooding rivers, are only doing what their nature impels them to do. Moral evaluation, discretion, choice, and responsibility are largely beside the point.

Think about what it means to say that, for example, it's human nature to be selfish. This claim might mean:

1. It is the way all people everywhere have always been, and must necessarily be. It is part of the essence of being a person. A person who wasn't selfish would be like a bird without wings. Thus the business practices we reviewed in chapter 2 are just the way of the world ("business is business").

Or it might mean:

2. It is the way some, most, or all people are and are likely to continue to be under a particular set of social, economic, and cultural circumstances that could be otherwise, may once have been otherwise, and may still be otherwise in different cultures. For example, people who grow up as part of the modern, "me generation" are selfish.

The first sense of "human nature" suggests the constrained vision, while the second suggests the unconstrained vision. And when we shrug our shoulders and say, "It's only human nature," to explain something or other that someone has done, it makes a big difference which of these meanings is intended, which frame is understood. Suppose we agree that selfishness is a bad thing, that people should not be selfish. Unfortunately, though, it's human nature to be selfish. What can be done about it? If it's "constrained" human nature, there is really nothing much to be done. If part of what it means and has always meant and must always mean to be a person is to be selfish, then we simply have to resign ourselves to the fact that people possess an ineradicable character flaw. Social intitutions can be designed to restrain people from exercising their selfishness. People can be policed and severely punished for displays of selfishness that are especially abhorent. But not much can be done to change selfishness.

If, on the other hand, selfishness is "unconstrained" human nature, there is cause for optimism. If it is human nature to be selfish under a particular set of social conditions, then selfishness can be reduced or even eliminated by changing the conditions.

Selfishness is in human nature in the same way that the sculpture of *David* was in the marble before Michelangelo touched it. In an important sense, the sculpture *was* in the marble; with a different block of marble, it would have come out looking different. But lots of other possible sculptures were also in the marble, and what actually came out was the product of the conditions to which the marble was subjected (Michelangelo's vision and his hands). In an unconstrained vision, selfishness is in the human marble, just requiring the right conditions to make its appearance. But so, for all we know, is selflessness. So are lust and chastity, greed and generosity, deceit and honesty. Clearly, though the *David* was in the marble, we are less interested in the marble than in the conditions that shaped it. And if selfishness is in people in the same sense, we should, here too, be less interested in the marble than in the conditions that shape it.

Thus it makes a big difference what meaning underlies the claim that such and such a trait is "human nature." Two people could agree that it is human nature to be selfish. This view might lead one of them, operating under the constrained vision, to a life of cynicism and suspicion. It might lead the other, operating under the unconstrained vision, to a life of commitment to producing social change. An appeal to an unconstrained vision of human nature preserves the significance of moral discourse. If it is human nature to be selfish only under certain conditions that can be controlled or changed, there is plenty of room for discussion of whether those conditions should or should not exist. On the other hand, an appeal to a constrained vision of human nature obviates much of the discussion of the moral significance of selfishness.

It is the hallmark of science that it seeks explanations that have the character of the constrained vision. It seeks the eternal regularities of things, the essential natures of planets, bees, and people. It is in the nature of being a person to need food to eat and oxygen to breathe; it is in the nature of being a person to see only certain wavelengths of light and to hear only certain frequencies of vibration of air. Moral and immoral are beside the point. What characterizes the human sciences is that they are endeavoring to extend explanations that have this character to domains of human activity that we are accustomed to regarding as discretionary—domains involving the pursuit and distribution of resources, patterns of mating and child care, patterns of aggression and cooperation, and patterns of social organization. If they are successful, it may become as idle to talk about the morality of selfishness as it is to talk about the morality of planetary motion. Thus, we have the paradox I mentioned before that an optimism about the liberating power of rationality and science can yield an account of human nature that is constraining and pessimistic.

Is there any reason for us to be concerned about the movement of science into previously moral human domains? On the surface, it seems not. It may be a little unsettling to have to give up some old, familiar moral concepts and learn to think and talk about ourselves in a new way with a new scientific language. But we'll get used to it. The important issue seems to be not whether this scientific development makes us a little uncomfortable but whether it is true. Like the sciences in general, the disciplines of economics, evolutionary biology, and behavioral psychology are making substantive, factual claims. Like all scientific claims, they must survive empirical test. If the claims are false—if they fail the test—then this science of human nature will die, of "natural" causes. If the claims are true, on the other hand, there isn't much to be done about them. So why worry? What's the big deal? To see what's the big deal, we must turn to an important, and often unappreciated aspect of science—something I call *idea technology.*

IDEA TECHNOLOGY

The technology of computers, of VCRs, of nuclear power, of microwaves, of medicine, and the like—what might be called thing technology—is what most of us think of when we think about the modern impact of science. But there is another kind of technology produced by science that has just as big an impact on us as thing technology, except that it is much less noticeable. We might call it idea technology. In addition to creating things, science creates concepts, ways of understanding the world and our place in it, that frame how we think and act. If we understand birth defects as acts of God, we pray. If we understand them as acts of chance, we grit our teeth and roll the dice. If we understand them as the product of prenatal abuse and neglect, we take better care of pregnant women.

It hardly needs to be said that people are profoundly affected by the material conditions of their lives, by the affluence of the societies they inhabit. The availability of necessities like food and shelter and the means by which individuals can obtain them may make all other influences on life seem insignificant. People without food will starve whether they accept their conditions tranquilly as God's will, accept them with depressed resignation as indications of their own inadequacy, or respond to them in anger at social injustice. No matter what ideas people appeal to in order to explain their lack of food, their bellies remain empty.

And yet it is clear that ideas matter, and matter a lot, even in the case of an obvious material condition like the availability of food. What a squirrel foraging for food in the park does in times of scarcity has nothing to do with how the squirrel understands this scarcity. The squirrel is not about to pray for food, cultivate trees, or organize its fellows to rise up in protest against people who have polluted the environment and diminished its food supply. But people aren't squirrels, and what *they* do about their lack of food depends a great deal on how they understand it—how they frame it. Tranquil acceptance, depressed passivity, and angry uprising are all possible human responses, as is the attempt to devise new methods of cultivation. Ideas have a lot to do with whether massive food shortages yield resignation or revolution. Ideas can transform our conception of how people can and should live. They can transform our culture's understanding of itself, so that after they appear, everything is different.

If we understand the concept of "technology" broadly, as the use of human intelligence to create objects or processes that change the conditions of daily life, then it seems clear that ideas are no less products of technology than are computers. However, two features of idea technology make it different from most thing technology. First, ideas are often quite subtle. They can suffuse themselves through the culture and start having profound effects on us before we even notice they are there, a little like low-level radioactive emissions whose presence goes unnoticed until the damage is done.

Second, idea technology, unlike thing technology, can have profound effects on us even if the ideas are *false*. Computers, micro-waves, nuclear power plants, and the like don't affect most of our lives unless they work. Companies can't sell technological objects that don't do the job. Technological objects may do bad things that we don't want them to do, but at least we don't have to worry about them unless they can also do the things they were designed to do in the first place. In contrast, bad (that is, untrue) ideas can affect how people act as long as people believe them. It works, after all, to advertise a "discount for paying cash" at the gas station, unless we can see through to the truth that the frame obscures or distorts.

There is a term that is sometimes used for "idea technology" that, even though false, is accepted by a culture as true and that thus profoundly affects the aspirations, expectations, and actions of the members of the culture. That word is "ideology." Because ideol-ogy—the belief in ideas that are false—often goes unnoticed and can have such profound effects, it is in some respects more dangerous and more in need of vigilant monitoring than the thing technology whose dangers we are all accustomed to worrying about.

The developments within areas of biology, psychology, and eco-nomics that I discussed are an example of idea technology that is extremely influential. These disciplines have told us that human beings are guided inexorably by the pursuit of selfish interests. They have suggested that human selfishness is, like gravity, a force of nature. In telling us this, they have established a frame for us to use in evaluating our actions and those of others that casts most of our moral considerations—considerations of honesty, integrity, fairness, and justice—aside. And we, as a culture, are increasingly coming to believe them. In consequence, individual actions and social arrangements that once were regarded as matters of moral choice, worthy of praise or blame, are coming to be regarded as matters of natural inevitability, met with only a shrug of our collective shoul-ders. The competitive market society that we inhabit, and that encourages each of us to "take care of number one," is coming to be viewed not as a subject for debate and decision but as a part of the natural order of things, like the planets revolving around the sun. The best we can hope to do is pass and enforce laws that restrain people, for we certainly can't expect people to restrain themselves.

I believe that this constrained vision of human nature shared by economics, biology, and behavior theory is false as a universal principle—that is ideology. But I also believe that it can be and is human nature at certain times and places. Moreover, the conditions under which it *is* human nature currently exist in our society, and ideas from economics, biology, and psychology have helped to bring these conditions into existence. In short, these disciplines provide a partly accurate description of human nature, but it is a human nature that they have helped create and perpetuate.

We seem, perhaps unwittingly, to be giving these disciplines more and more of our allegiance every day. When we examine aspects of our everyday life and of the social institutions that contribute to it, we find places where this Hobbesian view of human nature has already had a tremendous impact, as well as places where it may have an impact in the future. One reason why all these changes in our understanding of ourselves and our values are occurring is that social institutions that might offer some resistance to this economic view of life are eroding. We have already seen this exemplified in the case of medicine, law, and sports, and later we will see it in love, friendship, and family life, in work, in education, and in citizenship. Many of our traditional social institutions are no longer telling us convincing stories about what we should value and how we should act in our social lives. We are left to figure these tough things out for ourselves.

Why is all this happening? Why are traditional institutions and traditional values losing our confidence and commitment? This chapter has given you one answer. If human nature is as these sciences say it is, then most of what our traditional institutions tell us loses credibility. Moral exhortations may be based on superstition, on fantasy, or on wishful thinking, but they are not based on fact. And those who take them seriously will be exploited by the "realists" who know what people are actually like. Moreover, owing to the power of ideology, human nature doesn't even really have to be the way these sciences say it is. All that is necessary for the undermining of traditional institutions and values is that we *believe* that these sciences are right. And as modern, enlightened people, in awe of the explanatory power of science, we are inclined to believe what science tells us about ourselves. This makes it all too easy for us to justify as inevitable many actions we might once have regarded as reprehensible. It makes it all too easy for us to accept our unease and dissatisfaction with aspects of modern life rather than to work to transform them.

But the fact that we still feel dissatisfaction suggests that there remains an opportunity to resurrect and build upon traditional conceptions of what we can be and what we should value. What *do* we think is good and valuable in life? What *should* we think is good and valuable in life? What frames *should* we construct within which to evaluate possible courses of action and make decisions?

What We Value

What do we value? What kind of life do we want to live? It is very hard to know how to approach the various choices and activities that make up a life without knowing first what we want out of those activities. What is valuable about being a doctor or a lawyer? If we knew, we would know what is right and wrong about medicine and the law as they are currently organized and practiced. It is hard to know how to choose and pursue a career without knowing about the values that a career should help us realize. It is hard to know whether to choose a mate, and which mate to choose, without knowing about the values that intimate social relations should help us realize. It is similarly hard to know whether to have children and how to raise them, or whether to support the government or work to transform it unless we know what is valuable.

Questions of value are frighteningly difficult, so difficult that we tend to avoid them. What makes them so difficult is that the answers to them seem utterly individual and subjective. Different people want different things out of their careers, their marriages, and their societies. This diversity and subjectivity of values tempts us to forget about questions of value altogether and leave it up to each person to puzzle things out individually.

This is essentially what we do when we entrust so much to the market. With the market, we don't have to decide collectively what is valuable. Instead, we can let people buy and sell anything they want. The freedom of the market allows all of us to pursue whatever it is that we value. We're quite used to this freedom in the domain of consumer goods. We're perhaps less used to it in other domains, but, in principle, there is no reason why there can't be a market in everything, including even careers, marriages, and forms of government. People can opt for traditional or open marriages, corporate or public-interest-oriented law firms, progressive or conservative towns and states. In theory, it ought to be possible for all of us, no matter how peculiar our values, to find a place to live, a place to work, and people to live and work with that will enable us to realize our particular values. In allowing the market to be the ultimate arbiter of value, we may have stumbled onto the only viable solution to a seemingly intractable problem.

Alas, it's not this simple. For while the market is very good at catering to individual idiosyncrasy and at maximizing freedom of choice, it is not so good at other things. Suppose we value stability, commitment, and loyalty. Suppose we value community. Suppose we value justice and honesty. These are not values that can be realized by individuals in isolation. They require broad social and institutional support. And the market as an institution is not known for inspiring or promoting any of these values. In the market, people vote with their feet (or their pocketbooks), and they stay around only as long as wherever they are and whatever they are doing suits them. So if we are to pursue values like loyalty, community, commitment, honesty, and justice, we will have to pursue them collectively. And to pursue them collectively, we must decide they are valuable collectively. In other words, by choosing as a society to avoid difficult questions of value, and instead leaving them up to each of us as individuals, we are in effect providing answers to those questions. We are saying that the truly valuable things are the things that free individual choice on the market makes available.

I think that a little reflection about the kinds of things we value will convince us that this is a mistake—that we do have many values in common and that several of them are not well served by the market. Let us look, then, at some of the values that most of us share.

Let's begin with the obvious. We all value material things, including the good physical health that allows us to enjoy those things. We value material things that we need in order to survive, and we value material things that we don't need, but that give us pleasure and make our lives more comfortable. We tend to take the distinction between necessities and luxuries—needs and wants—fairly seriously. We try to teach it to our children when they tell us how much they *need* another pair of designer jeans or fancy athletic shoes. and we recoil when we hear someone say how much he *needs* that new Mercedes. Sometimes, the distinction between needs and wants is presented to us in a way that is truly painful to experience. For example, on January 3, 1993, the *New York Times Magazine* ran a stirring photo essay on the starving people of Somalia. Surrounding these horrifying photographs of people who were too weak to stand—collections of bones held together by the thinnest veneer of flesh—were advertisements extolling the virtues of luxury houses, expensive cars, jewelry, and watches, gourmet foods, and lavish vacations. The juxtaposition of these opposite ends of the spectrum of material life was startling, though of course one of the major goals of advertising is to blur the distinction between needs and wants, to convince us that we desperately need things that we only (and maybe not even) want.

Despite the occasional stark contrasts, the distinction between needs and wants is not always easy to make. We know that there are places in the world where people live without plumbing, electricity, telephones, or automobiles. It might seem that if people *can* live without these things, they cannot be regarded as needs. Yet, as virtually all members of a society come to possess certain things, society evolves in a way that presumes these things are available. Telephones are hardly a luxury nowadays in the United States, and they haven't been for quite some time. So things people want can become things they need when everyone else has them. This means that what counts as a material need will depend on which society you are evaluating, and that the list of human material needs will change as societies change.

To acquire the resources that enable us to satisfy our needs and wants, we work. Work is the means to consumption. If we don't work, we don't have money, and if we don't have money, we can't consume. There are some people who think—and act—as if this were all there is to work. These people seek jobs that maximize pay and minimize effort. While there is no denying that the most salient aspect of work for many of us is that it's the way we make our living, it seems equally clear that we value many things about work in addition to the opportunities it gives us for consumption. We feel incomplete and unfulfilled if we don't work. We value work when it challenges us to think and act creatively, and when it produces results that are meaningful, useful, and socially important. Work is valuable when it allows us to participate cooperatively with other people, and when it allows us to use our skills in the pursuit of excellence, to achieve results in which we can take pride. Work is valuable when we can say, at the end of a workday, that we have added something worthwhile to the world with our labor. Many of us are willing to sacrifice extra pay, and put in extra effort, to have work to do that possesses some or all of these characteristics.

We also value leisure. We value leisure time, and we value filling up that leisure time with activities. We like to do things. We fill up our days with games, sports, hobbies, trips, and the like. And these leisure activities are extremely important to us. Leisure is most often described in opposition to work. Work is drudgery; leisure is fun. Work is serious; leisure is playful. Work is hard and stressful; leisure is easy and relaxed. Work is done for someone else; leisure is for yourself. None of these oppositions is correct, at least not as a general rule. We can be very serious about our leisure activities. We can be driven. We can work hard to be the best golfers, tennis players, gardeners, woodworkers, bridge players, pianists, or cooks we can possibly be. In pursuit of these objectives, we can make extraordinary demands on ourselves and subject ourselves to training and practice regimes that don't look relaxed at all. It is hard for me to watch my friend preparing for the New York Marathon by getting up at five each morning and running eight hard miles, and then coming home tired from a full day of work and doing it again, and think about her leisure activity as relaxed, playful, and easy. Whatever it is, leisure is not just plain fun.

Many of the leisure activities that attract and consume people do so precisely because they permit people to realize many of the same values that they can realize through work. The activities are challenging, they demand creative intelligence, they are socially valued, and they allow people to pursue and achieve excellence. And frequently, they make their participants active members of a community of similarly committed people. So the real distinction between work and at least much leisure activity is that people get paid only for their work.

One of the reasons that we value work and leisure that permit us to think and act creatively and meet challenging standards of achievement is that these characteristics of our activities feed into another thing we value—control. We want to be autonomous. We went to be able to make our own decisions, to be able to determine our own destinies, to be responsible for the important things in our lives. We resist having to submit to the authority of others. At the workplace, we can forget that we have a boss if our own activities permit us to use our judgment and discretion. And one of the wonderful things about our hobbies is that, usually, there is no one telling us what to do or when to do it.

In the last few years I have encountered several former students who gave up jobs in large and prestigious organizations for jobs in smaller, less high-powered organizations that pay much less. Almost to a person, they made these changes because they came to realize that the things they thought they wanted—money, prestige, power—were much less important to them than autonomy.

Nowhere is the value of autonomy and control more important or obvious than in modern America. It probably undergirds the extraordinary importance we give to freedom of choice and the sanctity we give to the rights of the individual. We rebel against our social institutions (church, state, school) when they try to tell us what to do. Our children rebel against us when we try to tell them what to do. One of the reasons that the character of many of the things we do in life keeps changing is that we refuse to be constrained by the customs, habits, and traditions of those who came before us.

Modern American society provides us with an opportunity to control our lives to a degree that is surely unparalleled in human history. This is true both because technological change has freed us from many of the constraints imposed on us by nature and because cultural change has freed us from many of the constraints imposed on us by social institutions. So we are in a unique position to realize the values of autonomy and control. But this opportunity is something of a two-edged sword. To the extent that we can take responsibility for making of our lives what we will, we must also take responsibility for failing to do so.

There is another thing we value that contributes to our ability to exercise control and to achieve all that we value in our work and our leisure. We value knowledge. We want to know how the universe works and what makes people tick. We want to know about art, music, and literature. We want to know about the interplay of political forces and objectives. We want to know these things because knowing them enables us to get what we want, because knowing them makes us better people, and because knowing them satisfies our curiosity about the world.

And the fact that we are interested in becoming better people points to another of the things we value. We value *being* good people. We value virtues of character. What do we regard as virtues of character? What kinds of people do we think we and others should strive to be? What makes us label some people as good and others as bad?

These are all old-fashioned questions. Indeed, the very word "virtue" is an old-fashioned word, a throwback to a time when people believed that the line between good and evil was easy to draw. We now believe differently. We now believe that generations of people who came before us were forced to lead tortured and miserable lives in the service of a myopic conception of virtue, that "virtue" was an idea used to control people and get them to serve the interests of those with power. We are suspicious of appeals to our "virtue" on the part of others, and reluctant to make similar appeals ourselves. Indeed, we are tempted to do away with the idea of "virtue" altogether, to let each of us decide independently what kind of person we ought to be, and refrain from passing judgment on others.

Nevertheless, the idea of virtue is both inescapable and indispensable. We may have learned in modern society to tolerate styles of thinking, acting, and being of which we disapprove, so that people who display these styles are neither burned at the stake nor exiled. But our tolerance is often reluctant and our disapproval emphatic, as we use such people as models for ourselves and our children of what *not* to be. Conversely, we look for other people—people who do live what we regard as virtuous lives—to be models that we and our children can emulate.

What, then, do we take to be virtues of character? Here's one list: honesty, loyalty, courage, commitment, rationality, perseverance, dependability, empathy, and kindness. Cultivating and sustaining these virtues, in ourselves and in others, is hard. It takes work. Furthermore, how hard it is, and how much work it takes, will depend very much on how many of the people around us possess these virtues. It is easier—less costly and less risky—to be honest when everyone else is honest than when everyone else is duplicitous. The same is true of loyalty, of commitment, and of kindness. We are not at risk of exploitation if we can count on other people to behave the way we do. If we can't count on this, we are likely always to be played for suckers.

How easy and how rewarding it is to be virtuous will depend upon the kind of social institutions we live within and depend upon. The state, the local community, the church, the school, and the family can all play a role in nurturing virtue and protecting those who possess it. If these institutions value virtues of character, they help people develop and display them. If they don't value virtues of character, they don't help. So people are not, or at least need not be, out there trying to lead virtuous lives alone.

But one of the tensions and contradictions that we live with as modern Americans is that while we value virtues of character in people, we resent and resist the moralistic demands of the institutions that promote them. We want to get out from under the dictates of these institutions and make important life decisions on our own, and we assume or hope that we can also develop virtues of character on our own. One of the central arguments of this book is that this may be a vain hope. Thomas Jefferson and his peers could celebrate human freedom without fear because a strong set of character-forming social institutions was sitting in place in the background. But two hundred years of living out that dream of freedom has weakened these institutions. We can't count on them any longer. What we have instead is the market. And in the market little or no premium is placed on honesty, loyalty, commitment, empathy, or kindness. Remember, business (and medicine and law and sports) is business. To the extent that the market becomes our model for life in general, or to the extent that its operation penetrates those social institutions that do nurture virtue, our institutional support in the pursuit of virtuous lives will be undermined. Furthermore, if we take our lessons about what human nature is and can be from science rather than from the social institutions that nurture virtue, the very idea of virtue may rapidly disappear.

All the things discussed thus far that we find valuable involve people as individuals. What has been left out, and what may be most important of all, is that we value other people. We are social beings. We live with other human beings, and we care a great deal about what our relations with other human beings are like. We place enormous value on certain kinds of social relations, and we work very hard and sacrifice a great deal to foster and sustain them. Why? For friendship, for love, for experiences of intimacy, and, sometimes, for sexual satisfaction. Successes are hollow and failures are tragic when they must be experienced alone. Successes are fulfilling and failures bearable when they can be shared with others.

In addition to valuing meaningful personal social relations, we desire to belong to a community, to be a part of something larger than ourselves. The community may be defined geographically, ethnically, politically, or religiously. However it is defined, the community comprises people with a common history, common values, common concerns, and common projects. Community members look out for one another's welfare. The life of each individual is inextricably bound up with the lives of others.

The word "community" is used rather casually these days. Witness the retirement "communities" or singles "communities" that are now common in many parts of the United States. These instant communites actually wrench people away from their genuine communities and bring them together with little in common except perhaps their age and their taste in leisure activities. They are bound together only because their individual interests happen to coincide. They have little knowledge of or concern for one another as individuals. They have no communal ties and feel perfectly free to leave if their current interests change. In contrast, genuine communities bind people to one another. There is a sense of mutual obligation that makes leaving difficult, if not unthinkable.

Indeed, this feeling of obligation, or responsibility, or loyalty is a characteristic that love relations, friendships, and community membership share. We are born into families and communities; we don't choose them. And except in extraordinary circumstances, we carry our ties to them around with us, wherever we go. We do choose our friends and our lovers, but once having chosen them, we feel a lingering responsibility that makes us not quite free to abandon them when they stop serving our purposes.

Albert Hirschman, in his book *Exit, Voice, and Loyalty*, has suggested that we have two general classes of responses available to us when things are not as we want them to be. We can leave, or *exit* the situation, or we can protest, or give *voice* to our concerns. In the domain of goods—in the market—exit is the characteristic response to dissatisfaction. If a restaurant no longer pleases us, we go to another. If our once favorite breakfast cereal gets too expensive, we switch to a different one. If our favorite vacation spot gets too crowded, we find a new one. One of the principal virtues of free-market choice is that it gives us the opportunity to express our displeasure by exit.

In the domain of social relations, things are different. We don't dismiss lovers, friends, or communities the way we dismiss restaurants, cereals, or vacation spots. Treating people in this way is unseemly at best and reprehensible at worst. Instead, we give *voice* to our displeasure, hoping to influence our lover, our friend, or our community to change. And even when our efforts fail, we feel bound to keep trying. Exit, or abandonment, is the response of last resort.

This difference in our response to dissatisfaction in the material as opposed to the social domain points up a tension that many of us experience between market and nonmarket approaches to the things we value. The rules of the game in the market are different from the rules of the game outside it. If we frame love as a market commodity, then exit is an appropriate response to dissatisfaction. If we don't frame love as a market commodity, then exit is inappropriate. And we can't have it both ways, for if one of the things we value about love is the loyalty and commitment it entails, treating it as a market commodity deprives it of this value.

Of all the communities to which we might belong as individuals, one deserves special attention. That is the state. Different states pursue and protect different political values. In the United States, the central political values seem to be freedom, equality, and democracy. It is easy enough to state these values, but less easy to know how to realize them, since they often come into conflict.

The values of freedom and equality can conflict when the state tries to provide some people with things they have not been able to get on their own, by limiting, restricting, or taking away (through taxation) things from others. And the values of freedom and democracy can conflict when a majority tries to impose its views (about abortion, or sexual behavior, or what counts as art and good literature) on a minority. Most of the modern political debate that goes on in the United States between liberals and conservatives is essentially a debate about the relative importance of freedom, democracy, and equality. So agreeing that freedom, equality, and democracy are valuable does little to avoid the intense disagreements that characterize modern political life in the United States. Nevertheless, it seems fair to say that we value each of them and struggle among ourselves to figure out how they should be played off against each other.

Freedom, equality, and democracy conclude my list of things that people in the late-twentieth-century United States value. To summarize, the things we value are these:

- material things, including necessities and luxuries
- productive, meaningful work and active, fulfilling leisure
- knowledge and autonomy
- virtues of character
- close social relations, including love, sex, friendship, and membership in community
- freedom, equality, and democracy

This is a list of the best things in life, and the good life, the successful life, is a life that permits the realization of most or all of these values. Is it possible? Can we live good lives, understood in this way? Can we have it all? And if so, what must we do to have it all?

The obvious truth is that having it all is extremely difficult. Doing what we must to move closer to achieving some of these values moves us farther away from achieving others. We want to be wealthy enough to live lives filled with material pleasures and comforts. But we also want enough free time to be able to enjoy those pleasures and comforts, and we want our work to be meaningful and satisfying as well as financially rewarding. For most of us, some kind of trade-off will be necessary. We want committed, enduring relations with other people. But we also want to be free to come and go as we please, or at least to be able to extricate ourselves from relations that are unsatisfying. Again, trade-offs will be necessary. We want sufficient time to be able to devote ourselves to our friends, our lovers, and our communities; but taking the time often means sacrificing time that could be devoted to the pursuit of material success. We want social decisions to be made democratically; but we don't want to be told what to do. We want to be surrounded by virtuous people; but we don't want someone else's conception of virtue imposed on us.

As individuals, we find it extremely challenging to balance the conflicting demands that these various values we pursue impose on us. "Moderation in all things" is a useful aphorism from the past. But it is much easier to acknowledge the usefulness of this aphorism than to live by it. How much work is too much work? How much loyalty to friends and family is too much loyalty? How much material success is enough? When does democratic decision making become tyranny?

Each of us is expected to figure these things out individually. Each of us is expected to balance in our own way the conflicting demands that different values impose on us. This emphasis on the individual as the locus of decision making is what makes the market seem like such an ideal device for the pursuit of all that we value. Those of us who place a high value on material consumption will choose jobs that pay well and will compensate for long hours on the job by pursuing social relations that are undemanding. Those of us who value committed social relations will settle for jobs that demand less work and provide less pay. Those of us who value freedom of choice and movement will stay out of entangling relationships, while those of us who value stability and loyalty will seek them. Everything is possible. And if we fail we have only ourselves to blame.

Most of us will fail. Achieving moderation in all things is hard. And having to do it alone, as individuals, is especially hard. If there were "rules of the game," or frames, that we had to live by—rules that specify how much of our lives should be devoted to work, what our obligations to family, friends, and community should be, how much material wealth is enough—much of the onus for making these decisions would be taken off us as individuals. While there would still be room for individual freedom of choice, and still be domains in which the market could operate, much of the responsibility for the difficult balancing act that we now try to perform would be taken off our shoulders and placed instead in social customs, traditions, and institutions that would help us pursue all of the things we value. So social institutions could ease the burden on individuals by establishing rules of conduct that, while open to transformation, could not be violated willy-nilly by each of us if we so chose.

The price of accepting the rules of conduct imposed by social institutions is a restriction on our freedom. Is it a price worth paying? However much all of us might like to answer this question for ourselves as individuals, it isn't possible. A society that allows us to answer these questions individually has already given its own answer, for by giving us the choice, it has opted for freedom over rules. And a society that does not allow us to answer this question individually has also given its own answer, opting for rules over freedom. But if it should turn out that unrestricted freedom impedes the pursuit of our diverse values rather than enhancing it, then it may well be that the right kinds of restrictions make everyone better off. If it should turn out that "constraint" sometimes affords a kind of liberation while "freedom" affords a kind of enslavement, then we would all be wise to seek out appropriate constraint. I mention this paradoxical possibility only because I think it is true.

6

CONSUMED BY CONSUMPTION

How singular is the thing called pleasure, and how curiously related to pain, which might be thought to be the opposite of it; for they are never present to a man at the same instant, and yet he who pursues either is generally compelled to take the other; their bodies are two, but they are joined by a single head.   —PLATO

Finally, there came a time when everything that men had considered inalienable became an object of exchange, of traffic, and could be alienated. This is the time when the very things which till then had been communicated, but never exchanged; given, but never sold; acquired, but never bought—virtue, love, conviction, knowledge, conscience—when everything, in short, passed into commerce. It is the time of general corruption, of universal venality.   —KARL MARX

If it's true that people value productive, meaningful work, autonomy, honesty, loyalty, kindness, love, friendship, and membership in community, how is it that "business is business" and that professional and recreational activities are becoming business too? Why is there so much deception, fraud, and abuse in the marketplace, and why are many doctors, lawyers, and professional athletes giving themselves over so completely to the marketplace? Surely, many of the people who are caught up in the pursuit of wealth can afford to forgo a little bit of their striving for material success and pursue some of these other values—on and off the job—instead of neglecting or compromising them. How much money can you spend? Enough is enough.

153

Well, just how much is enough? How much work is enough work, how much money is enough money, how many things are enough things? Are people ever satisfied with what they have? Intuition might answer yes. As you look over the hedge at your neighbor's house, yard, furnishings, and cars, you might well believe that if only you had what he had, you'd be satisfied. Indeed, you might find yourself wondering why your neighbor is scrambling around all the time hustling a living—working long hours, in the office on weekends, away on business trips—instead of slowing down for a minute to enjoy all that he has.

Your neighbor, of course, is looking over *his* hedge, at his neighbor (not you), and telling himself that *he* would be satisifed with *his* neighbor's life, though his neighbor seems not to be. Meanwhile, your neighbor on the other side is making the same observations about you. "The grass is always greener," the truism goes. But is the truism true? If it is, what underlies it? If it is, are we condemned to a life of perpetual dissatisfaction, of endless striving for more?

There are three major reasons why we are so rarely satisfied with what we have, and so reluctant to conclude that what we have is enough. First, we care about status; part of the satisfaction we get from the things we have derives from the fact that not everyone else has them. As other people start to get these things, our own desires seem to escalate so that we can maintain our privileged position. Second, some of the things we desire are quite scarce, sufficiently scarce that it will never be possible for everyone to have them. As a result, our own ability to get those things depends not just on our being successful but on our being *more* successful than others. If we were satisfied with what we had, while others continued to pursue more and more, our position in the race for really scarce goods would deteriorate. Third, some of us are thing addicts. Consumption can be an addiction, and then it, like all addictions, can't be satisfied.

ADAPTATION AND ADDICTION

Imagine yourself out running errands on a hot, humid summer day. After several hours of sweating in the heat, you return home to your air-conditioned house. The feeling is spectacular. The cool, dry air in your house is immensely pleasurable. It invigorates you. But as time passes, the pleasure wanes. It is replaced by a feeling of comfort. While you don't feel hot, sticky and tired, you don't feel cool and energized either. In fact, you don't feel much of anything. You've gotten so accustomed to the air-conditioning that you don't even notice it. You don't notice it, that is, until you leave it to go back out into the heat a while later. Now the heat hits you like a blast from an open oven, and you notice the air-conditioning that you no longer have.

This is a common enough experience. People get used to all kinds of things, both pleasant and unpleasant. They adjust or *adapt*. Many people who suffer chronic pain (say from a bad back) learn to live with it, so they can go about their business and hardly notice sensations that for others would be extremely debilitating. And people whose life circumstances suggest that they "suffer" chronic pleasure (the idle rich, the "beautiful people") get so accustomed to it that they take for granted things that would make others ecstatic.

Several years ago, economist Tibor Scitovsky explored some of the consequences of the phenomenon of adaptation in his book *The Joyless Economy.* Human beings, Scitovsky said, want to experience pleasure. And when they consume, they do experience pleasure— as long as the things they consume are novel. But as people adapt— as the novelty wears off—pleasure comes to be replaced by comfort. It's a thrill to drive your new car for the first few weeks; after that, it's just comfortable. It certainly beats the old car, but it isn't much of a kick. Comfort is nice enough, but we want pleasure. And comfort isn't pleasure.

Scitovsky's account of the dynamics of consumption suggests that people will move from feeling good to feeling nothing in particular as they get used to consuming certain things, and that this will propel them to search for new things to consume. More recently, psychologist Richard Solomon articulated an account of the processes that underlie adaptation that suggests that the problem is even worse. From Solomon's point of view, the change we experience as we adapt to things is not from feeling good to feeling neutral; it's from feeling good to feeling bad. He argues that whenever we experience something that makes us feel either very good or very bad, that experience carries with it an automatic aftereffect that takes us in the opposite emotional direction. If being hot and sticky makes us feel bad, the aftereffect when that feeling ends will be pleasant. If we have a wonderfully pleasurable sexual experience, the aftereffect of that experience will be unpleasant. If we experience something extremely frightening (a horror movie, a ride on a roller coaster), the aftereffect of that experience will be a feeling of security and well-being, perhaps even euphoria. In general, every positive experience has negative aftereffects and every negative experience has positive aftereffects. The consequence of these aftereffects is to cancel out the initial effects and to move us in the direction of emotional neutrality—to a state of comfort rather than to a state of pleasure. This antagonistic relation between direct emotional experiences and their aftereffects Solomon terms *affective contrast*.

This description of affective contrast may not seem to square with your own experience. You may not recall feeling bad after sex, or feeling euphoric after a ride on a roller coaster. The reason for this, according to Solomon, is that the aftereffects may be quite small, sufficiently small that they are hardly noticeable. Their principal effects may be to diminish somewhat or to truncate the emotional states that precede them. So you might simply stop feeling good after sex faster than you otherwise would, or stop feeling scared after a roller coaster ride faster than you otherwise would. However, Solomon also suggests that the affective contrast can be dynamic. The first time you have a particular pleasurable experience, it may be followed by an aftereffect that is imperceptible. But if you have the pleasurable experience again, before too much time has gone by, its negative aftereffect will change. It will begin earlier, perhaps even while the positive experience is still occurring, it will be more intense, and it will last longer. As a result of this change, the negative aftereffect will start to cancel out some of the direct, positive effect, so it doesn't give as much pleasure as it did the last time. And when the direct, positive effect ends, you will be left with a more substantial, negative aftereffect—this time, perhaps, large enough to notice. As you continue to have the positive experience, the negative aftereffect will continue starting earlier, growing larger, and lasting longer. After enough experience, the once positive event will produce hardly any pleasure at all; the pleasure will be almost completely canceled out by the aftereffect. Indeed, the principal emotion you will feel at this point is negative. When the direct, positive effect wears off, you will be left with the now rather intense negative aftereffect. While you are having the experience, positive and negative will cancel each other out, so you feel roughly neutral. But when the experience ends, you will be left with a strong, negative aftereffect and feel awful.

The prime example of this kind of emotional dynamic is drug addiction. When a person first takes a drug like cocaine, there is a big positive emotional effect and only a small, negative aftereffect. But as the person continues to take the drug, the positive effect gets smaller and smaller, as it is being canceled by the ever growing negative aftereffect. This process, known as *tolerance*, pushes the user to take ever larger doses of the drug in order to recapture the initial high. And when each dose of the drug wears off, the user is left with a massive negative aftereffect. This aftereffect, usually called *withdrawal*, is what drives the user to find another dose.

Cigarette smoking offers another clear example. Indeed, nicotine, like cocaine, is an extremely addictive drug. Many heavy smokers will tell you that they derive almost no pleasure from smoking. What emotion they do experience is the negative emotion that occurs when they must refrain, as on an airplane, or in a theater, or nowadays, in almost any public place. They continue to smoke because each new dose of nicotine counteracts the negative emotion—the withdrawal—they are experiencing. If a once heavy smoker who has quit smokes an occasional cigarette, the pleasure he experiences from smoking is enormous. Once habitual but now occasional smokers will tell you that they haven't enjoyed a cigarette this much in years. But should the occasional cigarette lead to a return to the old habit, the smoker will again derive less and less pleasure from the act of smoking and feel principally the displeasure associated with abstinence. An old cigarette ad used to ask smokers if they were "smoking more but enjoying it less." The idea behind the ad, of course, was that if they switched brands, the pleasure would come back. The truth, however, is that virtually all habitual smokers smoke more but enjoy it less.

Solomon's account seems to fit the case of drug addiction well, but he suggests that it is not restricted to drugs. The same dynamic process of affective contrast can accompany many experiences of pleasure. We commonly assume that people pursue luxuries not because they need them but because they *like* them. One of the things that makes something a luxury is the substantial pleasure that it provides. But if Solomon is right, as people get accustomed to luxuries, these stop giving pleasure, and people feel mainly the *displeasure* of having to do without them. This process contributes to turning luxuries into necessities. Thus, air conditioners, cars, televisions, washing machines, dishwashers, and the like seem to many to be absolutely essential for existence. Microwave ovens and video recorders will soon join the list of necessities, as will car phones and fax machines, if they haven't already.

I don't mean to suggest that the *only* reason luxuries become necessities is that we *feel* bad without them. Other reasons are also very important. When we have time-saving luxuries like cars, telephones, washing machines, and microwave ovens, we organize our lives on the presumption that they'll be there to serve us. If we subsequently have to do without them for any reason, we find ourselves stretched too thin when we go back to doing things the old-fashioned way. We just can't get everything done without a car if we've set up our lives to be lived with one. My point here is that *in addition to* the inconvenience caused by the absence of accustomed luxuries, we *feel* bad without them.

I suggested in the last chapter that one of the things we value in life is the pleasure that material things bring us. But if Solomon's theory is correct, we cannot keep deriving pleasure from consuming the *same* material things. As we get used to these things, as the negative aftereffects catch up with the positive initial effects, pleasure essentially disappears. We are disappointed with consumption of the same old things because repeated consumption provides us with doses of pleasure that do not live up to our expectations—expectations that are shaped by our initial encounters with those things. Because of this process, the pursuit of pleasure from material things becomes the pursuit of ever new and different things.

The effects of this process are probably very different for different kinds of experiences. Experiences that don't give us much pleasure to begin with, that don't deflect us very far from emotional neutrality, probably have minimal negative aftereffects. We are thus unlikely to become especially addicted to eating potato chips (though it's hard to eat just one). And experiences that satisfy basic biological needs may be relatively immune to these aftereffects, because these needs renew themselves. If part (not all, but part) of the pleasure we get from eating and drinking comes from relieving hunger and thirst, we may continue to experience pleasure so long as we continue to experience hunger and thirst. However, much of the pleasure we experience from the sensory qualities of the particular things we eat or drink may well diminish as we get used to eating and drinking them. Thus the never ending search for new restaurants and new recipes. Thus the search, among fans of Szechuan cuisine, for ever hotter dishes. Thus the search, among chocolate fiends, for ever richer and more intensely chocolaty cakes and confections.

Even among the things we pursue that are luxuries, and thus don't satisfy any renewing biological needs, there may still be differences in the extent to which negative aftereffects cause disappointment or displeasure. When we spend our time and money on goods that are actually *consumed*—dinners out, or movies, or vacations—the magnitude of our disappointment may be limited. If, because of negative aftereffects, a dinner out isn't what we hoped it would be, at least it is brief, transient, and soon forgotten. However, when we shift our time and money to purchases of goods that are not consumed or, at least, are not consumed so quickly—goods that are durable and don't go away, like cars, houses, stereo systems, elegant clothes, jewelry, and computers—the problem is more severe. For after our brief period of real enthusiasm and pleasure with these things is negated by the aftereffects, we still have these things around us—as a constant reminder that consumption isn't all it's cracked up to be, that expectations are never matched by reality. Of course, very few of us can afford to get rid of these durable goods after they stop pleasing us. Indeed, in many instances, we may still be paying for them long after they have stopped pleasing us. And as economist Albert Hirschman has pointed out, as a society's affluence grows, consumption shifts increasingly to expensive, durable goods, with the result that disappointment with consumption increases.

Faced with this inevitable disappointment of consumption, what do people do? Some people (very, very few, I suspect) simply give up the chase; they stop valuing pleasure derived from things. Most people are driven instead to pursue novelty, to seek out new commodities whose pleasure potential has not been driven down by repeated consumption. But these new commodities will also eventually fail to satisfy. The lesson in this is that the pursuit of pleasure is a perpetual wild-goose chase. Nevertheless, people can and do get caught up in it, and if we think again about drug addiction, it isn't hard to see why. The cocaine addict may know that his next dose will produce very little pleasure, a barely perceptible high. However, at the time at which he is deciding whether or not to take another dose, his emotional state is far from neutral. Instead, he is experiencing withdrawal, the powerful negative aftereffect of the last dose. In the midst of this agonizing withdrawal, the addict's choice is between feeling terrible (as he does at the moment) or getting back to feeling neutral (as he will if he takes another dose). Only if he is willing to suffer through a prolonged period of abstinence agony, allowing the withdrawal to run its course, will he be able to get the monkey off his back. It is hardly surprising that few addicts make this choice. And so it may be with the disappointed consumer. Having bought the fancy new car, enjoyed it briefly, and then experienced a negative aftereffect, the consumer has to choose between waiting the aftereffect out, or attempting to override it with another dose of consumption. And the addicted consumer has no addiction clinics to help him get the monkey off *his* back. Indeed, his addiction is actively encouraged wherever he turns, in advertising that bombards him from every outlet of popular culture.

So, to return to the question with which I began this chapter, how much is enough? Ask the cocaine addict how much is enough. The answer, if you're an addict, is that you can never have enough. And so the thing addict is on a vicious treadmill of getting and spending with no relief in sight.

"Thing addiction" is certainly not as dramatic as cocaine addiction. The negative aftereffects are described better as disappointment than as agony. Furthermore, since consumption of things is quite legal, there is nothing (except for limited resources) to stop a thing addict from continuing to feed his habit, and thus never experiencing withdrawal at all. Nevertheless, the desire to continue feeding the habit certainly puts pressure on people to do things that they might never have imagined themselves capable of. It puts pressure on people to abandon themselves, and their friends and family, to the work that is the source of the cash that is the source of the things. It puts pressure on people to cut corners in their work, sometimes threatening public safety, sometimes violating public trust, and sometimes breaking the law. It puts pressure on people to go deeply into debt. Thing addiction may not be cocaine addiction, but it can be pretty destructive.

The phenomenon of thing addiction also speaks to the distinction we make between needs and wants. Addiction makes the distinction between needs and wants problematic. No one (except the heart-breaking infants of addicted mothers) comes into the world *needing* cocaine. Nevertheless, once a person becomes addicted to cocaine, thinking of it as a luxury is simply ridiculous. It follows from this that if people can become addicted to "things" more generally, many of the goods that we think of as want-satisfying luxuries may actually become need-satisfying, addiction-driven necessities. This implies that it's not so easy to get people to stop or even diminish their dedication to consumption. "Just say no!" won't do the job.

Indeed, even though the addiction to things may be less powerful than the addiction to drugs, it may be *more* difficult to overcome. Right now, there is enormous legal, moral, and social disapproval of drug production, sale, and use in this country. Aside from the stiff criminal penalties that are meant to act as a deterrent to drug use, children start hearing messages about the evils of drug use as soon as they enter school, and they continue to hear those messages, again and again, from different sources and in different forms, until they reach adulthood. Some kids, of course, will use drugs anyway, but very few of these kids can possibly be confused about what society's attitude toward drug use is. And when people do become involved with drugs, and try to end their addiction, they are provided with a vast array of medical, psychological, and social support services. Our daily newspapers make it clear that all these social forces do not stop people from using drugs or make it easy for them to quit, but there is no doubt that they do make starting harder and quitting easier.

Contrast this public attitude toward drug addiction with our attitude toward the consumption of things. The pursuit and consumption of things seems almost sacred in the United States. It may be the national sport. School kids are not warned repeatedly about the evils of shopping malls. On the contrary, kids seem to be getting initiated into the addiction earlier than ever before. All over the country, high schools are facing the problem of dealing with students who fall asleep in class and don't do their homework, because they are working full-time jobs after school—not so that they can bring money home but so that they can buy the things they "need." Getting and spending is actively promoted, encouraged, advertised, and revered. It is used by parents and school administrators as the carrot to be dangled in front of the noses of reluctant pupils. Overcoming or avoiding thing addiction in the face of almost univocal public pressure in the opposite direction is a very difficult task; it may be an impossible one. Until consumption stops being regarded as the national pastime, we can expect only that more and more individuals will develop thing addictions. Individuals can do their part in eliminating thing addiction not so much by reforming themselves as by contributing to a social discourse that actively discourages thing addiction just as it actively discourages addiction to other kinds of drugs.

Solomon's "addiction" account of the process of adaptation is controversial. There is uncertainty about whether it provides the right explanation of drug addiction and about whether it can be applied to the pleasure we get from other kinds of things. But the phenomenon of adaptation itself is not controversial. Whether we start feeling bad, or just stop feeling good, as we get used to things, the things we get used to clearly no longer give us pleasure. And if pleasure is one of the things we value, no matter how much stuff we have, it may not be enough.

STATUS AND SOCIAL SCARCITY

The disappointment we feel with consumption induces us to consume more and different things in the elusive pursuit of pleasure. This in turn induces us to attempt to amass greater and greater wealth. But it doesn't help much to amass greater wealth. About twenty years ago, a large survey was done in the United States in which people were asked how happy they were with their lives. A similar survey had been done twenty-five years before. During the intervening period (from 1946 to 1970), real (inflation adjusted) income had risen 62 percent. So people were, on the whole, much better off in 1970 than in 1946. Yet this large change in material welfare had no effect on happiness ratings. People were no happier in 1970 than in 1946, though if you had asked them in 1946 how happy they would be if they had the standard of living that they actually did have in 1970, nearly all would have answered that they would be thrilled.

The phenomenon of adaptation provides one account of why increases in wealth do not produce corresponding increases in happiness—why no matter how much people have, it may not be enough. But there are other possible accounts to consider, accounts I mentioned at the beginning of the chapter. It could be that material well-being is relevant to happiness only when it is evaluated relative to the material well-being of everybody else. It is possible that, for example, a 50 percent increase in real income will make someone happy only if not everyone else's income has also increased by 50 percent. If everyone is getting richer, then an individual's own gains are seen as only fair—as entitlements. They don't change his relative position in society at all, and thus they don't make him happy. It is certainly not implausible that, for many people, what matters is not simply how much they have but how much *more* they have than others. And this could account for why societywide changes in affluence do not affect individual judgments about happiness. Consistent with this view is another finding from the survey I just mentioned, this time comparing ratings of personal happiness across different nations at the *same* time—some very rich (the United States, the former West Germany, Japan) and some very poor (Nigeria, Egypt, India). The survey showed very little difference in happiness ratings even between people in nations that differed in per capita wealth by a factor of fifteen. The phenomenon of adaptation can't by itself account for data like these.

There are two different motivations that might underlie a person's concern with relative rather than with absolute wealth. One involves the importance of status; the other involves the importance of goods sufficiently scarce that not everyone in society can have them. Let's consider status first.

Most people care about status. It is important to them to be better, or more successful, than their neighbors. Material wealth is certainly not a direct reflection of either "goodness" or "success." Indeed, according to some notions of "goodness," the more wealth you have, the more your goodness is suspect. And in some domains of activity (for example, teaching, social work, games like badminton, volleyball, or chess), success simply does not, except in the rarest circumstances, carry with it material wealth. Nevertheless, for most people, in most circumstances, material wealth is as good an index, or proxy, of success as there is. While your neighbors will not be in a position to judge just how good a doctor, or lawyer, or banker you are, they will be in a position to judge how much stuff you have. And on the presumption that "to the victors go the spoils," they will assume that if you have a lot of stuff, you must be very good at what you do.

I suspect that very few people admit openly even to themselves that they are so concerned about status that they want things at least in part as a signal to other people of how successful they are. It indicates very low status to be openly concerned about status. Nevertheless, the interest that people show in what other people have, the injunctions against envy that have been a part of Western culture at least since biblical times, and the need that people feel to "explain" if they have less stuff than most members of their profession have ("I'm a lawyer; I work in the public defender's office." "I'm a doctor; I just got back from two years in Ethiopia.")—all strongly suggest that the desire for status plays a significant role in driving our desire for things.

Economist Robert Frank wrote a book a few years ago that was almost entirely devoted to demonstrating how important status, or relative position, is to people. He called it *Choosing the Right Pond*. The central idea of the book is that much of social life and group formation is determined by our desire to be big fish in our own ponds. If there were only one pond—if everyone compared her position to the positions of everybody else—virtually all of us would be losers. After all, in the pond of the whales, even sharks are small.

So instead of comparing ourselves to everyone, we try to mark off the world in such a way that in *our* pond, in comparison with *our* reference group, we are successful. Better to be the third-highest-paid lawyer in a small firm and make $120,000 a year than to be in the middle of the pack in a large firm and make $150,000. Frank marshals evidence from a variety of domains that people will work for substantially less compensation than they could get on the open market. And the reason they do this, he suggests, is that it allows them to maintain high status in the reference group to which they compare themselves. The way to be happy—the way to succeed in the quest for status that is so important to many of us—is to find the right pond and stay in it.

The quest for status is sufficiently important to many people that it leads them to make spending and employment decisions that are unwise—even irrational. Status is not served if we spend money on things that no one can see, for example, various kinds of insurance (life, health, homeowners') or retirement pensions. Nor is status served if we sacrifice salary in exchange for safe and comfortable working conditions. Someone who is at the margins of her own pond might be tempted to forgo these hidden expenditures, or costly but valuable working conditions, for opportunities to engage in what Thorsten Veblen called conspicuous consumption. This person might be tempted to seek out and purchase expensive things just because they are expensive. Frank suggests that much government regulation serves to counteract this quest for status, to protect us from ourselves. If one person in your pond were to decide to spend the several thousand dollars a year that you spend on insurance on a fancy vacation, or a sailboat, his decision would make you worse off, even though nothing about your own absolute financial circumstances changed. You would feel pressure to keep up, perhaps by giving up your own insurance, perhaps by taking another job, perhaps by going deeply into debt. Requiring workplaces to maintain certain safety standards, requiring people to pay social security taxes, requiring people to have insurance (as the mortgage company, if not the government, does), establishing a standard-length workweek, and the like protect us from the status race by preventing individuals from trying to surpass other members of their comparison group in this way. Of course, there is still plenty of opportunity for people to make foolish spending decisions that will signal to their neighbors that they are more successful (that is, more wealthy) than they really are. But regulatory measures like these serve to limit the damage that the status race can do.

The importance to us of status helps explain why we are always looking over our shoulders to see how our neighbors are doing. It helps explain why we can never be sure that what we have is enough. It helps explain why we are never satisfied with what we have. Together with the processes of adaptation and addiction, it makes the never ending quest for consumption seem not only plausible but inevitable. Adaptation has us continuing the quest for things because we stop getting pleasure from what we already have. And the desire for status has us continuing the quest for things because one of the things that gives us pleasure is simply having more than the people around us. Small wonder that people have a hard time getting off the get-and-spend merry-go-round!

If we stopped our discussion here, it would be tempting to conclude that dissatisfaction with consumption can be fixed by teaching people to care less about status and to change their consumption patterns so as to avoid thing addiction. In other words, we could produce a self-help book to join the hundreds already on bookstore shelves. Individuals could read the book, reform their attitudes and behavior, and solve the problem. Perpetual dissatisfaction, then, would be seen as a problem that affects society by affecting individuals and that can be fixed by fixing individuals, one person at a time.

But we can't stop here. We can't stop with an analysis focused exclusively on individual attitudes and behavior. For in addition to unfortunate habits and desires possessed by individuals, there is something about the social and economic system in which we live that propels people into lives of perpetual consumption and dissatisfaction, so a reforming of people without a reforming of the system is essentially impossible. In other words, even if we could teach people to give up some of their quest for pleasure, and to care less about status, they would still not be satisfied with what they have. They would not be satisfied because they actually have legitimate reasons for believing that no matter how much stuff a person has, it may not be enough.

In modern American society, relative economic position is

important not only because it makes people feel good (status) but because many of the things that people value most are in short supply. There are just not enough of these things to go around. And there never will be, no matter what technological marvels the future may hold. As a result, one individual's chance to get these things depends not merely on her absolute wealth but on her wealth relative to the wealth of other people who want the same things. In short, there are very real and good reasons for people in our society to be worried about their economic status. In the face of these real and good reasons, "fixing" people would do them a real disservice.

Economist Fred Hirsch argued in his book *Social Limits to Growth* that while technological development may continue to increase the number of people who can be fed from an acre of farmland, or the number of children who can be inoculated against polio for $1,000, there are certain kinds of goods that no amount of technological development will make universally available. For example, no matter how wealthy and technologically advanced society becomes as a whole, not everyone will be able to own a secluded acre of land at the seashore. Similarly, not everyone can have the most interesting jobs. Not everyone can be the boss. Not everyone can go to the best college or belong to the best country club. Not everyone can be treated by the "best" doctor in the "best" hospital. Hirsch calls goods like these *positional goods*, just because not everyone can have them. How likely anyone is to get what he wants depends upon his economic *position* relative to the position of others. What this means is that an individual's ability to procure and consume these goods depends upon the magnitude of his resources in relation to the resources of others—in short, on his *relative* economic position. No matter how much money a person has—no matter how much his income grows—if everyone else has at least as much, his chances of enjoying these positional goods are slim. Sometimes these kinds of goods are positional simply because there is a limited supply of them that can't be increased. Not everyone can have a Van Gogh hanging in her living room. At other times, the problem is that as more people gain access to these goods, they become less good, through overcrowding. The New York City area has several beautiful beaches, enough to accommodate thousands of people. But as more and more people use the beaches, they become so crowded that there is barely room to lie down, they become so noisy that people can hardly hear themselves think, they become so dirty that it is no longer pleasant even to look at them, and the highways that lead to them turn into parking lots. Under these conditions, the only way to get the kind of beach experience you want is to own (or rent) your own beach. And that's expensive.

Some people, like economist Lester Thurow in his book *The Zero-Sum Society*, have suggested that positional competition for consumption helps turn the economy into a "zero-sum game." Zero-sum games are games like poker, in which everything one player wins, the other players lose. Despite the suspicious claims that poker players are known to make about how they did at the end of a game, it is mathematically necessary that the total amount won in a poker game equal the total amount lost. The pie cannot expand during the game so that everybody wins. What both Hirsch and Thurow are suggesting is that, in important respects, the economic pie, like the poker pie, also can't be expanded. As a result, whatever an individual gains, he gains at some other individual's expense. Absolute improvements in prosperity don't get you the beach house; only relative improvements do.

Hirsch also suggests that as a society gets wealthier, more and more of the goods that people desire have this positional character, which can't be fixed by technological change. It is when basic material needs are easily met that attention turns to beach houses, fancy country clubs, servants, prestigious schools, and the like. And for these things, no amount of money is enough. Or at least, people can never be sure how much money is enough.

We might all agree that everyone would be better off if there were less positional competition. It's stressful, it's wasteful, and it distorts people's lives. Imagine being a parent wanting only the best for your child—a great education, a great job, good friends, lots of money, and so on. What do you do? You encourage your child to study hard so that she can get into a good college. But everyone is doing that. So you push harder. But so does everybody else. So you send your child to after-school enrichment programs and educational summer camps. And so does everyone else. So now you switch to private school. Again you have lots of company. So you nag at your kid to be a great musician or athlete or something that will make her distinctive. You hire tutors and trainers. And so, of course, does everyone else, or at least everyone who has not gone broke or died of a coronary. Your poor child, meanwhile, has been tortured by your ambitions for her and by now has no interest in any of the things you have forced her to do for the sake of her own future.

How sad! Students work to get good grades even when they have no interest in their studies. Many go to college not because they are interested in further education but to defend their position against everyone else who goes to college. People seek job advancement even when they are happy with the jobs they already have. If only we would all agree to stop. But we can't, because for each individual, the best situation is the one in which everyone stops but him. And the situation to be feared and avoided is the one in which he, and only he, stops. It's like being in a crowded football stadium, watching the crucial play. A spectator several rows in front stands up to get a better view. A chain reaction follows. Soon everyone is standing, just to be able to see as well as before. Everyone is standing rather than sitting, but no one's position has improved. And if someone, unilaterally and resolutely, refuses to stand, he might just as well not be at the game at all. Again, when people pursue goods that are positional, they can't help being in the rat race. To choose not to run is to lose. Nonparticipation is not an option.

If we wrote a self-help book to prevent positional competition, what could we tell people? How could we get them to stop always feeling that they need to have more? Do we want to teach them not to desire access to a beautiful, uncrowded beach? Do we want to teach them not to want a pretty, spacious house on a quiet street? Do we want to teach them not to want the best for their families? Of course not. But as long as goods like these are available to the highest bidder, endless acquisitiveness and dissatisfaction with what they already have will haunt people. It will haunt even people who don't give a damn about status and who have avoided thing addiction.

So the self-help book needs to be supplemented by societal help. Some kind of social reorganization must occur that prevents many of the things that people value from being available at auction on the open market. Only then can people learn to be satisfied with what they have. Only then can people avoid being forced into endless competition for what they want.

Right now, obviously, people are in serious competition with one another to improve their relative positions. And this competition has very significant social consequences, consequences that every day make the problem worse.

THE PROBLEM OF THE COMMON

Thing addiction leaves people frustrated, disappointed, and exhausted. Nowadays, we face many situations analogous to that of the crowd at a football game, where one person standing up to see better triggers a process in which all end up standing just to see as well as they did before from their seats. To prevent situations like these from occurring requires an appeal to people to restrain themselves. But, at the same time, the pressure to keep up with others (to join those who are standing so that at least you can see) makes restraint extremely costly. As fewer and fewer people are willing to restrain their pursuit of material goods, the costs to those who do show restraint escalate. Each time another person abandons ship, he makes it harder for those who remain on board to keep the ship afloat. In other words, as some people aggressively pursue *things*, they make it harder for themselves, and others, to pursue some of the other values I discussed earlier. And the more people feel the need to abandon concern for other values in order to get the material things they want, the less they are able to get. They keep running faster, but fall farther and farther behind.

Imagine a small village in the eighteenth century. Each family has a house with a small plot of land for raising vegetables. In addition, there is a large, common area used by all the villagers to graze their livestock. Each villager has a cow or two that provide the family with its milk. The common area is large enough to support the entire village. Then the village begins to grow. Families get larger and procure an extra cow. New families move in. Suddenly, the common is threatened; it is being overgrazed. Grass is being consumed so fast that there is not enough time for it to replenish itself before rains erode the topsoil. Each cow no longer has quite enough to eat and thus yields less milk than it did before. If the overuse of the common continues, there will be a slow but sure decrease in the number of animals it can support, until, finally, it becomes useless for grazing.

How can the overuse be stopped? Consider the issue from the point of view of an individual villager. He needs the milk from his two or three cows, and even if they give him less than they did before, less is better than nothing. Besides, how much difference will it make if he alone shows some restraint in his use of the common. Indeed, his temptation might be to add another cow, since each of the ones he already has is producing less than before. The slow decrease in overall production of dairy products in the village has little impact on him, especially in comparison to how he would be affected if he stopped using the common altogether. It would be best for this villager if everyone else in the village were to show restraint. Then he could continue to use the common as before, with plenty of grass to take care of his cows. He could, in this way, be a *free rider* on the restraint shown by others. But of course, this villager's interest, that he continue to use the common as before, is shared by all the villagers. Everyone could benefit from being a free rider. The result is that none of them modify their behavior, and the common is destroyed.

This is the *commons problem*, known to economists in one form or another for many years. The problem is one in which the interests of the collective, and even the long-term interests of each individual in the collective, are best served by the exercise of restraint, but only if everyone cooperates in showing that restraint. If there is no such cooperation—if some individuals are likely to take advantage of the restraint shown by others—then it is in no one's interest to show restraint.

Examples of the commons problem are plentiful. They include the overharvesting of trees by lumber companies, the overplanting of land by farmers, the overdevelopment of suburban communities, the extraction of petroleum from a common pool by oil companies, and the overcrowding of highways, beaches, libraries, and other public facilities so as to make whatever benefits its users derive from those facilities vanishingly small. They also include pollution of water by toxic wastes, pollution of the environment by noise and litter, overpopulation, hoarding of goods during shortages, using water to keep a green lawn during droughts, and keeping the air conditioner on during hot summer days when the community is threatened with a power shortage. In all of these examples, in the absence of any assurance that all individuals will exercise restraint for the common good, the rational individual will eschew restraint, rather than be exploited by free-riding others. And if others *do* show restraint, the rational individual will be tempted to be a free rider himself. If you do the right thing, you lose; you're a sucker. Doing the wrong thing at least keeps you even.

And when you do decide to do the thing that keeps you even with others, you (and everyone else) may still end up worse off than before. Consider the suburbanization of large cities. People move to the suburbs to get access to a little clean air, some grass, some peace and quiet, open space, and good uncrowded schools for their kids, without being so far away from work that commuting is intolerable. So you move to a suburb—and so does everyone else. The result is the same dirty air, crowded schools, and noise you left behind, shopping malls instead of grass, *and* a commute. So you move a little farther out—and so does everyone else. The crowds are as bad as before, but the commute is worse. You can continue moving farther out, until you are no longer in a suburb but in the country. The trouble is that the country isn't the country any more. At best, it's a moderately crowded suburb. And now the commute from crowded suburb to crowded city is ninety minutes each way. So, for most people, the end result of the pursuit of suburban tranquillity will be frustration. Either they won't be able to afford it, or it won't be tranquil. At best, people will end up expending extra effort (commuting time) just to maintain their position.

There is an important and quite general feature to the suburbanization process that should be pointed out—what economist Thomas Schelling has called "the tyranny of small decisions." When contemplating moving to the suburbs, you face the choice between crowds, noise, and a short commute and space, quiet, and a long commute. You may choose the latter. But because so many others do the same, the result is that what turns out ultimately to have been chosen is crowds, noise, and a long commute over crowds, noise, and a short commute. Anyone faced with that choice at the beginning would have stayed where he was.

This happens all the time. The choices people confront at the moment are very different from what they would be if people knew that everyone else confronted the same choices and was likely to make the same decisions. For example, imagine two bookstores coexisting in your little town. One is a discount chain, with little selection (only the best-sellers), but good prices. The other is an old-fashioned bookstore, with a diverse and interesting stock, and a knowledgeable proprietor, but list prices. You, as a rational purchaser, adopt the habit of buying at the discount store whenever they carry what you want, and otherwise buying at the old-fashioned store. So does everyone else. Why would anyone spend twenty dollars on a book when she could get it next door for fifteen. The problem is that since most of the books people buy are best-sellers (that, after all, is what makes them best-sellers), the old-fashioned bookstore doesn't sell enough books to stay in business. So it folds, and you are left either to be satisfied with an impoverished selection of reading material or with the chore of going downtown to buy your books. Faced with the choice between spending a few extra dollars now and then, and thus keeping the old-fashioned bookstore alive, or always buying at discount and putting the old-fashioned store out of business, would everyone still have chosen to save the money? Probably not. But you as an individual aren't going to make the difference between success and failure for the old-fashioned bookstore. And you as an individual have no control over what other book buyers do. So it doesn't seem to make much sense for you as an individual to contribute your hard-earned cash to the old-fashioned store. Unless others do it, your patronage won't help. And if others do it, your patronage won't be necessary. So you opt for buying cheap, and so does everyone else, and the bookstore closes.

It seems that part of what people purchase when they buy into the free-market, individualistic organization of society is a host of situations like the commons problem. Is the free market worth this price? Could people avoid these problems if they organized society in some other way? Could people avoid these problems if they just patched some restraints onto the free-market system? Or are these problems that people simply have to live with no matter how society is organized?

In recent years, social commentators have offered two basic types of answers to these questions. One of them appeals to the moral side of people. It suggests that we should educate people about the dangers and social costs of pollution, wanton use of energy and public lands, overpopulation, overcrowding of public spaces, and the like, and exhort them to do their duty as citizens and exercise restraint. If we tell people what the right thing to do is, and show that if they all do the right thing, society will be better off, we can count on them to do the right thing.

The other answer appeals to our economic side. It offers incentives for "good behavior" and punishments for "bad behavior." Nonpolluters and energy conservers get tax breaks. Nonsmokers pay less for life insurance, and safe drivers pay less for car insurance. Polluters pay fines. Purchasers of inefficient automobiles pay a luxury tax. Tobacco and alcohol are taxed, to help defray the social (medical) costs of tobacco and alcohol use. Permits are sold to regulate the use of parks and beaches. Access to highways during rush hours is restricted to force people to carpool. Restraints like these are designed to change the economics of each of the relevant situations, to make individual interest line up with collective interest. We can choose not to exercise restraint, but only at a price. And the price will be high enough either to induce restraint or to compensate society for profligacy.

The problem with these kinds of incentives and restraints is that they don't work very well. Regulations and laws that provide rewards for public-spirited actions and punishments for self-interested, harmful ones aren't very successful in achieving restraint. Why not? After all, we live in a society of laws, and our ability to enforce those laws is good enough that most people obey most laws most of the time. We live in a society in which people make legal or contractual commitments to one another, and our ability to enforce those commitments is good enough that most people honor most contracts most of the time. Why can't we make people toe the line and show restraint for the common good? Because our ability to enforce laws and contractual commitments depends critically on the fact that most people honor them not out of fear of being caught in transgression but because it's the right thing to do. Suppose that we all decided to do whatever we thought we could get away with, no matter what the law said. People would cheat on taxes, go through red lights, sign contracts and then ignore them, refuse to pay bills, and the like. How many people would get caught? And if they were caught, how long would it take for their transgressions to be adjudicated in the courts? Already our legal system is so jammed that civil suits take years and years to be decided. Already our prisons are so crowded that only people convicted of the most serious crimes are incarcerated.

And this is in a society of predominantly law-abiding citizens. As more people decided to ignore the law, the chances that any one of them would get caught and punished would grow smaller and smaller. If everyone decided to ignore the law, our system of taxes, fines, and other punishments would quickly become paralyzed and useless. It's a kind of "critical mass" phenomenon. If our system of legal constraints works, it is only because a critical mass of people has not yet decided to disregard laws and contracts.

And people need not totally disregard laws in order to subvert them. They can also subvert laws by honoring them to the letter, but ignoring their spirit, and thus twisting them to serve their own, individual interests. Even if we could enforce all laws and contracts, there would be big trouble if we had to depend exclusively on them to get people to act appropriately. You simply can't put everything in a contract. To a large extent, the smooth functioning of the economic and social system depends not on contracts but on a measure of good will. As evidence of the limited value of contracts, consider that one of the most effective devices workers have for exerting control over management involves not going on strike but honoring their contracts—to the letter. Such job actions—known as "working to rule"—paralyze productivity. For as soon as anything unanticipated in the contract comes up (as it inevitably will), workers substitute contractual obligation for judgment and do nothing. We count on workers to enter into agreements with their employers in good faith, to understand the point of their work activity, and to use their discretion in pursuing that point when unforeseen difficulties arise. Our system of legal and contractual constraint works precisely because, for most workers, it does not have to be applied.

Another example that laws are inadequate to induce people to do the right thing is the case of bankruptcy. The laws that permit people and organizations to declare bankruptcy are written in a way that protects people suffering financial reverses from total financial ruin, while still allowing their creditors to gain a piece of what is due them. Lenient bankruptcy laws make sense, both as a kindness to those who need their protection and as a recognition that if you protect people and organizations from total ruin, they may be able to bounce back and become solvent and productive once again.

We can afford such a lenient attitude toward people who can't pay their bills so long as bankruptcy is regarded as the option of last resort. And until recently it was so regarded. There was a general sense that people were under a moral (as well as a legal) obligation to pay their bills, so declaring bankruptcy was sufficiently shameful— a dramatic enough public admission of failure, both financial and moral—that we could be confident that people would do it only when there was no alternative. Because of the enormous social sanction against declaring bankruptcy, society could afford to be generous and lenient in structuring bankruptcy negotiations. No one dreamed of exploiting that generosity.

Times have changed. How much they have changed was made clear to me by a friend who told me of an incident in which she revealed to an acquaintenance the ordeal of her parents' bankruptcy proceedings, which occurred when my friend was a young adolescent. What my friend was trying to convey in telling her story was just how shameful her parents found the prospect of bankruptcy— so shameful that it was never discussed except in hushed whispers. On hearing the story, her acquaintenance's only comment was a question: Did they make any money on the deal?

Bankruptcy filings are now increasing at an astonishing rate. Last year was the seventh consecutive year of record filings. Almost a million people filed for personal bankruptcy, as did 87,000 businesses, with assets totalling over $100 billion (2 percent of the gross domestic product). This may partly be a reflection of hard economic times. But there have been hard economic times before. The bankruptcy rate in the recession of the early 1980s was less than half that in the current one, and the assets of companies filing for bankruptcy were only 0.3 percent of the gross domestic product. I think the primary reason for the rise in bankruptcies is that bankruptcy is now regarded as merely one economic strategy among many. And the only question that people now ask themselves before filing for bankruptcy is whether it will leave them better off than any of the alternatives. There is no longer any sense that it is shameful. There is no longer any sense that people owe their creditors anything beyond what the law requires them to pay. Should this current attitude toward bankruptcy persist, the laws will have to be changed to make bankruptcy much more stringent and punitive than it is now. The current laws make sense only if people honor the spirit in which they were intended. And, of course, if the laws are changed, we can be sure that an army of bankruptcy specialists will quickly turn their attention to finding ways to violate the spirit, if not the letter, of the new laws.

So economic incentives and disincentives will not do the job, at least not so long as people depend on them exclusively. Some appeal must also be made to voluntary restraint as an act of public virtue. But could it work? Clearly, it could not work so long as people were exclusively ruled by economic interests. Public virtue is for suckers. Economic rationality demands that we "free ride" if we can get away with it. But people are not exclusively economic agents. The trick, then, seems to be to appeal to our moral side to solve social problems created by our economic side.

MORAL RESTRAINTS ON ECONOMIC ACTIVITY

That our effectiveness in pursuing economic interests depends upon the simultaneous existence of moral commitments is not news. The father of the free market, Adam Smith, said it two hundred years ago:

> All members of human society stand in need of each others' assistance. . . . Where the necessary assistance is reciprocally afforded from love, from gratitude, from friendship and esteem, the society flourishes and is happy. All the different members of it are bound together by the agreeable bonds of love and affection. . . . Society, however, can not subsist among those who are at all times ready to hurt and injure one another.

For Smith, this need for love, friendship, and esteem was not a problem for the market system, because he thought that natural sympathy for others is as much a part of human nature as is the pursuit of self-interest. People simply won't do absolutely anything to secure their interests. What they will do is retrained by their social concern.

The modern economist might acknowledge both the need for and the presence of sympathy, but suggest that it can be viewed as an economic good. In this view, sympathy is triggered not by a sense of obligation or public responsibility but because it gets sympathetic individuals something they want. It is just another economic "strategy," another means to consumption. If doing harm to someone else hurts you, then it is in your interest not to do harm. Behaving "morally" is simply one way to maximize your own, personal welfare. If the satisfaction you gain by using less of the common than you might, and making your neighbor happy as a result, is greater than the satisfaction you lose in lowered milk yield, then restraint is the rational *economic* decision. No appeal to morality—no concern for the public good—is required. According to this point of view, all decisions have economic consequences and thus all decisions are economic decisions. This view is the hallmark of what has come to be called *economic imperialism*.

When people start to think about all decisions and actions in terms of their economic consequences, it changes the way they think about moral issues. It becomes easier to assess material and nonmaterial values and concerns by a common yardstick. So in deciding whether to exercise restraint in the interests of the public good, people can engage in *economic* calculations. How much material welfare will be gained by refusing to exercise restraint? What will it cost if I'm caught? How good will showing restraint make other people feel and how good will that make me feel? How many units of sympathy is that extra quart of milk worth? If the bottom line of these calculations says be restrained, people will be restrained; if not, they will not.

But just as a system of incentives and penalties can't ensure the public good, neither can acting because making others feel good makes you feel good. This might work in a small community, in which everyone knows everyone and the effects of one's actions on others are discernible. But it quickly breaks down as small communities become large cities, as buyers and sellers in the market become virtually anonymous—indeed, as many transactions occur by long distance. Under these conditions, in which increasing numbers of people now live, the pull of sympathy fades. Who is it that is hurt, or feels bad, if you neglect to pay your credit card bill? Who is the citrus farmer hurting if he charges as much as he can for the oranges that are about to be shipped halfway across the country? If we are to appeal to anything to induce people to act for the public good, it had better be to something other than this kind of sympathy.

What could that other "something" be? Economist Amartya Sen has suggested that sometimes people do the right thing not because it gets them a profit, and not because it makes them feel good, but just because it's the right thing. They do what will promote public welfare, quite apart from whether it promotes their own. They act out of a sense of responsibility as citizens. A small but significant example is the act of voting in large general elections. No matter how small the cost of voting may be to a single individual, in time or inconvenience, it will be larger than the benefit. One vote simply won't make a difference. Yet people vote, or at least many people do. Another example is coming to the aid of a stranger in distress, always at a cost of time and sometimes at considerable personal risk. Another example is doing your job to the best of your ability—going beyond the terms of the contract—even if no one is watching and there is nothing to be gained from it.

When making economic decisions, people will presumably choose the alternative that best serves their interests. But Sen points out that before they can do this, they must make another choice. They must first *choose* to frame their decision as an economic one, that is based on self-interest, as against, say, a moral one, that is based on concern for what is right. We want people to choose to frame their decisions on the basis of what is right. Such decisions are what we hope for and expect from our friends, our family, and our lovers. They are what we look for in people who possess the virtues of character that we value. Can we count on people to ignore or submerge their economic interests and act in this way? From where do they get the strength to resist their economic impulses and respond to their moral ones? Is doing what is right simply a part of human nature that will always be there to keep people restrained and keep society civil? Or does it require the right set of social conditions to make its presence felt?

Despite Adam Smith's recognition that the pursuit of economic interest is just a part of people, and despite his view that economic interests and moral interests can coexist, there is ample evidence from modern social and economic life that economic interests just won't stay in their place. They seem bent on encroaching on moral interests, determined to appropriate more and more aspects of daily life to their own economic domain. Remember the responses of the business school students to the questions about fairness I discussed earlier. And nowadays, after all, less than half of the eligible voters in this country vote. Could this lack of participation be the result of well-learned lessons in the economics of self-interest? Could this lack of participation be an example of the spread of economic considerations to previously noneconomic aspects of life, one that is undermining the set of social practices and institutions that nurture and strengthen moral concern? If so, the result of the undermining of these social practices is that we can count on moral concern less and less, even as we need it more and more. Preserving the moral domain in the hope that it will dominate or at least restrain the domain of consumption is extremely difficult. At the moment, the pressure is in the opposite direction. As the economic stakes in society increase, the economic consequences of acting morally increase. This increased cost forces at least some people to abandon their moral concerns. Thus, instead of having our moral values restrain our pursuit of things, they are being assimilated into the pursuit of things.

ECONOMIC IMPERIALISM AND THE UNDERMINING OF MORAL CONCERN

If a willingness to show restraint and moral concern are not, as Adam Smith thought, characteristics of human nature that we can always rely on to counter the worst aspects of material acquisitiveness, where do they come from? In part, they come from the pursuit of values other than material wealth that I have already discussed. In addition to valuing things, people value meaningful work, knowledge, virtues of character, love, friendship, community, freedom, equality, and democracy. Pursuing most of these other values requires and nurtures a sense of responsibility to others, as well as a degree of public-spiritedness and moral concern. Unfortunately, owing to the increasing pressure on us to achieve material success that I have already discussed, the pursuit of these other values is being submerged. And the domains in which they might be pursued are being corrupted by the very process of economic imperialism that they are meant to control.

To appreciate better the character and significance of economic imperialism requires a clear idea of what it means for a domain of activity to be noneconomic. If the pursuit of economic interest does not set the goals of a domain, then what does? What is it that participants in noneconomic activities strive for?

This question has been illuminated by philosopher Alasdair MacIntyre, in his book *After Virtue*. Central to the book is MacIntyre's concept of a *practice*. Practices are certain kinds of complex, cooperative human activities. Each practice establishes its own standards of excellence and, indeed, is partly defined by those standards. And each practice establishes a set of "goods" or goals that are internal or specific to it, and inextricably connected to engaging in the practice itself. In other words, to be engaging in the practice is to be pursuing these internal goods. Thus practices are established and developing social traditions, traditions that are kept on course by a conception of their purpose that is shared by the practitioners. And, most important, the goals or purposes of practices are specific or peculiar to each of them. There is no common denominator of what is good, like wealth accumulation, by which all practices can be assessed.

Many of the noneconomic values we share are realized through participation in practices. Knowledge requires participation in the practices of the educational institutions that transmit it and in the intellectual traditions that create it. Freedom, equality, and democracy require participation in the practice of politics, of governance. Social connectedness (to community, friends, and family) requires participation in the practices of community and family life. Traditionally, the goods people realized by participating in practices like these were not economic goods, and the rules by which these practices operated were not economic rules. And so they provided a space in people's lives in which alternatives to economic calculation could be fostered. But, as a result of economic imperialism, many of these domains of life that once were largely independent of economic considerations are now becoming increasingly pervaded by them.

We already encountered examples of this process in my discussion of the professions and sports. Physicians are finding the pursuit of the goods of medicine—healing and comforting the sick and maintaining the well-being of the healthy—compromised by economic considerations. Lawyers are finding the pursuit of the goods of law—just and fair treatment of citizens in a society that is based on law—compromised by economic considerations. And athletes are finding the pursuit of the goods of sports—individual excellence and team success—compromised by economic considerations. As this economic imperialism continues to occur, each of these domains of activity is eroded as a distinct practice; its goods are replaced by economic goods.

Another example of this process—one that I will be discussing later at some length—is education. The goal of education is to impart knowledge and to develop in people the ability to think critically. Education at its best creates well-informed, responsible, concerned citizens. Education at its best is essential both for the well-being of our economy and for the well-being of our democracy. What happens to the practice of education as increasing competition among members of society for material resources leads to increasing competition for good (that is, high-paying) jobs? In response to this competition, employers keep erecting new educational hurdles that must be jumped before job entry is possible. These hurdles have a profound effect on the way people view education. With education closely tied to job entry, job training, and material success, it becomes an "investment" (literally, not metaphorically) in your future. The money spent on school is expected to be returned, with interest, later on. You start putting a dollar value on a college degree by surveying the salaries paid on the jobs to which it gives access. It is easy to imagine deciding whether or where to go to college by engaging in the following kind of calculations: A degree from the state university will cost $40,000. If you took that money and invested it, and entered the job market four years earlier than you otherwise would, would the interest on investment coupled with the four extra years of earning power compensate for the higher-paying jobs forgone? If the answer to this question is yes, you don't go to college. Or perhaps the calculations might go like this: Harvard will cost $100,000, while the state university will cost $40,000. Will the job opportunities provided by the Harvard degree pay back the extra $60,000 invested? If the answer to *this* question is no, then you might go to college, but you won't go to Harvard.

Once people start thinking about education in these terms—as an economic investment—it affects what they want out of education and thus how they evaluate what they get. Suppose people stop valuing knowledge as an end in itself, or as an essential ingredient in the making of mature, responsible citizens, and start valuing it only as a means to material ends. If enough people assess their education in this way, what actually goes on in the college classroom will change. Colleges and universities will have to be sensitive to market demand; they will have to provide what students want, or the students will go elsewhere. The goal of education will shift from creating well-informed, responsible citizens to creating skilled, high-income workers. And in pursuit of that goal, the institution will change what it does. The very practice of education, defined as are all practices, by the goals that direct it, will lose its distinctiveness. It will simply become a part of the economy, an input, a cost to be factored in when the economic consequences of various possible life decisions are evaluated. To the extent that this "economization" of education occurs (and it already has at many, if not most, of our universities— even the "elite" ones), the practice of education will cease to be a counterforce to the pursuit of self-interest that governs behavior in the marketplace.

A personal illustration of this phenomenon occurred a few years ago when parents of high school students who had won recognition on a national scholarship test were invited to a little celebration at the high school. A daughter of mine was one of those being honored, so my wife and I were there. The principal greeted and congratulated the assembled students and their parents. He proceeded to tell us how wonderful it was that so many of the students at the school had succeeded on this examination. Not only did it mean for each of them a great chance to get admitted to a great college and start on the path to a great career; in addition it meant an increase in the value of all of our houses. For when the word got out about how many students had succeeded, people would be flocking into our community so that their kids could be educated in our high school. I waited for him to chuckle at his little ice-breaking joke. I'm still waiting.

So long as most of the people who engage in a practice pursue the goals that help define them—in medicine, healing and comforting the sick rather than gaining wealth and prestige—practices can remain true to their objectives. Proper practitioners will be able to recognize good and bad examples of the practice, and will be able to shake their heads at those of their colleagues who have lost their way. New practitioners can be brought into the practice with a clear indication of what its proper goals are. But as the pursuit of inappropriate goals grows more commonplace, practices become vulnerable to corruption. This is in part because practices develop, and the direction that development takes will be determined by participants in the practice. The way a practice might develop to maintain its pursuit of appropriate goods and the way it might develop to maintain its pursuit of inappropriate goods need not coincide. And if the practice is controlled by people with inappropriate aims, it may be corrupted to the point where it ceases to be a practice.

For MacIntyre, the concept of a practice has a central place in a theory of what it is to be a good person. Good people possess just those characteristics, or virtues, that permit them to engage successfully in practices. And successful practices strengthen these virtues at the same time that they depend on them. The list of these virtues is like the list I developed earlier—justice, honesty, courage, commitment, loyalty, perseverance, rationality, kindness, and so on. And the continued existence and development of practices depends upon the continued existence of people who possess these virtues. Thus our judgment of the moral character of a culture is bound up with our judgment of the set of practices that the culture encourages and supports. What, then, happens to the moral character of a culture if the practices disappear, if economic imperialism transforms them into simply means to economic goods? If that happens, there is only one practice—the practice of pursuit of economic interest. And the good person becomes the good pursuer of wealth. By penetrating and transforming the set of practices that make up human social life, economic imperialism will have created the conditions under which the conception of people as exclusively driven by economic interests is true.

If what it means to be moral depends in part on what our practices are, the elimination of practices will eliminate the meaning of morality. In a world made and run to serve economic interests—a world consumed by consumption—moral concerns will be idle concerns. People may continue to use moral language and continue to argue about right and wrong, but the language will lose its concrete significance, and the arguments will be unresolvable. In a world like this, people won't any longer possess the traditions with which to anchor their notions of good and bad, of right and wrong.

THE COMMERCIALIZATION OF SOCIAL RELATIONS

Education, medicine, law, and even sports and other recreational activities are examples of practices that can foster in people the commitment to communal, noneconomic goals that enables them to resist the pull of economic self-interest. But far more important than any of these practices are the everyday social relations that maintain friendships, families, and communities. These everyday social relations can all be viewed as practices. They are all complex, cooperative activities, with long histories. They all possess their own, unique ends, which continue to evolve. Some people are good and some are bad at these practices, though what it means to be good and bad changes as the practices change. Most of us expect good examples of these practices to be characterized by intimacy, trust, care, and concern—attributes that might be regarded as contributing to moral concern and, certainly, attributes that are very different from the pursuit of economic interest. But, here too, we can see the effects of economic imperialism. Increasingly, our ordinary social relations—as friends, neighbors, spouses, and parents—are taking on an economic component. Indeed, the spread of economic imperialism to these relations is changing what we want and expect out of them. Rather than intimacy, trust, and commitment, the goods of what might be called "commercialized" social relations are just the mutual satisfaction of individual interests—just another form of consumption.

In part, the commercialization of social relations comes as an automatic consequence of the increased pressure people feel both to make money and to spend it. No matter how rich a person is, time is a resource that cannot be increased; there are only 24 hours in a day. It takes time to nurture and sustain close personal relations. It also takes time to make money. (Between 1970 and 1990, despite an explosion of computer technology that presumably made all kinds of work easier to do, the average American's workweek *increased* by nearly three hours. The average American works 1,950 hours per year, which comes to 39 hours a week, assuming a two-week vacation. Only in Japan, among industrialized nations, do people work more; in Germany, for example, the average workweek is 32 hours.) And it even takes time to consume. If people have money only for the essentials of life, finding the time in which to consume them is not an issue. But when they have money for stereos, VCRs, dinners in nice restaurants, evenings at the theater, and weekend vacations, they must find the time to decide which stereo, restaurant, play, or vacation weekend to consume. In addition, they must find the time actually to consume them. Dinner at home takes an hour; dinner out takes an evening. Buying records takes time, and so does listening to them (that is, *really* listening, as opposed to having some noise in the background as you do other things). Recording a favorite television show doesn't take much time, but actually watching the recording does.

The pressure for time—both to make money and to spend it—has real costs. It produces what Fred Hirsch called "the economics of bad neighbors." Time spent being sociable is time taken away from getting and spending. Chatting over the backyard fence, or helping a neighbor cut down a tree, is an action taken at the cost of working on the contract that has to be ready next week for a client, or watching the show you taped on the VCR, or going into town for a nice dinner. Whether we like it or not, the decision to be sociable becomes an economic decision, another example of the spread of economic considerations to traditionally noneconomic domains.

Many people have experienced how much harder it has become to find the time to spend a quiet evening chatting with a few friends over beer. It is becoming increasingly rare for such occasions to develop spontaneously; they must be planned days, or even weeks, in advance. And of course it seems ludicrous to "plan" an evening of casual conversation. So instead it becomes a dinner party. This, in turn, only adds to the time pressure, since now food must be purchased and an impressive meal prepared. One of the few virtues of having limited resources is that you often can't afford to do much more than have an evening of casual conversation over beer.

This "economizing" of social relations can have profound effects. First, it can undermine the strength of the social relations themselves. It's hard to keep social relations going if people don't have time for one another. Second, it may undermine the strength of moral concern more generally. The strength of our concern for the public good may derive in part from the range and depth of our personal, social relations. It is from these relations, after all, that we learn much of what it means to approach domains of life from a noneconomic perspective. As these relations diminish, for lack of time, moral concern may diminish with them. And third, a general decrease in sociability is likely to change even the *economic* incentives to be a good citizen. Suppose that the good turns an individual does are motivated only by the expectation that they will one day be reciprocated, and nothing more. If you don't overuse the common, neither will I. If you don't dump toxic wastes in my stream, I won't dump them in yours. As an individual's network of social relations shrinks, the likelihood of reciprocation shrinks with it. Therefore, each decrease in social connectedness brings a corresponding decrease in the possibility of concerted action to solve the various commons problems each of us faces.

Since many of our social activities are increasingly taking on an economic aspect, some economists have suggested that we should take these domains out of the economic closet and treat them explicitly as part of economic life. We should enlarge the consumer's potential market basket to include not just stereos, vacations, and dinners out but time spent chatting with friends as well. Even if we don't literally put dollar values on the time people spend with friends, there ought to be some way to estimate the dollar value equivalents of social activities, perhaps by examining how many things that *do* have dollar value people are willing to trade for time spent with friends. Making this move has the virtue of revealing costs and benefits that may previously have been hidden from economic analysis. But making this move is also a major step in the direction of economic imperialism because it makes explicit the commercialization of social relations.

In the economic world, people get what they pay for. Certainly, they get nothing more, and vigilance is required to see that they don't get less. Business is business, after all. So what happens when the social world gets commercialized? Presumably, people start getting only what they pay for in social relations as well as in economic ones. In the economic world, people are prepared to operate on this assumption. Products come with explicit guarantees, services are provided in accordance with detailed and specific contracts. People enter into exchanges with their eyes open, expecting, and guarding against, the worst. They are not so prepared in the social world, or at least have not been until recently. People assume that their friends, their lovers, their parents, their siblings, their doctors, and their teachers will act with good will, doing, insofar as possible, what is best for them. As a result, they ask no guarantees and write no contracts. People trust that part of what it means to be a spouse, a lover, a parent, a sister, a doctor, or a teacher ensures that the people close to them will behave honorably, truthfully, courageously, and dutifully in social interactions.

As social relations become commercialized, however, this assumption grows more and more suspect. Increasingly, people feel the need to have things written down in contracts. Increasingly, they feel the need to be able to hold others legally accountable—whether doctors, lawyers, teachers, or even friends or lovers—to have a club to wield to make sure that they are getting what they pay for out of their social relations. For example, some people have come to expect the worst from marriage, to regard it, at best, as an arrangement in which the parties involved make equal individual investments and derive equal individual benefits. To protect themselves from exploitation, some men and women insist on marriage contracts that are not just metaphors. "For better or for worse, in sickness and in health, till death do us part" is replaced by a detailed specification of household and sexual obligation and entitlement, and asset ownership and control, to be reevaluated by both parties after a fixed term.

It is possible to see this shift from trust in what is implicit in various social relations to dependence on what is explicit and contractual as merely a recognition of cold, hard reality. It can be viewed as an extension of the consumer protection movement to social domains, to protect people from doctors who are callous, careless, or paternalistic, teachers who are indifferent, and spouses who are out to dominate and exploit.

What this view fails to acknowledge is that the process of commercialization of social relations affects the product. By treating the services of doctors and teachers as commodities being offered to the wary consumer, we change the way doctors doctor and teachers teach. Doctors practice defensively, doing not what they regard as the best medicine but what they regard as the best hedge against malpractice suits. Medical costs soar, but medical care does not improve. Teachers teach defensively, making sure their students will perform well on whatever tests will be used to evaluate their progress, at the expense of genuine education. Test scores go up, but students are no wiser than before.

There is, in short, a self-fulfilling character to the commercialization of social relations. The more we treat such relations as economic goods, to be purchased with care, the more they become economic goods about which we must be careful. The more an assumption of self-interest, rather than commitment, on the part of others governs social relations, the truer that assumption becomes. As Hirsch has said, "the more that is in the contracts, the less can be expected without them; the more you write it down, the less is taken—or expected—on trust." We replace the view that the people close to us love us and are deeply concerned for our welfare with the view that they are out only for themselves. And we change our actions accordingly.

●   ●

I'm sure that no one is sanguine about this somewhat apocalyptic vision of the world I've just presented. And things can be done to prevent it from becoming a reality. If it is true that moral traditions depend on practices, and that practices can be corrupted by the pursuit of economic goods, and that the pursuit of economic goods is encouraged by economic imperialism, then all we have to do is be vigilant and keep economic considerations from penetrating into all our practices. By keeping practices relatively pure, we can preserve a proper place for morality in a highly industrialized, productive, and affluent culture.

Can we live lives that are filled with both moral concern and affluence? This chapter has suggested why doing so will be difficult. As economic activity comes increasingly to be dominated by competition for positional goods, decisions about all aspects of life come increasingly to have an economic component. This happens whether people like it or not—whether they want it to or not. Choosing to keep the pursuit of practices pure—opting out of the race for positional goods—is not a refusal to make decisions on an economic basis. It is itself an economic choice, to forgo material goods in order better to secure others. It is an economic choice that will make our neighbors better off, and us worse off.

Furthermore, as fewer people make that choice and instead enter practices with economic orientations, the practices themselves will change and the pursuit of previously internal goods will no longer be possible. We might hope that economic interests can be pursued in moderation, but the problem is that there may be nothing left to provide that moderation. Sen's point, mentioned earlier, that before people make choices that will further their economic interests, they must choose to make those choices on the basis of their economic interests, will still be true, but it will lose all of its practical significance. For there will be no basis other than an economic basis on which choices can be made.

Are we prepared to opt out of the race for positional, material goods? Doing so as individuals involves substantial risk. In the short run, changing the way we live is going to mean substantial sacrifice. Even if society eventually swings around and heads in the same direction, it will take a long time for that to happen. In the meanwhile, changing our own direction will mean that we and our families will be getting fewer of the best things in life than we otherwise would. Why should we be the ones to go first, and let others benefit from our sacrifices?

This is a very reasonable question that poses a real problem. It reminds me of something that my younger daughter said to me a few summers ago. She had just finished spending eight weeks at a camp in which a bunch of teenagers lived a simple, communal life governed by simple, communal values. There were no fancy stereos and no fancy clothes. There was no posturing, no pretense, no back-biting, no meanness. It was an environment in which people found great meaning and satisfaction in tending a large, communal garden, preparing simple but nourishing communal meals, working together to maintain the camp's buildings, and entertaining themselves communally with real talk about real problems. The kids were completely open with each other, and genuinely concerned for each other's well-being.

My daughter just loved the camp. She had never imagined that it was possible to live this kind of life—to derive joy from the joy of another person and to be satisfied doing utterly mundane and sometimes arduous things, as long as other people did them alongside you. So I asked her if anything like this existed back home, and she said no. Then I asked her whether she thought it was because her camp friends were just special people. Again she said no. She was sure that when they went back home they were more or less the same as her own friends at home were. There was something about the atmosphere of the camp that transformed the people in it. There was an understanding that everyone was in it together, that there was a joint commitment to live a different kind of life, that no one there would exploit them or play them for fools. To live this kind of life, you had to be a part of a community that was committed to it. You just could not change the rules alone.

So I asked her whether she was willing to try the brave experiment of enlisting her friends back home to change the rules together. And she asked me the same question that I just posed. Why should she be first? Why should she make sacrifices and risk exploitation and ridicule? So I told her a story about penguins. I told her that penguins have the same problem. They stand together by the thousands on ice floes, looking longingly at the fish-laden waters beneath them. They want to jump in and hunt for fish. They *need* to jump in and hunt for fish. But they're afraid. Leopard seals might be lurking just beyond the water's edge, waiting to catch them, skin them alive, and swallow them whole. None of the penguins wants to be the first in. So they stand at the water's edge and start pushing each other toward the water—sort of trying to get volunteers in the way the army does. If one of them falls in and doesn't get eaten, then the others follow.

No one wants to be the first penguin in. But think about this. Suppose a pack of polar bears starts charging the penguins from the land. Now the penguins will get into the water soon enough, won't they. Now they'll be climbing all over each other to be the first in. Sure, they'll still risk being eaten. But they can see the alternative, and it isn't any better. It seems to me that if we do jump, we *might* get eaten. But if we don't jump, we'll surely get eaten. Or if not we, our kids. The time is right for taking the plunge.

7

ECONOMIZING ON LOVE

In the end they knew each other so well that by the time they had been married for thirty years they were like a single divided being, and they felt uncomfortable at the frequency with which they guessed each other's thoughts without intending to, or the ridiculous accident of one of them anticipating in public what the other was going to say. Together they had overcome the daily incomprehension, the instantaneous hatred, the reciprocal nastiness and fabulous flashes of glory in the conjugal conspiracy. It was the time when they loved each other best, without hurry or excess, when both were most conscious of and grateful for their incredible victories over adversity. Life would still present them with other mortal trials, of course, but that no longer mattered: they were on the other shore.　　　　　　　　　　　　　　　*—Gabriel García Marquez*

Each marriage bears the footprints of economic and cultural trends which originate far outside marriage.　　　　　*—Arlie Hochschild*

What does an economist economize on? Economist D. H. Robertson asked this question about fifty years ago. His answer: "The economist economizes on love." What he meant by this was that a competitive-market system gets people to serve one another's interests out of a desire for personal gain, for profit. Love is not required. So we can get by as a society with less love under a market system than under any other. The market economizes on love. The market establishes a system of human relations in which order, prosperity, peace, and even happiness can be achieved by people who don't care at all about one another's well-being. Within the system, people behave *as if* they cared about each other because by behaving in that way, people are able to serve their own interests. The system gets people to act *as if* out of care and concern because if they were to act differently, they would only hurt themselves. As Adam Smith put it, "it is not from the benevolence of the butcher, the brewer, or the baker that we expect our dinner, but from their regard to their own interest."

Competition in the market is what punishes us for failing to serve the interests of others. If we don't do it, someone else will, and he'll get the business and reap the rewards. Instead of depending on mutual obligation, concern, care, and trust, the market depends on mutual pursuit of profit. Instead of depending on relations between people and people, the market depends on relations between people and things. Instead of depending on informal personal *contact* between intimate friends, lovers, and family members, the market depends upon impersonal, formal *contract* between vast numbers of interchangeable buyers and sellers. In all of these ways, the market system economizes on love, a human quality that is presumably in short supply.

For most of us, words like "impersonal," "anonymous," "formal," or "contractual" have a negative tone. They are perhaps inevitable, but certainly undesirable, features of many aspects of modern life. But we should be mindful that people who do things *for* some people out of love may well do things *to* others out of hate. People who give special treatment to those they know and like may deny such treatment—or any treatment—to those they don't know or don't like. And as their feelings for the people they know change—out of envy, spite, or resentment—their treatment of these people will also change. Given the mercurial character of human emotions, and the dynamic character of personal relations, a social world based on these relations would be unstable and unpredictable. If, instead, people calculated their selfish interests in calm, cool, rational fashion and then relentlessly pursued those interests, social life would become much more stable and predictable. People would think twice about behaving hurtfully toward others, asking before they did so whether the outcome would also be hurtful to them. Thus a system of impersonal market relations might offer a calm and orderly alternative to the system of passionate, personal, nonmarket relations that makes daily life chaotic and hazardous.

This virtue of "interests" over "passions" is ironically reflected in the movie *The Godfather.* Repeatedly during the movie, as members of rival gangster "families" kill one another, they observe that "it's nothing personal; strictly business." The audience is meant, on the one hand, to appreciate the absurdity of regarding a violent killing as "strictly business" and, on the other hand, to understand that killing for profit really is more orderly and predictable than killing out of vengeance, or spite, or just for the fun of it. Bloodshed is expensive, the gangsters observe, and they wouldn't be doing it if it weren't necessary to preserve their market share.

Many of us have seen the dangers of passionate relations between people in our own lives. When love affairs turn sour, lovers rarely become neutral toward one another. Instead, there is an impulse to lash out, to be cruel, to hurt, even if doing so is hurtful to oneself. Imagine a world in which all social relations had the roller coaster character of our love affairs, and you will see why people can look so enthusiastically to the pursuit of selfish interests in the market as something of a social miracle. While the butcher, the brewer, and the baker aren't going to do us any favors, they aren't out to do us in either.

In the "market" view, economizing on love substitutes realism for romanticism. People are ruled by self-interest. They will act in the service of others only to the extent that it serves them. People *use* other people. Calling it love, and assuming that people will act with the best interests of their loved ones at heart, engenders expectations that cannot be met. And social systems that depend on the presence of love to work simply cannot provide what is demanded of them. It is better to understand that people derive utility from one another, better to understand that people will stay connected to others only as long as the cost-benefit calculations they engage in say it is worth their while to do so, better to understand that intimate relations are just an exchange of goods and services than to be deluded into thinking that love will rule over self-interest and lead people to act for the benefit of those they love no matter what the cost. Thinking "realistically" about love encourages us to develop a social system that protects people against the disappointment, exploitation, abandonment, and heartbreak that dependence on a romantic conception of love so often brings.

This market view of love is not the exclusive province of the economist. In recent years, it has become increasingly common among social scientists in various disciplines, leading the writer Daniel Goleman to conclude that "the mainstream of psychological research has looked at love almost as if it were a business transaction, a matter of profit and loss." The people who hold this market view remind those of us who are skeptical or disapproving of just how recent an invention "romantic" love is. Perhaps more common historically and cross-culturally than the "love marriage" that we now take for granted is the "arranged marriage," often an explicitly economic affair about which the bride and groom have little or nothing to say. And even the love marriages that have become commonplace in our culture may be better understood as economic transactions, with the word "love" merely a cover term for the variety of goods and services that the partners in the marriage are contracting to exchange. In support of this claim, the market realists can point to findings such as these: as the market value of the mother's labor increases, family size decreases; as the market value of the mother's labor increases, the likelihood of divorce increases; as the generosity of a state's welfare benefits increases, the likelihood of divorce increases. Such findings are taken to indicate that economic exchange, if not explicit, is at least *implicit* in most marriages.

What's wrong with this "realistic" (some would say cynical) view of people and of love? To begin with, it seems unnatural. We're accustomed to thinking about love quite differently from the way we think about exchanges in the market. We don't think about our spouse the way we think about our grocer. The "realist" might well agree that it's unnatural, but he might then point out that it was once "unnatural" to believe that the earth is round or that it was once "unnatural" to believe that people are descended from apes. The fact that a certain way of thinking about things is "natural" doesn't make it right. When we are properly educated about the true character of human relations, our "natural" view of love may join the flat-earth and creationist theories in the dustbin of intellectual history.

A more telling criticism of the conception of love as nothing but an exchange that provides mutual benefit would be that it leaves out much that is important—and true—about love. It isn't only that we don't think about our spouse the way we think about our grocer. We don't *treat* our spouse the way we treat our grocer either. Our relations with our loved ones are filled with compassion, care, tenderness, intimacy, openness, and vulnerability. Not so our relations with our grocer. To forget or ignore this is to make the mistake that mythic King Midas made—to turn people into gold and lose sight of all the things that people are that gold is not. To forget or ignore this is to forget or ignore the thousands and thousands of efforts that poets, novelists, and songwriters have made to get it right—efforts that have not been spent trying to capture the relations between people and their grocers.

This criticism is worth pursuing. But to take it seriously, we can't simply wave our hands indignantly championing all the things that love is and market exchange is not. Instead, we must carefully flesh out an alternative conception of love that makes explicit what a market conception leaves out—that makes clear what makes love valuable and what makes it different from the world of exchange and contract. Having done this, we must examine some of the obstacles that our modern world poses to successful, enduring love relations. In the process, we will see that while it is true that market systems may *need* less love than other social arrangements to work, it is also true that they engender less love than other social arrangements. And finally, we must ask whether, as a society, we can afford to "economize" on love.

THE COMPONENTS OF LOVE: PASSION, INTIMACY, COMMITMENT

In order to understand what the market conception of love leaves out, we must attempt to understand what a richer, more accurate account of love contains. Psychologist Robert Sternberg offers such an account; it captures well many of our everyday intuitions about love. Sternberg analyzes love into three components: passion, intimacy, and commitment. His central idea is that different kinds of love are made up of different mixtures of these three components.

Passion refers to the physical attraction and sexual consummation that are a part of some love relations. It is characterized by an intense longing for union and by kissing, hugging, touching, and making love. *Intimacy* refers to the feelings of closeness, bondedness, warmth, and openness that characterize loving relations. It is marked by high regard for the loved one, by mutual understanding, by the communication of inner feelings, the sharing of time and of possessions, the expression of empathy and compassion, the provision of emotional and material support, and the general concern for the other's well-being. Finally, *commitment* refers to the conscious decision to maintain a loving relation. It is expressed in the making of pledges, the maintenance of fidelity, the willingness to stay in relations through hard times, and, of course, in the institution of marriage.

Not all kinds of love, or of close relations, possess all three of these components. For example, relatively casual, short-term friendships may be marked only by intimacy. Intimate friends may like one another intensely, but without passion and without any expectation that the friendship will continue indefinitely. More enduring are friendships marked by intimacy and commitment. These are friendships for life, and friendships like these may characterize relations between parents and children, or between siblings. When we add passion to the intimacy of friendship, we get romantic love, and when we add it to intimacy and commitment, we get what Sternberg calls "consummate love."

The character of these various types of close relations will typically change over time. Sometimes, love affairs may begin based on only one of the three components, and as the affairs continue, the other components develop. And sometimes, love relations will lose one or more of the three components. Our stereotypical view of romantic attachments is that they begin with passion. An intense physical attraction brings the people together. Once they are together, however, intimacy begins to develop. In addition to enjoying physical contact and sexual stimulation, the partners come to like each other, to confide in each other, to do little things that make each other feel secure and comfortable. Out of this intimacy can come commitment, typically reflected in marriage. At the time of marriage, this stereotypical couple has it all—passion, intimacy, and commitment bound together in a consummate love. As the marriage continues, the contribution that each of these components of love makes to it can change. For stereotypical "old marrieds," passion plays a far less significant role than it did at the beginning. Young people observing a long married couple find it hard to believe that there was a time when they couldn't keep their hands off each other. Intimacy may also diminish, or at least change in form, as the members of a couple come to know each other so well that deep, personal thoughts and feelings rarely require overt expression. In long-term marriages like this, with passion and intimacy both on the wane, it is commitment that keeps the married couple together.

This is a stereotypical scenario, and it may be a common one. But it is certainly not the only possible one. Sometimes—perhaps often—intimacy can precede passion, as when people who are very close friends for a time drift into being lovers. In a case like this, the physical attraction seems to grow out of the intimate knowledge people have of each other. And sometimes, intimacy and passion can both grow out of commitment. This can happen in the case of arranged marriages. The partners in arranged marriages may hardly know each other at the time the match is made. But over time, as they are bound together by powerful social custom if not also by law, they actually come to love each other more fully. Far more commonly, this can happen in relations among family members. We don't choose our parents or our siblings. Family members are thrown together by chance and kept together by social custom. Nevertheless, powerfully intimate relations often grow out of this externally imposed familial commitment.

LOVE AND FRIENDSHIP: WHAT ARE FRIENDS FOR?

In Sternberg's account of love, intimacy and commitment are common to romantic and nonromantic love—to spouses as well as to parents, children, and siblings. But intimacy and commitment are also characteristics of friendship. To the extent that friendship involves intimacy and commitment, we should think about it as a kind of love. We may not love our close friends in the same way that we love our children or our parents, but we do love them.

In one respect, friendship is the sternest test of love. Unlike the relations between spouses, or between parents and children, relations between friends are totally free and unregulated. Society, both in custom and in law, places many requirements and restrictions on relations between family members. Parents are required to care for their children until the children are able to care for themselves. And "care" is understood to include some things (nutrition, shelter, education, medical help, physical and psychological comfort) and to preclude others (sexual contact, physical or psychological abuse). Children are expected to care for their parents when the parents are no longer able to care for themselves. Spouses (or, nowadays, cohabitants) are understood to have a wide range of obligations to each other. There are even strong social expectations (if not laws) about how siblings should get along with one another.

In contrast, friendship is wide open. Anything goes. Everything about it is totally voluntary. Friends can define their friendship in whatever way they want, and can end it at any time for any reason. It is, therefore, the purest kind of social relation people have with one another. If spouses become boring, or children become tiresome, or parents become a burden, and we are tempted to neglect or even abandon them, strong social and legal pressures force us to reconsider—at least for a little while. But friendships stand naked, with nothing to protect them but the qualities that make them worthwhile. Indeed, this openness is one of the things that makes modern friendships so attractive. With neither social convention nor law binding friends together, participants in a friendship can be confident that the intentions and feelings that are keeping them together are genuine.

What are the intentions and the feelings that keep friends together? Let me suggest, borrowing from the philosopher Aristotle, that friendships can rest on three quite different kinds of foundations. First, friendship can be based on virtue or goodness. In modern parlance, we might describe this as friendship based on shared values—religious values, moral values, political values, aesthetic values, or perhaps values of character. Friendship based on shared values will bring together people who are alike, at least in the significant respect that they share important values. It will take time to develop, because it requires that the people involved come to know each other quite well. And once developed, such a friendship is likely to last, based as it is on aspects of character that are likely to be rather deep and stable. Friendship based on shared values is a most demanding form of friendship. Friends of this type seek to give one another what is good, and to help one another stay true to the values that brought them together in the first place.

Second, there can be friendship based on pleasure. This kind of friendship is less substantial. People can enjoy being in one another's company, and participating together in various activities, without having an especially deep knowledge of one another's character. And just as its foundation is less substantial, so are the bonds that hold it together. People may tire of each other, or tire of the activities that they once enjoyed doing together. When this happens, friendships based on pleasure should dissolve, since nothing remains to hold them together.

Finally, friendship can be based on usefulness—what we might call instrumental friendship. This is the "you scratch my back, I'll scratch yours" kind of friendship—the friendship of convenience. Friendship like this requires little or no knowledge of the other person's character. It doesn't even require that the friends enjoy being together. All that is required is that each "friend" can provide something useful to the other. Instrumental friendships come very close to being marketlike, contractual relations, with personal contact and the knowledge of mutual interdependence substituting for formal contractual documents.

We probably all have friendships that fit into each of these categories. We give differently to each of them and get differently from each of them. Though we are reluctant to admit it—even to ourselves—there are some people whose friendships we maintain because they have some skill, or some contact, or access to some good, that someday we may want to exploit. We see friends like these infrequently, preferably amid groups large enough that the shallowness of our relation does not become painfully obvious through several hours of awkward, face-to-face conversation. We want to know as little as possible about such friends, and want them to know as little as possible about us. If we trust them, it is only in the narrow domain within which we use each other. It's a trust based on the possibility of retaliation. In friendships like these, we worry a great deal about being used or exploited. We want to make sure that we're getting at least as much as we're giving.

More common, perhaps, than instrumental friendships, and more acceptable for people to admit to themselves, are friendships based on pleasure. Friends who give us pleasure are the people with whom we have a good time, who like the same restaurants we do, who like the same movies we do, who like the same forms of exercise we do. It's fun to be with these people not especially because of who or what they are but because of what they like to do. In a sense, friendships like this are instrumental also, since we hang out with these kinds of friends because of what it gets us. But unlike nakedly instrumental friendships, friendships with people whose company we enjoy give everyone the same thing out of the relation. Doing things for yourself and doing things for your friend often amount to the same thing, since what your friend values about you are the kinds of things you enjoy doing. And the more pleasure you can give a friend, the more you will experience yourself. So there isn't the same kind of concern about exploitation. In addition, since friends like this actually enjoy being together, there is a reasonable chance that they will come to know one another more deeply than they expected or intended at the start of the friendship. That is, some amount of intimacy may develop.

Friendship based on mutual pleasure has in recent years been institutionalized in an odd sort of way, with the creation of "lifestyle communities." Apartment complexes for young singles, retirement communities for older people, summer camps that specialize in one or another sport or craft, all throw people together who are complete strangers and who wait for instant friendships to arise out of interests in the same activities. It is hard to imagine intimacy and commitment developing between people who come to know one another for the first time at the age of seventy. Yet retirees are lured away from lifelong relations in their old communities by the prospect of frequent and instant gratification—without complications—in their new ones. Without complications. What complications? The complications that arise out of loyalty and commitment that require us to be there when our friends need us. When friendship is based on pleasure, we can tell our friends to leave their troubles at home. If they are unwilling to do so, we simply terminate the friendship and strike up another.

There is, finally, the friendship based on shared values. This is friendship that takes time to develop, since it takes time to come to know someone well enough to know that values are indeed shared. It is friendship that rewards us with intimacy and trust, since we won't share our core values with just anyone. It is friendship where exploitation is not a danger. Giving more than we receive is not a problem, since our objective in such friendships *is* to give—to give what is good. And it is friendship that makes strenuous demands. We are committed to such friends, obliged to be there when they need us, obliged to help them achieve what is good, obliged to deal with them honestly, openly, and compassionately. Friendships like these are characterized by high regard for the friend, desire to promote the friend's welfare, mutual understanding and respect, desire to share oneself and one's possessions, giving and receipt of emotional support—all the things that are a part of genuine love relations.

PASSION AND INTIMACY: ADAPTATION AND ADDICTION

Sternberg's theory of love can incorporate the wide range of different kinds of close relations that we see around us in modern society. It can help us understand what various close relations have in common as well as what makes them distinctive. It can help us understand how close relations change over time. Finally, it can help us see how close relations go wrong. We turn to this feature of the theory next.

In the last chapter, I suggested that, through the processes of adaptation and addiction, we can come to experience less and less pleasure from the things we consume. We experience disappointment with consumption, disappointment that is especially acute in the case of durable goods (cars, houses), which stay around to remind us that they aren't as wonderful as we had thought and hoped. But it isn't only *things* that give us pleasure; social relations give us pleasure too. Whatever else passion may be, it is certainly pleasurable. So are the often intense emotional experiences engendered by intimacy. And just as we adapt to the pleasure provided by things, we seem to adapt to the pleasure provided by passion and intimacy. This process of adaptation may be as true of friends as of lovers. The pleasure we derive from being with particular friends may diminish with repeated contact.

If we apply what we know about adaptation to passion, it leads us to expect that while our first few encounters with a person with whom we are passionately involved may bring intense pleasure, as our relation with that person continues, and sexual encounters are repeated, the experience of passion will diminish substantially. As with cars, stereos, and hot tubs, there will be a growing disappointment in consumption associated with passion. That passion wanes over time is hardly news, as almost anyone who has been involved in a long-term passionate relation will tell you. The interesting question to consider is what do people do about this inevitable waning of passion?

What makes this question so interesting is that while cars are inherently durable goods, and meals in restaurants are inherently transient goods, intimate interpersonal relations are inherently neither durable nor transient. Whether people expect their marriages to last forever, or only as long as both partners are getting a kick out of them, is very much up for grabs. If we start out with the presumption that marriage is a durable good, then we must learn to expect and to live with the diminution in passion that occurs, and find other sources of satisfaction in the marriage. When our car stops being exciting, we derive satisfaction from its reliability, or from its fuel efficiency. On the other hand, if we start out with the presumption that marriage is a transient good, then the waning of passion can be a signal that it is time to move on, time to find a new restaurant.

Viewed through the lens of "market realism," the temptation is to view love affairs as transient goods and to expect people to leave them as soon as a cost-benefit analysis tells them that they would do better by leaving than by staying around. A typical cost-benefit calculation might consider the economic consequences of separation (alimony, child support, separate housing, and so on), the search costs involved in finding a new mate (singles bars, dating services, new clothes, membership dues to a fitness center), the uncertainty of finding a new mate, the increase in passion that a new mate will provide, and the residual passion that exists with the current mate. As we know, these calculations are typically very different for men than for women; for women, the outcome of the cost-benefit calculation is almost always negative. As we also know, cultural expectations and legal requirements can have an enormous impact on the cost-benefit calculations. When societies and laws view separation and divorce as a serious problem, a wide range of costs can be introduced that serve to keep people together. When the social and legal attitude toward separation and divorce is more casual, separation costs are reduced, and termination of relations becomes more attractive.

Another thing we know is that the divorce rate in modern America is extremely high. This is not because we are the first generation of human beings to experience the adaptation of passion. There is no reason to believe that passion wanes any more or any faster now than it ever did in the past. Far more likely is that we have come as a culture to expect and to demand that our consumption in passionate relations not be disappointing. We have come to think about these relations as transient economic goods, and we have insisted that our cultural and legal practices be changed so that our continual pursuit of these goods can go on unimpeded by ties that bind us to people we no longer find exciting. What I am suggesting, then, is that our high divorce rate may be taken as a sign that we have already embraced the market realist view of love. If the process of adaptation is an inherent part of our nature, then unless cultural and legal efforts are made to influence us to think of intimate relations as durable, and to focus on aspects of those relations aside from the passion they provide, we can expect unstable marriages to be with us for a long time to come.

It is important to emphasize three points about my account of relation between the waning of passion and the accompanying instability of marriage. First, the two do not go together inevitably; passion could wane and marriages remain stable. Second, if marriages are more unstable now than they were in the past, it is not because people get less out of marriage than they used to; it is because they expect more. And third, the responsibility for the growing instability of marriages should not be laid exclusively, or even principally, at the feet of the marriage partners. Individual responsibility is heavily leavened by changes in cultural norms and legal demands that do little to discourage marital instability and much to promote it.

If, in an effort to restabilize marriages, we were to minimize the long-term significance of passion, and emphasize instead the importance of other aspects of our social relations, a logical candidate would be intimacy. But like passion, intimacy also changes in character over the course of a long-term relation. The substance of the change is different, but unless people are prepared for the kinds of changes that occur, they may find themselves just as disappointed in the character of the intimacy they experience in a long-term relation as they are in the character of the passion they experience.

Imagine this picture of a young married couple, sitting down to dinner after a day of separation at work. They hold hands, look tenderly at each other, and speak with great animation about the events of the day. They talk about what they did, about whom they did it with, about what they were thinking and feeling as they did it. They talk about how often they thought of each other, and how eager they were to reunite. They talk about the meal itself, how crunchy the broccoli is, how tender and moist the fish, how dry and crisp the wine. The dinner goes on and on, as they find themselves with an almost endless supply of experiences and feelings to share.

Now imagine this picture of an older married couple, sitting down to dinner after their day of separation at work. Perhaps the television news is on in the background. Perhaps a newspaper is open beside one or both of their place settings. "How was your day?" says one. "Fine, and yours?" says the other. "Oh fine," says the first. And the meal proceeds in silence. There is nothing to say about their work, about their feelings for each other, about the meal, about anything.

These pictures are of course caricatures. The difference between new and old marrieds is not this stark. But there is surely a difference. And we might be inclined to say that what the difference reflects is that intimacy, mutual concern, empathy, and emotional involvement have gone out of the long-term marriage. The old marrieds are roommates. They share a bed, a bathroom, and a kitchen, but little else—little of their "true selves."

In his account of love, Sternberg acknowledges that overt changes of this type occur, but he interprets these changes quite differently.

Intimacy, he suggests, can be *manifest* or *latent*. When it is manifest, as in the case of the young couple, people wear their hearts on their sleeves. They say what's on their minds. They demonstrate their mutual commitment and emotional involvement overtly, over and over again. When it is latent, intimacy goes underground. The old marrieds may be just as concerned and involved as the young ones, but they no longer have the need for overt expression. They may know each other so well that each can finish the other's sentences. As a result, the sentences need not be uttered. They may be so secure in their commitment to one another that it does not require articulation.

The difficulty is that when intimacy becomes latent, it becomes difficult to distinguish a very close relation from no relation at all. An emotionally estranged couple may eat their dinner in the same silence as an emotionally involved couple. This difficulty may be a difficulty only to outsiders who want to know what kind of relation this is. The insiders—the partners themselves—may know quite clearly when silence is a subtle kind of conversation and when it is just silence. If, however, people come to expect overt expressions of emotional involvement and commitment as items to be "consumed," as "goods" that marriages should be providing—if they expect to experience emotion in the same way they experience passion—then the shift from manifest to latent intimacy may be a signal that it is time to find a new partner, one who doesn't know you so well that little needs to be said. As I suggested in the case of passion, people may be terminating marriages that no longer provide the goods of intimacy they want, not because marriages sustain *less* manifest intimacy than they once did, but because people expect and demand *more* manifest intimacy than they once did.

There is some research, conducted by M. S. Clark and J. Mills, that supports my suggestion that increases in marital failure arise from changed—"commoditized"—conceptions of the goods that marriages should provide. Clark and Mills tried to assess whether people differ in the degree to which they regard their marriages as marketlike exchanges. They found that people do differ and that— an important point—the more that people think about their marriages in terms of exchange, the less satisfied they are with them. This finding led Clark and Mills to conclude that "the idea that exchange is the basis for intimate relationships may even have the effect of impairing such relationships."

With both passion and intimacy subject to transformations over time that are likely to be disappointing, the best hope for long-term loving relations rests with commitment. Commitment is the key ingredient in maintaining stable, loving relations, and if stable, loving relations are becoming less common in our culture, it is probably because commitment is becoming less common. But why? The conventional wisdom is that people are reluctant to make commitments because they are unsure whether the relation they are in is the "real thing." They see relations around them that from the outside looked wonderful falling apart, and they are desperately seeking some clue that for them it will be different. Until they find that clue, they hold back.

This account is plausible, but I don't think it's the best account. I think that the main problem people face in deciding whether to make a commitment is not that they don't know whether this is the "real thing." Instead, what they are wondering is whether they are ready to treat marriage as a durable good, whether they are ready to settle for steadily decreasing levels of passion and intimacy. Instead of worrying about whether a particular relation is actually the real thing, people worry about whether the "real thing" is the thing they actually want. Until they are sure of this, they will be reluctant to give up the opportunity for a series of short-term passionate, intimate relations that is available to them. Until they are sure of this, the risk of making a commitment will be too high, the "opportunity cost" of making a commitment will be too steep, for them to undertake it. What combination of experiences and values is required for people to come to be sure of this is an open question. It is clear to me, however, that the market realist view of love makes no contribution to people's commitment to making commitments.

THE SECOND SHIFT: "FOOTPRINTS" ON OUR MARRIAGES

Changed expectations about passion and intimacy may be one reason for the fragility of marriages and other close relations in the modern world, but they are only part of the story—and probably not the most important part. Intimacy and commitment take time; they take time to develop and, once they develop, they take time to deliver. And as I suggested in the last chapter, in an age of growing affluence and growing attention to material consumption, time is the one resource that cannot be expanded. Time devoted to our friends, our families, or our lovers is time not devoted either to the achievement of material success at work or to reaping the benefits of that success in the marketplace. As our material desires and needs escalate, the "price" of intimacy and commitment escalates. People just can't afford to have many close relations. The demands, in time and in energy, are too great. Indeed, the real question is whether nowadays people can have *any* close relations. The pressure people feel to work harder and harder, to accumulate more and more, creates what Fred Hirsch called "the economics of bad neighbors." Time is a scarce resource. If we squander it on friends or our lovers, we incur significant costs, costs that we may be increasingly unwilling or unable to pay.

This analysis has recently been confirmed by sociologist Arlie Hochschild in her important book *The Second Shift*, which documents the stresses and strains faced by modern American families with two working parents and a home and children to care for. Hochschild interviewed many families and studied several of them extensively, following them around to see how they managed to meet the simultaneous demands of job, children, and housekeeping. She found that some families managed these tasks rather well, but that most were barely keeping their lives together. And she found, not surprisingly, that in most families the burden for household and family care—the "second shift"—fell principally on the women.

Hochschild's emphasis in the book is on what she calls the "stalled revolution." The rise of feminism in the last generation dramatically changed the expectations and aspirations that women had for themselves and their lives. The now familiar picture of the breathless woman racing around trying to "have it all"—significant career, devoted spouse, wonderful kids, beautiful home, plus abundant beauty and charm—has established a model of what life is supposed to be like for many women who have come of age since the early 1970s. This is truly a revolution—in expectation. The trouble is that it has stalled in realization. It has stalled because "having it all" is simply impossible without a cooperating spouse and cooperating social institutions. That is, women can't have it all without affordable child care, flexible working hours, generous family leave policies, and spouses who willingly do a significant amount of the household "woman's work." That social institutions have been almost uniformly unforthcoming in providing the needed support is a matter of public record. Hochschild shows that, inside the household, most men are also unforthcoming. In only 20 percent of the couples she studied was there a commitment to an egalitarian marriage. And even within that 20 percent, women tended to do the major share of the household work.

This finding probably comes as no surprise, especially to women now engaged in the struggle to have it all. The mismatch between expectation and reality can perhaps be understood as an inevitable consequence of the fact that there is a great deal of inertia to patterns of living. It takes a long time to change personal habits, and an even longer time to change institutions. So women in this transitional time, in which the rules of marriage are changing, must pay a heavy price as they drag their husbands into the next century. The task for their daughters will be easier and the price lower.

The difficulty, however, is that more than just a generation of women is being strained by this transitional time. Their marriages are also being strained, as is the very character of the family as a significant social unit. Part of the strain on marriages comes from what Hochschild calls "the economy of gratitude." Even in households in which a fair amount of burden sharing occurs, deep tensions lie just beneath the surface. The tensions arise in part because the marriage partners have quite different interpretations of what is going on in the marriage. The husband, who might buy the groceries, do the wash, and cook dinner once or twice a week, expects his wife to be grateful for all he is "doing for her." The wife, in contrast, doesn't think her husband is doing anything for *her*; he's doing it for the family. It's just as much his responsibility as hers, and she might be wondering why he isn't doing substantially more. So while the marriage partners might agree completely on an objective description of who does what around the house, the husband will walk around expecting gratitude, and be met instead with resentment. How long can any marriage survive this fundamental mismatch of perception?

That women who are twenty-something, thirty-something, and even forty-something are being burdened in their marriages to the point of cracking is a very serious problem. How can this pressure on women, and on the family, be eased? One thing that some families trying to have it all do is hire people to perform the housekeeping and child care tasks that the parents can't manage. My spouse and I used to joke when we were raising two young children while engaged in demanding careers that what our family really needed was a wife. We even considered advertising for one. But of course you can't hire a wife. You can hire someone to do the chores that wives have traditionally done, but this person's ties to your family will be based on contract and wages, not on love and commitment. Indeed, hiring people to do the household chores may solve the problem of getting everything done, but at the price of making the family even less resistant to the influences of commerce than it was before. After all, a commercial relation will sit at the heart of almost all family activity. And besides, only a handful of families can afford to hire a wife anyway. Even if this did offer a solution to the problem, it would be a solution unavailable to most people.

What else can be done? It seems clear that if the problem here is that the expectations and behavior of husbands are lagging behind the expectations and needs of their wives, efforts must be made to change men's expectations and behavior. Well, sure, but in order for husbands to change, the social circumstances of their lives must change. The pressure on them at work must decrease. The pressure of economic competition must decrease. But, as I have been arguing throughout the book, quite the opposite is happening. As long as people must provide for their needs by themselves, without institutional support, the economic pressure is relentless. So even men with appropriately egalitarian attitudes may find it impossible to do what is required.

For this reason, "each marriage bears the footprints of economic and cultural trends which originate far outside marriage." And the economic and cultural trends in modern America are serving to undermine marriage and family rather than to strengthen it, to increase the burden on spouses rather than to diminish it. It is partly because we use an economic yardstick to assess the value of people's time that maintaining the household is valued so little. After all, traditionally, housework was unpaid work. That it was unpaid implies, to the modern market mentality, that it was not valuable. But if women's time is not valuable or, at any rate, less valuable than men's, then they should be paid less than men for their time in the workplace, as indeed they are. And if women's time is less valuable than men's, then filling up the leisure of a working woman with household chores "costs" less than filling up the more valuable leisure of her spouse with household chores. As long as respect and worth are measured by salary, for men to do their share around the house will represent a substantial drop in their status. Economic and cultural forces like these make strong, egalitarian commitments to family and marriage almost impossible to sustain. And the weaker the family becomes, the less able it is to be a significant agent in restraining the very forces that are undermining it.

So while modern women may want it all, they can't have it all, at least not without a substantial amount of help. This help must come from their spouses, but it must also come from the workplace and the state. A serious commitment to preserving and strengthening the family requires a change in what the state is willing to spend its money on, and an equivalent change in what employers expect from their employees and are willing to provide for them.

Pursuing this sort of "pro-family" policy, both in the private sector and in the state, would make it possible for women—and their husbands—to get closer to having it all. But much more important (why, after all, *should* anyone expect to be able to have it all?), such pro-family policies would help preserve the family as a significant social institution, protecting it from assimilation by the market. It would enable the family to nurture concern, compassion, and responsibility to others.

WHAT MARKET REALISM LEAVES OUT

A "market realist" might respond to my discussion of the stresses and strains on the modern family by suggesting that it just makes his point. Marriages are economic exchanges. True enough, not all of the "goods" exchanged in marriages have "prices," as ordinarily understood, but they are prices nonetheless. We could go a long way toward reducing the strains on the family by acknowledging marriages as economic relations, examining the costs and benefits, and changing them. By clinging to a romantic conception of love, marriage, and family, we obscure what is really going on and impede any progress that might be made in solving modern family problems.

Is the market realist right? Is love just an exchange of commodities between consenting adults? Are passion, intimacy, and commitment merely goods, like any others, available on the open market? Is the marriage contract really a contract? If not, what is it about love that market realism leaves out?

To try to answer these questions, let's try to imagine what passion, intimacy, and commitment would actually look like as market goods. Let's begin with passion, because it's the easiest. Passion already is a market commodity; it is marketed by prostitutes. Passion is an intense longing for union with another person. It is marked by smoldering looks, touching, kissing, intimate caresses, and sexual union. Prostitutes do all of these things, and they do them well. They are professionally passionate. And yet, even though prostitutes are capable of providing their customers with intense arousal and pleasure, customers in general understand that what they are getting from the prostitutes is not real passion. It is an act, a simulation. The prostitute acts *as if* she were passionately involved with her partner when in fact she is not. What distinguishes the prostitute's simulation of passion from real passion is not action but intention. The prostitute's *reasons* for behaving as she does are economic. Acting passionate is a finely honed skill, and it is probably finely honed because the artful simulation of passionate involvement is important to the customer, enabling him to convince himself that he's experiencing the real thing.

What about intimacy? I said earlier that intimacy includes the desire to promote the welfare of the loved one, high regard for the loved one, sharing of one's self and one's possessions with the loved one, giving and receiving of emotional support, and being able to count on the loved one in times of need. Is this package of goods available on the market? I don't believe we can hire or rent all of these goods in a single person—at least not yet. We can, however, rent them in pieces. Housekeepers, secretaries, lawyers, accountants, and other service personnel can be hired to see to our welfare in the more prosaic details of daily life. And for our less prosaic needs, we can turn to an institution that has grown up in recent years that allows us to have relations with people who will provide us with all the goods that are a part of intimate friendships without making any complementary demands on us. These modern friends are friends for hire. We call them psychotherapists. For a fee, we can hire people who will care about us, provide us with guidance and emotional support, deal with us honestly, act as though they admire and respect us, and promote our welfare. And what they ask in return is bounded and predictable; it's just money. We don't have to be there for the psychotherapist; only our checks do.

In the modern world, psychotherapy is not reserved for those who are deeply troubled. It is also available for people who need someone to talk to, who need a friend. And especially in urban settings, where people are so busy and relations are marked by the impersonality—even anonymity—of the market, there is a seemingly infinite demand for psychotherapy. Friendship for hire substitutes for the real thing.

Some such package of people—housekeepers, lawyers, secretaries, accountants, and psychotherapists—can together provide the behavior that goes along with intimacy. But, as in the case of the prostitute, the intentions will be different. And it's the intentions that we care most about. Secretaries, housekeepers, lawyers, accountants, and therapists go home at the end of the day and attend to the needs of those they actually love. When they pay attention to us, we are ever mindful that the meter is running.

If intentions are crucial to passion and intimacy, they are essentially all there is to commitment. Commitment *is* the intention to be loyal and faithful to the loved one, for richer or poorer, for better or worse, in sickness and in health, and so on. Is commitment available on the market? Can it be purchased or hired? Well, yes and no. We can write long-term, "exclusive services" contracts, which in effect bind an individual to do whatever it is that he or she does for only the other party to the contract. But such contracts purchase only the services, not the commitment. Indeed, the need to write such a contact is good prima facie evidence that the commitment is absent. If it were there, the contract would be unnecessary. Loyalty simply cannot be purchased. So long as the basis of the relation is merely contractual, the "buyer" must always be on the lookout for violations on the part of the "seller." So long as the basis of the relation is merely that it serves the interests of the seller to be loyal to the buyer, the buyer must always be on guard against the moment when the seller's interests will be served better by treachery or abandonment than by loyalty. We sometimes hear it said of some employer or other that he "buys" the loyalty of his employees with extremely generous compensation and attractive working conditions. It must be understood, however, that if loyalty is available to the highest bidder, it isn't loyalty at all.

I'm suggesting that contractual "simulations" of love fail to capture the intentions and the loyalty that genuine passion, intimacy, and commitment possess. Does it matter? If we can hire the appropriate behavior, one might ask, who cares about the underlying intentions? We know the answer to this question: everybody cares. The real question is, Why? And the answer, I think, is that what genuine, as opposed to simulated, love relations make possible is trust. When people are doing the right things for the right reasons, we can trust that they will continue to do them. We can let down our guard, relax our vigilance as consumers. When people are doing the right things for the wrong reasons, trust is wholly unjustified. The people must be watched. Mechanisms of supervision and contract enforcement must be developed. And of course the supervisors and enforcers can't be trusted either, and must also be supervised. What a relief it is, after a hard day guarding your back in the marketplace against any and all adversaries who are trying to take what is yours, to be able to come home to your "haven in a heartless world," kick off your shoes, let down your guard, and relax. It's a relief indeed, but for trust to be justified, the intentions associated with genuine love must be present. As Fred Hirsch put it, "the more that is in the contracts, the less can be expected without them; the more you write it down, the less is taken, or expected, on trust."

If what distinguishes genuine passion, intimacy, and commitment from simulations is the intention that underlies the action, perhaps we could preserve the market realist view of love by making intentions available for exchange on the market. Instead of arranging contracts for services, we could arrange contracts for intentions. I suspect that the very idea of having intentions under contract sounds ludicrous—and for good reason. Intentions of the kind we're talking about here are not the sort of thing that people have under perfect voluntary control, to be turned on and off at the right contractual moments. People can't will themselves instantly to be genuinely committed, passionate, and intimate with others, nor can they alienate these internal states from themselves when a "contract" expires. One of the reasons that the presence of these internal states in our loved ones inspires trust and confidence in the quality and durability of our relations is just that they can't be turned off, or directed elsewhere, if the right deal comes up.

PARTISAN FAMILIES AND IMPARTIAL MARKETS: SHOULD WE ECONOMIZE ON LOVE?

I have presented a very positive view of love relations between people. If passion, intimacy, and commitment were at the foundation of most close relations, we would expect families and friendships to be characterized by care, concern, trust, respect, and devotion. Some close relations have these characteristics. Some families really are havens in a heartless world. But there are also families—many of them—that seem heartless. Instead of trust, concern, respect, and care, these families are characterized by suspicion, indifference, domination, and exploitation. For families like these, market realism seems wholly appropriate. Indeed, for families like these, taking the notion of a marriage "contract" literally may be the best way of protecting the most vulnerable members (typically women and children) from mistreatment by the most powerful members. The market realist might argue that we really must economize on love, because it is in very short supply. By assuming romantically that it exists as the glue that holds the family together, we are exposing people who need society's protection to the arbitrary excesses of those who rule the roost.

Furthermore, the rules by which families have traditionally operated and often continue to operate are rules that we find quite unacceptable in general. Families are authoritarian, not democratic. They are hierarchical, not egalitarian. They assign their members rigidly specified roles (the "breadwinner," the "homemaker," the "eldest son," the "marriageable daughter," and so on). Parents make decisions for their children, providing what they think their children need. While we may tolerate such "paternalism" in the family, we typically resent it when it comes from our friends, from our churches, from the market, or from the state. A democratic government and a market economy are intended to ensure personal freedom and provide equal opportunity. Why, then, do we exalt and romanticize an institution like the family, which denies both?

Indeed, even when a family *is* providing a haven in a heartless world—even when its hierarchical, authoritarian, paternalistic character is successfully protecting and nurturing its members—its structure raises problems for the ideals of fairness and equality that we try to maintain in the market and the state. We demand and expect that the market and the state will treat people impartially. For example, public policies are expected to be applied uniformly to all relevant citizens. Child labor laws apply to all children, not just to the children of the lawmakers. Jobs are made available to all qualified applicants, not just to the employer's family and friends or to his ethnic group. In the domain of public policy, when things are done right, rules and protections are applied universally and without partisanship. There is no distinction made between "us" and "them." Not so in the family. Distinctions between us and them are expected of family members. Partisanship is expected among family members. Parents make sacrifices for their children that no sane person would expect them to make for strangers.

There is thus a tension between universal principles of fairness that we expect to operate in public and standards of partiality and favoritism that we expect to operate in private. If we are concerned to achieve universal standards of fairness, using the family as a model for our social relations poses a real problem. As novelist Graham Greene has written, "You can't love humanity; you can only love people." It is fine to expect behavior toward family members to be based upon love. That much love is possible; you can love people. But it is foolish and even dangerous to expect that relations among strangers can also be based upon love. That much love is impossible; you can't love humanity. The knowledge of particular others that is necessary for genuine intimacy and commitment simply can't be developed for humanity in general. So a society that expects relations between its members to be governed by universal love is in trouble. This is just another way of saying that societies must find a way to economize on love, which is what the market realist has been telling us all along. In a society that takes universal fairness as a significant objective, efforts must be made to limit the extent to which familylike relations spread outside the family and dominate society as a whole.

How big a threat the family actually poses to universal fairness depends upon how far the tentacles of the family spread into social life in general. When, prior to large-scale industrialization, the family was an essentially independent economic unit, there was virtually no aspect of social life that it did not touch. And one was expected to do everything possible to make life better for family members, typically at the expense of outsiders. There was little or no attachment to a "civil society" that existed above and beyond the family, and to which all citizens bore an equal responsibility. With the growth of industrialization, and of the market, a sphere of life was created that operated by public rules, rules different from the rules of the family. Within that sphere, people were expected to treat all comers equally. Buyers and sellers were, or could be, anonymous. Everyone sought the best deal. Competition, price, and self-interest saw to it that partisanship and special pleading did not pay. With the economic sphere walled off in this way from the special interests of family loyalty, certain manifestations of partisanship inside the family could be tolerated without their effects' pervading society. So, in an important sense, it may be that it was the growth of the market system that made a romantic conception of love, family, and friendship possible. Partisanship, passion, intimacy, and commitment could be accepted—even celebrated—in some social relations as long as it was limited and prevented from spreading to all social relations. And the market is what set these limits. In the market, people neither love nor hate those with whom they deal. People's relations with others in the market are marked by a benign indifference. And the rules of market interaction are quite clear: one is expected to buy for as little as possible and sell for as much as possible, without regard for whatever special circumstances might mark the other party to the transaction.

Nothing is this clear in the case of the intimate relations of love and friendship. The actions required of friends (or lovers) are vague and indeterminate, not governed by rules. What is critical to them, as we saw before, is that they are governed by the right intentions, the right motives. We can give the people we love special attention and treatment. We can do things for them that we would not do for anyone else. We can protect them tenaciously against the assaults of strangers. We can give ourselves to them unconditionally. Democratic society can celebrate all of this special dedication as long as it does not extend to all of life, as long as strangers are protected, and can't be excluded from everything. And the market, along with the democratic state, extends this protection to strangers.

Think about what life would be like if special relations between people dominated everything. Imagine shopping for a television and discovering either that the shopkeeper wouldn't sell you one or that you had to pay twice as much as someone the shopkeeper knew. Imagine visiting a doctor and being told that the doctor treated only her friends or, perhaps even worse, that the doctor could be counted on to pay attention only if her patient was a friend. Imagine taking an exam in school and having the grade significantly determined by how close you were to the teacher. Imagine being involved in litigation and having to worry about whose side your lawyer was really on. "It's not what you know, it's who you know," we sometimes cynically observe when our social institutions aren't working as they should. Well, when social institutions are based on close personal relations, "who you know" stops being an aberration. It becomes the way the system is *supposed* to work.

When the marketplace is working as it should, the behavior of shopkeepers, doctors, lawyers, teachers, and the like becomes more evenhanded and predictable. While it is true that we can't count on these people to serve our interests out of personal devotion and loyalty, it is also true that we don't need personal devotion and loyalty. We can assume that as long as they need or want our business, doctors, lawyers, teachers, and shopkeepers will treat us fairly and that if they are competent doctors, lawyers, teachers, and shopkeepers, they will treat us well. We can even count on the competitive market to weed the incompetent ones out. For personal devotion and loyalty, we can seek out our family and our friends.

Furthermore, the presence of an impersonal and evenhanded market at work in much of our daily life makes our close personal relations seem more attractive. One reason that we value so much the devotion, intimacy, and commitment we receive from family and friends is precisely that the rest of our social relations are so impersonal. If life were nothing but close personal relations, they might come to feel oppressive. Everywhere we turned we would find people who knew everything about us and expected a great deal from us. We would be trapped in a web of intimacy from which there was no escape. What makes close personal relations so important and valuable to us is their scarcity in our lives.

This point is well illustrated by two modern social phenomena that exist side by side in striking contradiction. Many, if not most, city dwellers bemoan the absence of close personal relations in their lives. They live in anonymity, knowing almost none of the hundreds of people with whom they share a large apartment building, having little involvement in the private lives of the people with whom they work, being completely unknown to the people with whom they buy and sell, and they long for the small-town life, where neighbors know one another, care for one another, and get involved in one another's lives, and where shopkeepers can deal with each of their customers on a personal basis. Simultaneously, small-town dwellers can't wait to get out from under all this "neighborliness," which for them is often experienced as nosiness. They long for the anonymity of an apartment house, for the impersonality of a shopping mall. The lesson here is that there needs to be a happy medium, and the institution of the market, when it is working properly, contributes to that happy medium by keeping personal relations out.

The market keeps personal relations from becoming all encompassing and oppressive and thus solves the problem of the small-town dweller. But what gets the personal relations in? What addresses the problems of the city person? Presumably, it is the strength of the personal relations themselves. The city person needs a network of friends and family to protect her from an equally oppressive, all-encompassing anonymity. And here is where the trouble comes for the market realist view of love. Adam Smith and many of his contemporaries understood in the eighteenth century that, just as the market served as a needed restraint on the special relations between family and friends, family and friends served as a needed restraint on the harsh impersonality of the market. Each kind of relation had to be strong to keep the influence of the other within bounds. But the market realist view of love does nothing to keep special relations strong. On the contrary, it assimilates the relations between friends and family to the model of the market. This is what the "economic imperialism" I discussed in the last few chapters is all about. When the family becomes an extension of the market, with family members "contracting" with one another to provide goods and services, there is nothing left to soften or restrain the market. It becomes too much of a good thing.

We can think of impersonal market relations and intimate family relations as being on opposite sides of a seesaw. What is required is enough weight on both sides to keep the seesaw in balance. Prior to the growth of the market that took off in the eighteenth century, all the weight was on the side of the family and other special relations. As the market grew, it added weight to the other side until some kind of balance was reached. But the market continued to grow, so the seesaw started tipping in the other direction. And now, economic imperialism and market realism threaten to make the tip complete by taking weight away from the family side and relocating it on the market side.

There is a very important and general lesson to be learned from this seesaw metaphor. One generation's solution can become the next generation's problem. When we look at the effects of social institutions and social movements at a particular time and place, we must be very careful not to assume that they will have the same effects at other times and places. The historical context very much influences the kind of effect that any social practice will have. The virtues of the market in the eighteenth century depended upon restraints on the market that already existed. In the late twentieth century, those restraints are being very seriously eroded. It is one thing for the market realist to look at the nature of family relations in the past, and see how the market introduced impartiality, order, and stability into an otherwise chaotic social world. It is quite another thing for him to use this lesson from history to suggest a future world made up of nothing but contractual, marketlike arrangements.

This is a very important point, first made with remarkable foresight by Alexis de Tocqueville, a Frenchman who toured the United States to examine its experiment in egalitarian democracy more than 150 years ago. The product of his examination, *Democracy in America*, was and remains a landmark analysis of the character of American life. Tocqueville was impressed with the freedom and fluidity that characterized American society. Americans possessed a level of geographic, economic, and social mobility that was unheard of in a still rigidly class-based Europe. What made all this mobility possible was the American commitment to individualism. Individualism was the guiding ideology of the government, the economy, and the society.

Tocqueville observed this, and admired the freedom it made possible. But he also saw a grave danger in a commitment to unbridled individualism. It encouraged the naked pursuit of self-interest, and it broke down ties to family, community, and state. In the short run, this breakdown was fairly modest, because Americans retained deeply ingrained habits and customs from their more structured European past. But it was not clear to Tocqueville that, in the long run, as these customs and habits faded, American society could hold itself together if it continued to be guided by an individualist ideology that was unrestrained by countervailing forces.

What optimism Tocqueville could find for the long-term health and stability of American society came principally from his observation of American women. Individualism was mostly the province of men, and it was present mostly in their activities in the world of commerce. Inside the home, commitment to family, community, and church was demanded, nurtured, and valued. And all of this was accomplished by the woman of the house. By insisting on participation in religious institutions (which most men had rather little use for), women maintained in their men both ethical commitments and community ties. And by emphasizing the sanctity of the family, women maintained in their men a sense of responsibility to others. While it is, of course, true that men had almost all the real power in the society, the influence on them by the women with whom they lived served to provide the needed restraint on their tendency to pursue their individual interests no matter what the social consequences.

Thus, from Tocqueville's point of view, the counterweight to the pursuit of selfish interests in the marketplace was provided by the family, and largely by the women in the family. If we bring his perspective to bear on the present moment, we can see that there are far-reaching potential consequences when women leave the household to join men in the workforce and society finds nothing to replace their stabilizing, communitarian influence.

Let's look at what happens when women leave the household. Of necessity, a significant portion of their time, talent, and energy will now be directed toward their work. Also, (almost) of necessity, less of their time, talent, and energy will be devoted to the family. What will happen to the family if their husbands don't step in to fill the gap? Since families don't run themselves, cracks will start to develop.

The cracks will widen as the consequences of neglect of the household start to appear. Family life will be less satisfying to everyone because things won't be running as smoothly. Furthermore, as a result of mismatched "economies of gratitude," wives will resent their husbands for not doing more, while husbands resent their wives for not appreciating sufficiently what they already do. Such resentments lead to fairly careful scorekeeping, to make sure that neither partner is being exploited. Indeed, they can lead to rather specific marriage contracts, as legal protection against exploitation. And surely, as family life grows less satisfying to people, the value and the significance of the family as a social institution becomes more and more questionable. With women less willing and less able to provide the counterweight to individualism, and men unwilling to take up the slack, Tocqueville's dark vision of a society coming apart looks ominously real.

What do these cracks in the family do to the precarious balance of the seesaw? Can we embrace equity and fairness as principles that should operate within the family and still preserve intimacy, care, and nurturance? Is there a way to preserve what is good about family relations even as we encourage families to be more democratic? Is there a way we can persuade men to play the same role in the household that women do without resorting to contract? These tough questions are the questions we all face as we try to build loving family relations that are attuned to the modern world.

8

THE "DEMEANING" OF WORK

Without work all life goes rotten. But when work is soulless, life stifles and dies.
                                                            —ALBERT CAMUS

I understand that it's the music that keeps me alive. . . . That's my life-blood. And to give that up for, like, the TV, the cars, the houses—that's not the American dream. That's the booby prize, in the end. Those are the booby prizes. And if you fall for them—if, when you achieve them, you believe that this is the end in and of itself—then you've been suckered in. Because those are the consolation prizes, if you're not careful, for selling yourself out, or letting the best of yourself slip away. So you gotta be vigilant. You gotta carry the idea you began with further. And you gotta hope that you're headed for higher ground.
                                                            —BRUCE SPRINGSTEEN

Why do we work? This seems like a silly question. The answer is so obvious. We work because we have to. We work to put a roof over our heads, clothes on our backs, bread on the table, and oil in the furnace. When we've got that taken care of, we work to pay doctor bills and insurance premiums and send our kids to college. When that's taken care of, we work to maintain our automobiles, take an occasional trip, have a nice stereo, see a movie or a ball game now and then, and eat out once in a while. When that's taken care of, we work so that we can put a little away toward retirement. And when that's taken care of, we work for pasta makers, BMWs, elegant clothes, and summer houses. We work because work gets us the things we need and want; it's a means to the various opportunities for consumption we value.

This is all true, of course, but it's not the whole story. When I went to work, for example, it simply never occurred to me that there was an alternative to working. I just took it for granted that people worked. It was a natural part of people's lives, and an important part of what defined them. It never crossed my mind that the question "Why do people work?" needed an answer, any more than "Why do people make love?" needs an answer. Nor did I think about work as the means to food, shelter, clothes, and education for my children. People got these things by working, just as they got babies by making love, but the notion that people work *in order* to get the things they want and need seemed to me both inadequate and inaccurate as an explanation of work.

What would we do if we didn't have to work, if we inherited substantial wealth—if, as my mother likes to say, we were fortunate enough to have our parents born before us? Would we spend all of our time consuming? Would we live lives of leisure—playing tennis today, golf tomorrow; visiting Aspen this week, Palm Springs next? I don't think so, at least not most of us. While it is true that work is a means to many of the things we value, it is also true that work is valuable in itself. While it is true that we work to live, it is also true that we live to work. Repeatedly over the years, when people in a wide range of occupations have been asked in surveys about what they want and expect out of work, material rewards have emerged as only one of several significant aspirations—and typically not the most important one. People want work that is interesting, challenging, and socially valued. They want work with people they like. And they want work in organizations that treat them with respect. People continue working even when they no longer have to—indeed, even when they could make out better financially by retiring. Small-business owners, for example, characteristically work longer hours than they would if they worked for a similar income for a corporation, and they keep the business going even though they could do better by selling it and investing the proceeds.

Despite the evidence that people want more from work than their paychecks, according to what might be called the "official ideology" of our culture, people wouldn't work if they didn't have to. Work is regarded as inherently unpleasant—as a cost, a burden. And an elaborate set of incentives, coupled with vigilant supervision, operates in most work settings to get people to do what they're being paid to do. Advertisements repeatedly tell us that we live for weekends and that, if we could get away with it, we would make every day a weekend. Just as the official ideology tells us we must "economize on love" because we can't count on people to treat one another well out of a sense of care, concern, and respect, it also tells us we must "economize on work" because we can't count on people to do their jobs well out of a sense of pride, responsibility, and commitment. Just as we can get people to treat one another well only if, in some sense, we make it pay, we can get them to do their jobs well only if we make that pay.

Most of us know that this "official ideology" is false. In our own work, we aspire to more than just a healthy paycheck. We actually want to work, and we want work that is meaningful, challenging, and fulfilling. Obvious though this may be, the official ideology denies it. And in denying it, it encourages the creation of working environments in which meaning, challenge, and fulfillment are increasingly difficult to find.

What gives work meaning? What makes it fulfilling? Under what circumstances is work one of the best things in life? In this chapter, I address these questions. I also explore why the modern workplace has tended to minimize the value that people derive from meaningful work and to operate instead on the assumption that work is just an unpleasant means to material ends. Finally, I suggest that by making work meaningful, we can simultaneously improve the lives of the people who work and improve the quality of the work that they do.

THE JOY OF WORK

Let's begin by considering what it is that makes work meaningful and satisfying, focusing on my own work as an example. What's good about being a college professor? First of all, it's fun. Trying to develop insight into or understanding of the world, and then inventing ways to communicate that insight (and my enthusiasm) to students, is a pleasure. It's a pleasure for several reasons. It requires me continually to be learning and doing new things. It challenges me. It demands creativity. It affords enormous freedom of thought and of action. It brings me into contact with other people (fellow scholars) who share my expertise and enthusiasm, and it encourages me to work with them collaboratively. It gives me the chance to influence students to make my interests theirs and to join me in my quest for knowledge. In sum, it gives me the chance to use my intelligence creatively in the pursuit of excellence in a supportive social environment. That's why it's fun.

But in addition to being fun, college teaching and research are meaningful because they are highly valued by society. Even during those periods when new ideas won't come to me, and when my current group of students asks the same questions, and makes the same mistakes, that their predecessors asked and made for years—even, in short, when I get into a rut—my work has meaning because what I do is important. And knowing that what I do is important makes it a lot easier to get up and face the day, even when I know that it holds nothing new, exciting, or challenging.

I chose college teaching to exemplify meaningful work not because it is unique but because I know it. It's what I've been doing for twenty years. The things that make college teaching meaningful—that it offers people the chance to use their intelligence creatively in the pursuit of excellence and that it is socially significant—can apply to most of the different kinds of work that people do. Not all work provides equal opportunities for the use of creative intelligence, and not all work is equally highly valued by society, but virtually all of the work people do can have some measure of both of these components of meaning. For example, an automobile assembly line worker can find challenge in her work if she is encouraged to use her intelligence by involving herself in developing techniques that improve the quality or efficiency of production. She can take pride if the product she helps produce is a good one. And she can find meaning if, perhaps because of the quality of her product, her work is valued by her society. Similarly, the stereo salesperson (remember my fantasy in chapter 2) can find her work challenging if she conscientiously keeps abreast of rapidly developing technology; she can take pride if she helps customers select a stereo system that meets their aims without breaking their budgets; and she can find meaning in the knowledge that she is performing a real service for her customers. None of this is an automatic part of either assembly line work or retail sales. An effort must be made to create a workplace in which intelligence can be used and quality pursued. But none of it is automatic on a college campus either. Whether work permits the use of creative intelligence depends on how it is organized and on the attitudes that workers bring to it. And whether it is socially significant depends upon the way society views it.

The nature and organization of work, along with individual and collective attitudes toward it, affect more than just how much people like the work they do. They also have an enormous impact on how well the work is done. To see this point, it is useful to distinguish three different attitudes that people might have toward their work. Some may view their work as a *job*, some as a *career*, and some as a *calling*. People who have jobs don't expect them to have much meaning. They do the jobs for the material benefits they bring, and nothing more. Work is simply a means to consumption. I imagine that, for practically everyone who does it, slinging or serving hamburgers at a fast-food restaurant is just a job. Without close supervision and / or a system of incentives that rewards diligence, people with jobs can be expected to do as little as they can get away with. The jobs aren't challenging, and they are of little social value. So who cares?

For people with careers the situation is different. While people with jobs are just working for a wage, people with careers are going somewhere. There is a clear trajectory of advancement that defines success, and people derive satisfaction from advancing over and above the larger paychecks that it brings. So people with careers can be energized not just by the prospect of high wages but by the prospect of moving up the ladder. They will work hard and take initiatives, even without constant supervision, in the hope that such efforts will bring advancement. The hamburger slinger who hopes one day to manage a store of her own may see her work as a career.

The trouble with careers is that not everyone can keep advancing. The fast-food restaurant has many burger makers and servers, but only one manager. Owing to the pyramidal structure typical of workplace organizations, many people with careers are continually driven to do more and better work than their peers. The pressure to keep up is relentless, and time devoted to career advancement eats into time that might otherwise be available for other kinds of activity. One result of this pressure to work, as I've already discussed, is that it competes with the time required to be a good spouse, lover, friend, or parent. A second result is that because people are forced to work longer and harder than they want, they get less satisfaction out of their work than they otherwise might. And despite these great efforts, and neglect of friends and family, most people embarked on career paths will fail to reach the heights to which they aspire. By the time most people get to be about forty, if not before, the realization hits that they are stuck. They won't be getting to the top, as they might have imagined in their youthful, ambitious fantasies. They face twenty-five years or more of just holding on, with nowhere to go but down. As the realization sets in that they have gone about as far as they can go, diligence wanes, initiative-taking disappears, and close supervision is required to see to it that their work meets even minimal standards of acceptability. When a person's reason for doing her best is the prospect of advancement, as that prospect dims, enthusiasm dims with it.

For people with a calling, the situation is still different. For them, it is the concrete products of their work, and not just personal advancement, that provide meaning and satisfaction. People with a calling are doing something of value. It will not lose its value even if they are stuck doing it, with no prospect of moving up, for twenty-five years or more. The very unusual hamburger slinger who sees herself as providing nourishing food at moderate prices in clean, attractive surroundings to ease the pressure on modern, two-job families with modest incomes has neither a job nor a career but a calling. She can go to work each day knowing that just by meeting her responsibilities, she will be doing something of value for other people. People with a calling don't require careful supervision or an elaborate system of incentives. Their motivation to do their work well comes from inside. The work is just too important to be done carelessly or lazily.

If we use these three categories to understand different kinds of work, the most natural temptation is to assume that each of the various tasks people perform in society simply falls, by its very nature, into one of the categories. For example, fast-food workers, assembly line workers, government clerks, and retail salespeople have jobs, and their bosses must be sure to monitor their performance carefully; stockbrokers, lawyers, engineers, and professional athletes have careers, and their bosses must be sure that opportunities for advancement continue to be available; ministers, doctors, and teachers have callings, and they are so internally motivated that they don't even need bosses. I have tried to suggest, however, that this is the wrong way to think about work. Virtually any of the occupations people have could, in theory, fall into any one of these three categories. Where they fall will be determined in part by the attitudes people bring with them to their work. And these attitudes will in turn be influenced both by characteristics of the work itself and by the way society views it. While most fast-food workers may see their work as merely a job, it is possible, under the right circumstances, to see it as a calling. And conversely, while most teachers may regard their work as a calling, it is possible, under the wrong circumstances, to see it as just a job.

Let's consider the work of teaching a bit more carefully. For some people, in some settings, teaching is only about salary and benefits: short school days, long vacations, summers off, excellent retirement and health plans. The trick, for people like this, is to meet the requirements of the job while doing as little as possible. It goes without saying that these teachers, for whom teaching is a job, will not be very good at it, unless their performance is carefully monitored and various incentives can be brought to bear on it.

For other people, teaching is a career. In addition to wages and benefits, there is tenure, promotion, and perhaps administrative authority to be sought. There may also be various forms of recognition for excellence. People for whom teaching is a career may be fine teachers, especially if the criteria that determine advancement are actually connected to classroom performance. They may often do far more than the minimum required for them to keep their jobs. They may stay long after school is out to give students individual assistance. They may accompany kids on trips and supervise extracurricular activities. But it is very important to them to know that someone in authority is watching, that they will get credit for the extra work. These teachers' eyes are primarily on the next step on the ladder, not on the children in their classes. If the requirements for advancement and the requirements for classroom effectiveness ever start to pull in different directions, we know which direction these teachers will take.

Finally, there are some people for whom teaching is a calling. Their eyes are firmly focused on the real aim of what they do. They are interested in doing whatever they can to help their students learn. They do extra work, but they don't regard it as "extra," since the point of their work is to help students learn. They concentrate on the task and let the recognition and promotion take care of themselves.

We may be tempted to say to ourselves that teaching *ought* to be a calling, and to hold the teachers for whom it is a merely a job or a career responsible for their misguided attitude toward their work. It is, after all, interesting work, with new challenges arising almost every day. And it is important, socially valued work, since teachers are entrusted with the future of our children and thus of our society. But neither interest nor importance can be taken for granted. Much of what teachers do can be extremely repetitive and uninteresting. They teach the same material, and correct the same mistakes, year after year. Furthermore, efforts by administrators to develop a uniform curriculum and set of teaching methods can undermine the desires of teachers to be creatively involved in both the setting of educational goals and the development of methods to achieve them. If the structure of the work is made routine and repetitive, the people who value creative and challenging engagement will be driven away. People who want to use their intelligence in the pursuit of excellence will seek other kinds of work. We will be left at best with careerists and at worst with people who are just putting in time. And as to the importance of teaching, what is our typical response when we learn that someone we've just met is a teacher? Do we respond with respect and admiration? Or do we ask ourselves why he's *only* a teacher?

So there is nothing that is obvious or automatic to influence teachers to regard their work as a calling. And the same is true of other occupations. Treating the same illnesses year after year, or writing the same wills and contracts, or farming the same crops, or selling the same stereos—whether these activities are jobs, careers, or callings depends upon whether their products are generally regarded as valuable. Doctors, lawyers, salespeople, and farmers can keep boredom from the door, and be content doing the same thing over and over again, only if they can be convinced that what they do is important.

What signals do we give that various occupations are valuable? What standards do we use to measure and assign value? The only device we have available for assessing and assigning value is the market. Just as with goods, we determine the value of services by seeing how much people are willing to pay for them. Your value to society is then directly reflected in how much society is willing to pay you for what you do. So doctors and lawyers are far more valuable than teachers, though less valuable than investment bankers, athletes, and movie stars. Some notion like this must be lurking in the back of our minds when we note that so and so is *only* a teacher.

I know that most of us don't *really* believe that salary is the only, or perhaps even the primary, measure of value. We all believe that the practitioners of some occupations receive compensation that far exceeds their real social worth, while practitioners of other occupations are undercompensated. While we don't know quite what to do about this, we are quick to point out to people like teachers that we understand that they are worth more than they are paid. But such disclaimers are both unconvincing and inadequate. Disclaimers are only empty words. "Put your money where your mouth is," the teacher might say. And as long as people must have substantial amounts of money to provide the things that they and their families need—decent housing, education, and health care, for example— they will be faced always with doubts about whether their low salaries and consequent family sacrifices can possibly be justified. Imagine what goes through the mind of a diligent, dedicated teacher who does everything she can to provide a superb education for the children she teaches at a first-rate public school in an affluent suburb when she realizes that she can't afford to live in that suburb and send her own children to that first-rate school.

If it is useful to divide the kinds of work that people do into jobs, careers, and callings, and if it is true that which category a given type of work falls into is not inherent in the work itself, we must examine what *does* determine which kinds of work fall into which categories. One possible answer is that this determination has very little to do with either the work itself or with society's view of it. Instead, whether work is a job, a career, or a calling is determined by the attitudes that the people doing the work bring to it. Give two people the same work, side by side, and one of them will be enthusiastic, dedicated, and responsible while the other will just be working for a wage. For example, there was a man who worked for several years in my neighborhood as a church janitor and a school crossing guard. Neither of these tasks strike me as being either especially challenging or highly valued socially. Nevertheless, this man put himself into his work with a level of passion, care, and devotion that would be rare and admirable in a brain surgeon. He watched his corner like a hawk, stopping rush hour traffic fearlessly to allow the young children to cross the street safely. He knew all the little kids whose journey to school he protected, and engaged them in conversation regularly. He even knew the cars and faces of many of the commuters who drove by his corner every day, and never failed to give them a warm wave hello. And he maintained the church grounds as though they were an arboretum. Why this enthusiasm and commitment? Perhaps he had the view that *all* work is meaningful, that everyone contributes to society by doing his job well, whatever it is. Perhaps it was just his nature to find something valuable in any situation. Perhaps he thought that all people are called by God to do something, and that God does not distinguish between "significant" tasks and "menial" ones. Whatever the reason, my temptation, in watching him, was to want to bottle what's inside him and spread it around.

This man was admittedly unusual, but we all know of some doctors, lawyers, accountants, teachers, engineers, salespeople, restaurant workers, and house painters who are utterly dedicated to their work and do it as well as it can be done—even with no one watching—while other doctors, lawyers, accountants, and so on are only going through the motions. Given that individual variation in people's attitudes toward work is an obvious and undeniable fact, maybe the thing to do is find a way to bottle the attitude of my crossing guard and use it to inoculate everyone else.

This individualistic orientation to social phenomena is quite popular in our culture. We commonly tell ourselves that the problem, whatever it is, is not in society; it's in individuals. The right self-help book, or therapy regime, or training program can induce anyone to find meaning in anything. Our task, if we want people to regard their work as a calling, is to change the character of the people, not the character of the work. Without denying what is undeniable—that different people approach the same work differently—focusing on changing the attitudes of individuals might be the wrong way to proceed. It is easier to find meaning and challenge in some kinds of work than in others. And the work people do ought to have meaning and challenge. So, rather than finding ways to adapt people to work that has little challenge or social value, we could be looking for ways to adapt work to people who want and need challenge and social value. The people will be better for it, and so will the work.

WORK AND "MARKET REALISM"

I have made three claims in this chapter that create a puzzle when taken together. First, work can be viewed as a job, a career, or a calling. Second, any given type of work can, in theory, belong in any one of these categories. Third, when work is regarded as a calling, the work is done better and the people doing it are more satisfied. What these claims suggest is that society would be well served if work were structured so that as many people as possible saw what they did as a calling. This might lead us to expect that by now our society would have evolved so that most of us were "called" to do the work we do. And therein lies the puzzle. It is fair to say that few of us engage in work we regard as a calling. Why? Are my three claims false? Is it simply in the nature of things that most of the work that needs to be done to keep society going is essentially meaningless drudgery? Or is it simply in human nature to regard virtually any work as a necessary evil, to be avoided if possible or, if not, to be minimized? In the eyes of the market realists—the same ones who taught us about love in chapter 7—one or both of these suggestions are true. Work, except in unusual circumstances, is just the means by which people accumulate the resources that can then be devoted to consumption.

Why have so many of us allowed ourselves to be put in a position where we spend half our waking lives doing what we don't want to do in a place we don't want to be? Is there something about work as just a means to an end that serves the market system very well and thus has encouraged those in positions of power and authority to organize work in this way? To address this question, let's examine how it helps the market system to have a collection of workers who work only for the wages they receive.

Market activity is about buying and selling things. For the market to function effectively, it must be possible for the exchange of things to occur freely and easily. What makes this possible is a medium of exchange that all participants can use: money. But the market is also about buying and selling labor. The market requires that labor be mobile, that people be willing to move around from job to job as fluctuations in consumer demand increase the call for some kinds of work and decrease the call for other kinds. Unless people are willing to stop working in a hula hoop factory and go to work in a computer game factory if changes in consumer demand require it, manufacturers will not be able to switch their resources from hula hoops to computer games, and supply will not keep up with demand. And just as a medium of exchange is essential for the marketing of things, it is essential for the marketing of labor. What makes labor mobile is the same medium of exchange that works for goods—namely, money. If you work simply for the wage, you're a mercenary. You can easily be induced to change jobs for a better wage. Thus the market can induce the car mechanic to switch from fixing cars to fixing bicycles if consumer demand requires it. But if you work at least in part because of the meaning and significance of the particular work that you do, inducing you to change jobs is much, much harder. Meaning and significance simply can't be dispensed like money.

If, in general, people do work simply in exchange for money, then labor will be mobile and the market will run smoothly. The value of people's time and work will be equal to the price they fetch on the market and nothing more. People won't care about the character of the work they do, since work will simply be the means to consumption. People will sell their labor to the highest bidder, to maximize the rate of return on labor time and thus maximize opportunities to consume. And employers will dictate what the workers do so as to maximize their rate of return, or profit. So both workers and employers will strive to get the greatest return for the least effort.

If, in contrast, people do work that has meaning and significance, so that there is value in the activities themselves, how can we induce them to change their work? How can we induce them to do whatever we want them to do in exchange for a wage? People are not indifferent enough toward work that is challenging and meaningful to be willing to sell their time to the highest bidder. So, to establish a market system that functions effectively, work must be organized in such a way that people are willing to trade it on the market.

And there is another requirement that must be met for labor to be mobile. The training, knowledge, and skill demanded by the work must be minimal. To see why, think about a worker whose job requires a great deal of training and knowledge. Such a worker might not become productive until after a year or more of training. During that training period, her company is paying her a salary, but getting little or no production in return. The company finances the training as an investment in the worker's future productivity. But once the worker is trained, she can hold the company hostage, threatening to take her skills to a competitor unless her salary demands are met. What can the company do? It can't afford to let the worker leave and be faced with the expensive training of a replacement. Thus it must meet her demands. And even if she isn't making demands, when times are slack, the company will be reluctant to let her go, since all the time and money invested in her will then be wasted.

To respond to this problem, and keep labor mobile, companies can try to structure work so that it requires as little training, knowledge, and skill as possible. By doing this, the company will have only an insignificant investment in each worker. It can then afford to let workers come and go as they, and the market, please. But as a consequence of doing this, the company will deprive its workers of opportunities to use their intelligence in the workplace. All jobs will be as menial as possible, as interchangeable as possible. With a workplace organized like this, it is hardly surprising that most people will be driven to seek satisfaction in what their work buys them, rather than in the work itself.

ECONOMIC ACTIVITY AND HISTORY

If organizing work so that it is merely a means to consumption is good for the market system, it isn't so good for the person doing the work. The more mobile and interchangeable labor is, the less likely it is to provide workers with opportunities to find challenge, meaning, and significance in the work that they do. Why would workers accept this impoverishment of their work? The answer to this question is that workers didn't have much choice. With the coming of the industrial revolution in the eighteenth century, workers were subjected to a process of transformation of work that they did not want but could not prevent. The history of work over the last three centuries is a history of this process of transformation.

The industrial revolution brought with it an increase in the specialization and routinization of work, so very few of the people engaged in production had much opportunity to exercise intelligence, skill, or creativity. This process has been powerfully documented by historians like Karl Polanyi and E. J. Hobsbawm. In his book *The Great Transformation*, Polanyi traced the development of industrialization and the market system in western Europe, contrasting the market as an economic and social institution and exchange as an economic activity with the institutions and activities it replaced. His argument about the development of exchange and the market system can best be summarized in his own words:

> No less a thinker than Adam Smith suggested that the division of labor in society was dependent upon the existence of markets, or, as he put it, upon man's "propensity to barter, truck and exchange one thing for another." . . . In retrospect it can be said that no misreading of the past ever proved more prophetic of the future. For while up to Adam Smith's time that propensity had hardly shown up on a considerable scale in any observed community, and had remained, at best, a subordinate feature of economic life, a hundred years later an industrial system was in full swing over the major part of the planet which . . . implied that the human race was swayed in all its economic activities, if not also in its political, intellectual, and spiritual pursuits, by that one particular propensity.

The world into which Adam Smith injected his notion of man's "propensity to truck and barter" had very few factories. Even the people who worked for wages typically did the work in their own homes and were paid by middlemen who traded the products on the market. People integrated the work they did for wages into their other daily activities, which often included tending a small plot and a few animals that together provided the family with a subsistence living. Aristotle called this form of economic life "householding," perhaps to emphasize the essential economic independence of each family or household. In providing for most of its basic needs by itself, the family or household did not depend on wages or exchange for its survival.

Whether the people engaged in householding were producing things for their own use or producing for sale, the kind of work they did, as well as the way in which they did it, was determined more by social custom than by market demand. Men did the work of their fathers before them, in the way their fathers had done it, for the price their fathers had charged. The kind of work they did, and the way they did it, was part of what defined them; it was part of their personal identity. A man could no more switch from being a blacksmith to being a cooper than he could switch from being an Englishman to being a Frenchman. Indeed, even their surnames (like Smith and Cooper) reflected how much their work was a permanent part of their identity. And people did their work to meet established standards of quality rather than to maximize their daily rate of return. "A fair day's work for a fair day's pay," and not "Buy cheap and sell dear," seemed to be the watchword of the time.

Over a period of many years, with the emergence of the factory system, customary work for a customary wage was slowly replaced by a labor market much like the one that exists today. By the end of the eighteenth century in England, many of the descendants of householders were not only working for wages but freely hiring themselves out to the highest bidder. Moreover, with growing mechanization and division of labor, work became increasingly specialized and routinized. Opportunities to derive value from the work activities themselves were correspondingly diminished. A central component of the final stages of development of the workplace was a movement at the turn of this century that came to be known as the "scientific management" movement. Its founder and leader was Frederick Winslow Taylor.

Taylor argued that traditional or customary ways of working interfered with efficiency and productivity. It did no good to develop efficient and powerful machines if the people hired to run them wanted to continue to produce in the old-fashioned way they had been brought up on. Industry needed a set of techniques for controlling the behavior of the worker that was effective enough to turn workers into efficient cogs in the production machinery. Accomplishing this control involved two different lines of human engineering. First, it was necessary to discover and implement pay rates and patterns that kept people working hard and resulted in maximal output. Second, it was necessary to break up customary ways of doing work and to substitute for them minutely specialized and routinized tasks that could be accomplished mechanically and automatically. The idea was to strip work down to its simplest possible elements—to eliminate the need for judgment, intelligence, and skill. Under these conditions, labor would be maximally mobile. With work requiring little skill, people could be moved from job to job without much training. And with work providing little or no satisfaction other than the wage, bosses could control the behavior of their employees simply by manipulating rates of pay. Thus it came to be that the workplace as we know it in the late twentieth century is indeed a place in which work is just a means to an end. Work does not provide people with the opportunity to exercise their skill and intelligence in a way that allows them to take pride in accomplishment. It does not have meaning. It is not socially valued. In a properly engineered workplace, people are just interchangeable parts in a production machine.

It is interesting to realize, as we read modern cries of alarm about the "deskilling" of labor, that it didn't happen by accident. A century ago, the deskilling of labor was the explicit objective of management. And as more and more of the U.S. economy has shifted from production industries to service industries, the routinized, deadening methods of the factory have been imported into the service sector. People who work for airline companies, telephone companies, mail-order houses, and government agencies, and who spend their days talking to customers on the telephone, are being subjected to a degree of performance monitoring and regimentation that would have made Taylor proud. Thanks to the modern computer, it is now possible to monitor automatically how long such workers take on each call, as well as when, and for how long, they are away from their stations. In one company, the computers keep track of how much time workers take between calls (they are allowed seven seconds), how much time they take for lunch away from their stations (they are allowed thirty minutes), how much time they take on their breaks (two fifteen-minute breaks per day), and even how much time they spend in the bathroom. Each employee gets a grade (automatically computed) each week. Good grades bring workers small bonuses (an hour off with pay), while bad grades bring them penalties (an hour of extra work with no pay). Supervisors can listen in on calls, to make sure that the proper service is being provided and no time is being wasted. There may be as many as twenty million American workers whose work is being micromonitored in this way. They report a much higher incidence of work-related ailments (back pain, eyestrain, and the like), and a much higher incidence of depression, than workers doing similar jobs who are not being micromonitored and managed.

A defender of modern workplace organization might concede that it didn't *have* to go the way it did, but argue that the astonishing productivity and efficiency it made possible made it far superior to previous forms of work organization. As a result, it represents a kind of cultural evolution. The cultures that develop practices and modes of organization that best meet the demands imposed on them by the environment are the ones that survive and flourish. Modern industrial society is no cultural accident. It is the most efficient and productive system ever known. The industrial revolution is still with us because nothing can match it.

Is it true that the modern workplace replaced its predecessors because it was so much more efficient and productive? Economist Stephen Marglin has attempted to show that the case *cannot* be made that workplace organization evolved on the basis of efficiency and productivity. He has argued that key developments in early industrialization had almost nothing to do with productivity and efficiency. Instead, what industrialization and division of labor did was give the boss much greater control over the production process than he had previously had. And it was this increase in control, along with the opportunity for profit it provided, that was the point of industrialization.

Consider what has become perhaps the most famous, and most often quoted, historical example of industrial specialization and division of labor, the pin factory that was singled out for praise by Adam Smith. Smith describes the pin factory this way:

> One man draws out the wire, another straights it, a third cuts it, a fourth points it, a fifth grinds it at the top for receiving the head. . . . I have seen a small manufactory of this kind where ten men only were employed. . . . They could . . . make among them upwards of forty-eight thousand pins a day. . . . But if they had all wrought separately and independently, . . . they certainly could not each of them have made twenty.

Surely, there was an efficiency advantage in breaking pin production down into component tasks and in performing each of those tasks hundreds or even thousands of times before moving on to the next one. But there is no appreciable gain in efficiency by having each of these component tasks done by *different* people, by instituting what is called the "*social* division of labor." It may be that some tasks require so much skill that it is unreasonable to think that a single individual could become a master of all the components. In such cases, division of labor among people makes sense. But many, many tasks, from those performed in a "scientifically managed" factory to those performed in retail sales, to those performed in most service professions, do not require that degree of skill. In these cases, we cannot explain the *social* division of labor by appealing to efficiency.

Indeed, if anything, dividing a task among different people *decreases* efficiency, since the efforts of different people need to be coordinated by someone who could otherwise be directly involved in production. It is just this need for coordination that gives the boss the crucial and controlling hand in the production process. It is in his hands, and his hands alone, that the finished pin resides. And that fact, according to Marglin, was the real motivation for industrial development as we know it. It is interesting to note, in this regard, that in Japan and Germany, now widely regarded as the world's models of productive efficiency, there are roughly one-third as many managers per production worker as there are in the United States.

Furthermore, the social division of labor into minuscule components has another negative effect on efficiency; it is not conducive to innovation. It is the person with a view of the task as a whole who is most likely to have imaginative ideas about what a good innovation will be. Think about being faced with the task of designing an elephant mover. Do you consult the dozen blind men who happen to be surrounding the elephant, each manually exploring a different part, for advice about the best design? When people spend all their time engaged in a minute component of a large and complex production process, each is a metaphorical blind man when it comes to understanding the whole.

This point seems obvious. The more anyone knows about all aspects of an operation, the more likely she is to keep it afloat when things go wrong, or to design significant improvements in it. But few modern American factories are organized to take advantage of this obvious fact. Nor, for that matter, are most white-collar bureaucracies. They seem increasingly to operate on a "need to know" basis, jealously guarding information and meting it out as if it were gold, one speck at a time. Yet when people observe modern foreign industrial operations, which are increasingly organized to involve individual workers in larger and larger chunks of the production process, they marvel at the productivity and reliability of their methods and talk about bringing this new "industrial revolution" home to America.

Even Adam Smith, at the same time that he was extolling the efficiency of the division of labor, recognized that it had a dark side, a deadening effect on the capacity of workers to exercise judgment and intelligence:

> The man whose whole life is spent in performing a few simple operations . . . has no occasion to exert his understanding, or to exercise his invention. . . . He naturally loses, therefore, the habit of such exertion, and generally becomes as stupid and ignorant as it is possible for a human creature to become.

There is one final respect in which the minute social division of labor is inefficient. When work is organized in this way, it is deprived of almost all challenge, meaning, and significance. As a result, it is nothing but a job. If the sole point of a job is to get as much as possible for doing as little as possible, then people will be tempted to cut corners—to lie, to cheat, to steal, to break the law—in the service of increased profitability or decreased effort. Why not? There is nothing—no pride in craft and no social responsibility—to hold them back. And the temptation to cheat requires a host of (unproductive and inefficient) inspectors and regulators to make sure that quality is being preserved and that customers are being treated honestly and fairly. Some economists who are critical of the current character of workplace organization have estimated that as many as 34 million people in the American workforce are engaged in monitoring, supervising, and policing production workers who would rather not be doing what they do for a living. This amounts to about one policer for every 2.3 productive workers.

Why would anyone willingly submit to a life of work that is menial and deadening? Marglin points out that most early factory workers really had no effective choice. They were either country people who had been driven off their land, or paupers, or disbanded soldiers, or women and children who had been offered to the factory by their husbands and fathers. Eventually, the problem of inducing workers to put up with the conditions of the factory disappeared. As Marglin notes,

> Recruiting the first generation of factory workers was the key problem. For this generation's progeny the factory was part of the natural order, perhaps the only natural order. Once grown to maturity, fortified by the discipline of church and school, the next generation could be recruited to the factory with probably no greater difficulty than the sons of colliers are recruited to the mines or the sons of career soldiers to the army.

So it is that what for one generation is intolerable becomes for the next "only natural." So it is that ways of being that are forced upon people by the social and material circumstances in which they happen to live come to be viewed as "human nature"—eternal, inevitable, and unchangeable. The historical deskilling of work is another manifestation of what I referred to earlier as idea technology, or ideology. Once we realize that there is nothing inevitable about the character of work as we know it, we have to ask ourselves what work *should* be like, and how work *should* be organized.

What, then, is to be done? How can meaning and significance be restored to the work that people do? Turning back the clock is not an option. We can't go back to the days of independent house-holding family units. The large-scale technology of the modern workplace is here to stay. The genie is out of the bottle. If we are to reintroduce meaning and significance to work, we must do so within the structures of society that currently exist. But even within these constraints, there are significant possibilities for change.

MAKING WORK A CALLING

If the only point of your work is to make as much money as possible, whether for yourself as an employee or for the company as an employer, concerns about product or service quality, consumer sat-isfaction, consumer safety, and the like will fade into the back-ground. These aspects of your work will be relevant only to the extent that they contribute to profit. They will simply be means to an end. If you can find other means that are more effective, you will leave concern for customers and quality behind. When work comes to be defined or framed strictly in terms of the making of money, rather than the making of things, then sources of satisfaction with a job well done, a product well made, a customer well served erode. Those people who continue to care about the quality of what they do find themselves subverted by management decisions that sacrifice quality for profit. Under conditions like these, the only satisfaction that remains available to the worker is the satisfaction that comes from earning and consuming a large salary.

So the temptation to view work as a job must be eased. The way to do this is to reintroduce challenge, meaning, and significance into work—to reemphasize the service to the community that work can provide. Saying this is one thing; doing it is quite another. But there are steps that can be taken that would encourage people in all lines of work to behave like the stereo salesperson in my recurring fantasy.

Think about what happened to the banking industry. When I was a child, the local banker (whoever he might be) was regarded as a pillar of the community. He was a Citizen. He had the stature of an elected official. The place he worked in looked almost like a government building, replete as it was with marble floors and counters. The presumption was that the banker was responsible and responsive to us all. He could be counted on to pursue the best interests of the community he served. I remember thinking that if you spoke at all in the bank, it had to be in a whisper. The institution commanded respect, even awe.

Why was the banker so respected? Well, we gave him our life savings to look after. We entrusted him with knowledge about our financial circumstances that even family members didn't have. And he responded appropriately. He gave us the mortgage that allowed us to buy a home, first taking care that we did not pay more for the home than it was worth. He lent us money that allowed us to purchase inventory for the next season, or to expand our business, first taking care that our purchases were prudent and our expansion justified. He lent us money to plant that year's crops. And if things didn't go as planned, he did what he could to allow us to get over the hard times without having to give up the house, the business, or the farm. While he wouldn't extend credit indiscriminately, he could use his intimate knowledge of the character of the people with whom he dealt to ease the pressure when the circumstances and the people warranted it. The entire community depended on the discretion, the good judgment, and even the kindness of the banker. If the community prospered, his behavior had a lot to do with it.

What did the banker get out of this? He certainly made a good living, but he rarely got rich. Many of the people who depended on him made more money than he did. But getting rich wasn't the point, or at least not the sole point. On top of his income, the banker enjoyed the respect of the community. And on top of that, he could justly feel that he played a central part in keeping the community working—keeping businesses going, keeping people employed, keeping families together. It is not so hard to see the local banker regarding his work as a calling and deriving considerable satisfaction from a job well done apart from the money it put in his pocket.

Several different factors contributed to making this kind of banking possible. Banks were *community* institutions. They dealt with the same people day after day. The banker socialized with the same people he did business with. His kids and their kids went to school together. Even if he was inclined to be in banking only for the money, it's much more difficult to be ruthless with the people with whom you live your life than to be ruthless with strangers. In addition, a variety of government regulations essentially required banks to be community institutions. But the regulations by themselves would not have been sufficient. They were important because they set standards of conduct, and because they could be used to discipline and punish the occasional wayward bank executive. But had the *typical* and not just the occasional banker been inclined to violate or circumvent regulations, the system would have been helpless to stop such large-scale abuse.

So government standard setting together with community involvement and repeated interaction with the same customers helped make the banker of old something of a public servant. What about the banker of today? The virtually unregulated, long-distance, anonymous banking industry of the 1980s produced what is surely the greatest financial scandal in the history of the United States, if not the world. Banks opened overnight, made virtually unsecured loans to uncreditworthy people all over the world, offered absurdly high rates of interest to electronic depositors whose money was moved around in $100,000 lots by brokerage houses that got huge fees from each transaction. Banking became a casino game, and bankers became players. Banks either joined the game, or they went under. The community-oriented banker and the community-oriented bank disappeared. And now society must pick up the pieces.

There are several very detailed accounts of what went wrong with the banking industry in the last fifteen years or so, to which I have nothing to add. Instead, I want to focus on what may have been right about it before: small scale, community involvement, repeat customers, and a mission aside from making money. There are plenty of local businesses, of all types, that seek to serve rather than deceive customers. They do so partly because they know the people with whom they deal. Could you imagine picking up a piece of chicken that had fallen on the filthy floor, dusting it off, and serving it to your mother or your best friend? Could you imagine being careless about installing brakes in a new car if the car was going to be driven by your daughter? Well, it becomes similarly difficult to do such things to people you get to see every day and to know, people who come to depend on you for whatever good or service you provide. In my discussion of love, I talked about how family relations are being assimilated to the model of the market, with literal contracts replacing metaphorical ones. I suggested that we might all be better off if the reverse occurred, if market relations were assimilated to the model of the family. The repeated interactions between workers of all types and their regular customers is an approximation to the family model of doing business.

Can we afford it? Can shopkeepers afford to take the time to see to the well-being of their customers? Can they afford to pass up or discourage potential sales because they don't think the purchases will really serve their customers' interests? I think it depends on how they do the accounting. If customers realized how much they are cheated and exploited in the markets in which they are treated anonymously, they might be willing to pay the extra few cents that the local merchant requires for the personalized service he provides. If customers realized how much time they spend making sure they are not being taken advantage of, they might be willing to pay the extra few cents and place their trust in the local merchant. And if shopkeepers could count on customer loyalty, they might be able to stop wasting money on advertising and spend it instead to keep the place clean, keep the stock fresh, and serve their customers while keeping their prices down.

There is a model of the kind of retail setting in which the proprietors and the customers see themselves as on the same side. It is the consumer cooperative. In a consumer co-op, the customers *are* the proprietors. They own shares in the co-op, and any profits are either distributed to the shareholders or put back into the business. Employees in the co-op truly are there to serve the customers. Since the customers are the owners, no one is served by selling stale food, or by price gouging. Accomplishment is measured by finding good-quality products at reasonable prices, and by keeping customers as informed as possible about what they are buying.

The co-op does not require people of exceptional honesty. It does not require extensive government protection of consumers. It does not demand of each customer that she be an expert on nutrition, or drugs, or automobile repairs before she enters. Instead, it creates a structure in which people of ordinary honesty and sophistication can behave honestly, selling what they claim to sell and getting what they pay for, because buyers and sellers are not engaged in a competitive, zero-sum game. Buyers and sellers can both come out winners.

A similar kind of structure can make for dramatic changes on the production side of business as well. In company after company, management control has shifted out of the hands of people who know about production and into the hands of people who know about finance. The result has been a shift in company mission—from making things to making money. When making money becomes a company's sole mission, concerns about the product fade. You make it well only if your advertising department can't find a way to sell it when it's made poorly.

When the company's sole mission is to make money, the work of the people who make the product is slowly but surely degraded. When workers see their efforts to make quality products subverted, diligence, initiative, creativity, and care on the shop floor are undermined. If the company is in it only for the money and the boss is in it only for the money, what can we expect of the people who actually make the product?

Putting control of companies back in the hands of people who know about production is a step toward reintroducing concerns about quality to the workplace. But it's too small a step. It still leaves the problem of a workforce whose intelligence and talent are underutilized, and whose ability is not respected. More is required. People on the shop floor need to become involved at all levels of production. They need to feel that the product they are making is *their* product. If they are given the opportunity to use their talent and intelligence on the job, they will start getting more out of their work than just a paycheck. When they can legitimately take responsibility for a product well made, a job well done, they will begin to care that the product is well made. And, as a result, well-made products will become more common than they now are—without extensive government regulation or plant supervision.

Steps along these lines have been taken in various forms of producer cooperatives. What producer cooperatives have in common is that they give the workers a stake in the company. But there are many different ways to do this, and not all of them will be equally effective in changing the character and quality of the work that is done. Least effective is the approach that gives workers the opportunity to share in the profits, either through cash bonuses or through the award of company stock. Under arrangements like this, the more money a company makes, the more money the workers make. But nothing about what the workers do and how they do it is affected. Managers still make all the decisions, and the talents of workers continue to be underutilized. Meaningless work may be more tolerable if, when the company prospers, you prosper, but if the company's prosperity is not tied to the quality of its products, an incentive system like this is not going to produce better-quality products. The interests of the workers, like those of any other shareholders, will be tied to profit, not to production.

Far more powerful is an arrangement in which workers take on a significant share of decision making, quality control, and supervision. They sit on the board of directors, participate in long-range planning, and contribute to decisions about how their work should be organized and executed, and what standards it should meet. In the limiting case, in which the company is wholly owned by the workers (a true producers' cooperative), they don't merely sit on the board; they make up the board. But even when the company continues to be owned by the shareholders, and continues to have a level of senior management that is removed from the shop floor, workers can be given a fair measure of control over what they do.

How do companies that are partly or entirely run by workers fare? How does breaking the barrier between labor and management affect product quality and company profitability? There is no universal agreement on the answers to these questions. Some worker-managed firms fail; others succeed. In some worker-managed firms, product quality is not enhanced; in others it is. In some worker-managed firms, worker satisfaction does not go up; in others it does. So the turning of control over to the workers is no guarantee of anything. It has to be done right, and what it means to do it right may vary from case to case. But when it is done right, worker engagement and satisfaction rise dramatically, and so does the quality of what is produced. And it is becoming increasingly clear that, worker satisfaction aside, some kind of worker participation in the running of companies is essential if American industry is to be successful in an increasingly competitive global economy. As one group of commentators on the current world economic scene put it, it is vital to the well-being of the American economy that employers "replace the iron fist with the sustained handshake, improving economic performance by giving workers a stake in their enterprises and economy rather than clubbing them into submission."

It is unlikely that producer cooperatives can achieve the same results that consumer cooperatives do. In consumer cooperatives, the adversarial relation between buyer and seller vanishes; both are after the same thing. In producer cooperatives, this isn't true. Especially when workers share in company profits, their financial interests are served by selling as much of the product as possible for as big a profit as possible. However, what producer cooperatives can do is introduce interests to the workforce in addition to financial ones. Having responsibility for the product, and the opportunity to make it well, encourages workers to care not just about how much they make but about how they make it.

So restructuring the way in which commercial activity occurs— both the making and the selling of goods—can go a long way toward bringing challenge, meaning, and significance back to work. It can increase the satisfaction that people get out of making the things they make, which in turn will increase the satisfaction that people get out of buying the things they buy. It just isn't true that "business is business," nor is it true that work is inherently dissatisfying. Business can be the ruthless pursuit of self-interest, or it can be in the service of the public interest. Were it to become the latter, everyone would be better off. Work can be meaningless and alienating, or it can be meaningful and involving. And were it to become the latter, everyone would be better off.

But we have to be realistic. We should heed Marglin's warning about how quickly people can come to view meaningless, alienating work as the natural order of things. Undoing this perception will be a laborious and time-consuming process. It should probably begin not in the workplace but in the school, the institution in which we get our first instruction about the nature and meaning of work. So let us turn to the school and see what it is teaching our children about what work is for and what work is like.

9

THE DEBASING OF EDUCATION: TURNING PLAY INTO WORK

When one of my daughters was about three years old, our family set off on a long drive to a house we had rented for our summer vacation. While my wife and I chatted in the front seat of the car, our daughter was amusing herself in the backseat singing songs. We recognized them from the "Sesame Street" show, but we weren't really listening. Before long, though, the singing drifted into something that was unfamiliar, and my wife and I stopped talking and listened. Our daughter was making up a song of her own. When she finished, we turned to her, beaming, and told her how wonderful her song was. She smiled happily and sang it again. We enthused again. She sang it again. We enthused again. She sang it again. We enthused again. Then she politely asked us to go back to talking to each other so she could have fun. So we went back to ignoring her, and she went back to making up songs.

· ·

Most of the residents of my community teach their kids from a very early age to value education and take it seriously. Many of the kids are reading early, even before kindergarten, and those who aren't reading by then are being read to constantly. Whatever problems the elementary school teachers may have in running their classes, motivating the kids to read and to learn is not one of them. One year, a long-term substitute teacher came to the school to teach fourth-graders. Her previous experience had been at a school in which developing discipline and willingness to do schoolwork had been a major challenge. She introduced to our school a technique that had been quite effective in her previous one. Every time one of her students read a book, he or she would get a point. By accumulating a certain number of points, the kids could win prizes. And whichever kid accumulated the most points would win a grand prize. The results of this procedure were amazing. The kids were reading like demons. Some were reading more than a book a day. I learned this from a neighbor, whose daughter was in the class. When I told her how impressed I was, she told me that things were not as impressive as they seemed. Her daughter, who had already been a pretty voracious reader, was now choosing books to read on the basis of two criteria: how long they were—the shorter, the better—and how big the print was—the bigger, the better. And she seemed unable to remember what was in the books almost immediately after she finished them. She was certainly reading an enormous amount, but the only point to her reading seemed to be to get to the end of one book so that she could start another.

•   •

Several years ago, a team of psychologists conducted an experiment with nursery school children. They gave the children an opportunity to draw with special felt-tipped drawing pens, an activity about which the kids were extremely enthusiastic. After a period of observation, in which the psychologists measured the amount of time the children spent drawing with the pens, the children were taken into a separate room, given the pens, and asked to draw pictures. Some of the children were told they might receive "Good Player" awards for their drawings; others were not. A week later, back in the regular nursery school setting, the drawing pens were again made available, this time with no promise of any award. The children who had received awards previously were *less* likely than the others to draw with the pens at all. And if they did draw, they spent less time at it than other children and drew pictures that were judged to be less complex, interesting, and creative. Without the prospect of further awards, their interest in drawing was now only perfunctory.

Three stories. Two anecdotes and an experiment. They converge on the same point. Young children are intensely interested, active, and inventive. They derive enormous pleasure from learning and doing. They love to make up little songs, to draw pictures, to read. They love to experiment with their world and to develop mastery over it. They are curious about everything. Learning and doing are their own reward. No external incentives are required.

And yet, when external incentives are introduced—whether attention and praise from parents, prizes from teachers, or "Good Player" awards from experimenters—these external incentives exert a substantial influence on the activities that produce them. Instead of singing songs for the sake of the songs themselves, kids may come to sing songs for the praise it gets them. Or they read books not to find out about the world but to win prizes. Kids will produce for rewards, but the quality of their activity and their interest in it will be dramatically altered. Spontaneity, exploration, and inventiveness will be replaced by mechanical, perfunctory efficiency. And if the external incentives are removed, the activities may cease all together. The introduction of external incentives may succeed in turning play into work—into the most limited kind of work.

This chapter is about how, with the help of pressure from the market, we have turned play—the excitement of education—into work. It's about the instrumentalization of education. It's about how five-year-old kids who enter school full of enthusiasm and alive to everything get turned into bored adolescents who would rather be anywhere than where they are. It's about how various efforts to prop up motivation to learn by introducing external incentives—rewards and punishments of various kinds—actually make the motivation problem worse. It's about how the dependence on external incentives, established early in the grade school years, carries all the way through the educational process. It's about how kids who start out their education seeking knowledge move from seeking knowledge to seeking approval and, from there, to seeking good grades, to seeking admission to good colleges, and to seeking good jobs. And finally, it's about how the instrumentalization of education affects not only the *process* of education but its *product*, making many of the best things about education increasingly difficult to achieve.

THE "GOODS" OF EDUCATION

What are the goods of education? Why is it valuable? First, we look toward education as job training. We try to persuade adolescents not to drop out of school, so that they will be able to get decent jobs. Hence we teach them to read and write, to add and subtract, to type, to work in machine shops, and to fix cars. But we also teach children history, literature, foreign languages, art, music, politics, philosophy, physics, and chemistry. Why? These aspects of the modern curriculum go beyond simply job training.

So a second value of education is that it contributes to understanding—of the physical world, of societies, of ourselves. And we value understanding both for its own sake and because it is empowering. Ever since the eighteenth-century Enlightenment, our culture has been dominated by the view that knowledge is power, that the world and human life can be improved if we understand how things work, how people behave. Change—whether in our own lives or in the larger society—is possible only through understanding how things came to be the way they are. So we teach the natural sciences in order that we will understand how nature works, and be able to harness it and improve it—in effect, bend it our way. We teach history, literature, philosophy, art, and foreign cultures and languages to understand who and what we are, how we came to be that way, and how we both resemble and differ from others. The understanding of society, like the understanding of nature, enables people to improve it.

We also teach these subjects for another reason. We teach history, literature, philosophy, and culture so that we will understand, appreciate, and conserve what is good. In order to care about conserving what is good, you must learn that it *is* good. You must learn to value what those around you value. It may seem obvious, for example, that a democratic political system is good. But what makes it so obvious? Democracy takes a lot of work, and it is extremely inefficient. Without having been taught what is valuable about democracy, we might be tempted to trade some of it for efficiency, especially when times are hard and things must get done. When we teach people about democracy and about some of its historical alternatives, we are teaching them why it is valuable. We are also teaching them what they must do as citizens—to work hard, to stay informed, to deal with inefficiencies—in order to preserve and protect it.

Indeed, it is in a democratic culture that education is especially important. The commitment of a democracy to let the people decide how their society should be run demands an informed public. If the people are ignorant, they will make bad decisions. If the people know only about the narrow set of issues that come up in their daily lives, they will be tempted to leave decisions about other matters to the "experts." The more they do this, the less democratic their society will be. Think, for example, about how you would go about deciding whether to vote for a political candidate who wanted to build nuclear power plants in order to reduce our dependence on foreign oil, or enact strong antipollution measures to protect the ozone layer, or decrease the minimum wage to lower unemployment, or put money into programs that taught kids how to read in preschools. You would want to know whether nuclear power plants were safe enough, whether the ozone layer was really threatened, whether a minimum wage actually caused unemployment, and whether kids could profit from reading instruction at such a young age. If you had the knowledge and intellectual resources to figure these things out for yourself, you could remain a political decision maker. If not, you would be forced to give up your responsibility to the experts. And as more and more of the political decisions people face involve assessments of complex, technical issues, giving up control to the experts will entail giving up more and more democratic participation.

Finally, the things we teach in school are guided by two other objectives. We hope that we are teaching our students how to learn, so that as new things arise in the rapidly changing world, they will be equipped intellectually to keep up, long after they have left school. And we hope that we are teaching our students that learning is fun—that it is enormously satisfying to be curious about the world and to feed that curiosity regularly throughout your life.

If our educational system produces people—and, in a democracy, *all* people—who are intellectually skilled, curious, and socially responsible, we will have produced an active and alive political and technological culture, in which new ideas and possibilities abound. And we will have produced people who can get good jobs as well.

We come, then, to the key question. Does education work? Do we succeed in producing such people? Many would say no, and for various reasons. If we read enough popular books, magazine articles, and reports from government commissions and private foundations, we cannot help seeing that every aspect of the educational system comes in for substantial criticism. Incompetent or uninterested teachers, unmotivated students, uninvolved parents, undemanding curricula, unnecessary and constraining administrators—all are viewed as part of the problem. Most of the various criticisms of contemporary education that focus on one or another of these factors contain a piece of the truth. But in criticizing uncommitted teachers or undisciplined students, they tend to miss a crucial causal factor that underlies many of the problems they do discuss—the penetration of contemporary education by the ideology of the market. It is on this factor—the instrumentalization of education—that I will focus. It is illustrated by the examples with which this chapter began. My reason for this focus is that, paradoxically, many of the remedies that are now being proposed for problems of teacher competence and motivation, student motivation, absence of standards, and the like promise to make education even more instrumental than it already is. And by doing so, by turning play into work, they will create problems that are just as severe as the ones they are trying to solve.

TEACHERS AND THE MARKET

Let's begin with teachers. The claim of many critics of education is that children don't learn what they should in school, because teachers are either untalented or unmotivated, or both. Standards are lax because it is easier to let children move through the system than to struggle to make sure that they learn what they should at every step of the process. Suppose this claim is true. How do you go about getting more talented people to go into teaching, keeping them interested in their work, and holding their performance accountable to reasonable standards? Most of the measures that have been proposed are predicated on the idea that teaching is a job, or maybe a career, but certainly not a calling. That is, the presumption is that people teach in order to get the salary and benefits that teaching provides. To get better teachers, we need to offer better salary and benefits. To keep teachers motivated, we need a set of incentives—bonuses of various sorts, or opportunities for advancement—that are contingent on the performance of their pupils. And to make sure that reasonably stringent standards are being maintained, we need close and careful monitoring, largely through standardized tests, of what the children are actually learning. In other words, to get good people into teaching, make it pay to be a teacher. To keep good people involved, make it pay to be a *good* teacher. And to prevent standards from slipping, make it cost if student performance slips.

The logic of these kinds of recommendations is straightforward. It's the same logic that guides our approach to transactions on the market. Right now, too many talented people are becoming lawyers and not enough are becoming teachers. Why? Because lawyers earn several times what teachers earn. If we reduce the earnings discrepancy between the two occupations, some potential lawyers will become teachers instead. And it isn't just the money; it's also the prestige that comes along with the money. Though we claim to value education enormously as a society, we don't think much of the people who provide it. "Those that can, do; those that can't, teach," the saying goes. We ask ourselves why anyone who is really good would settle for the salary and status that comes with teaching instead of something else? And this suspicion about the talents of those who enter teaching is reinforced by patterns of career choice among college students. It is rare to find students at the top of the class preparing for careers in education. Much more commonly, it's the C students who do it.

It's probably true that teaching is not attracting the best people, because of the relatively low salaries that teachers earn. But the explanation is more complex than a market orientation would suggest. Teachers have never been paid high salaries. Indeed, they probably do better now in comparison with other, similarly trained people than they ever have before. Nevertheless, a few generations ago, teachers were deeply respected by society despite their low salaries. Two things have happened in recent years to make the combination of low salary and high status virtually disappear from the social landscape. The first is the growth of economic imperialism. Values and standards that were internal to certain social practices and institutions and unique to them have slowly been replaced by external economic standards that are meant to be common to all practices. Increasingly, we have come to use the amount of money society is willing to pay people as the primary indication of the value society places on what those people do. Well, there goes the value of teaching.

Ironically, a second factor is the growth of modern feminism. For much of our history, the majority of teachers were women. Teaching was one of the few professions that was open to women. Teaching also afforded a short school day and a summer vacation, both of which left time for raising children. Women could be paid less than they were worth because they would willingly sacrifice some salary for the other benefits that teaching afforded, and because women were paid less than they were worth in all domains anyway. But they were talented and enthusiastic, and society respected and admired them. Their low salary was not equated with their social worth. Modern feminism has successfully opened up many other professions for women, where they receive both respect and higher salaries than those of teachers. So education has lost many of its best and most dedicated teachers.

Many suggest that we try to get better teachers by offering better salaries, and a handful of communities have done this. For most, though, there simply isn't enough money. While token increases in salary might be possible, substantial increases—of the kind that might make the financial returns for teaching comparable to the alternatives—are just not in the cards. Perhaps this is a lucky break. Perhaps paying teachers more is not the way to get better teachers. We have to pay teachers enough that they and their families will not be deprived of access to the most important things in life. But salary increases beyond this might only succeed in attracting those people who are interested primarily in money. It does not guarantee getting any more people who regard teaching as a calling—who believe they are performing a service of enormous social value and who derive their principal reward from performing that service well. To get, and to keep, people like this requires not increases in salary but improvements in the conditions under which teachers work so that they can freely exercise their intelligence, creativity, and judgment in the service of the goals—all the goals—of education.

And in this domain, education is moving in precisely the wrong direction. It is subjecting itself to the rules of the market. In the name of maintaining standards and holding teachers accountable for the success or failure of their students, the last few years have seen public education in America embark on a frenzied program of standardized testing. Virtually every recent effort for educational reform has had a substantial testing program at its core. The people who pay the bills, and the legislators they elect, are demanding a good "product." And the quality of the product is usually assessed by measuring how local schools stack up against the national average in this or that subject, as measured by this or that standardized test. It is estimated that more than fifty million standardized tests of basic competency are administered to students each year in the United States. More than half the states now require students to pass stan-dardized tests to graduate from high school, a number that is double what it was only five years ago. And in some areas the fate of teachers is in the hands of students as they take the tests. Salary increases, and even continued employment, depend on how well the students do.

It is certainly important to have a means of assessing how effective an educational program is. And it is certainly reasonable to expect individual teachers to take some responsibility for the performance of the students in their classes. The trouble is that assessments of student performance are helpful only in the hands of dedicated teachers. They don't succeed in *making* teachers dedicated; and in the hands of the wrong kinds of teachers, standardized assessments can be a disaster.

Let's look at an example. For years, New York has depended on statewide exams, given in all the major high school subjects, to ensure a certain degree of commonality of curriculum across the state. Students can get a high school diploma without passing all the exams given in each subject at the end of the year, but they get a special diploma if they pass the exams. Passing the exams and getting the special diploma are testimony that a student has met the state's rather high standards of competency.

I had a high school chemistry course that was a joke. I mean this quite literally; the teacher came into class each day and provided us with an extended, often riotous monologue, which only occasionally had anything to do with chemistry. Neither I nor any of my classmates were troubled by this. The class was fun, and the exams were tailored to cover the very little bit of chemistry that we had actually learned. So we were quite satisfied. But then, as spring came, we began to realize that we would soon be facing a state exam. And the people who made up the exam were unlikely to know or care about our chemistry teacher's jokes. Exam day drew nearer, and still we were learning almost no chemistry. About a week before the exam, the teacher started filling all the blackboards in the room with notes. Memorize this stuff, he was telling us, and you'll pass the exam. He had seen state exams many times before, and each year's edition was more or less like the previous year's. So I did a week's worth of memorizing, learned no chemistry, got a B+ on the exam, and went on to my next year of science.

What my chemistry teacher did was, of course, appalling. Standardized tests, given over a three-hour period, can't possibly measure everything a student has learned in a full year. Instead, the tests ask about a representative sample of the material that should have been covered. The assumption that underlies such a test is that since the test is representative of the class material as a whole, the more students have learned of the material, the better they will do on the tests. The tests are meant to be not an exhaustive measure of what was learned but an *index* of what was learned.

My chemistry teacher subverted the rationale and the legitimacy of the test by teaching us what he thought would be on it, and nothing more. In the case of my class, our performance on the test was not an *index* of what we knew—it was *all* we knew. Any reasonably clever teacher who worries that his or her future salary and employment depend on how well students do on these tests can tailor what goes on in the classroom to fit what is usually on the tests. Student performance on the tests may keep getting better and better, while students are actually learning less and less. If we thought that, in general, the answers to standardized test questions were becoming all that students learned in the course of a school year, we would abandon them altogether as a yardstick for assessing the performance of teachers and their students. But if a teacher regards his work as a job, what will stop him from doing precisely what my chemistry teacher did? In the case of teachers who take their work seriously, we don't have to worry about subverting tests. But in the case of these kinds of committed teachers, we probably don't have to worry too much about how well their students are doing in the first place.

My chemistry teacher was not unique. Consider the work of a watchdog group known as Friends for Education. Its founder, a physician named John Cannell, was struck a few years ago when he heard a report from the State Department of Education in West Virginia that their children had performed above the national average on standardized reading tests. Since West Virginia has one of the highest illiteracy rates in the United States, Cannell began to wonder whether there was any state that performed below the national average. So he did some research, and he was unable to discover a single state that ranked below average. This essentially impossible statistic came to be known as the Lake Wobegon Effect, after humorist Garrison Keillor's mythical Minnesota town where "the women are strong, the men are good looking, and all the children are above average."

Cannell and his associates probed further, and they discovered that 83 percent of all elementary school districts and 73 percent of all secondary school districts reported test scores that were above national averages. In effect, it was my chemistry teacher multiplied a thousandfold. Not only were teachers teaching just what was on the tests, but they were also offering monetary rewards to the highest scorers. They were also engaging in out-and-out cheating, by giving students extra time and altering their answers. In some cases, teachers would spend the morning teaching the *actual* test—not previous years' versions but the *current* version—and the afternoon administering it. Obviously, maintaining standards and accountability with this sort of "bottom line" orientation makes the problems of education worse, not better.

To make it clearer exactly what's wrong with teaching the tests instead of the subject, I need to discuss the logic that underlies such tests. As I said above, good performance on standardized tests is meant to be an index of educational achievement. It is not the achievement itself. Tests are constructed that are representative of the material being tested, on the assumption that the better a student knows the material in general, the more likely he or she will be to know the particular things that are asked on the test. It is this assumption that allows us to make inferences about years of schooling on the basis of a few hours with a test booklet, a pencil, and an answer sheet.

An assumption like this is probably not unreasonable, *as long as children are not being specifically trained to answer test items.* If they are indeed being taught to take the tests, then the assumption becomes very suspect. One could imagine drilling children to memorize the answers to the hundred questions that will appear on the test, and teaching them nothing else. Such children would know the answer to 24 + 12 and 42 − 21, but not 24 + 11 or 42 − 20. Children "educated" in this way would score way above average on tests of educational achievement, but be hardly better educated than their pet golden retrievers.

With education under attack, and communities insisting on quality control and financial accountability in their schools, administrators know that heads will roll if evidence appears that their schools are not doing the job. Pressure on administrators is transferred onto the teaching staff, and before long children are being taught how to take tests. Perhaps in the course of learning how to take tests, children will also learn some of the skills that the tests are designed to measure. But even if they don't, teachers and administrators will be able to wear good test results as armor against the slings and arrows of their communities.

And once a few communities start teaching children how to take tests, others must follow suit, in self-defense. It may look bad that, say, 70 percent of all elementary school kids in a given community score below grade level on an achievement test. But it won't look nearly so bad for local personnel if these low scores are occurring everywhere. It is one thing to find out that Washington, D.C., test scores are low. It is quite another to find out that they are *lower* than test scores in New York, Los Angeles, Philadelphia, Chicago, and Detroit. And so, before long, kids are being taught to take tests everywhere, and we face a situation in which 90 percent of all American children are above average—at the same time that thousands are graduating from high school as virtual illiterates.

School administrators and teachers are not the only ones who are teaching kids the tests. Parents have joined in with college entrance exams, the Scholastic Aptitude Tests, or SATs. They regularly enroll their high schoolers in very expensive SAT preparation courses. In effect, these courses teach kids only how to take the tests, and they can improve scores by more than 100 points, often enough to make the difference between acceptance and rejection at many selective colleges and universities. And once a few students take these courses, others feel compelled to take them also, again in self-defense.

This rash of SAT prep courses has created quite a problem for college admissions offices. When they look at a score of, say, 1200, they don't know whether it's a real index of college aptitude (to the extent that even "pure" SAT scores are indices of college aptitude) or merely an index of how much time and money the student's family spent on training for the SATs. As a result, colleges have been giving SAT scores less and less weight in their admissions decisions. Ironically, the lesson here is that if you don't approve of standardized tests, the best way to undermine them is to teach your kids how to take them.

Accountability in education is important, and standardized tests can provide useful information. But the intentions and goals of teachers matters. The effectiveness of standardized tests depends upon a dedicated teaching force that will use tests appropriately to guide what it does in the classroom. Testing will not root out bad and unprincipled teachers. They will find ways to use the tests to their own advantage. So testing programs may have the perverse effect of making the bad teachers look good and the good ones look bad. If untalented or unmotivated teachers are indeed a significant source of the problem with contemporary education, testing does not appear to be the way to solve it.

Teaching kids how to take tests is not the only way to improve test scores. We can also do it by teaching kids the skills that the tests are designed to measure, that is, teaching them what they are supposed to be taught. But this strategy involves something of a risk. It is ever so much more difficult and time consuming to teach real skills. It takes patience on the part of teachers and commitment on the part of students. It may even take some cooperation from parents and communities. So teaching the test is a kind of insurance policy. It is insurance against lack of dedication and resolve on the part of all the relevant parties. Of course, in the long term, such an insurance policy is a sham. Scoring well on tests doesn't serve the kids, or anybody else, once school is behind them. It protects educators from criticism or dismissal, and it protects communities from having to commit significant additional resources to education. But it serves no one else.

STUDENTS, MOTIVATION, AND THE MARKET

While some critics of modern education focus on the teachers, others focus on what they see as unmotivated students. But do students really lack motivation? There are two ways to tackle the problem of student motivation. One is to look for things that are *intrinsic* to the tasks at hand that will generate and sustain interest, enthusiasm, and commitment—that is, to make the work children do interesting and important to them without the prodding of the teacher. The other way is to look for things that are *extrinsic* to the tasks at hand that will keep kids attentive and involved. A system of rewards for good work and punishments for bad work is the most obvious example of this sort of approach. The incentives may be honors and awards, attention and approval from teachers, good and bad grades, special privileges, and even material things like money, or toys, or candy. Because these rewards and punishments are extrinsic, that is, because they bear no special relation to the tasks that children are actually being asked to perform, they can be almost anything.

The examples that began this chapter were about the difference between extrinsic and intrinsic incentives. My daughter was simply having fun learning to "compose" new songs. Our rewarding comments were a distraction; they put a damper on her fun. The fourth-grade kids read more when they competed for points, but they remembered little of what they read, and read less when not rewarded. Reading became work for hire. These examples suggest that while learning isn't always work, and doesn't have to be work, a system of extrinsic incentives can turn learning into work. If this suggestion is correct, relying on a system of external incentives to increase student motivation may be a mistake. Let us, then, examine this suggestion more carefully.

It's hard to find a very young child for whom learning is work. Little kids are extremely curious. They try to do things that they've never done before, things that the people around them are doing. They invent new ways to play with old toys. They invent ways to turn pots and pans and large cardboard boxes into an afternoon of fun. They learn an enormous amount every day, and each new bit of knowledge, each new skill, each new sign of mastery of the world, is a source of intense delight. Most kindergarten and first-grade teachers will tell you that motivating little kids to participate in school activities is not a problem. The problem, if anything, is to restrain their enthusiasm, so that large groups of kids can learn the same things together.

As schooling proceeds, much of this early energy and enthusiasm disappears. It's possible that the waning of enthusiasm has nothing to do with what happens in the schools themselves, but instead is the result of developmental changes that all kids go through. It's possible, in other words, that "natural" curiosity and enthusiasm for learning just diminishes as kids get older. Possible, but I think unlikely. Children who come to regard school as a boring, irrelevant chore somehow become alert, inventive, and intellectually alive in the streets after school. I believe that what goes on in school makes a substantial contribution to the motivation problem. Children are taught in school that learning is work, not play, and they are further taught that the kind of learning that does go on in school—book learning—is reserved exclusively *for* school. Kids learn that there's school and there's life, and what goes on in one place has nothing to do with what goes on in the other. So if you learn from books in school, that's the only place you learn from books. If I'm right, then at the same time our schools are teaching kids the basic skills and facts that will be the building blocks of all future learning, they are also teaching them that learning stops, and fun begins, when the school doors close at three.

A growing body of psychological research illustrates what I think is going on in schools. In a typical example, adult subjects are asked to participate in an experiment that requires them to solve various imaginative and engaging puzzles. Many of them like solving this type of puzzle. So they're looking forward to participating in the experiment. The experimenter sits the subjects down and explains that they will be paid five dollars for each puzzle they solve. Then the subjects dig into the puzzles. Afterward, the experimenter returns. The subjects are asked to fill out a form that inquires, among other things, about how much they liked participating in the task. They are also given several additional puzzles and told to feel free to work on them while they are waiting for the experimenter to return.

What researchers have found in experiments like this is that, in comparison with other people who did the same task but were not paid five dollars for each puzzle, the people who were paid reported that they liked the task less. In addition, they were less likely to work on any of the extra puzzles while they were waiting. The payoff seems to have communicated to them that this activity, which they thought they enjoyed, wasn't really fun after all. "People get paid only for work, not for play," they seem to be saying to themselves. "So this task must have been work."

And other experiments have shown that in addition to having an adverse effect on people's *motivation* to engage in puzzle-solving tasks, payoffs also adversely affect how people perform the tasks. For example, another experimenter asked college students to try to discover the rules that determined whether or not they would score points in a simple computer game. The students could get information about the rules of the game by playing it themselves and observing what happened. The best way to set about trying to discover the rules of a game like this is to vary how you play it from one time to the next, just as an experimental scientist discovers the "rules" of nature's "games" by varying the conditions from one experiment to the next. If you happen to find one way to get points, and then repeat it over and over again, you'll never be able to discover *all* the ways of getting points. Most of the students in the experiments understood this and varied what they did in systematic fashion from one game to the next. But students who were paid money on the basis of the number of points they collected tended to repeat what had worked in the past rather than varying their behavior in an intelligent and systematic fashion. Having found *a* way to get points and make money, they were less inclined to deviate than were those students who could not get money for points. Again, we have a task that is of intrinsic interest turned into work for hire, with a resulting drop in the quality of the performance.

This effect observed in a laboratory is not limited to artificial games in artificial settings. Think, for example, about what you would do if you wanted to learn how to bake bread. You might find a recipe, and follow it carefully, step-by-step. Suppose you did this, and the bread turned out delicious. If all you cared about was *a* way to make good bread, your troubles would be over; you would simply follow this recipe whenever the need for bread arose. (Similarly, if all that someone playing the computer game cared about was finding *a* way to get points, once she found one way, she might never deviate from it.) But suppose you wanted to know more than *a* way to make good bread. Suppose you wanted to make different kinds of bread. Or suppose you wanted to discover the most efficient way to make good bread. Now what you would have to know is the essentials of good bread baking, what is *necessary* to make good bread— the rules, as it were, of bread baking. And as in the case of the computer game, this requires careful and systematic variation or experimentation. Steps in the recipe are omitted, combined, reordered; different kinds of flour or shortening are substituted. To engage in this program of experimentation, you must be willing to tolerate occasional or even frequent bad outcomes. That is, sometimes the bread you bake when you vary the recipe will be inferior, even inedible. But ultimately, by varying what you do in this systematic way, you can improve your bread-baking. You might be quite willing to experiment with your bread-baking techniques at times when a bad outcome won't matter much—when, for example, the only people eating it will be family members. What you learn from your mistakes will make up for the inferior outcomes. However, when you are baking for casual acquaintances who are coming to dinner, the outcome is too important for you to risk experimentation. In other words, when outcomes loom large, experimentation is inhibited. So it would be with our hypothetical bread baker, so it was with the students in the experiments, and so it is when people face the choice between playing it safe and risking innovation in the classroom, the boardroom, the shop floor, or the laboratory bench.

When extrinsic incentives are used in the classroom, they may

have both of the adverse effects I just described. They may undermine motivation to learn, by teaching children that what they
thought was play is actually work. And they may interfere with imaginative problem solving, by teaching children to be safe and repeat
only solutions that have worked in the past. And much that goes on
during the typical school day contributes to both of these effects.
From about the third grade on, the school day is very much driven
by the rhythm of tests and grades. Weekly spelling tests, math tests,
science tests, social studies tests; interim reports sent home to parents, official report cards, honor rolls—before long, students learn
that you work to do well on tests and get good grades. You study for
tests, and only for tests. You study only the material that will be on
tests. You try to "psych out" the teacher, guessing at what he usually
asks, and learn just that material. And you try to get by by doing as
little work as possible.

Several years ago, to examine how malleable this motivational
effect is, I did a little experiment in a class I was teaching. At the
first class meeting, I read off the names of the students and then
held up a final grade sheet, the thing we normally turn in at the end
of a course. Next to each name was a B. I told them that if they
chose to stay in this class, all of them would get a B, no matter what
they did. There would be regular reading assignments, exams, and
even term papers, and the exams and papers would be evaluated,
but none of the evaluations would affect their final grade in the
course. They could walk out of the class right then, never appear
again, and still get B's in the course. A few students protested: "Why
a B and not an A?" One or two dropped the course. One stood up,
asked me if I was serious, and when I said yes, he thanked me very
much for the B and left, never to be seen by me again. But most
were enthusiastic. For the moment, they appreciated being treated
as serious, committed students.

For the first several weeks of the course, all went well. Everyone
came to class—prepared. But as the students experienced the
demands of other classes (midterm exams and papers), their work in
my class dropped off. More and more students skipped class, and
those who came were less well prepared. As the course drew to a
close, only a handful of the original forty students were still participating. Only two of them turned in their required final paper. The

experiment was clearly a failure. These students and I discovered that they had become so dependent on exams and grades to provide them with motivation to do their work that when these external incentives were removed, they were left with a motivational vacuum. And these were students who were as dedicated as any college students in the country.

None of this discussion is meant to suggest that we should not have tests in school. Tests provide an extremely important source of feedback—of information—to the teacher and the student about how things are going. Tests, or something like them, often offer the best way to diagnose problems and correct them. So tests as a source of *information* are good and important. The problem is that in addition to providing information, tests provide outcomes that students, and their parents, and their teachers, want and like—outcomes like approval, prizes, awards, honors, and special privileges. The hedonic character of these outcomes is what gets students to orient their work to passing the tests, and to regard what they do in the classroom as merely instrumental, as merely a means to various rewarding ends. In the computer game experiment, the points students won were an important source of information. Without points, they could never have discovered the rules of the game. But they got just as much information about the rules of the game on those occasions on which they didn't get points as on those on which they did. Informationally, getting points and not getting them were essentially equivalent. The problem came when getting points earned the students money. This added a hedonic dimension to the informative one, which in turn made it so that getting points and not getting them were no longer equivalent.

To see the difference between the informative and hedonic aspects of feedback (like grades on tests), imagine having to choose between two tennis instructors. One of them is a source of lots of positive feedback; no matter how you swing the racket, no matter how you hit the ball, he's always patting you on the back, encouraging you, telling you you're getting better and better. The other is brutally honest; he tells you when you do something right, and he tells you when you do something wrong. Ask yourself which of these instructors will leave you feeling better after a lesson, and ask yourself which of these instructors is more likely to improve your game.

The answers to these two questions are probably different. If people care about tests because they want to get A's, and not because they want to learn from what they're doing wrong, tests come to distort and impair learning rather than enhance it.

That there are important differences between children oriented to getting A's and children oriented to learning from their mistakes has been documented by psychologist Carol Dweck and her associates. They have spent more than a decade studying the incentive systems that govern the learning of children throughout the educational process. They have uncovered two fundamentally different approaches to learning in kids that can often lead to profound differences in how well kids learn. Dweck has suggested that we can distinguish among kids on the basis of the goals that seem to be operating while they learn. One group of kids has what she has called *performance goals*; the other group has what she has called *mastery goals*. Children with performance goals are primarily interested in gaining favorable judgments of their competence. They want to do well on tests. They want social approval. They want awards. Children with mastery goals are primarily interested in increasing their competence rather than in demonstrating it. They want to encounter things that they can't do and to learn from their failures. As Dweck puts it, performance-oriented children want to *prove* their ability, while mastery-oriented children want to *improve* their ability.

Children with performance goals avoid challenges. They prefer tasks that are well within the range of their ability. Children with mastery goals seek challenges. They prefer tasks that strain the limits of their ability. Children with performance goals respond to failure by giving up. Children with mastery goals respond to failure by working harder. Children with performance goals take failure as a sign of their inadequacy, and come to view the tasks at which they fail with a mixture of anxiety, boredom, and anger. Children with mastery goals take failure as a sign that their efforts, and not they, are inadequate, and they often come to view the tasks at which they fail with the kind of relish that comes when you encounter a worthy challenge.

Dweck has shown that when classroom tasks become moderately difficult, there are substantial differences between these two types of children in task performance. Mastery-oriented kids do much better than performance-oriented kids. It seems fairly obvious that we would much rather inspire a mastery orientation in our children than a performance orientation, and not only because they do better on difficult tasks. Perhaps more important, a mastery orientation that encourages people to continue to seek new challenges is likely to keep people intellectually engaged throughout their lives—to keep them involved and learning. A mastery orientation is likely to keep people learning because they find things of intrinsic interest and value, and not because of possible extrinsic payoffs and punishments.

Most colleges encourage the mastery orientation by allowing students to take a certain number of classes "pass-fail." Since in pass-fail courses students are essentially ungraded (they might fail, it is true, but they don't have to worry about A's, B's, C's, and D's), the hope is that students will choose courses that they might be afraid to take for a grade. That is, the hope is that students will choose courses that both interest and challenge them. This is a nice feature of the college curriculum, but notice what it says, by implication, about why students choose the courses they do when they are being graded. The implicit message is that most students have a performance orientation and care more about doing well than about learning. The pass-fail option allows them to pursue what they're interested in, and not just what they're good at. But it typically can be used for only about one-eighth of the student's total program, hardly enough to create or encourage a mastery orientation that a person might carry with her throughout her life. In effect, people with a mastery orientation treat all of life as if it were a pass-fail course. They take risks and seek challenges in public that the rest of us are willing to do only when no one is looking.

What is it that determines whether people will go through life with a performance or a mastery orientation? A complete answer to this crucial question is not yet at hand. But, importantly, Dweck has shown in laboratory studies that it is possible to get people to adopt one orientation or the other by tailoring task instructions to focus either on the intrinsic value of the skill to be learned (inducing a mastery orientation) or on the evaluations of individual performance that will be made (inducing a performance orientation). It is not hard to see that a curriculum structured by exams, grades, honors, awards, social approval, and the like is going to induce in most people concern with performance rather than with mastery, exactly the opposite of what is desirable.

I can imagine someone reading this discussion and responding that a willingness to experiment, to take risks, to fail, is all well and good—but only under a set of very limited circumstances. You don't want people experimenting with the bread they bake and learning from their failures if their family has to eat those failures for dinner. You don't want engineers building bridges in experimental new ways and learning from their failures if people actually have to drive over those failures. You don't want subsistence farmers experimenting with their agricultural techniques and learning from their failures if their failures mean that their families will have to go hungry. Much of life demands results, demands successes. When the consequences of failure are severe, you want people to know *a* way to do things successfully, even if it isn't the best way.

This observation is true and important. There are many situations in life where people can't afford to fail and thus can't afford to experiment. But school isn't—or shouldn't be—one of them. If the only consequence of doing something wrong is that you learn from your mistake, you can risk doing things wrong and thus learn from mistakes. But if the consequence is bad grades, disapproval, failure to get into a good college, and failure to get a good job, then experimentation is risky—perhaps too risky.

Perhaps the main reason that modern science offers the most powerful techniques in human history for finding things out about the world is that science invented the laboratory. In the laboratory, you can risk failure. In the laboratory, you can try new ways to build bridges or to plant crops without worrying that people will fall into rivers or starve to death if the new ways are unsuccessful. The laboratory, like the classroom, is a place where people can afford to learn from failure and can afford to take risks. But if the scientist's entire career—including promotion, tenure, salary, research grants—depends on success, it becomes harder to take risks, because the costs of failure have escalated. The result is less informative, less imaginative science. And if the student's entire future depends on classroom success, it becomes harder to take risks, for the same reason. By instrumentalizing education—by relying on a system of extrinsic incentives—we raise the stakes for what goes on in the classroom. We engender a performance orientation in students and thus undermine their inclination to learn. By doing this, by making the consequences of failure in the classroom just as steep as the consequences of failure in life, we undermine the classroom as a kind of "laboratory for life."

COLLEGE AND THE "MARKETPLACE OF IDEAS": FROM METAPHOR TO FACT

The focus of Dweck's research is young children, and this makes good sense. Chances are that the orientations she has identified get established pretty early in the educational process and then perpetuate themselves. Thus a child who begins to develop a performance orientation to win approval from parents may move on to seeking good grades to win approval from teachers, and from there to seeking academic honors, admission to a select university, and either a good job or admission to a select professional school. At every step of the way, the student's goal is to prove (rather than improve) herself so that she can take the next step. Each educational stage is just a means to the next stage, with the last stage a means to a lucrative career. The snowball starts to roll down the hill in first grade; by the time it gets to college, it's the size of a glacier.

Nevertheless, it's worth spending some time thinking about the end of the educational process along with the beginning. Even though it may be hard to change well-established motivational orientations in college, college does offer opportunities that are not available earlier. By the time secondary school begins, there are already plenty of children in school who don't want to be there and who won't do any work or learn anything unless an elaborate system of rewards and punishments is established. Establishing and relying upon a performance orientation in these children may be the best that teachers can do. If some mastery-oriented children get swept along in the process, and thus turned into performance-oriented children themselves, that may just be the unfortunate but inevitable consequence of the heterogeneity of universal secondary education in the United States. But in college there are many fewer students who attend against their will. This opens up the possibility that external incentives can be relaxed and mastery orientation rekindled. Besides, college is the last chance that the educational system has to create mastery-oriented people who will continue to pursue knowledge throughout the rest of their lives. So let's examine the extent to which colleges manage to undo the motivational damage that has been done in high school.

From what I have already suggested, you might guess that college doesn't do much along these lines. The experiment I conducted by eliminating grades in one of my own classes suggests that most college students have a performance orientation. So does the existence of the pass-fail option. If students didn't have a performance orientation, it wouldn't be necessary. But these little bits of evidence might be interpreted as showing only that college doesn't reverse patterns that are well established by earlier schooling—that while it doesn't provide a solution, it's not a part of the problem. There are other aspects of modern college education that encourage the far more pessimistic view that college actually contributes to the problem.

For the last half of this century, the United States has had the luxury of regarding university education as an institution for the creation not just of skilled workers and professionals but of informed, responsible citizens. The modern educational revolution in this country has been the extension of the ideal of general education from the wealthy classes to the population as a whole. But this conception of university education is now changing. Growing competition among members of society for good jobs has been altering the character of the university. With college education so closely tied to job prospects, it is increasingly being thought of as an "investment" in the student's future. The money spent on school is expected to be returned, with interest, later on.

Universities have contributed to the problem in the last twenty years by increasing fees at a rate that was often twice the rate of inflation. There are many reasons for this dramatic rise in college costs, and the market has had its hand in several of them. As universities compete in the "market" for good students, they are pressured to offer increasingly elaborate support and social services (athletic facilities, telephones in rooms, good food, career and psychological counseling, and a wide variety of entertainments) that are very expensive. And as they compete in the "market" for star professors and research support from private industry, they are pressured to provide high-tech laboratories and equipment, low teaching loads, high salaries, and plentiful research assistants. As a result of financial pressures like these, the cost of college has loomed as a larger and larger bite out of the family's resources. It is hard not to think about what college is going to "get you" in terms of a job and an income when your family is faced with paying $25,000 a year. It is hard not to think about what college is going to get you, in terms of a job and an income, when you may be faced with thousands of dollars worth of student loans that have to be paid off. The more expensive a college education becomes, the more people are pushed to think about college as a means to financial success.

And thinking of a college education as an economic investment can affect what people want out of education, and thus how they evaluate what they get. It encourages people to take an instrumental view of education, a performance orientation instead of a mastery orientation. An instrumental orientation emphasizes the kinds of careers that a college degree makes possible. It emphasizes curricular and extracurricular choices that will enhance the student's résumé. Courses are taken on the basis of how impressive they sound, and of how likely they are to yield good grades, which will "cash in" as impressive résumés. At prices like these, pursuing one's intellectual interests is a luxury that few can afford.

As people begin to assess their education in these economic terms, what actually goes on in the college classroom changes. Because colleges and universities have to be sensitive to market demand, they provide what students want. And, increasingly, what students (and their parents) want is an education that will pay them back, in kind, for their huge financial investment (in the decade between the early 1970s and the early 1980s, the number of business majors in college doubled while the number of literature majors halved). The goal of education shifts from creating well-informed, responsible, and enlightened citizens to creating highly paid workers (in 1987, 73 percent of the college students surveyed said that being well-off financially was their top goal, as compared with 39 percent in 1970). Extra salary potential becomes the yardstick for evaluating the effectiveness of an educational institution. What happens as considerations like these come to dominate the university is that institutions change what they do, so the creation of extra salary potential becomes the goal itself, instead of just a measuring stick. Once again, the index of a thing replaces the thing itself, as in the case of tests of basic competency in grade school. The "marketplace of ideas" is transformed from a metaphor that describes the free and open inquiry that characterizes the college curriculum into a literal description of that curriculum.

An example of the extent to which a college education has come to be regarded as an economic tool recently surfaced when several prestigious private universities were charged with violating the Sherman Antitrust Act. These institutions were sharing information with regard to matters of financial aid to students. Their intent in doing so was to maintain roughly uniform policies regarding financial aid, so that all aid was awarded solely on the basis of demonstrated need and so that prospective students would not find themselves having to factor in financial considerations when they were deciding which of these schools to attend. These schools wanted differences in educational program, and not differences in cost, to determine where students chose to go to school. In effect, this sharing of information among schools resulted in a kind of price-fixing, since the costs of going to any one of them would be essentially equivalent. The Sherman Antitrust Act is intended to prevent price-fixing and maintain competition, so its application in this instance might seem appropriate. But the Sherman Antitrust Act is concerned with profit-seeking firms in the market. Universities are not profit seeking, and they are not, or were not, competing on the market. Their intent in sharing information was not to price gouge in the service of profit but to make price irrelevant in students' school choice. The antitrust suit is trying to force schools to compete with one another not just in program but in price. It is trying to enable students to induce schools to engage in bidding wars.

If this antitrust action is upheld, it may result in an end to financial aid decisions that are based solely on need. Schools may start attracting the most talented students by offering them substantial financial inducements, whether or not the students need them. This will leave less money for students who really need it and will price all but the wealthiest schools out of the market for the best students. That an antitrust action would even be considered, let alone pursued, is a powerful sign that the distinction between profit seeking and nonprofit is disappearing, that economic imperialism is becoming so widespread that it seems quite natural and straightforward to apply market regulations to everything.

As educational institutions, whether by choice or by outside pressure, come increasingly to be literal marketplaces of ideas, they teach their students the *implicit* lesson that knowledge is a means to extrinsic ends, that knowledge can be sold, that credentials pay for themselves on the market. And this implicit lesson not only shapes the programs of study that students pursue but also affects the way in which they pursue them. Students find the most efficient ways to do well in school. In some cases, this means choosing easy courses. In other cases, it means cheating.

There are clear indications that cheating—at all levels of education—occurs with much higher frequency now than it did in the past. A recent survey of almost 300,000 college freshmen indicated that 30 percent had cheated at some time during their senior year in high school (and other studies come up with higher estimates— some as high as 50 percent). When a similar question was asked in 1966, the number was 20 percent. Moreover, indications are that cheating gets more and more frequent as you move up the educational ladder; more in high school than in junior high, and more in college than in high school. In addition, cheating seems to be more common among gifted students than among mediocre ones; more common in high-powered academic high schools than in trade schools, and more common in honors classes than in ordinary ones. It is the honors students who feel the most intense pressure to do well, so that they get into the best colleges or, later, the best medical or law schools.

At the university level, more and more institutions are finding it necessary to educate faculty about some of the ingenious ways that cheating occurs so that they can be on the lookout for instances of it. It's no longer a simple matter of looking at the paper of the person sitting next to you. Miniature cassette recorders, or files hidden away on a computer disk, make for much more effective cheating than wandering eyes. Those schools that depend on honor codes (systems in which exams are unsupervised and students are expected to moni-tor the honesty and propriety of one another) are experiencing a substantial increase in alleged violations. And an entire industry, the term-paper industry, has grown up in recent years. With thinly disguised ads in college newspapers, or fliers that appear on bulletin boards in student hangouts, term-paper companies advertise exten-sive product lines. They offer a wide selection of already existing papers as well as a service for the custom production of papers. One company has a stock of more than 16,000 papers (available for $6.50 a page) and produces custom jobs for $20 a page. These companies avoid detection by keeping very careful records, by school, of which papers were sold when, so as to avoid the problem of having the same paper turned in by two students in the same year. Cheating like this marks the apotheosis of Dweck's performance orientation. If for the performance-oriented person it is *proving* your ability rather than *improving* it that matters, for the cheater the proof with-out the ability is good enough.

What is it that influences students to cheat? No doubt the intense competition to succeed in school and in life is part of it. No doubt the pervasive cheating that they see around them in the adult com-munity—both petty and serious—is part of it. And perhaps the casual neglect of instruction in ethical values by their parents and their teachers is part of it. But I think the largest and most significant influence on cheating is the instrumental orientation to education. It is only if you have this orientation that cheating even surfaces as an option. If you have a mastery orientation rather than a perfor-mance orientation, cheating simply makes no sense.

THE VALUE OF EDUCATION AND THE EDUCATION OF VALUE

There is a very important lesson to be learned from my discussion of the instrumentalization of education. The lesson is that while students are learning all the things that are explicitly taught to them in school, they are also learning other things that are being taught implicitly. No one may intend the system of tests and grades that operates in school to teach children to view their education as instrumental. The tests may be intended only to monitor student progress and to provide feedback to the teacher on the effectiveness of her instruction. Nevertheless, the tests *will* teach the children to view learning as instrumental.

If we don't want children to think of education as instrumental—if we want them to be mastery oriented rather than performance oriented, and to continue to derive joy from meeting new challenges and learning new things, what are we to do? Must we abandon tests and grades all together? A radical move like this is, I think, as unnecessary and undesirable as it is impractical. Students and teachers alike need feedback, and tests are a good way to get it. What we *do* need to do is make sure that students and teachers alike understand what tests are really for, that they are primarily tools for learning and only secondarily, if at all, tools for individual evaluation. And what we need to do is make sure that students and teachers alike know what education is really for. Rather than taking it for granted that everyone knows that an informed citizenry is the lifeblood of our society, or that individual freedom and autonomy depend upon knowledge and understanding, these goods of education must be made explicit. Perhaps the most important explicit lesson that should be taught in schools is why schools are important, and why the things people do in them are important. In short, people must be taught about the real value of education.

This means that the way to preserve the value of education is to engage in the education of values. Nowadays, any talk of values education in the classroom makes many people nervous, nervous that schools will attempt to impose some "official" moral code on everyone. A typical institutional response to this appropriate nervousness is to avoid teaching about values all together. But the problem with efforts to steer clear of teaching and thus imparting values to students is that the very effort itself constitutes a lesson in values. Specifically, the lesson is that values are a world apart, that while schools can give us powerful intellectual tools and show us how to use them, they can't tell us what to use them for. Often efforts to maintain value neutrality in education actually teach value irrelevance.

There is certainly good reason to be very careful when it comes to teaching values in a pluralistic society like ours, especially in public schools that are open to all comers. If we maintain our commitment to pluralism, we must avoid offering up views as accepted truth about which there is actually significant disagreement among different social groups. But we can also be too careful. If educational institutions avoid developing and teaching a particular view about the value of education, then the goals that guide education will surely erode. They may even eventually disappear. And if educational institutions fail to teach people why education is valuable, everything else that they do teach becomes a waste of time.

Right now a debate is raging in many universities about why education is valuable and about what should be taught. The terms of the debate often involve matters of curricular diversity, of standards of evaluation, and of what constitutes truth or understanding. The debate is often about what is called the "canon," the set of historical texts and ideas that have traditionally been taught as the core of Western civilization. And the content of the debate is another reflection that some understand the university as a "marketplace of ideas" literally, not metaphorically.

Some critics of the traditional curriculum have suggested that the primacy of traditional works stems from the fact that educational institutions have historically been run by white European men for white European men. Traditional works are taken to be central not because of the insight or understanding they provide but because they enable the white men who have dominated the culture to perpetuate that domination by inculcating in new generations the very ideas that have made domination possible. There are no standards of quality or truth by which these classic works stand out and command attention over other works that have been regarded as marginal or even ignored all together. These works command attention because the people who run the intellectual world want them to. The classical college curriculum, critics contend, reflects the truth of power disguised as the power of truth.

Many of those who defend the traditional curriculum will admit to a certain myopia in the Western intellectual tradition that has led to the exclusion of works and ideas that are just as powerful and insightful as the ones that have traditionally been taught. But, at the same time, they will insist that the work that has comprised the core belongs there. Shakespeare is not taught because powerful people want him taught so that they can remain powerful. Shakespeare is taught because he was a great writer, a significant figure in the development of our culture's self-understanding. And so, these traditionalists argue, while the canon must be expanded, it must not be abandoned.

There are two ways to interpret this debate that is absorbing so much time and energy among modern intellectuals, one rather benign and the other quite malignant. The benign interpretation is that people are arguing about which texts are insightful, about whose ideas are true. Is it Isaac Newton or Albert Einstein, John Locke or Karl Marx, Henry James or Virginia Woolf, John Updike or Toni Morrison? Arguments like this are what intellectual life has always been about. The practice of education grows and develops as a result of the work of its practitioners. As practitioners struggle to realize the goods of the practice—truth, knowledge, and understanding— their conception of those goods changes.

The malignant interpretation is that the argument is really about whether truth, knowledge, and understanding are indeed the goods of education. If they are, the application of standards by which these goods are assessed is appropriate and necessary. But what if, as some have claimed, "truth," "knowledge," and "understanding" are just cover terms for *power?* What if there really are no standards and if in the intellectual world, as in most others, might makes right? What if the old truism "Knowledge is power" has things exactly backward? What if, instead, power is knowledge, in the sense that the people who have power get to decide what truth, understanding, and knowledge are?

If you hold this view, then you want the university to open up its curriculum, to relieve the stranglehold of the powerful and create a free market. On this "idea market," people will be free to buy and sell whatever ideas they like, with no standards for assessing value other than the fact that people are willing to buy. An idea will be judged to be good on the basis not of its truthfulness or insightfulness but of its popularity.

It may seem that the current debate about curriculum in the university is of no interest or importance to those who live and work outside it, but it is. What's at stake in this debate is not only what books students will read in college but also how they will interact with ideas and with one another. At stake in this debate is the meaning and value of understanding, and of reason, of rationality.

Most of us place a high value on being "reasonable." We aspire to it in our own lives, admire it in others, and value it in our social institutions. We want the people we live with to do things for *reasons*, reasons that make sense. And we hope and expect that they will change what they do if we can give them good reasons for changing. Living with "reasonable" people is what makes real conversation possible. Reason allows us to influence one another with ideas and arguments. The alternative to reasoned conversation is the exercise of power. And reason denies privilege to power. Or better, it substitutes the power of evidence and argument for the power of physical force, or of position, or of money.

Reasonable people who disagree talk, argue, attempt to persuade. They engage in conversation with one another, conversation based on mutual respect. But conversation is not the only means at our disposal to get people to go along with us. Instead of reasoning with people—instead of giving them *reasons*—we can try to manipulate them. We can manipulate people by means of bribery ("Say you agree with me, and I'll give you a thousand dollars), or by means of threat ("Say you agree with me, or you won't get promoted"). We can manipulate people by intentionally misleading them, as advertisers routinely do, by giving them distorted or incomplete information. When all we care about is results, the various techniques of manipulation that are available to us look very tempting.

What keeps us from resorting to manipulation all the time is that we care not only about results but about how those results are achieved. We want people to agree with us, but we want them to agree for the right reasons—because our view is correct, and not because of who we are or who we know or how much we're willing to pay. Conversation rather than manipulation is the proper stance to take with people we respect and value. To manipulate people is to use them, and you don't use people if you respect them.

But however much we may aspire to reasonable conversation in our relations with other people, we don't always attain it. The possibilities for conversation, as opposed to manipulation, vary with the social conditions in which we live. The competitive individualism of the market, for example, undermines, or at least discourages, conversation. If the point is to get what you want as efficiently as possible, power and manipulation may well be the most effective means to given ends. If competitive individualism so pervades social life that we are interested in other people only to the extent that they can serve our individual desires, conversation loses its privileged position and becomes merely one technique among many for getting what we want. With conversation just instrumental—just a means—rather than a reflection of a fundamental moral stance toward other persons, the presumption of respect and value for others disintegrates. What disintegrates with it is the social character of intellectual life, and of the practice of education more generally.

You might suppose that our regard for other people as worthy of value and respect is so deep and basic a part of us that it—and we—will resist social forces that threaten it; that, in effect, we will correct changes in our social institutions that challenge this fundamental stance we take toward others. But I have been suggesting throughout this book that this hopeful supposition is mistaken. As practices like education and the institutions that embody those practices lose sight of the goods that make them distinctive, as they join the march to the drumbeat of the market, not only is their own integrity threatened but so is the integrity of our moral stance toward other people. Thus, by attempting to combat the instrumentalization of education—by attempting to prevent the measurement of educational goods with an economic yardstick—we will not only be protecting the distinctive values of one of the best things in life. We will also be protecting an institution that teaches us how to interact with other people as agents worthy of respect rather than as objects worthy only of manipulation.

10

THE SELLING OF DEMOCRACY: PUBLIC LIFE AND PRIVATE INTERESTS

The danger to liberty lies in the subordination of belief to the needs of the industrial system. —*John Kenneth Galbraith*

We Americans value freedom of choice perhaps above all else. In the economic domain, the social arrangement that best caters to our desire for free choice is the market, and we have turned to the market and embraced it, despite its many failings and excesses, for just this reason. But putting *everything* on the market leaves us dissatisfied. Relying on the market to allow us to pursue the best things in life makes many of those things less good—less valuable. Economic imperialism erodes the goods that we derive from our work, our education, our relations with family and friends, our recreational activities. The price we seem to be paying for the freedom to pursue whatever we want is that there is less and less that is worth wanting.

Furthermore, economic imperialism affects us whether or not we approve of it. We can't avoid having our education affected by economic considerations if all educational institutions are penetrated by economic considerations. We can't avoid having the way we practice medicine affected by economic considerations if we've got malpractice premiums to pay, nurses, receptionists, technicians, and bookkeepers on the payroll, a mortgage to satisfy, and a family to feed. We can't avoid pursuing profits at all costs if doing otherwise will get us fired from our jobs. And we can't avoid thinking about the costs and benefits of our involvement with family and friends if our family and friends are thinking about the costs and benefits of involvement with us. Economic imperialism does not spare anyone; indeed, it extracts an especially heavy price from those who don't participate.

It is tempting to try to solve the problem of economic imperialism by appealing to individuals to mend their ways and restrain their pursuit of economic interests. But this appeal to personal restraint won't work. The problem, which we encountered earlier, is known as the *free-rider* problem, and it appears whenever the actions of an isolated individual are neither necessary nor sufficient to affect the practices of society as a whole. One person's willingness not to sue for malpractice won't change the cost of malpractice premiums. One person's commitment to honoring contracts and making safe products won't change the practices of others. One person's willingness to refrain from using tax dodges won't change the tax rates. So long as a single individual alone shows restraint, she will be much worse off than before. She will pay her fair share of taxes, but the tax rates will remain high as all others pay less than their fair share. For individual, voluntary restraint to be effective, everyone has to do it. But once everyone, or almost everyone, is doing it, individuals can really serve themselves by continuing to sue for malpractice, use tax dodges, and make unsafe products. So long as self-interest is the sole motive for action, the most effective strategy is to take merciless advantage of the restraint or public commitment shown by others.

If we can't solve the problems of economic imperialism by relying on ordinary individuals to restrain themselves, perhaps we can rely on our industrial and economic leaders. Economist John Maynard Keynes did this more than half a century ago when he introduced the system of "state-managed capitalism" that has come to dominate the economies of virtually all developed nations. He was confident that "captains of industry" had motives considerably loftier than mere economic self-interest. Influenced, no doubt, by the fact that so many of these "captains" came from the British aristocracy, for whom, as a class, the pursuit of profit was a bit crass, Keynes assumed that the leaders of the economy would themselves show restraint in seeking profit for their companies. They would consider and act in the public interest. Not that their business activity was a charity; by no means. But there were bounds on what a business could legitimately do in the service of profit—bounds dictated by custom and by an aristocratic tradition of public service.

But as economist Fred Hirsch pointed out in his book *Social Limits to Growth*, Keynes was mistaken. Keynes failed to realize that the aristocratic tradition of public service on which he counted was a slender and ephemeral reed on which to rest an economy, let alone a whole society. Keynes failed to realize that the very act of participation in the market system would turn his lofty aristocrats—or if not them, then their children—into self-seeking egoists. It should be clear from my discussion in chapter 2, or from the pages of our daily newspapers, that the era of "captain of industry as public citizen" is on the wane in the United States. The dominant attitude of high-level management at present seems to be "Get as much as you can as fast as you can, and let someone else worry about picking up the pieces." But who is that someone else, and where will he come from? In the case of the recent disaster in the banking industry, that someone else is all of us, and our children, and our children's children.

We could probably survive the loss of restraint and public-spiritedness on the part of industrial leaders if it were true that whatever serves the interests of big corporations also serves the interests of the United States as a whole—if it were true that "what's good for GM is good for the nation." Whether this was ever true (as opposed to being propaganda for big business), I don't know. But it certainly isn't true now. The last twenty years or so has witnessed the internationalization of business to such a remarkable degree that it is no longer clear that major corporations even *belong* to any nation, let alone serve its interests. Major corporations do not hesitate to move production operations to foreign locations where labor costs are cheaper. For example, while the share of world manufactured exports made *in* the United States dropped from 17 percent to 13 percent between 1966 and 1985, the share made *by* U.S. corporations increased from 17 percent to 18 percent. Thus U.S. corporations were making more of the world's goods in 1985 than in 1966, but they were making a lot of those goods outside the United States. Movement of production operations outside the country means lost jobs and devastated communities, hardly a result that is "good for the nation." The corporations might claim that since these moves increase profits, they benefit shareholders and thus are good for the nation. But ownership of U.S. corporations is increasingly moving into foreign hands. More than $200 billion of American capital is now owned by foreigners, double what it was ten years ago. In addition, there is significant foreign ownership of many of the major U.S. financial institutions. I don't mean to suggest that there is anything necessarily wrong with foreign investment in U.S. corporations. What I *do* mean to suggest is that when a significant proportion of both the operations and the ownership of these corporations has moved offshore, the presumption that what is good for these corporations will automatically be good for the people of the United States is extremely suspect.

Faced with free-rider problem, the internationalization of business, and the erosion of personal moral principles that might restrain economic activity, we seem to be left with nowhere to turn except the state. It may be that only the state possesses the character and the power to restrain economic activity, to control economic imperialism, and to preserve what is good about some of the best things in life. But if we look to the state, to our institutions of political democracy, to control economic imperialism, we will be disappointed. For rather than controlling economic imperialism, modern democratic politics has already been pervaded by it.

ECONOMIC IMPERIALISM AND DEMOCRACY

The roots of American democracy were grounded in morality. Discussions of "justice," "equality," "freedom," and "authority" derived from ideas about right and wrong, and presupposed public commitment and responsibility. As citizens, people owed it to the state to be concerned about the public interest. People owed it to the state to be loyal. People owed it to the state that they would participate in public life, at least by voting. The right to vote was more than just a right; it was a responsibility. The franchise was *inalienable*; people couldn't sell their votes for cash even if they wanted to. Participation in a democracy was thus a kind of calling, and a democratic state would not be worthy of the name unless the bulk of its citizens honored that calling. The state truly served the people only if the people were willing to serve the state, by accepting the responsibilities that citizenship demanded. The preservation of democracy itself depended on this moral core, and the resolution of disputes about the extent of government responsibility depended on a common moral vocabulary. Most accounts of democracy in the past argued that democratic political systems cannot be sustained in the absence of a set of shared values and moral precepts that unite the citizenry into a moral community.

At least, that's the way things were historically. They seem to be no longer. Instead of being grounded in principles of morality, democracy is coming to be grounded in principles of the market. According to what is called the "economic theory of democracy," the democratic state runs exclusively on market principles, with no presumption that people are guided by anything but self-interest. The origins of the economic theory of democracy can be traced to economist Joseph Schumpeter, in his book *Capitalism, Socialism, and Democracy*. According to the theory, the political sphere of life is accurately modeled on the economic sphere, with both spheres inhabited by the same self-interested people. Groups of political entrepreneurs—the elites—seek the rewards of political power by offering goods (programs) in the political market. Larger groups of people—the masses—purchase (vote for) the goods they want. Not only *can* people sell their votes, but they do so routinely—not, of course, for cash, but for programs that are eventually convertible into cash. Political participation is essentially the making of demands on government, and the democratic process is a way of bringing together individual political demands in the same way that the market brings together individual economic demands. And the aim of the elite is to stay elite, that is, to stay in power. To this end, they offer whatever goods it takes to "buy" the votes of the masses.

This very simple theory of democracy has the virtue that it has very low expectations and makes almost no demands of the citizenry. Morality, public commitment, and even serious political participation are unnecessary. All this is required is the pursuit of self-interest, which is presumed to be what human nature is about anyway. However, this simplicity has a price; it doesn't work. The analogy between government and the market is not perfect.

The market, when it is functioning smoothly, is governed by Adam Smith's famous "invisible hand," which ensures that supply will equal demand. The price mechanism sees to this equilibration; prices rise or fall as demand and supply rise and fall. The government has no such built-in equilibrator. There is nothing to check the growth of aggregate demand for government programs. Thus individual interest groups or lobbies keep yelling "more, more, more," and "me, me, me," and the people in power promise anything to stay in power. Superfluous military bases should be closed, but not the one in my congressional district. Extravagant defense contracts should be eliminated, but not the one that keeps the local company in business and employs a thousand voters. Social programs should be cut. Which ones? Not support for the elderly, says the senator from Florida. Not support for minorities, says the senator from New York. Not support for farmers, says the senator from Iowa.

Once, these various demands could be kept in check by the mechanisms of party politics. The leadership of each party could influence party members to toe the line and submerge their own local interests for the good of the party, if not the country. Then political debate and horse trading had only two voices—those of the Democrats and the Republicans. Now individual legislators are much less party loyalists and much more free agents. Congressional debate involves five hundred voices, all screaming at once, often for incompatible things. Little gets done, and the country simply can't afford to satisfy everyone's demands. In the political market, demand now vastly exceeds supply. The result is what has variously been called an "overload of democracy," a "crisis of democracy," or, nowadays, "gridlock." America can no longer afford all the democracy it has. We can't keep buying everyone's votes. Excess demand must somehow be checked.

But how can it be checked? If a member of the office-holding elite says no to enough demands, he will not be elected to carry out his policies. People will elect a "yes-man" instead. And if the yes-man then goes back on his promise, he won't be reelected. It seems that so long as people are selling their votes for programs, there is nothing to check the impulse not to sell cheap. The current U.S. fiscal crisis offers an excellent example of this process in action.

Even though virtually everyone knows that revenues (taxes) must be increased if the United States is ever to reduce or eliminate its massive deficit, it is almost suicidal for any candidate for national office to run on a platform that calls for tax increases (except maybe for the very rich, which won't cost many votes, but won't raise much money either). At best, tax increases will get snuck in after the election, usually disguised as something else, and former President Bush can testify to the consequences of that strategy. The alternative to tax increases—spending cuts—is also unacceptable, because such cuts will alienate whatever groups are affected by them. Only something like across-the-board spending cuts, in which no groups are hurt worse than any others, are deemed to be politically possible.

As for the elite, they are not only at the mercy of their always demanding voters (which is not, after all, so bad, since people elected in a representative democracy are supposed to represent the views and the interests of those who elect them). Even more, they are at the mercy of their sources of money. The costs of campaigning in this media age are astronomical. In 1988, an average campaign for a Senate seat cost over $3 million, or about $10,000 per week for the elected senator's entire six-year term. To win a seat in the House required about $400,000, or $5,000 a week for the elected representative's two-year term. This means that politicians are always raising money. And what this means is that people with money, whether individuals or lobbies or political action committees (PACs), will have a disproportionate influence on what the politicians do. The incredibly high cost of a successful political campaign virtually guarantees that incumbents will retain office (the retention rate of incumbents in the U.S. Congress is about 96 percent, higher than the retention rate was in the former Soviet Union). Challengers have a very hard time raising money. PACs would rather give money to incumbents as a way of influencing how they vote on legislation than risk their money on challengers who have little chance to win. Thus the economic theory of democracy has become less metaphorical, as "one dollar, one vote" has come to replace "one person, one vote" in the political arena. And in case you are wondering why it is so difficult to get Congress to enact significant campaign reform legislation, asking congresspeople voluntarily to change a system that so favors their retention of power is a little like asking the white minority in South Africa voluntarily to give full voting rights to the black majority.

In response to this crisis, that democracy can no longer afford to meet the demands of all of its citizens but has no means for restraining those demands, the state can try to persuade individual people, or interest groups, to restrain their demand voluntarily for the greater good of everyone. There are two possible grounds on which to appeal to people to restrain their demands. We can appeal to their self-interest, or we can appeal to a set of democratic values about the common good that they all share. Appeals to self-interest won't work, because of the free-rider problem. Even if people were convinced that social cooperation and restraint are essential to preserving democracy, it would be in the best interests of every individual to be a free rider and to let everyone else exercise restraint. Thus if every lobbyist and interest group agreed to put less pressure on congresspeople, the road would be clear for *your* group to press its demands and get them satisfied. If every candidate agreed to limit campaign spending, the road would be clear for *your* candidate to buy the election with a media blitz. If every government employee organization agreed to take a cut in benefits or give up some job security, the government could afford to give *your* organization everything it wants.

If appeals to self-interest won't secure restraint, what about appeals to shared democratic values? Can appeals to trust, compassion, social responsibility, and public mindedness get people to restrain their demands? If people actually shared these values, such appeals might be effective. But where are these shared values to come from? That they don't come from the market is obvious. And as economic imperialism turns other aspects of life—aspects I've discussed throughout this book—into extensions of the market, they won't come from there either. Indeed, the one place they might have come from is the political sphere itself. But it is just the "economization" of this sphere that has produced the problem in the first place. The only value people may be said to share in a world of commercialized social institutions is the value of individual preference satisfaction. And this is a value that *produces* excess demand rather than restrains it.

So it seems that voluntary restraint is not a possible solution to the crisis of democracy, at least not as long as democracy is conceived and practiced in accord with the market model. The alternatives seem to be somehow to abandon the market model or to abandon democracy. The second is unacceptable, but the first may be unattainable.

There is an extraordinary irony in this turn that democracy has taken in its commercialization. Economic historian Albert Hirschman, in the book *The Passions and the Interests*, discussed how the notion of "interest" as distinct from "passion" was born a few hundred years ago. Enlightenment thinkers realized that some kind of restraint was needed on the monarch's reckless attempts to satisfy his passions that led him and his subjects into one foolish venture after another, fighting wars and exhausting national treasure out of vanity, anger, jealousy, or pure whimsy. Some order and stability was needed in life. That stability came, it was thought, by substituting interest—rational commercial interest—for passion. The pursuit of rational commercial interest would be orderly and predictable rather than capricious. It would be benign rather than malignant. The clockwork of the market provided a remarkably civilized alternative to what it was intended to replace. But now we find ourselves in need of something to check, restrain, rationalize, and civilize the pursuit of self-interest. It turns out that the pursuit of self-interest has much in common with heroin. Both are human inventions. Both slowly destroy the fabric of whatever social institutions they invade. Both are addictive. And heroin was introduced as a cure for the evils of morphine.

If we resign ourselves to the idea that democracy is now just another market, and one that doesn't work very efficiently, there is a temptation to try to solve the crisis of democracy by reducing the number of functions that government performs. That is, there is a temptation to put government functions on the real market—to privatize them. If government can't satisfy the demands of everyone, let it stop trying. If it can't provide enough police to keep the streets safe, or enough medical care to keep everybody healthy, or enough sanitation workers to keep communities clean, or enough teachers and books to get everyone educated, then let it turn these domains over to the private sector. Let individuals and communities decide what services they want, and have them purchase these services with their own money. Of course, government will continue to provide services for people and communities with no resources. But these services will just be minimal—a real safety net. Government can afford to meet minimal demands so long as people are left to their own devices if they want more than the minimum.

This strategy is precisely the opposite of the one I have been suggesting throughout this book. Instead of moving in the direction of easing the economic pressure on people, it increases that pressure, by making things that are currently available to everyone available only to those who can pay the price. By the logic of the arguments that I have been making, a move like this will increase the need for people to accumulate wealth. It will deform life even more than life is already deformed. It will enlarge and strengthen the iron cage. It will further erode values that are noneconomic.

Despite all this, many people nowadays are suggesting precisely this kind of move, and many communities are making it. This is especially true among the wealthiest members of society, who, as Secretary of Labor Robert Reich puts it, are "quietly seceding from the rest of the nation." They watch public parks and playgrounds deteriorate, and join private recreational clubs of every possible description. They watch public safety deteriorate, and hire private security guards (the number of private security guards in the United States now exceeds the number of public police officers). They hire their own garbage collectors and street cleaners to supplement the work of public employees (one neighborhood in Manhattan raised almost $5 million for these supplemental services from its residents in 1989, of which $1 million went to support a private security force, a police within a police to protect a city within a city). They finance education with local real estate taxes, so schools in adjacent communities can be as different from one another as schools in First and Third World countries. In Texas, for example, the richest school district spends $19,000 a year per pupil while the poorest spends $2,000 a year per pupil. In Massachusetts, one suburban town pays its teachers an average salary of $37,000 while the town right next to it pays $26,000. Or, if people are led, by convenience, to stay in a city that mixes together rich and poor, the rich vote to keep taxes low and then send their kids to private schools (almost 50 percent of all white children in Los Angeles go to private or parochial schools).

The wealthy even make many of their (tax-deductible) charitable contributions to organizations (orchestras, museums, private hospitals, elite universities) of whose services they will be the principal beneficiaries.

We can understand some of the impulses behind this move on the part of the wealthy to secede from the nation, and to privatize as many services as possible so that their tax dollars don't go to serving the needs of others. Not only can government not afford to provide all needed services, but those services it does provide are often horrendously expensive, inefficient, and inadequate. Given the reputation that the competitive marketplace enjoys for generating productivity and efficiency, the temptation to take services out of the hands of government and put them into the hands of the market can be very strong.

Economist John Donahue has recently done a study of privatization, with an eye toward examining how often, and under what circumstances, taking public services private actually is efficient. He looked at the defense industry, at the penal system, at various job-training programs, and at a host of services (trash collection, street repair, street cleaning, park maintenance, janitorial service, and the like) normally provided by local governments. He contrasted the *public* provision of services (services paid for by government and provided by government employees) with the *private* provision of services (services *also* paid for by government but provided by private, for-profit contractors). Thus, in all cases, the source of the money was the same, and the question of interest was whether tax payers get more for their money from private contractors than from public employees. The results of his analysis, described in his book *The Privatization Decision*, carry a surprising message. Despite our almost universal cynicism about the effectiveness of public employees, it is only under a rather special set of circumstances that privatization seems to increase efficiency. And often these increases in efficiency come at a rather steep price.

According to Donahue's analysis, the private provision of services works well only when we are interested entirely in results, in ends, and not in the means by which those ends are achieved. If we want clean streets for the lowest price, and we don't care how it's done, then private contractors may do better than public employees. If we *do* care how it's done (if, for example, we don't want big, noisy street-cleaning machinery riding up and down our streets at six in the morning, or we don't want to support firms that hire part-time help, pay them the minimum wage, and provide no benefits), then the advantage of privatization may disappear.

Even if we do care only about ends and not about means, in order for privatization to work, we must be able to specify those ends very precisely in advance, and we must be able to evaluate performance very clearly after the task is performed. In other words, we must be able to specify, in a contract, the details of what is to be done by the contractor. Furthermore, we must be sure that there is genuine competition among potential contractors. Otherwise, there will be no pressure on the contractor to get the job done cheaply and efficiently.

There may be services for which these requirements can be met. It may be that when it comes to picking up trash, caring for parks, painting and cleaning public buildings, and the like, all we care about is that the jobs get done, the requirements of the jobs can be precisely specified, and there is plenty of competition among potential contractors. Donahue discusses some services that meet these requirements, and he finds that they are indeed provided more cheaply and efficiently by private contractors than by public employees. However, he also finds that the bulk of the savings comes from wages and benefits. Private contractors pay their employees much less (10 to 40 percent less, depending on the job) than people doing similar jobs in the public sector earn. They employ a good deal of part-time help and offer very little in the way of benefits. Since these are jobs that, even when they pay relatively well, are hardly providing people with lives of luxury, we can imagine that when they pay poorly, they may not even be adequate for subsistence. And even if we don't care about having our tax dollars go to companies that don't pay their employees a living wage, we may well care when our tax dollars end up subsidizing these very same employees for essential services, like health care, that they can't afford to pay for themselves. In other words, some of these savings may be more apparent than real. Less of our tax money goes to cleaning the streets, and more of it goes to public health care facilities.

Whatever the financial (and the ethical) bottom line may be with regard to the privatization of services that do meet the requirements set out by Donahue, there are plenty of other services that don't meet these requirements, and when these services are contracted out, the result can be a fiasco. The defense industry exemplifies the importance of these requirements beautifully. The armed forces devote enormous energy and personpower to drafting specifications for goods and services that range from simple supplies for foot soldiers to complex missile systems. Specs for trivial things like metal whistles or oatmeal cookies can be a dozen pages long. The reason for all this detail is both to set the precise terms for competitive bidding and to have clear and rigorous standards to which contractors can be held accountable. The problem with it is that it costs a fortune, in the time both of the people who draft the specs and of the contractors who have to meet them. Military contractors are constantly complaining about being regulated to death. On the other hand, whenever there is a dispute about whether a contract has been adequately fulfilled, contractors point to ambiguities and omissions in the specifications. At the same time that one representative of an aerospace firm complains about the 24,000 specification documents it has on file, another member of the same firm insists that quality lapses result from written specs that were incomplete or unclear. As one military procurement official observed, military specs are "the sum total of all our past mistakes; they are lists of lessons learned." What he meant is that whenever the results of a contract are unsatisfactory in any way, specs are added to the next contract to prevent whatever went wrong with the last one from going wrong again.

Several years ago, David Packard, the head of a hugely successful electronics firm (Hewlett-Packard), was brought into government to oversee defense procurement and make it more efficient. He was appalled by the overregulation and overspecification of contracts that seemed to be wasting so much of everybody's time, and he sought to liberate private contractors from several layers of bureaucracy so that they could exercise the discretion and ingenuity that a competitive market rewards. He was dismayed to discover that when specifications were relaxed and individual discretion was encouraged, the results were often unacceptable. When faced with a choice between doing it right and doing it cheaply, companies chose to do it cheaply and make extra profit, if the specs were vague enough to let them get away with it. Faced, in other words, with the choice between business and patriotism, they chose business (remember why the butcher puts his finger on the scale but the postal clerk doesn't). They owed it to their shareholders. Or so the ideology of the market tells us. Thus, it seemed to him, in the defense business, you either spent enormous amounts of time and money and got what you wanted, or you saved time and money and didn't get what you wanted.

There are a few reasons for this kind of problem in the defense industry. One is that, in many domains, so much expertise is required that there isn't much competition. There are only a handful of companies actually in a position to produce complex, state-of-the-art military hardware. And once a particular company has spent time and money developing the expertise and equipment to meet one contract, it will have an enormous advantage over its potential competitors when the time comes to bid on the next one. So there isn't as much competition as one might like. Another reason is that in the defense procurement business, people often care not only about ends but also about means. They have security and secrecy requirements. They may want to be able to shift production priorities and timetables as needs shift. They may care about whether component parts are American made. They may care about whether the workforce has a sufficient number of women and minorities. The more they impose means requirements on contractors, the less efficient private contracting will be.

Finally, it is often true that even if the people concerned with defense procurement care only about ends, it is not so easy to specify exactly what ends they want in advance of the process of design and production. With virtually all tasks of any complexity at all, insight and expertise develop as the task is being executed that will cause a thoughtful person to revise the aims of the task. The goals of defense systems are to deter or contain the enemy. These goals are not nearly specific enough to become the terms of a contract. On a more specific level, there may be goals like building planes that are fast, maneuverable, and capable of flying low to the ground; or building tents that are light, water resistant, and easy to assemble; or meals that are nutritious, tasty, easy to transport, and resistant to spoilage.

Even these goals are not specific enough to become the terms of a contract. How fast do the planes have to fly, and how maneuverable do they have to be? How light must the tents be and how quickly assembled? How tasty must the meals be, and how nutritious? Of course, it is possible to provide specs that can become terms of a contract, but when you do this, you negate the special expertise that people who are in the middle of a job may be able to bring to it.

And this situation is not unique to defense. We want a wildlife service that will protect the ecological balance, an air traffic control system that will make flying safe, a teaching corps that will educate our children. It makes sense for the specific goal setting, and modification, to be done by the experts in the field—by the wildlife specialists, the air traffic controllers, and the teachers. But if we are going to give people in the field the discretion to use their expertise in the most effective manner, we can't contract out for their services.

At this very moment, a debate is raging about whether national education can be improved by privatizing it. This idea was initially given serious attention during the presidential administration of Ronald Reagan, and it was one of the central planks in the educational platform of former President Bush. It has been given perhaps its fullest form in the recent book *Politics, Markets, and America's Schools*, by John Chubb and Terry Moe. What proponents of privatization have in mind is continued public funding, but of private rather than of public schools. Some sort of voucher system would enable parents to shop around for schools for their children. Some might choose traditional schools, while others chose experimental ones. Some might choose religious schools, while others chose secular ones. The schools themselves would be forced to compete for students and the voucher checks they brought with them. The rationale behind this proposal is that if they are forced to compete for students in order to stay in business, schools will be driven to improve what they do. Only excellent, or at least very good, schools will be able to attract students and stay in business. Bad schools, like bad businesses, will go under.

From what I've described of Donahue's work, we can anticipate that privatization of schooling can work only if (*a*) we care only about ends, not means, and (*b*) we can be clear in specifying the ends. Both of these preconditions are problematic. We certainly care about more than ends in education. We care not only about how well our children learn but also about how well they are treated. Few of us (or our children) would put up with a draconian educational regime that terrorized and humiliated children into doing their work, no matter how much they ended up learning. And as to specifying ends, the most obvious way to do this is with a set of competency exams, and I showed in the last chapter how a system of competency exams can be abused by teachers and administrators whose jobs depend on the performance of their students. Privatization will do nothing to prevent or counteract this kind of abuse. Only integrity—a commitment to the mission—will do that.

There is something good about the suggestion to privatize education. It lies not in privatization per se but in the decentralization that would accompany it. Whether schools are public or private, if a substantial amount of control is given over to the teachers and administrators in the individual schools to shape curriculum and educational methods, we can benefit from the local expertise that develops in dealing with particular groups of children. We can also benefit if, as I think is likely, increasing the autonomy and responsibility given to individual teachers increases both the quality of people who enter the profession and their level of commitment to their work. Local control of public schools will allow different schools to try different things and thus compete with one another to meet a wide range of standards for success. It will be a competition that has no losers. Since no one will be in education to make money, innovations that work in one school can be shared openly and readily imported and adopted by others.

John Donahue has written that "profit-seekers cannot be expected to exceed the literal specifications of a contract. The less completely can duties be specified in advance, the more valuable is bureaucratic honor." Bureaucratic honor. Where is that to come from? It certainly won't come from people who subscribe to the economic theory of democracy. Bureaucratic honor depends upon people who take their work seriously, who want to do the right thing, who view public service as a calling. Privatization may be the best we can do on the assumption that bureaucratic honor is a bygone trait. But we should not be misled into thinking that privatization is the cure for what ails the bureaucratic system. All it actually does is substitute the inefficiency of rigidly specified contracts for the inefficiency of bureaucratic indifference. The real cure for what ails the current system will be one that finds a way to rekindle bureaucratic honor, by reinvesting public service with civic rather than economic values.

And this brings me to my last point about privatization. This chapter began by asking what we might do to restrain economic imperialism, to keep the market from entering domains where it doesn't belong. The state seems like the best candidate for restricting the scope of the market. And this remains true even if the state seems itself to be operating in accordance with economic principles, as the economic theory of democracy suggests. If restraining economic imperialism is an important goal, and if the state is the leading candidate for pursuing that goal, then we may have to resist privatization and accept public provision of services, even if that means a certain amount of bureaucratic inefficiency. We can't restrain the economy or revive a sense of civic virtue if we give up our public responsibilities to the marketplace, which is just the institution that we are trying to restrain. Donahue puts it this way:

> It is not simply the emergence and entrenchment of special interests that has bedeviled postwar American politics, but also the erosion of traditional public values and the failure to restore them or to replace them with a new consensus on the claims citizens can make on their fellows. . . .
>
> Insofar as we renounce the common realm and restrict ourselves to endeavors that do not burden our weak and vulnerable procedures for collective choice, we opt for a safer but a bleaker path.

The question before us, then, is how do we make our procedures for collective choice less weak and vulnerable by restoring traditional public values.

SPHERES OF SOCIAL LIFE

One step that we could take to restore traditional public values is to control the forces that are eroding them. But how do we stop economic imperialism? How do we contain the economic pressure on

individuals and on institutions? The way to stop economic imperialism is to erect barriers or walls around domains of social life that are
designed to keep domination by economic interests out.

The beginnings of a rationale for doing this were provided a few
years ago by philosopher Michael Walzer, in his book *Spheres of
Justice*. He suggested that we think about our lives as organized into
distinct spheres that operate, or at least should operate, according to
different rules. Central to Walzer's thesis is the idea that different
aims or values are appropriate to different spheres of life. There is
no common denominator that unites them. The values served by
religious or civic participation, say, are incomparable with the values served by material consumption. Money can't buy ecclesiastical
office, and piety does no good in the market. There is no sensible
way to equate so many mornings in church with so many evenings
in the theater. In short, neither money nor anything else can or
should buy everything.

That spheres of life serve distinct values is acknowledged both by
social convention and by law. People can't buy or sell human beings
(including themselves), criminal justice, civil rights, marriage and
procreation, exemption from military service, political office, prizes
and honors, divine grace, friendship, and love. But the point I have
been making throughout the book is that these prohibitions on buying and selling are much less secure than we might think. Considering the cost of legal services, justice is to a large extent for sale.
According to the economic theory of democracy and to the practical
realities of the modern political campaign, so, effectively, are political power and political office. To the more enthusiastic economists,
so are love and marriage. Friendship must now be purchased at the
cost of opportunities to consume. With the development of artificial
insemination techniques and "rent-a-womb" practices, procreation
has become an exchangeable commodity. And members of the
wealthy classes have always managed to find (not quite illegal) ways
to buy their way out of military service or, if not that, to buy their
way into military service away from the front lines. The buying and
selling of these goods that are "not for sale" is not yet completely
open, but there is no reason to believe that, as people become accustomed to the more subtle forms of exchange that now occur,
exchange won't become more and more brazen.

And this would be a disaster. Not only would the spread of exchange into nonmarket spheres of life undermine the values unique to those spheres; in addition, it would lead to a kind of tyranny, a tyranny produced when one good comes to dominate all others. Economic imperialism threatens to make money a *dominant good*, one whose influence extends beyond the market, to all spheres of social life. Were this to happen, success in the market would come to mean success at everything. Success in the market would then reach into all aspects of life. Those who dominate the market would then dominate the lives of other people. If money were to buy not only cars and houses but education, political power, love, friendship, divine grace, respect, and prestige, then those who have money would necessarily tyrannize those who do not.

Walzer's views have recently been echoed by journalist Mickey Kaus, in his book *The End of Equality*. Kaus argues that the focus of modern American liberals on economic policies that are directed at moving toward equality of income among all American citizens is misguided both in theory and in practice. Far more important than economic equality to the democratic spirit of America, he suggests, is social and political equality. And these forms of equality can be achieved without economic equality, so long as significant aspects of our lives are protected from the tyranny of the market. Leave income inequality alone (except for a safety net), he argues, and make sure that education, health care, access to public parks and highways, and other crucial goods are equally available to all, and independent of economic status. Money inequality really matters, according to Kaus, only when it corrodes social and political equality. But, of course, the central argument of this book is that, as a result of economic imperialism, money inequality is doing precisely that.

An extreme but instructive historical example of the tyranny that results when money is a dominant good is provided by the town of Pullman, Illinois. Founded in 1880, Pullman was a company town, and the company was George Pullman's railroad car company. There are plenty of company towns around, towns most of whose residents are employed by a single company. In towns like this, company and town—market and polity—are inextricably linked, since what is good for the company is good for virtually all of the town's residents. But Pullman, Illinois, was a different kind of company town. Not only did almost everyone there work for the company, but the company literally owned the town. Pullman built the town from scratch, creating houses, shops, medical facilities, schools, playgrounds, a hotel, a theater, a library, and a church. And he owned it all. The town was governed in the same way stereo equipment is governed—by its owner, as a property right. Pullman had clear ideas about how people should live, and he imposed his ideas on the residents of the town. A certain measure of tidiness and decorum was expected, and violaters could be fined by Pullman's inspectors or, worse, evicted on ten days' notice. Alteration of houses was strictly controlled, and no private construction was permitted.

Pullman's intentions were benevolent, and he ran the town with a generous, if iron, hand. The housing was good, and it was kept in good repair. The rents and prices were modest. But benevolent or not, all decision and control rested with one man—not the man chosen by the people, but the man who owned all the resources. That this mode of governance violated the principles of American democracy was eventually recognized by the Supreme Court, which required the Pullman company to divest itself of all property not used for manufacturing purposes. In reaching this decision, the court was in essence enforcing the distinction between different spheres of life. Companies could be owned; towns could not. Property rights extended to commodities, but not to communities.

It certainly seems clear that Pullman had no business owning a town and telling its residents how to live. But how clear would this be if economic imperialism swept aside the barriers between spheres of social life? All Pullman was trying to do was run his town the way he ran his factory. He didn't force anyone to work in his factory, and he didn't force anyone to live in his town. If they did either, however, they were going to live by his rules. What's the difference, after all, between the town and the factory? Pullman owned them both. He had complete control in the factory, by virtue of his ownership. Why not also in the town? We can give no coherent answer to this question unless we keep the economic sphere distinct from the political one and insist that different goods be attainable in the two spheres and that different rules govern them.

Indeed, there is a need to keep the economic and political spheres distinct even within the factory. When a woman goes to work in a factory, economists argue, she is selling her labor. But it is not just her labor that walks through the factory gate every morning; it is all of her. The laboring woman is also the political woman, the family woman, the consuming woman, and the worshiping woman.

How much of this woman is the employer "renting" with the weekly wage he pays? Is he renting the right to tell the woman what to wear or how to comb her hair? Is he renting the right to tell the woman whom to vote for, how to raise her children, or how to treat her husband? Is he renting the right to tell the woman what religion to practice or what products to buy? Of course not. It seems obvious that he is renting only those aspects of the woman that are relevant to the successful discharge of her duties.

But it is not so easy to say where relevance stops. A woman who doesn't drink off the job will probably do better work on it. A woman who keeps herself trim and fit will be sick less often. A woman who doesn't cheat on her husband may be more honest and reliable on the job. A woman who votes for one candidate may help create a better business climate than a woman who votes for the other. A woman who buys only the company's products and not those of its competitors will aid the company's profitability. A woman who speaks well of the company outside it will encourage others to buy its products. A woman who practices a religion that advocates hard work and material achievement will be more productive than a mystic. And a woman who raises her children to value material consumption will create more customers for the company in the long run than a woman who does not.

It is not very farfetched to say that all aspects of a person's life, and not just her labor, are relevant to the success of the commercial enterprise she works for. Yet her employer is not allowed to control all aspects of her life. We implicitly acknowledge that when a person goes to work in a particular factory, she is choosing a way to make a living, not a way to live. We therefore restrict the prerogatives of her employer, so that how the person lives can be subject to other sources of control and influence—those of her family, of the government, of the church, and of her own conscience.

Where, then, does the line fall between what an employer does control and what he doesn't? As in the case of all social practices, the answer here is subject to continual disagreement, struggle, reevaluation, and change. For example, right now there is a significant controversy about whether employers have the right, or perhaps even the responsibility, to require employees to take drug tests and, if so, whether that right extends to times when the employees are not on the job. The matter of drug testing arose at first in domains where customer safety was at stake (for example, among train conductors, air traffic controllers, pilots, and the like), but it has been extended to many other domains. Estimates are that more than fifteen million people must now submit to drug testing each year as a condition of employment. One company went even further than this, firing two employees because they refused to refrain from smoking cigarettes *at home*. Being a nonsmoker was a condition of employment, the company said. The company argued, correctly, that it had a financial stake in whether its employees smoked. Smokers get sick more than nonsmokers, thus costing the company money both in lost productivity and in higher health insurance premiums. There is no doubt that whether or not people smoke or use drugs is relevant to their effectiveness as employees. But whether this fact gives the company the right to insinuate itself into its employees' "private" lives is at present an unsettled issue. In the years to come, the limits to a company's involvement in its employees' lives set by the Supreme Court's *Pullman* decision may be changed.

On the other hand, there is now a movement, in many different industrial societies, to democratize the workplace. Instead of bringing principles of ownership and commerce into the polity, as Pullman did, workers are attempting to bring principles of democratic politics into the factory. They are seeking a voice in determining when they work, what they make, and how they make it—to bring areas of decision authority that have traditionally rested exclusively with ownership onto the shop floor. They are seeking to establish the principle that ownership of a company's assets does not give someone the right to do anything he wants with the company, that companies owe something to the communities in which they operate and may not simply move out when an attractive economic opportunity arises. Just where this movement to democratize the workplace will come to rest is at present also an open question. But it depends upon the realization that, even in the factory, not all of the goods available are commercial, so not all of the rules that apply should be the rules that govern the exchange of commodities.

If people are to keep different spheres of social life distinct, they must be committed to preserving the noneconomic character of nonmarket social institutions. This will involve resisting the pull to think of marriage and family life as a contractual, economic arrangement whose goods can be judged in terms of money equivalents. This is not to say that people will be required to remain loyal to the family as a patriarchal institution, in which the husband has ultimate control of all resources and all decisions. There is plenty of room, and plenty of justification, for transforming the family so that it is less authoritarian than it has traditionally been. It *is* to say that when people attempt to change the structure of traditional family life, it should be with an eye toward increasing participants' access to the goods that are appropriate to it, and not to economic goods. It is not communal access to stocks, bonds, and bank accounts but communal access to intimacy, care, and emotional attachment that should be the principal concern.

Similarly, people can struggle to preserve the relative autonomy and independence of the school from the market. The goods of education—the provision of critical awareness of self, of others, and of one's social and political institutions—should not be replaced by job training. People will need the resolve to resist the temptation to ask whether college study gives them their money's worth. This is no easy matter, especially as the costs of a college education continue to skyrocket. But it could be made a good deal easier by, for example, making education—at any level—something that money can't buy.

This discussion of the need to preserve distinct spheres of life that are not dominated by money calls to mind my discussion of *framing* in chapter 5. Recall that one of the issues raised there was that whether a particular choice people make is rational will depend on how people keep their accounts, how they decide to keep track of gains and losses. As with formal accounting, everyday accounting practices are shaped by the goals people have, by the things they are taught, and by the accounting traditions of their culture. Insisting that people keep different spheres of life distinct amounts to an argument for a particular way of keeping accounts. People have an education account, a piety account, a family account, and a political account—as well as a bank account. And their holdings in each of these accounts should not be transferable into any of the others. In this way, social institutions can be preserved, and perhaps economic imperialism can be stopped.

PRESERVING SPHERES OF SOCIAL LIFE: WE CAN'T DO IT ALONE

A decision to preserve distinct spheres of social life is not something that all of us can make on our own as individuals. We can't do it alone—for two reasons. First, if we decide to restrain our pursuit of economic interests, and to live a significant portion of our lives pursuing noneconomic objectives by nonmarket means, we will be dominated, exploited, and crushed by those who won't hesitate to have everything they do guided by economic objectives and market rules. These people will be free riders, taking advantage of our restraint to pursue their interests. And second, the character of any sphere of life is determined by the people who participate in it. If everyone around us has accepted economic imperialism, then all spheres of life will be turned into extensions of the market whether we like it or not, whether we ourselves do it or not.

This point can be made somewhat clearer with an example, one discussed by Walzer. Consider the evolution of an institution that has become commonplace in modern industrial society—the institution known as the vacation. The vacation is a modern phenomenon, perhaps a century old, and its extension to any but the very rich is more modern still. The institution that it has gradually replaced is the "holiday" (holy day). Dating at least from ancient Rome, the holiday was a time of public and communal celebration, a time to commemorate some event of civic or religious significance in which all citizens participated. The set of holidays observed by a given community was a way of defining that community. Each holiday, with its unique history and set of rituals, connected the members of a community to one another and to the community's collective past. Everyone participated, independently of economic circumstances. Indeed, often everyone was *required* to participate, as in the case of the Jewish Sabbath, so the holiday did not even involve much cost in material opportunities forgone (that is, people were not permitted to work and thus gain an advantage over those who observed the holiday).

In contrast to the public and communal holiday, the vacation is thoroughly private and individual. People negotiate for paid vacations with their employers. They decide whether to spend their money on vacations or on things, in a way that they never would with holidays. Imagine asking whether to buy a new car or celebrate Easter. The point of a vacation is not to join in celebration with other members of the community but to escape it—at least for a while. People take vacations for a change of scene, and they take them alone or just with their families. When vacations are at different times and when they take people to different places, they do not contribute, as holidays did, to keeping the community together.

As must be obvious, holidays are disappearing from American life. Within the rhythm of the week, there is no longer a period when everyone rests or has the free time to join with others in some kind of communal activity. Shops are open seven days a week, and "weekends" occur on different days for different people. The few national holidays we do observe are increasingly being separated from their histories, from the dates they are intended to commemorate. The birthdays of George Washington and Abraham Lincoln are now observed on a "Presidents' Birthday" weekend—always a weekend so that the number of people who can actually escape is maximized. If these holidays mark anything, it is not great events or persons in American history, but the opportunity to go on ski trips and to take advantage of sales in retail stores.

Certainly, the vacation offers advantages that the holiday does not. The holiday does not offer freedom from having to be at a certain place at a certain time doing a certain thing, as is the case on the job. People may be at a different place, doing a different thing, but their obligation to participate in the holiday is no less strong than their obligation to participate on the job. The vacation, in contrast, truly does afford a kind of liberation. However, the benefit of the vacation carries with it an attendant, somewhat hidden cost. It eliminates a major source of communal identity and strength. One person's vacation can't be another person's holiday.

If a significant component of what makes something a holiday is communal participation, the failure of some people to participate has an inevitable effect on others. As people choose to turn holidays into vacations, our own holidays become vacations whether we want them to or not. Communities can, of course, decide to take their leisure as some mix of holidays and vacations, but for holidays themselves to persist, there must be community agreement on what they are.

In our very pluralistic society, we can expect that different holidays will be especially significant to different groups of people— Christmas for some, Passover for some, the birthday of Martin Luther King, Jr., for some. But as long as these days are still celebrated *as* holidays, they can be a source of community cohesion and strength. When they get turned into vacations, the communities that celebrate them are communities of one.

The general consequence of turning holidays into vacations is the undermining of public life and of the social institutions that support it. When an individual decides to treat free time as a private economic good, the decision affects not only his behavior but the behavior of others who have not made that decision. The social norms governing the use of this "free" time slowly change, making it increasingly difficult to support a public, social, and noneconomic stance toward it. Eventually, one has no choice but to "consume" vacation time. Without strong social institutions that nurture and depend on public involvement and participation, the orientation of people to pursue and protect the general good weakens. Eventually, it must disappear altogether. When this happens, people have no choice but to turn to the competitive marketplace, as a supplier not just of food, clothing, and other commodities but of goods that once were provided in other ways.

THE LANGUAGES OF AMERICA: INDIVIDUAL FREEDOM AND COLLECTIVE RESPONSIBILITY

We live in a time and a place where it is possible to experience a degree of freedom that our ancestors could not have imagined. The Constitution has guaranteed certain freedoms for two hundred years.

But it is one thing to have freedom by *law* and quite another to have freedom by *more*, by social custom. And whereas legal freedom has virtually defined the United States from its beginnings, freedom by social custom is only a few generations old.

Americans have always been free by law to decide for themselves what is important and valuable in life. They have been free to choose how to live their lives; what kind of work to do, where to live, whom to live with, whom to love, what kinds of things to have, and what kind of spiritual or familial commitments to make. But until recently most of these choices were made by default. People essentially lived the lives that their parents lived. Of course, there were differences between generations. By and large, each new generation was better educated than its predecessors, and achieved greater material success. What for the parents were often only dreams, for the children became realities. Importantly, though, parents' dreams and children's realities were the same. The children were perhaps more fortunate, and went further, but their parents would have done the same thing in their place.

The making of significant life choices by default has been disappearing. Probably, the change has been continuous over America's two hundred years. Indeed, historian Gordon Wood has suggested that what was most radical about the American Revolution was not the political freedom it aspired to but the social freedom it aspired to. However, in the last generation or so, the change has been especially dramatic. It is a legacy handed down to this generation of young adults by their parents that nowadays anything is possible; everything is up for grabs. No choices are made by default. The door is open to all kinds of occupations. Liberalized social practices have made it acceptable to have intimate relations with several people of the opposite (or the same) sex before, or instead of, settling on a marital partner. Furthermore, there is no longer any expectation that marriages last forever. They are subject to continual reevaluation, with the possibility always open that they will be terminated if they stop being mutually satisfying. There are no longer clear expectations about relations between family members. Some families stay close; others drift apart. As with marriage, commitment to family life has become a matter of genuine choice. Children cannot divorce their parents, but allegiance and respect must be earned; they are not automatic. Finally, people must decide whether to pursue a spiritual life and, if so, what kind of spiritual life. The religion people are born into is not the one they are stuck with. They can convert, be born again, even create their own, personal religion.

What has all this genuine freedom of choice brought us? As has been widely reported, many members of this first generation of truly liberated Americans are experiencing—no, have invented—a collective midlife crisis. Their jobs are not all they had hoped they would be. The material rewards of their jobs do not yield satisfactions that quite match expectations. Their marriages are coming apart. They are not enjoying the close, friendly relations with their children that they thought would be the product of modern, enlightened child-rearing. Home is no longer, as it was for Robert Frost, "the place where, when you have to go there, / they have to take you in." These Americans feel disconnected from their communities and find themselves with many acquaintances, but few friends. They are distrustful of their political leaders and cynical about the moral principles for which their country stands.

What has gone wrong? How can there be so much dissatisfaction in the face of so much opportunity? An answer to this question is suggested in the book *Habits of the Heart*, an analysis of several hundred detailed interviews with Americans from all over the country, with a wide range of backgrounds, aspirations, and life paths. The unease that grips modern Americans is clear in these interviews. It is not so much that they are unhappy as that they are unsure. They don't seem to know where they belong. They don't seem to know that they are doing the right things with their lives. They don't seem to know what the right things are.

The source of this uncertainty lies in the phrase that gave the book its title, "habits of the heart." In *Democracy in America*, an analysis of American life in the early nineteenth century, Alexis de Tocqueville observed that what might be called the first language of America, as embodied in the Constitution and as lived in daily life, was individualism. America was a collection of social atoms, each in pursuit of his own interests. In America, individualism was a matter of principle, a matter of right. But this individualism was also tempered, by several "second languages" that united individuals into communities and bound them together. These second languages—

one of religious conviction and one of civic virtue—were sources of moral tradition, of social mores, of habits of the heart. They were what made it possible for people in pursuit of private, individual interests nevertheless to share public, communal purposes.

People with a common religious or civic tradition could live in genuine communities, in which at least some convictions, aspirations, and motives were shared. Their tradition could define for them a goal—something that told them what the point of life was—so they could tell whether they were on course, and they could help one another stay on course. Their tradition could also serve to restrain the pursuit of self-interest. On this, Tocqueville's position was clear. He said, "The main business of religion is to purify, control, and restrain that excessive and exclusive taste for well-being." It was these second languages of religious and civic virtue that convinced the founders of the Republic that European philosophers of the time were wrong to think that a free society, not run by aristocrats, would run amok. Virtue could substitute for aristocracy in guiding society.

Tocqueville also made it clear that the first and second languages of America—individualism and religious and civic virtue—would be in constant tension. There was no guarantee that the traditions that were keeping America civilized when Tocqueville made his study would remain strong without eternal vigilance. And Americans have not remained vigilant. In choosing to be free to choose, we have let traditions weaken. The price for the liberation of modern America seems to have been paid in these habits of the heart. In consequence, modern society *has* run amok. In an attempt to restore order and purpose to modern life, our current political leaders appeal to us to display those virtues that are part of our national heritage. They appeal for a return to the "old values" of religious commitment and civic participation. And their appeals are not falling on deaf ears. In a national poll conducted in September of 1992, more than two-thirds of all Americans indicated that they believed that the United States is in a serious, long-term moral and spiritual decline. People expressed fear that the American Dream is slipping away, that greed and materialism are ruining the country, and that their children will lead less fulfilling lives than they do. In response to this crisis, people expressed a willingness to sacrifice—to pay more taxes, to do community volunteer work, to reconnect with their civic and religious communities—but only if (and here is where the free-rider problem rears its head) other people are willing to do the same.

But as *Habits of the Heart* documents, these efforts, for many, are marked by a deep, underlying confusion and conflict. The problem is that, as a result of economic imperialism, our second languages are slowly being infused with terms from the first language, that of individualism. Civic participation is increasingly understood to be nothing but the pursuit of self-interest in the public arena. This is what the economic theory of democracy is all about. Similarly, for many of us, religion is increasingly understood to be an individual, private affair, whose function is to serve the particular needs and desires of each individual who participates. Where once most people belonged to the "church," a public institution that always had its eye turned to the secular world, now many of us find the church unsatisfactory and turn instead to sects, which set themselves apart from the world, or even to individualistic religious observance.

In addition, we are voicing serious and appropriate doubts about the legitimacy of the second languages themselves. Women are pointing out how oppressive and autocratic the second languages of religion and family can be. African Americans, Latino Americans, and Asian Americans are pointing out that "everybody's" second languages aren't, and never were, *their* second languages. And many of these groups of nonwhite Americans, who have never been fully embraced by America's first language, have retained strong commitments and social ties to the second languages of their own communities, with the result that many of the problems discussed in this book are problems for the white middle class, but not for them.

It seems clear that if they are to play a positive role in modern America, these second languages, and the institutions that embody them, will have to be modified. But it also seems clear that they cannot simply be abandoned to the freedom of the market. I say this because the members of the first generation of truly liberated Americans have not fared well with their unprecedented freedom of choice. They have had what the first governor of Massachusetts, John Winthrop, called "natural freedom," the freedom to do whatever they wanted. But in gaining this natural freedom, they have given up what he called "moral freedom," the freedom to do what is good. For the price of natural freedom is that no one is sure what "good" is any more. This seems like too steep a price to have to pay.

It's hard to work to maintain an orientation to do what is good. It's hard work to maintain a moral stance toward other people, regarding them as subjects worthy of respect rather than as objects to be manipulated for our own satisfaction. Indeed, without help—institutional help—it may be impossible for us consistently to act in this way. We can't simply teach our children in school to value other people and to take their community responsibilities seriously. As philosopher and educator John Dewey said, "the only way to prepare for social life is to engage in social life."

Can we provide the help that we all need? Can we somehow reverse the erosion of America's second languages? Can we reinvigorate public morality, the traditions of religious commitment and civic virtue? To do so, we must find a way to revive our traditional institutions, transforming them so that they retain what is good, purge what is unacceptable, and rid themselves of the influences of economic imperialism. Doing this will not be easy, but we have no alternative but to try.

11

FROM PROFITS TO PROPHETS

The real problem of our time is to restore the sense of absolute right and wrong when the belief that it used to rest on—that is, the belief in personal immortality—has been destroyed. This demands faith, which is a different thing from credulity. —GEORGE ORWELL

Sure a bird could marry a fish. But where would they live?
—TRADITIONAL YIDDISH SAYING

As many of us go through life trying to get the things we think we want out of it, we discover either that we can't have them or that they aren't worth having. The conditions of modern life have conspired to take the value out of much of what we pursue, leaving us sometimes with the frustration of failure and sometimes with the disappointment of success. The task before us, as we look at lives in which material things are disappointing, work is unsatisfying, families are coming apart, and education, leisure, health care, and justice are very expensive, is to find a way to restrain the market—to reverse economic imperialism or, at least, to keep it from spreading.

We might be tempted to try to do this as individuals, by turning inward, by reforming ourselves so that we are less interested in the things that money can buy. But at this time, living as we do in a society in which almost everything we value must be bought, the only result of our becoming less acquisitive as individuals is further deprivation and disappointment.

Alternatively, we might try to restrain the market by looking to the state to regulate and control the things that money can buy. But, as we've seen, the state has already largely given itself over to the market. It has become a part of the problem. People who are in power will listen to us politely and then ignore us as they cater to the demands of the "economic realists" on whose support their future power depends.

If as individuals we are too vulnerable and as a nation we are too unresponsive to restrain the influence of the market and change our collective social direction, where else can we turn? A possible candidate, suggested by Tocqueville, is our religious institutions. As he pointed out almost two hundred years ago, it is religious commandments—largely mediated by the family and, within the family, by its women—that rein in the pursuit and abuse of political and economic power. By strengthening our religious institutions, and by strengthening our commitment to participation in those institutions, we might thus be able to reintroduce the language of responsibility and morality into our public life. Membership in religious communities might protect us from the very harsh consequences we would otherwise face if we chose as individuals to reject the pursuit of material wealth as our primary objective in life. And religious communities might become a significant force in our social and political life, redirecting the state in a way that restrains the market and restores and protects nonmaterial values that people in our society cherish.

For this to happen, serious obstacles must be overcome. Many of us have a deep and well-justified suspicion of religious institutions as a potential source of good in the world. The mere mention of the possibility that we will turn to religious communities and institutions to seek solutions to many of the social, political, and economic problems that dominate modern social life raises a host of red flags. One flag warns against mixing religion and politics and reminds us that one of the great achievements of American constitutional democracy is the guarantee of religious freedom that comes with the separation of church and state. A second flag warns us of the *destructive* potential of religious commitment and reminds us of the bloody horrors that have been perpetrated in the name of holiness throughout history, as well as in our own time, when religious institutions have succeeded in gaining political power. A third flag warns us of the tendency of religious institutions to be slavishly bound to traditions that are oppressive, dominating, and totally at odds with the spirit of egalitarianism that guides our modern secular society when it is functioning at its best. A fourth flag reminds us that religious institutions are already involved in politics and that the politics they push seems bent on imposing their particular view of morality on everyone. And a final flag reminds us that many churches, in their modern institutionalized forms, have themselves become a part of the problem, losing touch with both the moral impulses that originally inspired them and the needs and concerns of their congregants, and seeking instead to wield power in ways that are indistinguishable from the ways of the secular institutions that we want them to restrain.

All these red flags raise appropriate concerns, legitimate fears. In addition, women, the people who have sustained the influence of religious values in the practices of daily life—who have been carriers of the "word"—have special reasons for being concerned. For women have traditionally been excluded from full participation in the very religious institutions whose word they carry. Nevertheless, it is true that religious institutions are opening themselves up, however grudgingly, to women. And it is true that there are movements within religious institutions to bring them back in touch with the values and the moral commitments that once defined them—commitments to justice and to social responsibility—which are just what we need to provide resistance to the spread of economic imperialism. Indeed, throughout the history of what is called the Judeo-Christian tradition, religious institutions have repeatedly lost touch with their core values, only to be scolded and reformed by some within those institutions who were able to see that the institutions had gone wrong. Traditionally, this scolding has been done by the prophet. The prophet does not see into the future so much as remember the past. And the prophet takes on the task of reminding people of that past and pointing out to them how far they have strayed from the initial vision that gave their religious commitments the moral force they had.

That past is a past in which religious commitments were social and political commitments. It is a past embodied by the story of the Exodus from Egypt, a story of human liberation from both material and spiritual bondage. It is a past reflected in the current practices of some modern religious institutions, from the black church in the United States to the "people's church"—the church of "liberation"—throughout Latin America.

From our vantage point as modern Americans, living in a secular society in which church and state are constitutionally separate, it seems like a corruption of religious principles when religious institutions get involved in worldly affairs. As political scientist Glenn Tinder puts it, "We are so used to thinking of spirituality as withdrawal from the world and human affairs that it is hard to think of it as political. Spirituality is personal and private, we assume, while politics is public." But, he goes on,

> such a dichotomy drastically diminishes spirituality, construing it as a relationship to God without implications for one's relationship to the surrounding world. The God of the [Judeo-]Christian faith . . . created the world and is deeply engaged in the affairs of the world. The notion that we can be related to God and not to the world—that we can practice a spirituality that is not political—is in conflict with the [Judeo-]Christian understanding of God.
>
> And if spirituality is properly political, the converse is also true, however distant it may be from prevailing assumptions: politics is properly spiritual. The spirituality of politics was affirmed by Plato at the very beginnings of Western political philosophy and was a commonplace of medieval political thought. Only in modern times has it come to be taken for granted that politics is entirely secular. The inevitable result is the demoralization of politics. Politics loses its moral structure and purpose, and turns into an affair of group interest and personal ambition.

And so, according to Tinder, and to the ancient prophets, and to many modern theologians, it is the separation of worldly from spiritual, of political from religious, that is the corruption, the deformation, of the founding vision. The task we face is to reconnect these realms, in a way that promotes liberation rather than oppression.

Can such a formidable task be undertaken successfully? I think so. Even as many of us lead what seem to be thoroughly secular lives, lives taken up with the pursuit of our individual desires, our second languages whisper to us. They whisper to us in dozens of very particular ways. They whisper to us in the meals we eat at holiday family gatherings, in the tunes of traditional songs, hymns, and prayers that we find ourselves humming or hear snatches of on the radio, in the stories and jokes that are told and retold, in the reminiscences of our elders, and in works of art and literature that surround us and live through generations. When we put all these bits and pieces together, they can amount to a sizable chunk of our daily life.

In my own childhood, for example, Friday night (Shabbat) dinners were always special. We used our "good" dishes and a fancy tablecloth. We had a meal consisting of several courses. We had challah instead of ordinary bread. We did this only on Friday night, and we did it because Friday night was Shabbat and we were Jewish. We almost never went to synagogue services. We never said any of the traditional prayers associated with eating and drinking at our special Shabbat meal. Nevertheless, it was clear to me from family activities like this that I was a Jew and that, whatever that identity might mean, it could not be casually discarded. I can still see the well-set table, still smell the food, still hear my grandmother's Yiddish-Russian-English voice. The cultural vestiges of Judaism with which I grew up are in my bones; they're a permanent part of me. An unobservant Jew is still a Jew. A lapsed Catholic is still a Catholic.

Most of us have traditional practices like this somewhere in our past and feel pulled by them. We may not think of them as religious. We may think of them as cultural. Nevertheless, they may provide a solid foundation on which our second languages can be strengthened—strengthened to restrain the individualism that is our first language. We may be able to rekindle our second languages by reconnecting the traditional practices we value to their religious sources. And we may be able to use these foundations to transform our religious institutions so that their oppressive and dominating features, which make us afraid to enhance the role they play in our individual and collective lives, can be replaced by features that are liberating and just.

As people contemplate returning to the fold, or entering the fold for the first time, they may find themselves confronted with a variety of conflicts and hard choices. People may find that while their religious institutions tell them one thing, their various secular commitments tell them something else, so they are faced with the very difficult task of weighing and balancing different goals and different standards in different domains of their lives. For example, their religious institutions may tell them that they owe a special loyalty to people of their own faith, while their secular commitments tell them to care about all people equally. Their religious institutions may tell them that abortion is a mortal sin, while their secular commitments tell them that abortion is a civil right. Their religious institutions may tell them to accept authority, while their secular commitments tell them to question it. Their religious institutions may tell them to put the welfare of others first, while their secular commitments and experience tell them they have to look out for themselves. People may find themselves unwilling to regard religious teachings as *commandments*, about which they have no choice, rather than as *suggestions*, about which they are the ultimate arbiters, and thus they may be unwilling to accept the hierarchical, authoritarian structure of their traditional religious institutions. Having been thoroughly immersed in a culture dominated by economic imperialism that speaks only the language of individualism, people may look upon participation in a religious community as a way to satisfy very personal desires. Some may be seeking particular kinds of emotional experience. Some may be seeking particular kinds of social experience. Some may be seeking ethical guidance and assistance with specific problems in their lives. All such people may think it appropriate that individuals seek to make religious activities and experiences into whatever they want them to be. Religious institutions then become a kind of market in comfort, tranquillity, spirituality, and ethical reflection, and "religion consumers" shop in that market until they find what they like. Or, if not that, people may think it appropriate that the religious institutions to which they belong are flexible enough in their teachings and their practices to accommodate a diverse set of congregants with a diverse set of interests, needs, and desires.

It may seem odd to talk about religious institutions in these kinds of shopping mall terms, but I think such descriptions are often accurate reflections of what people want and expect from their religious activities. With expectations about individual choice and personal satisfaction as dominant as they are in all other domains of life, it is hard to imagine that they could be kept out of the daily functioning of religious institutions. Even when people join communities of faith and expect to participate in the life of those communities and embrace (at least some of) the practices of those communities, they simultaneously expect the communities to be responsive to *their* needs, *their* tastes, and *their* desires. It is hard for people to spend the bulk of their lives engaged in the marketplace, living by America's first language and suffering the effects of economic imperialism, without having some of this concern and activity spill over into the domains of their second languages. By importing the goals and expectations of the marketplace into their religious institutions, people reduce the tension between these two languages. At the same time, of course, they reduce the extent to which the second language can restrain the first.

We don't customarily think of religious affiliation as a matter of taste or desire. More commonly, we think in terms of commandment, ethical commitment, and moral obligation. We think of people who join religious institutions as having chosen a path that is full of social and moral responsibilities. But in order for a religious affiliation to have this customary meaning, its tenets must derive from some kind of authority. Traditionally, that authority was, of course, the authority of God. Either God, or God's messengers, revealed to the people the divine word, the sacred laws by which people were to live their lives. In the late twentieth century, dominated as it is by a materialistic, scientific conception of the universe, it is very difficult for many people—even people who participate in religious communities—to accept and embrace such a view of God and God's word. It is very difficult to accept a supernatural God, a maker of miracles, a knower of all things, an author of divine and eternal law. Many people find themselves drawn to a much more naturalistic conception of God, one in which the "word of God" was written by people, and in which "divine laws" are actually human laws. In this view, "God" represents a kind of force for good that exists within us, within human beings. If God's word is a human word, and God's law is a human law, and God itself is a human ethical impulse, then God's authority is a human authority. It was created by people, and it can be changed by people. While this view makes it possible to transform religious institutions and practices in keeping with modern conceptions of justice and freedom, it also opens the door to condoning and even celebrating whatever form of religious participation any individual finds meaningful. Tastes and preferences in religious activity become no more peculiar than tastes and preferences in literature, or in music, or in ice cream. And this view also opens the door to a wide array of different, and even incompatible, ethical commitments and, in so doing, undermines the sense of absolute right and wrong about which George Orwell was concerned in the passage with which this chapter began.

Such a view of God and of people is perfectly compatible with a social system organized around the individualism of the market-place. When Fyodor Dostoevsky contemplated what a world like this might be like, he said that "if God is dead, everything is permitted." He imagined a world of callousness, indifference, and outright hostility as the strong trampled the weak—a world that was a jungle. If my arguments are correct, we now live in such a world. And yet, harsh as it may be, it doesn't seem to be the nihilistic nightmare of Dostoevsky's imaginings. We all know many people who either hold a naturalistic conception of God or don't believe in God at all. And, for the most part, these people try to lead decent lives, showing concern for the well-being of others, being honest and caring in their social relations, taking on community obligations, and offering help to those in need. They don't act as if "everything is permitted." It is possible, then, that secular moral principles, of human rather than divine authorship and authority, can substitute for religious principles. But it is also possible that the decency and respect that people display in their everyday dealings with one another are vestiges of customs and habits that developed in a time when commitment to divine law was commonplace and that, as that commitment disappears, the customs and habits will slowly disappear with it. It is possible, in other words, that the civility we now observe in society is parasitic on a view of the world that people no longer hold and that, as time passes, that civility will be replaced by precisely the nihilism that Dostoevsky feared.

Dostoevsky also said that a person "cannot live without worshipping something." If God, as traditionally understood, is either dead or dying, what is that something to be? There is no shortage of candidates. Some people worship science, which has slowly replaced religion as the final authority on the state of the world and our place in it. Some people worship pleasure, and devote all of their energy to its pursuit. Some people worship political leaders, and commit indescribable atrocities in their names. Some people worship themselves, as the notion of God as a human creation sometimes invites. And some people worship commerce, the world of getting and spending, in which "business is business" and requires no further justification.

Much that I have discussed in this book is about the consequences of the worship of commerce. Enthusiastic supporters of the free market see it as a device for channeling the sins of greed and selfishness so that they serve the common good. They suggest that it is far more effective in this regard than any religious appeal to justice, love, charity, or mercy. But, as Tinder sees it, the principles that govern the free market are antithetical to the religious principles they are meant to replace:

> Insofar as the market governs social relations, people are forced into acquisitive rivalry; to count in any way on a gift of "daily bread" rather than on money in the bank would be the mark of a fool. Acquisitive success is candidly equated with virtue and personal worth naively measured in material terms. Charity . . . is a matter of personal generosity, not of justice or community. . . . No principles could be more thoroughly anticommunal than those of capitalism. Indeed, capitalism is probably more anticommunal in theory than in practice, for human beings cannot be as consistently selfish and calculating as capitalist doctrine calls on them to be. . . . Even if capitalism worked as well as its supporters claim, it would by Christian standards fail morally and spiritually.

●   ●

My discussion has left us (or at least me) on the horns of a dilemma. People seem to need and want a spiritual life in a religious community. And society seems to need and want such people. However, without a belief in a supernatural God, a spiritual life in a religious community can degenerate into the exercise of personal taste in the worship of almost anything. This is one horn of the dilemma. The other horn is that many people find it difficult to accept a supernatural God. And they find it difficult to accept religious codes of conduct as commandments rather than as mere suggestions. They expect to be able to pick and choose among commandments—to observe just the ones that suit them. Is there someplace we can turn to resolve this dilemma? I cannot answer this question with any certainty. What I can do is offer an example—a case study—of a group of people that has been grappling with this dilemma for several years. The efforts of this group may provide a useful illustration both of why resolving the dilemma is so difficult and of why it is worth the struggle.

The Bird and the Fish

So let me tell you about the bird and the fish. Each of them is exquisitely adapted to survive and even flourish in a particular environment. Each has evolved mechanisms for respiration, locomotion, feeding, and reproduction that meet the unique challenges and demands imposed by the environment in which it normally lives. The trouble when you try to bring them together is that the mechanisms each has evolved for its own niche are totally unsuited to the other's niche. There just isn't any place where a fish and a bird can live together successfully and still remain a fish and a bird. No compromise is possible. Either the bird becomes a fish, or the fish becomes a bird, or both perish trying to become some third thing.

This incompatibility between fish life and bird life is obviously nothing that should trouble us, since no one with any sense would try to "marry" a fish and a bird. But the point of the traditional saying is that sometimes different people live lives made up of rituals and customs, hopes and aspirations, that are as different from each other and as incompatible with each other as the worlds of the fish and the bird. With these people, as with the fish and the bird, there is no possibility for compromise, no neutral place where they can live together successfully. When they try, either the bird becomes a fish, or the fish becomes a bird, or both perish trying to become some third thing. And even within a single individual, there may be hopes and aspirations that are also incompatible, and that can't be served at the same time and the same place by the same activities. The marriage of bird and fish within a single person is at least as difficult as it is among different people.

When a group of people to which I belonged set out to start a new kind of Jewish community, we were faced, though we didn't know it, with the problem of the fish and the bird. Each of us was both a Jew and an American, and we wanted to create an institution that incorporated what was good about each of those identities. Judaism, it is said, is a religion of laws. What this means is that Jews are told by their traditional teachings what to do in almost every aspect of daily life—secular or religious, significant or mundane. And America is the culture of freedom, a culture in which individuals are empowered to decide for themselves how to live their lives. So when a group of very American Jews gets together to form a congregation, it is faced with the task of marrying a fish and a bird, of marrying traditional constraint and regulation to unfettered freedom. As my congregation discovered, figuring out how to do this—figuring out where and how the "married couple" should live—is no simple matter. It is no simple matter for the group as a whole or for any of the individuals within the group. We performed the marriage five years ago, and we're still not sure that the bird and the fish have a place to call home.

It all began over politics. My family belonged to a small Jewish congregation that operated out of a plain, old, converted three-story house in a Philadelphia suburb. My participation in the congregation was at first quite minimal. Membership in an organized Jewish community had never been especially important to me. Indeed, for many years I found the prospect of participation in an organized Jewish community almost unthinkable. Then I fell into what has become quite a common pattern among Jews in the United States, disparagingly referred to by some as "pediatric Judaism." A pediatric Jew is someone who becomes Jewish, or "remembers" that he's Jewish, at the time that his children are old enough for a Jewish education. Most pediatric Jews maintain some involvement with the congregations they join until their children reach middle adolescence, at which point their involvement begins to diminish, or even disappears altogether. I fully expected to conform to this pattern. But then something unexpected happened. Our congregation hired a new rabbi, who was committed to the view that religious involvement demanded social and political activism. For this rabbi, being a "good Jew" required more than attending services and participating in rituals. It required more than giving charity to the needy. It also required engaging in political activity in pursuit of justice—social justice, economic justice, and political justice—for non-Jews as well as for Jews. This commitment to marrying spiritual observance with political and social action got me interested and engaged.

Despite the long history within Judaism of emphasis on political activity as a part of religious observance, it did not sit well with most members of the congregation. It wasn't so much that they disagreed with the rabbi (though some did) about which injustices required attention and action. Rather, it was more that they thought it inappropriate for a *religious* organization to be doing political work. They thought that people could do political work on their own, or as part of *explicitly* political organizations—that politics was not what religious organizations were for. Many people who participated in our congregational life did so explicitly to separate themselves for a few hours each week from the trouble and sadness of the everyday world, not to immerse themselves in it.

Nevertheless, the rabbi was insistent in his view that religious observance required political involvement. And the underlying tension that existed about matters of political and religious philosophy came to the surface when the rabbi, along with several members of the congregation, engaged in public political activities that came to be identified with the congregation as a whole. Several members of the congregation demanded that the rabbi restrain his public political activity. He refused, claiming not that the demand for restraint violated his right to free speech but that it violated his conception of what a good Jew as part of a good community must do. There was a vote of confidence. And the rabbi and his supporters lost.

I had by now become thoroughly embroiled in the community conflict. Pediatric Jew or not, I found the vision of a religious community committed to political and social activism to be wholly appropriate and deeply appealing. It seemed like the antidote to a secular world in which economic imperialism had bleached all morality out of politics. There was simply no political organization left in which a person could work and expect to hear discussions about what was right rather than about what was expedient. To speak in such organizations about right and wrong was to guarantee that you would not be taken seriously. Faced with the moral vacuum of secular politics, individuals were left with two equally unattractive choices. They could maintain their moral concerns and opt out of politics all together, or they could engage in political activity and leave their moral concerns at the door. The involvement of religious organizations in politics offered a possible third way, a way to combine morality and politics within and through a strong and committed organization. Whether being a good Jew required this, as my rabbi contended, I could not say. But it did seem to me that being a good *American* required it. It did seem to me that this might be the best way to begin to build a social movement that would work to reverse some of the developments I have outlined in this book— that would work to preserve and reconstruct some of the best things in life by freeing them from the grip of economic imperialism. So when the rabbi lost his vote of confidence, I and many of my fellow congregants thought there was too much stake for us simply to be good losers and give up the fight. We felt compelled to try to create a new institution.

And so we did precisely that. At meetings in people's living rooms on sweltering summer nights, the forty or so families that had supported the rabbi gathered to plan and to create a new institution. Many of the people involved had joined the congregation as pediatric Jews like myself. They had abandoned Judaism—they thought permanently—in late adolescence or early adulthood, only to find themselves drawn back as their children started asking them why *they* didn't celebrate Christmas. It had never been their intention to become active in the congregation. They had been drawn into active involvement by the rabbi, who showed them that Jewish life and observance could be quite different from what it had been in their childhood. And now they found themselves not only active but deeply engaged in the process of establishing a new institution.

Many of the people who planned the new congregation were among the religious walking wounded. They had not left organized Judaism casually. They had not left it because their lives had become too busy. They had not distractedly neglected it until it seeped, like sand through a sieve, out of their lives. They had left it consciously and deliberately because they had found aspects of its doctrines and its practice hurtful, offensive, and unjust. They had left congregations where money talked—where the biggest contributors ran the institution, where people with small incomes were made to feel unworthy, and where community events became opportunities for people to display their wealth to one another. They had left congregations in which people could chant ritual pieties at weekend services and then ignore them in their dealings with the world during the rest of the week. They had left congregations in which the traditional treatment of women as second-class was left unchanged and, indeed, unexamined. They had found in the practices of the congregations of their past the very same patterns of hierarchy, domination, injustice, and hypocrisy that they spent their time combatting in the secular world. This new institution was going to be different, different not just in matters of practice but in matters of principle. In fact, this new institution was going to start with a statement of principles, so that people would know, explicitly and unequivocally, what it stood for—what made it different from other Jewish congregations.

And so, while some planners worried about finding a place for the congregation to meet, and some worried about finding money for the rent and for the rabbi's salary, and some worried about setting up a school for the children, others set about to write the principles that would define our community. They set about to try to adapt or reconstruct the long-standing traditions and teachings of Judaism to the particular circumstances that faced people in a contemporary America that was dominated by economic imperialism and the language of self-interest. And it was in the course of this process of community definition that the bird and the fish got together and tried to figure out where to live.

For the traditions we had to work with, as Jews, were traditions of commandment, law, and regulation. The traditional community of Jews has something to tell its members about what they eat, what they wear, what kind of work they do and how they do it, whom they marry, how they engage in sex, and how they should behave with their children, their parents, their spouses, their friends, other Jews, and even non-Jews who live among them. Traditional Judaism has little use for a distinction that most Americans take for granted— the distinction between public life and private life. Modern Americans attach a great deal of importance to the distinction between the public and the private aspects of their lives. And while they are willing to have their public lives regulated, both by law and by custom, they expect freedom in their private lives, and they support an elaborate system of laws whose principal function is to protect their private lives from meddling both by the state and by other citizens. For traditional Judaism, basically all aspects of life are public.

On the other hand, as modern Americans, we expected that all decisions about how to live and what to do were up to the individual. Individual freedom and empowerment are deeply valued by Americans, and they were deeply valued by the members of my Jewish community. Indeed, much of their commitment to the pursuit of social justice was a commitment to help make the kind of personal freedom that they enjoyed as well-educated, middle-class Americans available to the millions in their culture, and around the world, who didn't possess it. So our task in drafting a statement of principles was to find a way to marry traditional restraint and regulation with modern freedom. Where would they live? How would they live?

The task we faced was one of making a coherent conversation out of the two languages that Tocqueville had noticed in his observations of American culture two centuries before. The language of individualism whispered into our ears advice to do whatever we wanted, whatever would give us satisfaction. The language of religious commitment whispered into our ears advice to do what was right, what was good for everyone. These two languages were often explicitly incompatible and contradictory. The only place they were united was in the heads of individuals, where they established conflicts between rights and duties, between pleasure and virtue. Tocqueville's confidence (or faith) that sometimes these conflicts would be decided in favor of duty over rights, virtue over pleasure, was what inspired his confidence (or faith) that the American experiment would succeed.

What we were trying to do was eliminate the conflict. We were trying to invent or discover a third language, into which these incompatible first and second languages could be translated, that would somehow reconcile rights and duties. Rather than allowing the fish and the bird to fight it out for our allegiance, we were trying to develop a new creature—neither fish nor fowl—that respected individual freedom and privacy at the same time that it established community standards and obligations. And we discovered that the task was exceedingly difficult, perhaps even impossible.

We considered the extreme of Jewish Orthodoxy, of taking all the commandments that were meant to regulate our lives seriously, as community imperatives. It was immediately apparent that Orthodoxy was not a viable candidate. Not only was it highly impractical to try to live an Orthodox Jewish life in a non-Jewish world. Even worse, many aspects of Jewish Orthodoxy were explicitly incompatible with some of the commitments that had brought us together.

The extreme of complete individual autonomy seemed much more attractive, much more in keeping with the language of individual freedom that was everyone's first language. The language of freedom could embrace gender equality, toleration of spiritual and sexual differences, and respect for privacy, while traditional Orthodoxy could not. The problem was that, in its extreme form, individual autonomy offers no community-defining principles at all. Each free-flying bird is entitled to make of her community commitments whatever she wishes—to observe what and when and how she wants to observe, to participate when and how she wants to participate. A community of birds is no community. It's just a collection, one that may, at times, happen to fly together, but cannot be counted upon to do so. So the extreme of complete individual freedom also wouldn't do.

Although we knew from the beginning that traditional Orthodoxy was not a possibility for our community, the problems with the opposite extreme, of complete individual freedom, were less obvious. We had come together as a collection of like-minded people, people who had many, if not most, values in common and who, if completely free to choose how they and others should live, would probably make very similar choices. And so it seemed to us that if we embraced individual freedom of expression, observance, and religious commitment as a principle, we would form the kind of community we wanted to be. But as we talked more about it, we realized that this was only because of the happy accident that we happened to agree about most things. There was no guarantee that this uniformity of vision would continue. A commitment to individual freedom of expression and observance also meant giving freedom of expression and observance to people who thought men and women should have radically different roles in a Jewish community, who thought homosexuality was an abomination, and who thought politics had no place in a religious organization. And so we came to realize that our commitment was not really to individual expression and observance. Instead, it was to some forms of expression and observance—including some that had been excluded from traditional Jewish practice—and a rejection of others, many of which had been embraced in traditional Jewish practice.

When we came to this understanding, we realized that we could not avoid producing a statement of principles that excluded some Jews (that is, made them feel unwelcome) and rejected some practices. And we realized that our statement of principles had, to some degree, to tell people how we thought they should be living their lives. None of this sat well with people who had themselves abandoned Jewish practice years before precisely because the things it told them about how to live their lives they found unacceptable. But any community worthy of the name is a community of some but not all people; it celebrates some but not all ways of life.

Faced with the daunting task of melding our first and second languages, we drafted a statement of principles. It identified our community as "committed to the integration of the three primary areas of Jewish life; prayer, study, and acts of care and repair of the world." With this statement, we not only made clear our commitment to political activism, but, by focusing on *integration*, we made clear that activism was integral to what we believed and did. It was informed and guided by our prayer and study; it was not merely added on. On this general statement, there was broad community support and agreement. The problems came when we began to specify more concretely what kind of prayer, study, and repair of the world we were committed to.

With regard to prayer, we faced two significant problems. First, different members of our congregation had very different conceptions of God. At the extremes, some members held rather traditional views of a supernatural God, while others believed that "God" was a human invention. Second, women are virtually absent from the language and the content of the traditional liturgy. Everyone agreed that this was unacceptable. But people differed as to what might be done about it. Many of our members found it difficult or impossible to say prayers that in effect were institutionalizing the insignificance of women. They argued that the content of the liturgy should be changed. But other members thought there was value in saying the same words that had been said by our ancestors for thousands of years and that were still being said, in synagogues all over the world, every Friday night and Saturday morning. They argued that the liturgy should be retained, but supplemented with suitable commentary.

Our statement of principles resolved these disagreements by means of the word "and." We would accommodate views of God as a force of nature, *and* as a force of human agency, *and* as something transcendant and mysterious. We would change some of the content of our prayers to reflect the equal status of women, *and* we would retain the original prayers in our prayerbooks so that people could experience a bond with their traditional past. All these "and" 's make for prayer services that are sometimes rather long and sometimes rather incoherent. They make for prayer services that give everybody something and nobody everything. Though these compromises by conjunction left most of us a little uncomfortable, our community accepted them with good will and in good faith, understanding that if things got too sexist (or too feminist), too mundane (or too supernatural), too insular (or too universal), our spiritual practices would be open to continuing discussion and revision.

When we turned to study, the second leg of our tripod (of prayer, study and repair of the world), similar issues arose. We were committed to study, but study of what? Clearly, because we were Jews, our focus would be on the sacred texts of our tradition, the Torah and the Talmud. But how open should we be to other texts, including both secular texts and the sacred texts of other religious traditions? And how were we to approach our sacred texts? For traditional Jews, the Talmud was the law. It laid out, in extraordinary detail, the rules by which people were to live their lives. But many of these laws were for us either impractical or unacceptable. This meant that we would have to read the laws critically, picking and choosing from among them the ones that seemed appropriate. The trouble was that we had no principles that could govern our picking and choosing. Different members of our community found different laws unacceptable. Some members found the very notion of a *law* unacceptable. In their view, it was up to each of us to decide individually how to live a life—what to observe and what to disregard. The notion of law, as articulated and enforced by a community, deprived individuals of the freedom and autonomy that the first language of America had given them as their birthright.

In our statement of principles, we resolved some of these difficulties by again resorting to "and." We would study sacred texts *and* other sources. And we resolved other difficulties by being silent altogether about whether any of the teachings of our sacred texts would have the status of law. But this silence as to law only postponed problems; it didn't solve them. Within the first year of our existence, several issues arose regarding matters of law. We had to struggle over deciding which, if any, of Judaism's traditional dietary laws (the laws of kashrut) to observe on occasions when food was served at one of our gatherings. Should we ignore dietary laws, and just let individuals bring and eat whatever they wanted? Should we adhere strictly to the traditional laws of kashrut? Should we adhere to a modified version of kashrut by observing the prohibition against mixing meat and dairy and prohibiting meat from being served at community gatherings? Or should we create a new kashrut, one that was sensitive to issues of ecology, health, and problems of world hunger? We also had to struggle over deciding which, if any, of Judaism's traditional laws governing the Sabbath to observe. The Sabbath is meant to be a day of prayer, study, and rest, a day that separates us from the normal activities of daily life—no work, no handling money, no cooking or cleaning. So we had to decide whether we could have congregational committee meetings (surely a form of work) on the Sabbath. We had to decide whether we could allow people to perform their assigned synagogue cleanup and maintenance chores on the Sabbath. Strict observance of the Sabbath was impossible. Almost none of our members could even have attended Sabbath services if they had observed the prohibition against driving. So we either had to abandon Sabbath restrictions altogether or, once again, pick and choose among them, in the absence of any principles that would guide us. And some of our members resented any prohibitions or restrictions, arguing that what was important about Sabbath observance was not so much what one did as how one did

it ("God loveth adverbs," the saying goes). Even cleaning the synagogue bathrooms might be a holy activity if it was done with the
right attitude, and it was up to each of us to decide, as individuals,
what kind of activity made the Sabbath separate and holy for us.
The sacredness of the Sabbath was, in other words, a private and
not a public matter.

Except, unfortunately, that it wasn't. Almost all "private" matters
have a public aspect. If for some, a sacred Sabbath requires people
gathered together for rest, prayer, and study, it just won't do to have
a vacuum cleaner humming in the background, no matter how
sacred the vacuuming might be to the person doing it. Indeed, more
generally, if for some what makes the Sabbath sacred is that it brings
the members of the community together in the common pursuit of
rest, prayer, and study, then any principle that encourages or allows
people to observe the Sabbath in whatever way they find meaningful
is unsatisfactory.

What's at issue here echoes some points in the last chapter.
Recall my discussion of the difference between vacations and holidays. Vacations are private and typically encourage us to escape
from the community. Holidays are public and typically encourage
us to interact with the community. It is simply not possible to allow
people to decide for themselves whether their lives will contain vacations or holidays. When people are allowed (I mean by custom, not
by law) to do whatever they want about holidays, holidays perforce
stop being holidays. If some members of the community choose to
work and some choose to get away, the holiday as an occasion of
communal observance and celebration has been destroyed. And the
Sabbath is the prototype of the holiday (holy day).

It is in matters of observance of Jewish law that America's first
and second languages come most directly into conflict. It is here
that people face most starkly the choice between giving free rein to
their individual tastes and preferences or submerging them in the
service of a communal vision. It is in these matters that the fish
and the bird face their problems of incompatibility most vividly. In
traditional Jewish communities, picking and choosing among the
laws in a way that suits individual tastes and life circumstances was
and is simply not an option. Such notions of personal choice and
discretion were and are unthinkable. In nontraditional Jewish com-

munities, like ours, personal choice and discretion are inescapable. So are the problems for communal practice and character that they pose. At this writing, as my congregation celebrates and struggles through its fifth year of existence, we have not yet developed a way to discuss matters of Jewish law as they might apply to our community in a way that does not offend or threaten many of our members. Whether such a discussion is possible in a community that gives primacy to the first language of America is an open question.

Agreeing on what our statement of principles should say about acts of care and repair of the world, the third leg of our communal tripod, was relatively easy. We were bound together by the story of the Exodus from bondage in Egypt. We viewed the Exodus as a model of how religious commitment and commitment to the pursuit of justice go together. "Exodus morality" we called it, the morality of liberation. And there was general agreement among us about which side we were on in many of the struggles for liberation that were going on both inside and outside our national boundaries.

But here, alas, was the problem. There was no shortage of liberation struggles to get involved with. There was the struggle of blacks in South Africa. There was the struggle of homeless people in Philadelphia. There was the struggle of Jews in the Soviet Union. There was the struggle of peasants in Central America. There was the struggle of Arabs in the West Bank and the Gaza Strip. There were the struggles of women and of homosexuals. There was the struggle of the disabled. There were the struggles against age, sex, and race discrimination in jobs and in housing. Many worthy projects. Much work to be done. Community support, in theory, for all of them. But not nearly enough community resources—in people, in time, or in money—to follow through. So which ones should be chosen? And according to what principles? Different individuals in the congregation had very deep involvements with one or another of these struggles. But what lay behind the particular struggles they had chosen usually involved idiosyncratic personal history or secular political involvement. They could appeal *personally* to other members of the congregation to become involved ("I think this is very important, and you respect me and my judgment, so you should think it's important too.") They could not appeal to religious principles generally, or to the particular principles that united our community, to justify our involvement in one struggle rather than another. As a community, we lacked a language that might enable us to prioritize projects and choose among them. The only language we had was the language of individual preference and choice. Thus, even when our focus was on getting outside ourselves to engage in activities that would contribute to the care and repair of a broken world, the fact that we spoke to one another in America's first language made it difficult to agree on what to care for, what to repair.

In addition to the difficulties we had in specifying our basic principles in specific detail, we also had difficulty in deciding just how seriously the members of our congregation were supposed to take their membership. Was our community supposed to become the center of our lives—spiritually, ethically, politically, and even socially and economically? Were our members supposed to treat fellow congregants differently from the way they treated the rest of the world? Did congregants have special responsibilities and obligations? Could they command special attention? If, by some chance, our community was able to agree on what kinds of worship, of diet, of sexual practices, of living arrangements, of political involvements, were "kosher," and if it was to proclaim its "kosher laws," were the members of the community expected to abide by those laws? If they didn't, could they be publicly sanctioned, or even expelled from the community? Was it possible, in a society in which there were almost no social or economic rules, for a small community to establish its own and demand that its members follow them?

Questions like these go right to the heart of what it means to be a community, whether Jewish, Protestant, Catholic, or Muslim, whether religious or secular. As sociologist John Murray Cuddihy has pointed out in his book *No Offense*, what it means to belong to a religious community has changed dramatically over the last century in the United States. Owing perhaps to the multiplicity of religious groups in the country, and perhaps to the fact that the United States has no established religion, we expect people in our society to be Americans first and Jews, Protestants, Catholics, or Muslims second. We expect people to be Americans who "happen to be" whatever religion they are. We value second languages and support them, but it is essential that they stay second languages, that they stay in their place. We value religious commitments and support them, but we expect that people won't take their religion too seriously, that they won't let it show in public, that they won't let it spill over into America's pluralistic, secular life. We expect people to be Jewish, or Protestant, or Catholic, or Muslim in the same way that they are Yankee, Dodger, Cub, or Red Sox fans. (When I say "we," I don't, of course, mean everybody. There are certainly people whose religious commitments suffuse everything they do, and who think that others should be similarly guided. But I believe that most modern Americans, and certainly most university-educated, urban, professional Americans, believe that if religion has a place in life, that place is not everyplace.) Cuddihy suggests that while Protestantism developed with this kind of part-time view in mind, it is inimical both to traditional Judaism and to traditional Catholicism. Traditional Judaism and Catholicism are total ways of life, and not just flavors of religious belief that can get tacked on to an otherwise secular existence.

If you are faced with an all-encompassing religious community, you have but one question to answer, one choice to make: Do you join up or not? Once you decide to join up, you simply understand and accept the fact that this decision will affect everything you do. You may decide to work within the community to change it, to change the specific instructions (commandments) it gives you about the various aspects of your life (sexual conduct, Sabbath observance, diet, politics), but you expect it to give you some instructions about everything. If, in contrast, you are faced with a religious community whose scope is more modest, you confront myriad questions and choices. In addition to deciding whether or not to join up, you are also faced, again and again, with decisions about whether to allow this or that aspect of your life (your work, your hobbies, your diet, your charitable activities, your sexual preferences, your reading habits) to be influenced by your religious affiliation. In each case, the decision is entirely up to you; it is personal and private, a matter of taste.

Many Americans, thoroughly imbued as they are with the first language of individual freedom, would find an all-encompassing religious commitment unacceptably oppressive. And true as this is in general, it is even truer of the members of my congregation, many of whom had fled the congregations of their youth precisely because these congregations were telling them how to live and, worse, telling them that they should live in ways that violated their own beliefs. So there was strong sentiment in our community to resist any tendency to total commitment. On the other hand, there was a very deep longing in people to belong to something, something that was larger than any individual, would last longer than any individual, and would accept, nurture, and protect those who had made commitments to it. There was a very deep longing in people to make this congregation, this community, their "haven in a heartless world." And it wasn't clear that any institution that allowed each individual member to pick and choose among the principles that defined and governed it could ever develop the strength and continuity to become that haven. So over and above the conflicts between first and second languages that were reflected in our discussion of the various principles to which our community was committed, there was this more general conflict, over how much individuals could be expected to submerge their first language when they chose to adopt our particular second language. What, in other words, was a person giving up, and what was she getting, if she decided to become one of us?

We grappled with all of these questions, resolving none of them, as we formulated our statement of principles, as we ratified it, and as we began to function as a community. Some people became angry while others approved when we decided that the members' cleaning of our communal space could not be done on the Sabbath. Some people became angry while others approved when some women in the congregation tested our commitment to the full participation of women in congregational life by holding "alternative" Sabbath services that were open only to women. Some people became angry while others approved when we decided that there were some roles in the Sabbath service that could not be taken by the non-Jewish partners of members, though, for the most part, non-Jewish partners were welcome to full membership and participation. Some people became angry while others approved when we took a public stand opposing the launching of a ground war by the United States against Iraq after Iraq's 1990 invasion of Kuwait. And some people became angry while others approved when we failed to oppose the U.S. bombing raids against Iraq that preceded the ground war. Through all the disagreement, conflict, and uncertainty, we were kept together, and are still kept together, by the realization that none of us alone could create a safe, just, and caring world for ourselves and our families. None of us alone could resist the force of economic imperialism and the competitive pressure of the market. None of us alone could instill in our children the kind of values we thought they should have, and the kind of strength to resist corruption we thought they would need. None of us alone could make political organizations talk in the language of justice rather than in the language of interests. We were willing as individuals to pay a price to help make a world in which the best things in life were available to people, and in which the best things in life were still worth having. But acting as individuals, without a supporting community, the price was too steep and the goal too remote. Our hope was that by acting in the world as part of a strong and supportive organization, some of our burden would be eased. And it couldn't be just any supportive organization. It couldn't be an interest group, a political lobby. Such groups are more a part of the problem than of the solution. It had to be an organization with moral force and vision. It had to be an organization that reflected what we were. And what we were, each of us, despite the many differences among us, was Jewish.

What many of us did not know at first, and came slowly to realize in the course of our community's struggle for self-definition, was the extent to which the price we would have to pay for membership in a strong and supportive community was in the coin of our individualism. We simply could not, each of us, be whatever kind of Jew we wanted to be. We would surely have to sacrifice some of our individualism in our public lives, and we might even have to sacrifice it in our private lives as well. Yes, a bird could marry a fish. And perhaps the bird could avoid having to develop gills. But it would surely have to be willing to give up flying, to have its wings clipped.

Exodus, Community, and Liberation

The Exodus story is the story not of individuals but of a people. The phrase "the people of Israel" is first used in the Book of Exodus. Prior to the Exodus, the Hebrew Bible tells the stories of individuals and of families. In the Exodus, these individuals and families become fused into a "people," a community. It is an intergenerational community, united not only by blood but by common religious commitment. It is a community whose spirit has been crushed by years of bondage and domination under the rule of the pharaoh in Egypt, sufficiently crushed that, despite their impressive numbers (600,000 or so), the members of the community quake in fear rather than rise up to fight against the pharaoh's tyrannical rule. It is a community whose spirit is sufficiently crushed that, despite God's promise to deliver them from bondage, there are many who resist the uncertain future of freedom and prefer the safety and security of servitude. It is a community whose spirit is sufficiently crushed that it must learn the ways of freedom—it must be made to wander in the desert for forty years so that the generation raised in slavery can learn the possibilities and responsibilities of freedom or else die off and be replaced by a generation born and raised with those possibilities and responsibilities. The move from bondage to freedom is not easy. Even with God's help it is a struggle, a struggle that takes faith, courage, patience, and time.

What unites the Jews in Egypt and makes them a people is a covenant, an agreement they make—with God and with one another—to be bound by a set of religious and moral commandments. As Michael Walzer points out,

> The covenant is a founding act, creating alongside the old association of tribes a new nation composed of willing members. In Egypt, . . . [the Israelites'] identity, like that of all men and women before liberation, is something that has happened to them. Only with the covenant do they make themselves into a people in the strong sense, capable of sustaining a moral and political history, capable of obedience and also of stiff-necked resistance, of marching forward and of sliding back.

The importance of the covenant—the idea that group identity is something you choose rather than something that "happens to you"—is reflected in Judaism in the annual telling of the Exodus story at the Passover seder. The emphasis in this Passover ritual is on the children. They must be told the story so that they may elect to enter the covenant. Being born into it is not good enough, for being born into things is also something that "happens" to people. It is not something they choose, and for people to be bound by any commitments, they must have freely chosen them. Of course, the Exodus story is told in such a way that each new generation of Jews is made to feel a part of an ongoing peoplehood, so that choosing to enter the covenant will seem clear and compelling. Nevertheless, it is a covenant and thus does require choice by all parties.

The significance of the idea of covenant, and of an Exodus-inspired commitment to the pursuit of justice and liberation, can also be seen in a modern Christian movement, inspired by what is known as the "theology of liberation," that has been transforming the Christian church throughout Latin America. Liberation theology is deeply rooted in faith. But it is also deeply rooted in covenant—in community. Both the word of God and the word of the priest require extensive discussion and interpretation for them to become a useful guide to daily life in the modern world. And the process of discussion and interpretation is a communal process. Sacred texts and doctrines become authoritative only as they are understood by the community. And in the reaching of understanding, all community members have a voice. Importantly, however, while community members are encouraged to participate in the interpretation of sacred texts, they are not free to make of their religion whatever they want as individuals. As members of communities of faith, they are bound by the understandings and the practices of those communities. Their identities are bound up with the identities of those communities. Their goals are bound up with the goals of those communities.

In general, the goal of those communities is to turn faith and religious and moral commitment into practice—practice that serves human liberation, human freedom. Their understanding of what freedom means, and what it requires, is different from our own, and thus requires some discussion. When we talk about freedom, we usually mean freedom *from* constraint—freedom to do what we want. When the faith communities of Latin America speak of freedom, they usually mean freedom to do what is good, and freedom to flourish as human beings. It is this kind of freedom that is embodied by the Exodus story, and also by many of the writings of Karl Marx—not the freedom to live without any commandments, but the freedom to live by just commandments; not the freedom to live without any regulations, but the freedom to live by regulations to which community members voluntarily assent.

In this conception of liberation, the point of freedom is not merely to encourage human choice but also to nurture human flourishing. And for people to flourish, several conditions must be met. First, bodily needs must be satisfied. People must have food to eat, clothing to wear, a place to live, and care and treatment when they are ill. Second, people must be able to act in the world in a way that permits them to use their intelligence to formulate and pursue worthy projects and plans. They must be able to work, and they must be able to work in a way that is meaningful. Third, people must be able to live as participating, contributing members of communities, communities whose projects and plans they have a role in shaping and pursuing. They must be able to express themselves freely in these communities, and they must be able to count on the willingness of other members of the community to try to understand them and take what they say seriously.

Human flourishing requires all of these things, and people are free only when they are able to flourish. A conception of freedom that is based on the nurturing of human flourishing leads to social and political policies that would be anathema to a conception of freedom based on the encouraging of individual choice. Typically, in communities inspired by the theology of liberation, there is an emphasis on communal rather than on individual values, on social control of the means of production so that everyone's needs can be met, and on opposition to those instruments of control that allow some to exercise power over others. Each of these facets of social policy can restrict the choices of individuals rather than enhance them. People are not free to pursue whatever values they want, they are not free to do whatever they want with the resources they own, and they are not free to dominate and use other people. So while in communities like these everyone has a voice and everyone's voice is taken seriously—both in interpreting the word of God and in deciding on the practices of daily life—it is not true that "everything is permitted." It is understood by all that people's responsibilities to one another and to the community as a whole take precedence over their individual desires and choices.

This may seem like an extremely restrictive way to live, an invitation to a kind of tyranny of the majority, in which people are forced repeatedly to give up their individual prerogatives. And for people who grow up totally immersed in the language of individualism, it may actually *be* an extremely restrictive way to live. But for many of those who live in the small urban neighborhoods and rural peasant communities of Latin America, individualism isn't much to give up. For these people, a significant part of what they are as individuals is tied to their membership in their communities. For these people, the North American conception of freedom really is, as Kris Kristofferson said, "just another word for nothing left to lose." So what we might experience as a stark conflict between what we want and what our community wants will not be experienced in the same way by the Latin American community member. If community membership goes a long way toward defining people as individuals, then it will usually be true that what the community wants is, or becomes, what the individuals who compose it want.

Is it possible to create such communities in the United States? If so, need they be religious communities or can they be secular communities as well? Is it possible to pursue a vision of human liberation and human flourishing as a group that takes each of its members seriously, but at the same time expects them to make their individual desires and values responsive to the desires and values of the group? Or is the cultural background provided by America's first language so insistent and so dominant that people will recoil from any communal demands of this type? I don't know the answers to any of these questions. I believe that it would be a mistake to try simply to import the Latin American model wholesale into U.S. society. Any effort to build a significant community—religious or secular—must be based upon the religious and ethical traditions that already exist in a society, and must be responsive to the particular circumstances and particular problems that that society experiences. The religious liberation movements in Latin America are trying to adapt *their* religious traditions to *their* current social circumstances.

The problems that they face are not the same as the problems we face, and the obstacles to building communities that they must overcome are not the same as the obstacles that we must overcome. We must find a way to adapt and reconstruct *our* religious and ethical traditions to meet *our* problems. And doing this will not be easy.

●   ●

In offering a covenant to the Israelis, God made them a promise, or actually two promises. In return for their commitment, God would bring them "into a land flowing with milk and honey." In addition, God would make them "a kingdom of priests and a holy nation." But these promises were conditional, and they were connected. To have the milk and honey, and to be a holy nation, the recipients of God's promises had to earn them. They had live as a holy nation, to obey God's commandments. They had to live good and righteous lives. It was only for a "holy nation" that the promised land would fulfill its promise. In such a nation, there would be no oppression or domination of others, there would be no pharaohs, no kings. If the people failed to live up to God's commandments, if they failed to fulfill their end of the bargain, then neither would God fulfill the other end.

And of course, the people did fail. They pursued luxury, they worshiped idols, they oppressed the poor, they sought to dominate one another. They forgot that they had once been oppressed as slaves themselves. And when they failed, prophets rose up to remind them—of where they had been, what they had promised, and what they had become. The potential for oppression and domination is everywhere, and must be resisted at every opportunity. The ultimate lessons, then, of the Exodus story, according to Michael Walzer, are these:

> —first, that wherever you live, it is probably Egypt;
> —second, that there is a better place, a world more attractive, a promised land;
> —and third, that "the way to the land is through the wilderness." There is no way to get from here to there except by joining together and marching.

Even in our land of milk and honey, there is bondage. Even in our land of apparently limitless economic and political freedom, there is oppression. Even those who succeed in our land of opportunity seem trapped in Weber's iron cage. And just as "a people trained for generations in the house of bondage cannot cast off in an instant the effects of that training and become truly free," so too a people trained for generations to live in an iron cage cannot in an instant see the need and gather the strength to break through the bars. But, indeed, there seems to be no way to get from here to there except by joining together and marching, inspired by a moral vision that, whether religious or secular, is communal.

Credit: Danziger in
The Christian Science Monitor.
Copyright © TCSPS.

12

THE NAME OF THE GAME

I used to tell my students that the difference between economics and sociology is very simple. Economics is all about how people make choices. Sociology is all about why they don't have any choices to make.
                                                    —JAMES DUESENBERRY

Let me tell you a story. It's a true story, about an experience I had some ten years ago. The experience was quite trivial, but it changed my life. It happened at a softball game, and to understand it, you need to know a little bit about softball.

Imagine a situation in which there is a runner at first base, and one out. A ground ball is hit to the pitcher. The pitcher fields the ground ball and wheels around to second base. The idea is to try for a double play by throwing to second ahead of the runner arriving from first, and then having the throw relayed from second to first, in time to beat the batter. Typically, when a ball is hit up the middle of the diamond, the second baseman and the shortstop converge at second base. When the pitcher fields the ball and turns to throw, the proper play is to throw the ball to the shortstop. The shortstop is moving toward first base, while the second baseman is moving away from it. So the shortstop's momentum will carry him in the direction that the ball must be thrown, while the second baseman will have to stop, pivot, and then throw. The throw from second to first is much easier for the shortstop than for the second baseman.

Now, here's what happened. It was a gorgeous early fall morning in Boston—Red Sox town—and I had just begun a year's sabbatical

from teaching. I was pitching in a relaxed, mostly social, coed softball game. It was a game in which the participants played hard,
played by the rules, and wanted to win. But the game was largely an
excuse for some postadolescent fooling around in the sun. Winning
at all costs was not the idea. Players on opposing sides were courte-
ous, friendly, and careful to avoid doing anything that might risk
injury. There was one thing about the game that was notably more
serious than anything else. The women in the game did not want to
be patronized; they wanted to be treated by the men as full-fledged
competitors. No concessions were asked, and none, in general, were
given. I was not used to friendly, coed games like this. My own
softball experience had been on all-male, highly competitive teams.
But I hadn't had much trouble adjusting to the more casual atmosphere that dominated the games played by this particular group
of people.

So I was pitching, and there was one out and a runner on first. A
ground ball was hit to me. I fielded it cleanly and spun around to
begin the try for a double play. Both the shortstop, a man, and the
second baseman, a woman, were converging on second base to
receive my throw. I wound up to throw and then was stopped in my
tracks. Whom should I throw to? I knew, as I just told you, that the
"right" play was to throw to the shortstop. But I hesitated. Would
the woman understand that I was throwing to the shortstop (who
happened to be a man) because it was the right play? Or would she
think that I was excluding her and throwing to the man (who happened to be the shortstop) because he was more likely to catch it and
throw accurately on to first than she was? Would she think that I
regarded her as an obstacle to be avoided rather than as a teammate?
Did she know enough about the game to know what the right play
was? Or was she so touchy that she would be offended anyway?
What would she think of me? Would she think I was an enemy of
one of the major social movements of our time? Small wonder that
I hesitated, wrapped up as I was in this existential and moral crisis.

All of these questions washed over me in what couldn't have been
more than half a second. And I never answered them. To this day,
I don't know what I should have done. Not only that, but all during
my year off from teaching, as I worked on the book that I had gotten
the time off to write, the incident kept popping into my head. Why

had I been so indecisive? What was the right play? The more I thought about it, the less sure I was of the answer. Yes, I *knew* that the right play was to throw to the shortstop. But I slowly realized that the rightness of that choice depended on what I thought the game was that we were playing. If we were merely playing softball, then the shortstop should have gotten the throw. But we were playing more than softball. We were in the middle of a social movement, one that is struggling to eliminate certain well-established gender roles and replace them with a gender-neutral social orientation. And we were involved in a complex social interaction, in which the feelings and objectives of all participants were to be taken seriously. What's the right play in that kind of game?

When I finally threw the ball, I found an ingenious though unintended way out of my indecision. My agonized delay had forced me to rush my throw. So I "solved" my problem in deciding whether the second baseman or the shortstop should get the ball by throwing it to *neither* of them. I threw it three feet over both of their heads into centerfield. No double play. No single play. And that's no way to play at all. I was confused about what to do, and I screwed up.

This innocent, trivial experience of mine on the softball field a decade ago was the germ for this book. Many Americans—those unlucky enough to be born into circumstances of economic hardship and deprivation—face a life of continual scrambling to provide the necessities of life without much opportunity for choice. But I believe that among the lucky ones—the members of the privileged middle and upper classes—practically everybody faces situations just like this one almost every day. Repeatedly, people are forced to ask themselves what kind of game they are playing, and what the right play is in that kind of game. And a lot more rides on the answers to the versions of these questions people face in real life than just the completion of a double play.

What kind of game is being a student? Are the objectives of the student game to get the best grades possible? If so, a good student will find the easy courses, borrow (or buy or steal) other students' assignments, and ingratiate him or herself in every way possible with the relevant teachers. Are the objectives of the student game to prepare for a career that will be financially rewarding? Are they to prepare for a career that will be intellectually rewarding? Are they to prepare for a career that will serve the public? In any of these cases, a good student will map out a program that provides appropriate training, and then work hard to develop the skills necessary for success in that career. Or perhaps the objectives are not to *prepare* for a career at all, but simply to get the credentials that make it seem that you are prepared for a career. In this case, the good student will be one who substitutes form for substance, concentrating on looking good while doing little. Possibly, the objectives of the student game have nothing to do with careers, but instead involve becoming a knowledgeable, sensitive, compassionate, committed, ethical person who will be an informed and responsible citizen. The good student at this game will look very different from the good student at the other games. Today's confused eighteen-year-old must face simultaneously the challenge of being away from home, dealing with difficult roommates and demanding professors, and figuring out how he or she is supposed to be playing the college game. All together, this seems like quite a burden to have to bear.

What kind of game is being a businessperson? Are there any limits to what a businessperson should do in the service of corporate interests? If so, who sets the limits, and what are they? Should a businessperson be concerned about ethics and fairness? Should she seek to provide a good or service that the world genuinely needs. Should she be honest with her customers and clients? Or should she make whatever people will buy, tell them whatever she thinks they will believe, and break any law if she thinks she can get away with it?

What kind of game is being a spouse or a lover? To what extent are lovers supposed to submerge their own interests or desires to serve the interests or desires of their partners? At what point does devotion turn into subjugation? At what point does self-actualization turn into selfishness?

Finally, what kind of game is being a citizen? Are we obliged to be loyal to our country? Are there limits to these obligations? Is our public responsibility discharged when we vote, or are we required to do more?

Most of us are playing in several of these games simultaneously, and find ourselves trying to answer questions like these about each of them. For the world in which we "modern, enlightened, rational" people live is one in which the objectives and the rules of each of our games are very much up for grabs—more so now than ever before.

I use the words "modern", "enlightened", and "rational" deliberately, for our world of unsettled games is the product, perhaps the culmination, of several centuries worth of modernism, enlightenment, and rationality. For about three hundred years, we have gradually been throwing off the shackles of rigid social structure (by class, by race, by ethnicity, by religion, by gender), of authoritarian rule, and of dictatorial tradition. We have learned not to accept doing things in a certain way just because they have always been done in that way. We have learned not to accept doing things in a certain way because we are ordered to do them in that way or because others do them in that way. We have learned to celebrate our individual freedom and autonomy, perhaps to value it above all else. We have learned not only that we needn't accept the limits imposed on us by society but also that we needn't accept the limits imposed on us by nature. The development of science has taught us that if we're clever enough—open enough, rational enough—we can understand nature and that, if we understand it, we can master it, harness it, control it, and force it to do our bidding. We have come to believe that the power of the human mind and the individual will is such that, with suitable knowledge, determination, and discipline, everything is possible.

This long-standing love affair with modernity, enlightenment, and rationality has been true of the Western industrialized world in general, but it has been especially true of the United States. The worship of modernity, enlightenment, and rationality is built into our very foundations. As social critic Garry Wills points out, the Declaration of Independence, at least as understood by its principal architect, Thomas Jefferson, was not just about the independence of the colonies from England; it was about the independence of individuals from the various metaphorical Englands that restrained and hindered them in their pursuit of life, liberty, and happiness.

Although the exaltation of independence, autonomy, and freedom goes back to our very beginnings, embracing independence and freedom *in principle* does not lead automatically to embracing them *in practice*. Long after Jefferson wrote, and his colleagues and their descendants endorsed his manifesto of individual freedom, there were still slaves in the United States. The freedom of women was significantly restricted. So was the freedom of those who did not own property. Religious puritanism dominated the culture, legislating how people were to live their private lives. Traditional values, traditional institutions, and traditional practices imposed a tight rein on individual behavior. Though it was less true in the United States than in Europe, by and large, each new generation was expected to live where its parents lived, worship where its parents worshiped, work the way its parents worked, and raise its children the way it had been raised. Even as legal restraints on individuals were being removed, restraints imposed by social custom and religious doctrine remained. Although there were differences between generations, such differences tended to be small and subtle. Each new generation was better educated than its predecessors, and achieved greater material success. What for parents were often only dreams, for the children became realities. Importantly, though, parents' dreams and childrens' realities were usually the same.

There were, however, some people who did break dramatically with their traditional past. Slowly but surely, people left the small towns of their birth to make new lives for themselves in the rapidly industrializing cities. And with that, one after another traditional constraint on individual freedom weakened. People used their enlightenment-honed rationality to ask themselves whether traditional ways of doing things had any justification—any legitimacy. As they moved about in cities, people encountered others who did things a little differently, and so discovered that there were alternative ways of living, that their way of doing things was not the only way. With their confidence in rationality, in science, and in progress more generally, people came to believe that almost anything could be changed, and always for the better. And over the last few generations, the pace of change has accelerated and the domains of change have spread. Communities, cultural traditions, and social ties have grown steadily weaker. As they have weakened, so also have the boundaries on our freedom of choice. Nowadays, it is possible for individuals to experience degrees of freedom that their ancestors could not have imagined. Nowadays, it is possible, maybe even necessary, for individuals to make up the rules of games as they go along.

This book has illustrated the freedom that now exists in several of the most important domains of our lives. In most universities, people can study almost anything they want. In the world of work, many people are free to select and change their careers and to write their own job descriptions. Furthermore, there is increasing opportunity for people to enter occupations from which they were previously excluded for reasons of race, gender, religion, or class. In the family, people are free to marry or not, to have children early or late or not at all, to have open marriages or traditional ones, to have common-law marriages or legal ones, to have heterosexual partnerships or homosexual ones. People are free to terminate their marriages when they stop being satisfying, and to make a host of different arrangements afterward for taking care of their kids. People are free to move in and out of different religious affiliations and, within a particular religion, to shop around until they find a congregation that suits their individual tastes and desires. Certainly, there are still strong vestiges of traditional restraints that remain in all of these domains; as a result, many freedoms that exist for everyone in theory can't be realized by everyone in practice. But there is no question as to the direction in which things are moving. Every day it gets a little bit easier for individuals to do exactly what they want to do, and to live exactly as they want to live.

Obviously, all of this freedom from traditional constraint brought on by modernism is cause for celebration, particularly for those for whom traditional constraint was painful and oppressive. Traditional values and traditional practices are authoritarian; they tell people what to do. They are exclusionary; they deny many groups of people the opportunity to participate. They are inflexible; they are not completely open to argument about how they might be changed. Largely because traditions are authoritarian, exclusionary, and inflexible, modern Americans have fled from traditional institutions and values. Americans have chafed at being told what to do, at being told what is good for them. Traditions didn't merely *offer* order and structure to people's lives; they *insisted* on it. And to this inflexible insistence many Americans have said good riddance. It's much better to make up the rules of the games you play as you go along than to be forced to play those games by other people's rules—rules that don't seem to serve you and make no sense to you.

But we have seen a dark side to all this freedom from constraint and tradition, to all this emphasis on the individual as the maker of her own world, her own destiny. It leaves people frighteningly alone—indecisive about what to do and why, unsure of whom to trust and depend on, unprotected from the harsh misfortunes they may encounter. Modernity is a two-edged sword, a fundamental contradiction, for just on the other side of liberation sits chaos and terror. Poet W. B. Yeats probably had it right when he warned, "Things fall apart; the centre cannot hold; / mere anarchy is loosed upon the world. . . . The best lack all conviction, while the worst / are full of passionate intensity."

Thus there is a price for freedom—danger. There is a price for individualism—loneliness. There is a price for autonomy—vulnerability. And there is a price for enlightenment—uncertainty. There is a price for being able to change the rules of softball. You may not know what the new rules should be, and playing by new rules may ruin what was good when you played by the old ones.

And these prices can be very, very steep, for the significance of cultural traditions and social ties can scarcely be overestimated. We can be taught—sermonized—about what it means to be a good parent, a good doctor, a good businessperson, a good teacher, a good softball player, and the like. But we really learn what it means to be good in these roles by seeing how they are practiced by actual practitioners. No matter what we learn at business school in a course on business ethics, for example, our real education comes when we enter the world of business and see how business ethics are actually practiced—particularly in our modern era. Nothing taught in business school can withstand the lessons taught in the marketplace.

More generally, we have honest businesspeople only if honesty is actually valued in the practice of business. We have compassionate doctors only if compassion is valued in the practice of medicine. We have devoted parents and children only if devotion is valued in families. We have informed, responsible citizens only if such traits are valued in politics. The various practices that make up our lives as members of a culture establish and shape the goals, the values, the aspirations that we pursue and live by. Our culture's values are embodied in its practices and strengthened by them. These values tell us what the point of the culture's practices is. And the practices reinforce values by making us live in accord with them. We can't know how to play the game unless we know what the point of the game is. And we learn the point of the game by seeing how it has traditionally been played.

But inspired by the desire for unlimited freedom, and moved by the forces of modernity, we have created a culture in which individuals (at least those who can afford to) are free to decide for themselves what they will do and how they will do it. Our collective cultural response to the oppressiveness of tradition has been to reject it and to let each individual decide for her or himself what is valuable, and how valuable. What happens to the guiding role that practices play when people are allowed—even encouraged—in this way to make up the goals and rules of the games they play as they go along?

As an example of how extensive the freedom of modern life is, consider how the character of a college education has changed over the years. A century ago, a college curriculum entailed a rather fixed course of study. One of its principal goals was to educate people into their various ethical and civic traditions—to make them citizens with common values and aspirations. Often the capstone of a college education was a course in moral philosophy, taught to seniors by the college president. The aim of that course was to integrate the various fields of knowledge—the arts, literature, science, and religion—to which the students had been exposed. But, more important, it was to draw the implications of their college work for living a good life, both as an individual and as a member of society.

This is no longer true. There is no fixed program of study. There is no required course in the senior year. There is no attempt to teach people how they *should* live, for who is to say what a good life is? Professors teach what they know, and hope that somehow each of their students will turn these lessons into a personal vision of the good life. When "should" is removed from the public discourse, as it has been in the university, the appropriate goals of our social practices—our games—become unclear. It is "should" 's, after all, that tell us what it means to be a good lawyer, student, spouse, and citizen. A good lawyer, student, spouse, or citizen does what a lawyer, student, spouse, and citizen *should* do.

Virtually all universities embody—even celebrate—this modern view of liberal arts education. Teachers work hard to break down their students' unreflective suppositions about how things are. It takes them the better part of four years to succeed. But they do succeed. And when students come to their teachers asking what set of rules to what set of games should replace the ones they inherited from their families, their religious institutions, and their local communities—when students come asking, in effect, how they should live their lives—we teachers answer with a shrug of our collective shoulders. We answer with a shrug because we don't know. And we don't know as a matter of institutional principle. The modern university is a kind of intellectual shopping mall. It offers a wide array of different "goods" and allows, even encourages, students—the "customers"—to shop around until they find what they like. Individual customers are free to "purchase" whatever bundles of knowledge they want. The university provides whatever its customers demand. In some (rather prestigious) institutions, this shopping mall view has been carried to a ludicrous and even offensive extreme. In the first few weeks of classes, students sample the merchandise. They go to a class, stay ten minutes to see what the professor is like, and then walk out, often in the middle of the professor's sentence, to try another class. Students go into and out of classes just as shoppers go into and out of stores in a mall. "You've got ten minutes," the students seem to be saying, "to show me what you've got. So give it your best shot." In this way the university has substituted the ethic of individual choice for the ethic of intellectual tradition.

There is much that is good about the true liberalization of the liberal arts institution. The traditional values and traditional domains of knowledge and inquiry passed on from teachers to students were always constraining and often myopic. Interesting and important ideas, reflecting the values, insights, and concerns of people from different traditions and cultures, were systematically excluded from the university curriculum. The tastes and interests of idiosyncratic individual students were stifled and frustrated. In the modern university, each individual student is free to pursue almost any interest and cultivate almost any value, without having to be harnessed to what his intellectual ancestors thought was worth knowing and doing. But, as in other domains of life, this liberation comes at a high price. Students are left to make educational choices that will affect them for the rest of their lives without the intellectual resources to make those choices intelligently. Students find that each of their peers is studying something different, or studying the same thing for a different reason, or with different preparation, so it is hard to find a common language, a common background, and a common set of concepts from which to build a coherent and meaningful intellectual community. In the university, as elsewhere, the price of freedom, individualism, autonomy, and enlightenment can be loneliness, uncertainty, and danger.

If modernity carries with it the danger that "things fall apart; the centre cannot hold," where can people turn to protect themselves from the social chaos born of complete freedom? What can we appeal to to introduce a little bit of order, coordination, and stability into our lives? I'm reminded of a segment from the children's television program "Sesame Street," which I used to watch with my kids, in which the characters decide to have a picnic. Everyone is told to bring something. The big day arrives, and everyone does indeed bring something. The trouble is that everyone brings the *same* thing—potato salad. In a world that caters to the freedom and autonomy of individuals, how do we keep everybody from bringing potato salad? I compared the modern university to a shopping mall because the comparison points us to what has become the model for a solution to the problem of creating order and coordination in a modern world of free individual choice. That model is the marketplace. The "free" market allows each individual to pursue his or her own interests and values to the hilt, without regard to the wishes or the dictates of others, while still preserving a substantial amount of social order and coordination. It is the noncoercive substitute for tradition. As long as there is demand for things, enterprising individuals will find a way to supply those things—at a profit. And as long as anyone is free to be a supplier, competition will keep society productive and efficient and keep consumers from being deceived, overcharged, or otherwise manipulated.

When it first became a dominant social institution, the market offered people things—commodities. But, in response to the influence of modernity, it has been extended, at least metaphorically, into almost all corners of our lives. Our language is suffused with market terminology. The university is a "free marketplace of ideas." We "spend" time with our friends. Athletes who want to succeed must be willing to "pay the price" of rigorous training. We "invest" a great deal in our children. We enter into marriage "contracts." So long as these terms are just metaphors, I suppose they are fairly innocuous. But as we come to take the market increasingly seriously as an alternative to traditional ways of doing things—indeed, as the *only* alternative that produces social order while permitting individual freedom—the terms become less metaphorical. Can we "buy" ideas on the idea market and "own" them? Can we make up stories and present them as fact to anyone who is willing to "buy" (accept) them? In the real market, all's fair. Caveat emptor. If we can get people to buy hula hoops, ragged "new" designer jeans, or pet rocks, then why not? The only criterion for selling things is that someone be willing to buy them. But is that true of ideas as well? Should teachers tell students what they want to hear? Should doctors tell patients what they want to hear? The tradition of intellectual life has as its principal value the pursuit of truth—honesty, not flattery. A good idea is not good in the same way that a good breakfast cereal is. This distinction can be maintained, but only as long as the traditions and standards governing intellectual life are maintained. As the market metaphor grows less metaphorical, the distinction between buying ideas and buying cereal starts to vanish. A free marketplace of ideas, as fact rather than as metaphor, corrupts intellectual life. It undermines honesty, because the motive of the "seller" is not the truth but a sale.

And when we "spend" time with friends, what do we expect to purchase? Do we expect to get our "money's worth" out of each social engagement? Is time with a friend like a dinner at a restaurant? Do we ask ourselves if we're getting what we pay for? Do we abandon friends when better alternatives become available? Time *spent* with friends, as fact rather than metaphor, corrupts friendship. It undermines loyalty.

And what about our "investment" in our children and our "debt" to our parents? What kind of "return" do we expect here? Should we be constantly looking around for possible investments that might yield greater returns? Are there times when we should consider getting out, and either taking our profits or cutting our losses? Should we consider declaring filial "bankruptcy" and thus reducing the size of our debt?

Finally, what about the terms of our marriage "contract"? Is the contract a symbolic and spiritual bond, a public affirmation of enduring commitment, or is it just a deal? When the terms of the contract are not precisely met, should we take legal recourse? Should we always be on the lookout for a better deal?

We may all want to say that, *of course*, no one takes these market metaphors literally. Everyone knows that the rules of the game in the real market are different from the rules of the game in marriage, family life, friendship, and intellectual pursuit. But the examples throughout this book tell us differently. They tell us that along with the language of the market, people have increasingly adopted the practices of the market.

We all know how to behave in the market. The point of each transaction is to serve our interests. When we buy a stereo, we want our money's worth from *that* stereo. When we eat dinner out, we want our money's worth from *that* meal. It is small comfort to know when we make a purchase that it contributes to the well-being of the market system in general, making possible many future purchases, if this particular purchase is unsatisfactory. In contrast, we don't normally analyze a marriage, a friendship, or other social relations into a series of individual "purchases," and ask whether each social action has been appropriately compensated. What matters instead is a long-term assessment of the marriage or friendship as a whole. And this assessment involves our responsibilities as well as our satisfactions.

We don't assess marriages the way we assess dinners in restaurants, but we could. And as people start looking at their social relations as nothing but a series of exchanges, the norms that govern these social relations change to reflect this economic orientation. People start expecting, and guarding against the worst. They defend themselves against dishonesty, exploitation, and manipulation. They do so in friendships and in marriages just as they do so in the marketplace. The shopkeeper, after all, is pursuing *his* interests, not ours. And if we don't watch out, he'll take advantage. So also will the doctor, the lawyer, the teacher, the lover, the friend. Isn't that right? To believe otherwise is to be a naive romantic.

Furthermore, once we start using the language of the market to describe our nonmarket, social activities, it becomes easier and easier for us to trade off market, economic goods against nonmarket, social ones. When we ask ourselves whether we can "afford" to spend an evening with friends instead of finishing a legal brief or cultivating a new client, we are implicitly putting a price on our friendship. How else, after all, can we begin to answer the question? Several of my economist colleagues tell me that the single concept that is most difficult to convey to beginning economics students is the concept of *opportunity cost*. The opportunity cost of some activity is the gain that we would realize by doing something else. If working on a legal brief at night instead of being with friends would have gotten us a $500 bonus, then that $500 bonus forgone is the opportunity cost of our decision to be with friends. What the concept of opportunity cost does is put a literal price on everything we do. We could always work a little harder or a little longer. The "cost" for not doing so might be promotion, partnership in the firm, or even keeping our job at all. When we think in terms of opportunity costs, the impetus is always there for us to keep working. Lurking in the back of our minds is the likelihood that if we don't, surely someone else will.

Think about the pressure this puts on us all. Consider the young lawyer, who loves her work, but also wants to do other things in life, like raise a family. The lawyer thinks that fifty hours a week is dedication enough to the job. But the firm expects total commitment—eighty hours a week in the office and availability at all other times. Can the lawyer argue that such expectations are unreasonable? Can the lawyer suggest that people *shouldn't* be called upon to work so hard? Can the lawyer even say that such single-mindedness is a deformation of the human character? From what basis can such an argument be made? What stops the employers from translating a claim about what people *ought* and *ought not* to be doing into a mere statement of personal preference on the part of the lawyer. "You say that people shouldn't live this way," they respond. "But what you really mean is that *you* don't want to. Fine. *You* don't have to. You can work somewhere else, and we'll find someone to replace you who shares our values and our expectations." If the rules of the lawyering game are up to individuals, if there are no traditional or institutional constraints on what can reasonably be expected, there is really nothing the young lawyer can do but put in the time or leave the job.

The reason, I suspect, that economists have so much trouble teaching their students about opportunity costs is that the students don't naturally put a price on everything they do, and are inclined to resist the encouragement to do so. It reflects not a lack of understanding but a lack of agreement with the economists' way of looking at the world. Economists don't see it this way, because they regard opportunity costs simply as matters of *fact*. If you could earn a bonus by working on a brief, then, as a matter of fact, your night with friends cost $500. But opportunity costs are not matters of fact. While there is no doubt that a price *can* be put on everything, I believe it is very much up for debate whether a price *should* be put on everything. Indeed, I believe that there are severe consequences to becoming accustomed to thinking about our lives in terms of opportunity costs—to pricing all of our activities. The "opportunity cost" of thinking in terms of opportunity costs will be paid in the degradation of many forms of civilized, communal, social life. It will be paid in the degradation of all kinds of value except market value, the degradation of all kinds of goods except market goods, the degradation of all kinds of games except market games. This price for unlimited freedom is too steep a price to pay.

No one wants to give up the freedom and autonomy that modernity has brought. No one wants to give up the transformation of our material lives that the enlightenment commitment to rationality and science has brought. And even if we did want to give these things up, we couldn't. At this point in our social history, we have to figure out how to live with modernity, because we can certainly no longer live without it. But at the same time that we value modernity, we are beginning to see the need to find a way to balance the guidance and constraint of tradition with the chaos and openness of modernity. It's a very difficult challenge, like trying to balance a seesaw on the blade of a knife. Right now, we are hearing people from almost all corners of society asking what's become of traditional values and practices. What's become of honesty, loyalty, courage, patriotism, discipline, hard work, commitment to marriage and the family, or a pitcher who knows how to make the double play? Many of the people who ask these questions believe that, whereas their parents had too much of these things, their children have too little, and that this is a potential disaster for their kids and, ultimately, for society. The implication of such beliefs is that modernity has gone too far, that the wholesale abandonment of traditional values is a big mistake. It's a mistake because these values are good—good for the people who live by them and good for the people with whom they share a culture.

In this book, I have tried to show how our pursuit of individual freedom and our reliance on the marketplace as a device for catering to individual freedom have been excessive. I have tried to develop an analysis of the uncertainty and malaise of modern life that helps point the way to steps that can be taken to correct it. Those of you who hoped or expected to read this book and come away with a set of specific recommendations about how to transform your lives, recapture those traditional values worth recapturing, and thereby enrich yourselves and those you live with, while still maintaining freedom of choice in all domains where it really matters, may be disappointed. First, it is probably not possible to save, nurture, and strengthen what is good about traditional values and institutions without being willing to sacrifice a certain amount of individual freedom and autonomy. We simply can't have everything. And second, we cannot approach the future as an exercise in self-help. There are certainly some things that individuals can do to mitigate the conditions that result in the confusion and dissatisfaction they experience in their lives. Each of us can become a better person. But there are very real limits to what we can do as individuals. The price for being a good person in modern America is very steep. Without the encouragement and support of other people and, even more important, of the institutions that are most responsible for the fostering of traditional values, it may be too steep a price for us to expect anyone to pay. People may have been willing to support the major income-redistributive social welfare programs of the "Great Society" in the 1960s, because they were confident that everyone would be doing his part and that everyone's basic needs would be met. People were willing to make sacrifices for the common good so long as there was a social safety net to protect them. In contrast, in the mean-spirited 1980s, with the safety net full of holes and fast disappearing, people were resentful of efforts to provide for the common good at their expense. In the depression-like atmosphere of the 1990s, people will be even more resentful, unless their safety net of protective institutions is reconstructed. So, instead of reforming ourselves as individuals, we must as a group reform our institutions so that being a good person is less costly. This is a difficult task, one that may require a lifetime of commitment, but it is the only realistic way to succeed. And even if we are not around to enjoy the benefits of our social labors, at least we will have left a socially habitable world for our children and grandchildren.

Americans are not accustomed to arguments and discussions that focus on social structures or institutions as significant causal agents. We are much more comfortable focusing on individuals. When stockbrokers cheat, we throw them out and replace them with honest ones. When athletes use drugs, we throw them out and replace them with clean ones. When presidents lie, we throw them out and replace them with truthful ones. We keep looking for and replacing the bad apples, and rarely examine the tree. This book has examined the tree—our market-based society—and the responsibility it bears for the kinds of apples that have been growing.

I've been working with people about to embark on careers for twenty-five years now. I don't think I've ever met one whose ambition was to take over companies, cannibalize their assets, shut them down, and put people out of work, or to sell women birth control devices that would cause them serious, even fatal illnesses. I've never met one whose ambition was to produce automobiles that were safety hazards, or to expose employees to deadly carcinogens, or to reduce the costs of doing business by dumping poison in the community water supply, or to run a chemical company with unsafe plants in Third World countries that would explode and kill or deform thousands of people. I don't think I've ever met one whose ambition was to become a U.S. senator who sold votes for campaign contributions, or to achieve scientific fame and fortune by reporting fraudulent findings. I've never met anyone who *wanted* to do these things. Yet people do them, in what seems to be ever growing numbers. And as long as we focus on individuals, and attempt to reform their character, the supply of bad apples will continue unabated.

So this book has attempted to provide us with a framework for understanding and thus changing social life that appeals to factors considerably larger than the individual. It has tried to show what the real "costs of living" in modern society are—how the character of individuals is affected by the character of the social institutions and practices with which they live. And it has tried to show how the continued spread of economic objectives and tactics into domains of life that people have traditionally regarded as governed by other goals and rules are turning social life into a jungle. Economic imperialism must be stopped. And the way to stop it is to reduce the costs of living, to protect noneconomic domains of life from being turned into extensions of the market.

NOTES

Because this is not a scholarly work, a full bibliography is inappropriate. Instead, what I have done is gather references that should be both interesting and accessible to the general reader who wants to go beyond what is in this book. In addition to these references, I have provided full bibliographic information for each work mentioned in the book and for each quotation. The information is keyed to the page on which the reference or quotation appears.

CHAPTER 1: THE IRON CAGE

p. 17 M. Weber, *The Protestant Ethic and the Spirit of Capitalism* (1904) (New York: Scribners, 1958), p. 181.

p. 25 R. H. Tawney, *The Acquisitive Society* (New York: Harcourt, Brace, 1920), pp. 183–84.

CHAPTER 2: BUSINESS IS BUSINESS

p. 26 The source of this quotation is a friend, who could not track down its place of origin.

p. 31 P. Blumberg, *The Predatory Society* (New York: Oxford University Press, 1989).

p. 43 On the corporate excesses of the 1980s, see S. Bartlett, *The Money Machine: How KKR Manufactured Power and Profits* (New York: Warner, 1991); M. Mayer, *The Greatest Ever Bank Robbery: The Collapse of the Savings and Loan Industry* (New York: Scribners, 1990); S. Pizzo, M. Fricker, and P. Muolo, *Inside Job: The Looting of America's Savings and Loans* (New York: McGraw-Hill, 1991); and J. B. Stewart, *Den of Thieves* (New York: Simon & Schuster, 1991). For an extended journalistic account, see R. Sherrill, "S & Ls, Big Banks, and Other Triumphs of Capitalism," *The Nation*, November 19, 1990, pp. 589–623. And for a sampling of day-to-day journalism that provides a flavor of reactions to disclosures of wrongdoing as they were being uncovered, see W. Williams, "White Collar Crime: Booming Again," *New York Times*, June 9, 1984, sec. 3, pp. 1, 6; K. W. Arenson, "How Wall Street Bred Ivan Boesky," *New York Times*, November 23, 1986, sec. 3, pp. 1, 8; and S. Bartlett, "Curbing Excess on Wall Street," *New York Times*, December 25, 1988, sec. 3, pp. 1, 5.

p. 46   D. J. Ravenscraft and F. M. Scherer, *Mergers, Sell-offs, and Economic Efficiency* (Washington, D.C.: Brookings Institution, 1987). For a vivid example of a merger that went wrong, see M. Holland, *When the Machine Stopped* (Cambridge: Harvard Business School Press, 1989).

p. 47   A. D. Chandler, *Scale and Scope: The Dynamics of Industrial Capitalism* (Cambridge: Harvard University Press, 1990). See also L. Thurow, *Head to Head: The Coming Economic Battle among Japan, Europe, and America* (New York: Morrow, 1992).

p. 48   See Stewart, *Den of Thieves*.

p. 51   R. Mokhiber, *Corporate Crime and Violence: Big Business Power and the Abuse of the Public Trust* (New York: Sierra Club Books, 1988). On the space shuttle disaster, see the memoir of one of the key members of the commission that investigated it, R. P. Feynman, *What Do YOU Care What Other People Think: Further Adventures of a Curious Character* (New York: Norton, 1988).

p. 51   On the marketing of tobacco, see M. Mintz, "Marketing Tobacco to Children," *The Nation*, March 6, 1991, pp. 577, 591–96. On the World Bank memo, written by Lawrence Summers, see *The Economist*, February 8, 1992, p. 66, and *The Nation*, March 2, 1992, p. 257.

p. 51   For discussions of whistle-blowing and its consequences, see M. Glazer and P. Glazer, *The Whistle Blowers: Exposing Corruption in Government and Industry* (New York: Basic, 1989); D. Rasor, *The Pentagon Underground* (New York: Times Books, 1985); and, for an earlier view, C. Peters and T. Branch, *Blowing the Whistle: Dissent in the Public Interest* (New York: Praeger, 1972). For an annotated collection of further sources, see J. S. Bowman, F. A. Elliston, and P. Lockhard, *Professional Dissent: An Annotated Bibliography and Resource Guide* (New York: Garland, 1984).

CHAPTER 3: AND PROFESSIONS ARE BUSINESS TOO

p. 55 A. S. Relman, "The Health Care Industry: Where Is It Taking Us?" *New England Journal of Medicine* 325 (1991): 855; G. B. Shaw, *The Doctor's Dilemma*, preface.

p. 57 P. Starr, *The Social Transformation of American Medicine* (New York: Basic Books, 1982), p. 39 (much of my discussion of the development of medical practice in the United States is based on Starr's book). See B. Bledstein, *The Culture of Professionalism* (New York: Norton, 1976), for a discussion of the development of professionalization more generally.

p. 59 Starr, *Social Transformation*, p. 94.

p. 61 American Medical Association Principles of Medical Ethics, 1980.

p. 62 Starr, *Social Transformation*, p. 217.

p. 63 The statistics cited here and on the next few pages come from a special section of the *Journal of the American Medical Association* 265 (1991): 2491–576), which was devoted to a discussion of the skyrocketing of medical costs and what might be done to contain them.

p. 64 The changing role of medical insurance is discussed in Starr, *Social Transformation*, p. 260.

p. 66 See ibid., pp. 420–50, for a discussion of the history of HMOs, and Relman, "Health Care Industry," for a current perspective.

p. 67 Starr, *Social Transformation*, p. 436.

p. 69 For evidence on the fate of the uninsured in hospitals, see M. Gladwell, "Uninsured Fare Worse in Hospital," *Philadelphia Inquirer*, May 9, 1991, p. A1. For a discussion of competition for patients, see W. Bogdanitch and M. Waldholz, "Hospitals That Need Patients Pay Bounties for Doctors' Referrals," *Wall Street Journal*, February 27, 1989, pp. A1, A4.

Pp. 70–72 For a discussion of the growing dissatisfaction among physicians with medical practice, see a series in the *New York Times*: L. Altman and E. Rosenthal, "Changes in Medicine Bring Pain to Healing Profession" (February 18, 1990, pp. A1, A34–35); L. Belkin, "Many in Medicine Are Calling Rules a Professional Malaise" (February 19, 1990, pp. A1, A13); and G. Kolata, "Wariness Is Replacing Trust between Healer and Patient" (February 20, 1990, pp. A1, D15). For a discussion of the economic pressure induced by medical school debts, see C. Caruthers, "Ever-Mounting Medical School Debt Is Spurring Search for Solutions," *Physicians' Financial News*, January 30, 1991, pp. 1, 17.

p. 70 On self-referral, see A. S. Relman, "What Market Values Are Doing to Medicine," *The Atlantic*, March 1992, 99–106); and idem, " 'Self-referral'—What's at Stake," *New England Journal of Medicine* 327 (1992): 1522–24. For evidence on the negative medical and economic effects of self-referral, see J. M. Mitchell and J. H. Sunshine, "Consequences of Physicians' Ownership of Health Care Facilities—Joint Ventures in Radiation Therapy.," ibid., pp. 1497–501); and A. Swedlow, G. Johnson, N. Smithline, and A. Milstein, "Increased Costs and Rates of Use in the California Workers' Compensation System as a Result of Self-referral by Physicians," ibid., pp. 1502–6). The self-referral problem is also reported in W. Bogdanitch and M. Waldholz, "Doctor-Owned Labs Earn Lavish Profits in a Captive Market," *Wall Street Journal*, March 1, 1989, pp. A1, A9; and it is discussed in "When Doctors Own Their Own Labs," *New York Times*, August, 11, 1991, sec. 4, p. 11.

p. 70 Relman, "Health Care Industry," p. 859.

p. 71 D. Hilfiker, "A Doctor's View of Modern Medicine," *New York Times Magazine*, February 23, 1986, pp. 44–47, 58.

p. 72 Relman, "Health Care Industry," p. 859.

p. 74 This quotation appears in R. Jack and D. C. Jack, *Moral Vision and Professional Decisions: The Changing Values of Women and Men Lawyers* (New York: Cambridge University Press, 1989), p. 156. Much of my discussion of law in this chapter was informed by this book.

p. 75 S. Turow, *One L* (New York: Putnam, 1977); Jack and Jack, *Moral Vision*, p. 46.

p. 75 R. V. Stover, *Making It and Breaking It: The Fate of Public Interest Commitment during Law School* (Champaign: University of Illinois Press, 1989), p. 22; ibid., p. 49.

p. 76 Jack and Jack, *Moral Vision*, p. 29.

p. 76 Ibid., p. 30.

p. 76 Ibid.

p. 77 Ibid., p. 29.

p. 78 R. L. Abel, *American Lawyers* (New York: Oxford University Press, 1989), p. 97. See this book for detailed data from surveys of lawyers.

p. 79 A. Hochschild, *The Managed Heart* (Berkeley: University of California Press, 1983).

p. 81 The estimate of the number and percentage of lawyers comes from P. Blumberg, *The Predatory Society* (New York: Oxford University Press, 1989), p. 211.

p. 82 See R. A. Posner, *Economic Analysis of Law* (Boston: Little, Brown, 1986).

p. 83 Data on the percentage of female lawyers come from Jack and Jack, *Moral Vision*, p. 21.

p. 83 C. Gilligan, *In a Different Voice* (Cambridge: Harvard University Press, 1982).

p. 83 Jack and Jack, *Moral Vision*, p. 155.

CHAPTER 4: AND GAMES ARE BUSINESS TOO

p. 85 A. B. Giamatti, "Morality Strikes Out," *CBA Record*, February 1988, p. 20; P. Simon, "Mrs. Robinson" (New York: Paul Simon Music [BMI], 1967).

p. 86 S. Stout, "A Mom's Plea to a Ballplayer," *New York Times*, June 25, 1989, p. A31.

p. 90 Santayana's words are cited in R. A. Smith, *Sports and Freedom* (New York: Oxford University Press, 1988), p. 142.

p. 91 C. Lasch, *The Culture of Narcissism* (New York: Norton, 1978), pp. 122–23.

Pp. 96–102 For very recent discussions of the economics of modern baseball, see N. J. Sullivan, *The Diamond Revolution: The Prospects for Baseball after the Collapse of Its Ruling Class* (New York: St. Martin's, 1992); and A. Zimbalist, *Baseball and Billions: A Probing Look inside the Big Business of Our National Pastime* (New York: Basic, 1992). For a discussion of the incentives involved in moving sports teams from city to city, see C. C. Euchner, *Playing the Field* (Baltimore: Johns Hopkins University Press, 1993). For a more general discussion of modern sports, see R. Roberts and J. Olson, *Winning Is the Only Thing: Sports in America since 1945* (Baltimore: Johns Hopkins University Press, 1989).

p. 100 For discussions of amateur sports, see Smith, *Sports*, Roberts and Olson, *Winning*, and J. Dorschner, "College Sports: Fraud or Cesspool," *Philadelphia Inquirer Magazine*, October 15, 1989, pp. 16–17, 34–41.

p. 109 W. C. Rhoden, "Michigan State Coach Bothered by Ruling," *New York Times*, March 25, 1990, sec. 5, p. 5.

p. 110 The coments of this football player come from B. Moyers, "Sports for Sale" (produced and directed by Howard Weinberg, PBS, 1990).

CHAPTER 5: WHAT WE ARE AND WHAT WE VALUE

p. 114 F. Nietzsche, *The Gay Science* (1882), in *The Portable Nietzsche*, ed. W. Kaufmann (New York: Penguin, 1976).

p. 115 See A. Tversky and D. Kahneman, "The Framing of Decisions and the Psychology of Choice," *Science* 211 (1981): 453–58; D. Kahneman and A. Tversky, "Choices, Values, and Frames," *American Psychologist* 39 (1984): 341–50.

p. 121 D. Kahneman, J. L. Knetsch, and R. H. Thaler, "Fairness as a Constraint on Profit-Seeking: Entitlements in the Market," *American Economic Review* 76 (1986): 728–41.

p. 123 H. Kunreuther, "Comments on Platt and on Kahneman, Knetsch, and Thaler," *Journal of Business* 59 (1986): 329–38. For a related point, see R. Frank, T. Gilovich, and Dennis Regan, "Does Studying Economics Inhibit Cooperation?" *Journal of Economic Perspectives* 3 (1993): 111–25.

p. 128 T. Hobbes, *Leviathan* (1651).

p. 130 A. Smith, *The Wealth of Nations* (1776) (New York: Modern Library, 1937). For a clear, elementary discussion of the foundations of economics, see C. Dyke, *Philosophy of Economics* (Englewood Cliffs, N.J.: Prentice-Hall, 1981). A somewhat more sophisticated discussion can be found in M. Hollis and E. Nell, *Rational Economic Man* (Cambridge: Cambridge University Press, 1975). For still more sophistication, see T. Koopmans, *Three Essays on the State of Economic Science* (New York: McGraw-Hill, 1957). A very readable account of the history of economic thought is R. L. Heilbroner, *The Worldly Philosophers*, 5th ed. (New York: Simon & Schuster, 1980). Another historical story, on how the notion of "interest" was born, is told by A. O. Hirschman, *The Passions and the Interests* (Princeton: Princeton University Press, 1977). For a discussion of the application of economic principles to the whole range of human concerns and activities, see G. Becker, *The Economic Approach to Human Behavior* (Chicago: University of Chicago Press, 1976).

p. 130 C. Darwin, *The Origin of Species* (1859). Three nontechnical accounts of the new evolutionary biology worth reading are R. Dawkins, *The Selfish Gene* (Oxford: Oxford University Press, 1976); D. Barasch, *The Whisperings Within* (New York: Harper & Row, 1979); and E. O. Wilson, *On Human Nature* (Cambridge: Harvard University Press, 1978). More technical discussions are Wilson's *Sociobiology* (Cambridge: Harvard University Press, 1975), which started it all, and Barasch's *Sociobiology and Behavior*, 2d ed. (New York: Elsevier, 1982). A good account of the origins of Darwinian theory is M. Ruse, *The Darwinian Revolution* (Chicago: University of Chicago Press, 1979).

p. 131 A. Tennyson, "In Memoriam A.H.H." (1849); M. Ghiselin, *The Economy of Nature and the Evolution of Sex* (Berkeley: University of California Press, 1976), p. 247.

p. 131 For a sophisticated but readable discussion of the fundamental assumptions, commitments, and principles of behavior theory, there is no substitute for reading B. F. Skinner, the intellectual leader of the discipline. In *Science and Human Behavior* (New York: Macmillan, 1953), he presents the basic principles in nontechnical language and extrapolates them to countless situations in daily life. In *Beyond Freedom and Dignity* (New York: Knopf, 1971), he presents a challenging alternative to our everyday conception of human nature that follows from the fundamental principles of behavior theory. In *About Behaviorism* (New York: Knopf, 1974), he discusses the methodological commitments that behavior theory makes in striving to attain a science of human nature. For discussions of basic principles and applications of behavior theory that are more up-to-date and detailed than Skinner's, see B. Schwartz and H. Lacey, *Behaviorism, Science, and Human Nature* (New York: Norton, 1982); or, for a more sophisticated treatment, B. Schwartz, *Psychology of Learning and Behavior*, 3d ed. (New York: Norton, 1989). For a discussion that focuses on what the disciplines of economics, evolutionary biology, and behavior theory have in common, see B. Schwartz, *The Battle for Human Nature* (New York: Norton, 1986).

p. 132 J. J. Rousseau, *The Social Contract* (1762) (London: Penguin, 1968), p. 7; A. N. de Condorcet, *Sketch for a Historical Picture of the Progress of the Human Mind* (1793) (Westport, Conn.: Hyperion Press, 1979), p. 4; and W. Godwin, *Enquiry Concerning Political Justice* (1793) (Toronto: University of Toronto Press, 1969), vol. 2, pp. 193, 313, vol. 1, pp. 434–35.

p. 132 J. S. Mill, *Utilitarianism* (1863), in his *Collected Works* (Toronto: University of Toronto Press, 1969), vol. 10, p. 215. These quotations from Condorcet, Godwin, and Mill, and others that make a similar point, appear in T. Sowell, *A Conflict of Visions* (New York: Morrow, 1987).

p. 133 For a discussion of Jefferson's views about human nature, see G. Wills, *Inventing America: Jefferson's Declaration of Independence* (New York: Doubleday, 1978). For discussions of Marx's conception, see Sowell, *Conflict of Visions*, and M. Berman, *All That Is Solid Melts into Air* (New York: Simon & Schuster, 1982). Berman's book focuses on the challenge that the political and cultural freedoms of modernity have posed for the maintenance of a solid, coherent set of social practices that connects the present to the past.

Pp. 134–137 For a more extended discussion of the difference between scientific and everyday conceptions of human nature, see Schwartz, *Battle for Human Nature*.

p. 145 For evidence on the importance of autonomy and control for human well-being, see M. E. P. Seligman, *Helplessness* (San Francisco: W. H. Freeman, 1975) and *Learned Optimism* (New York: Knopf, 1992).

p. 146 See J. Q. Wilson, *The Moral Sense* (New York: Free Press, 1993).

p. 149 A. O. Hirschman, *Exit, Voice, and Loyalty* (Cambridge: Harvard University Press, 1970).

CHAPTER 6: CONSUMED BY CONSUMPTION

p. 153 Plato, *Phaedo* (New York: Liveright, 1927), p. 52; K. Marx, *The Poverty of Philosophy* (London: Lawrence & Wishart, 1955), p. 29.

p. 155 T. Scitovsky, *The Joyless Economy* (Oxford: Oxford University Press, 1976).

p. 155 R. L. Solomon, "The Opponent Process Theory of Acquired Motivation," *American Psychologist* 35 (1980): 691–12.

p. 159 A. O. Hirschman, *Shifting Involvements* (Princeton: Princeton University Press, 1982).

p. 160 There is a growing movement in the psychotherapeutic community to treat excessive consumption—thing addiction—as a form of pathology to be treated. See C. Perez, *Getting Off the Merry-Go-Round* (New York: Simon & Schuster, 1990).

p. 163 R. Easterlin, "Does Economic Growth Improve the Human Lot? Some Empirical Evidence," in *Nations and Households in Economic Growth: Essays in Honor of Moses Abramowitz*, ed. P. David and M. Reder (Palo Alto: Stanford University Press, 1973), 96–122.

p. 164 R. Frank, *Choosing the Right Pond* (New York: Oxford University Press, 1985).

p. 167 F. Hirsch, *Social Limits to Growth* (Cambridge: Harvard University Press, 1976).

p. 168 L. Thurow, *The Zero-Sum Society* (New York: Basic, 1980).

p. 170 G. Hardin, "The Tragedy of the Commons," *Science* 162 (1968): 1243–48; see B. Schwartz, *The Battle for Human Nature* (New York: Norton, 1986), chap. 9, for discussion of many of the points raised in the remainder of this chapter, and see M. Olson, *The Logic of Collective Action* (Cambridge: Harvard University Press, 1965), for a more general discussion of the logic by which the pursuit of individual interests fails to secure the collective interest, and may even interfere with it.

p. 172 T. C. Schelling, *Micromotives and Macrobehavior* (New York: Norton, 1978).

p. 176 For a discussion of contemporary bankruptcy filings, see K. Delaney, *Strategic Bankruptcy* (New York: Morrow, 1990); and D. Henwood, "Behind the Bankruptcy Boom," *The Nation*, October 5, 1992, pp. 345, 360–64.

p. 177 A. Smith, *The Theory of Moral Sentiments* (1753) (Oxford: Clarendon Press, 1976), pp. 124–25. For a recent similar argument, in modern theoretical dress, see R. H. Frank, *Passions within Reason* (New York: Norton, 1988).

p. 178 The idea of economic imperialism is developed in detail in Hirsch, *Social Limits*.

p. 179 A. Sen, "Rational Fools," *Philosophy and Public Affairs* 6 (1976): 317–44.

p. 181 A. MacIntyre, *After Virtue* (South Bend: University of Notre Dame Press, 1981). See also J. Stout, *Ethics after Babel* (Boston: Beacon Press, 1988).

p. 185 For a discussion of the commercialization of social relations, see Hirsch, *Social Limits*; for a discussion of the commercialization of feeling, see A. Hochschild, *The Managed Heart* (Berkeley: University of California Press, 1983).

p. 186 J. B. Schor, "Americans Work Too Hard," *New York Times*, July 25, 1991, p. A31; and see her *The Overworked American* (New York: Basic, 1991).

p. 186 Hirsch, *Social Limits*, p. 88.

CHAPTER 7: ECONOMIZING ON LOVE

p. 193 G. García Marquez, *Love in the Time of Cholera* (New York: Knopf, 1988), p. 224; A. Hochschild, *The Second Shift* (New York: Viking, 1989), p. 11; and D. H. Robertson, "What Does the Economist Economize?" in his *Economic Commentaries* (London: Staples, 1956).

p. 194 A. Smith, *The Wealth of Nations*, p. 14.

p. 195 See A. O. Hirschman, *The Passions and the Interests* (Princeton: Princeton University Press, 1977).

p. 196 D. Goleman, "Psychologists Pursue the Irrational Aspects of Love," *New York Times*, July 22, 1986, C1, C8. For the most thorough economic analysis of intimate relations, see G. Becker, *A Treatise on the Family* (Cambridge: Harvard University Press, 1981); and idem, *The Economic Analysis of Human Behavior* (Chicago: University of Chicago Press, 1976). For some supporting data, see G. Becker, E. M. Landes, and R. Michael, "An Economic Analysis of Marital Instability," *Journal of Political Economy* 85 (1977): 1141–87. For similar perspectives in other social sciences, see P. Blau, *Exchange and Power in Social Life* (New York: Wiley, 1964); G. Homans, *Social Behavior* (New York: Harcourt, Brace and World, 1961); and E. Walster, G. W. Walster, and E. Berscheid, *Equity: Theory and Research* (Rockleigh, N.J.: Allyn and Bacon, 1978). For a critical discussion of these views and a persuasive alternative, see R. H. Frank, *Passions within Reason* (New York: Norton, 1988).

p. 197 R. Sternberg, "A Triangular Theory of Love," *Psychological Review* 93 (1986): 119–35.

p. 200 Aristotle, *Nicomachean Ethics*.

p. 207 M. S. Clark and J. Mills, "Interpersonal Attraction in Exchange and Communal Relationships," *Journal of Personality and Social Psychology* 37 (1979): 12–24.

p. 209 F. Hirsch, *Social Limits to Growth* (Cambridge: Harvard University Press, 1976); Hochschild, *Second Shift*.

p. 210 Hochschild, *Second Shift*, p. 11. An important and in some respects similar argument about how the character of intimate social relations is affected by societywide economic relations was made many years ago by psychoanalyst Erich Fromm in *The Art of Loving* (New York: Harper and Row, 1956).

p. 215 On the importance of intentions—of doing things for the right reasons—see J. Baron, "Utility, Exchange, and Commensurability," *Journal of Thought* 23 (1988): 111–31. For persuasive suggestions about some of the mechanisms that influence people to do things for the right reasons, see Frank, *Passions within Reason*; Hirsch, *Social Limits*, p. 88.

p. 216 For an interesting argument about just how recent (and perhaps temporary) an invention the "nurturing family" bound by "romantic love" is, see A. Skolnick, *Embattled Paradise* (New York: Basic, 1991).

p. 219 Philosopher Virginia Held has made a challenging argument that a democratic society like ours might not be so badly served if some of the care and concern that govern relations within families were imported into the state. See her "Mothering versus Contract," in *Beyond Self-Interest*, ed. J. Mansbridge (Chicago: University of Chicago Press, 1990), pp. 287–304.

p. 221 A. Smith, *The Theory of Moral Sentiments* (Oxford: Clarendon Press, 1976).

p. 222 A. de Tocqueville, *Democracy in America* (1835–40) (New York: Doubleday, 1969).

CHAPTER 8: THE "DEMEANING" OF WORK

p. 225 A. Camus, cited in J. O'Toole, *Work in America* (Cambridge: MIT Press, 1973), p. 186; B. Springsteen, in *Rolling Stone*, December 6, 1984, pp. 18–22, 70.

p. 226 For a recent discussion of work motivation, see E. A. Locke and G. P. Latham, *A Theory of Goal Setting and Task Performance* (Englewood Cliffs, N.J.: Prentice-Hall, 1990). On the small-business owner's nonmaximizing decision to keep at his business, see J. Fallows, "What Can Save the Economy?" *New York Review of Books*, April 23, 1992, pp. 12–17.

p. 238 K. Polanyi, *The Great Transformation* (New York: Rinehart, 1944), pp. 43–44; E. J. Hobsbawm, *Labouring Men* (London: Weidenfeld and Nicholson, 1964).

p. 240 F. W. Taylor, *Principles of Scientific Management* (1911) (New

York: Norton, 1967). For more detailed discussion, see B. Schwartz, R. Schuldenfrei, and H. Lacey, "Operant Psychology as Factory Psychology," *Behaviorism* 6 (1978): 229–54.

p. 241 P. J. Kilborn, "Workers Using Computers Find a Supervisor Inside," *New York Times*, December 23, 1990, pp. A1, A18.

p. 241 S. Marglin, "What Do Bosses Do?" in *Division of Labour*, ed. A. Gorz (London: Harvester, 1976), 13–54.

p. 242 Smith, *Wealth of Nations*, pp. 4–5.

p. 242 On the ratio of managers to workers, see S. Bowles, D. M. Gordon, and T. E. Weisskopf, "An Economic Strategy for Progressives," *The Nation*, February 10, 1992, pp. 145, 163–65. On the difference between U.S. and Japanese factories in the range of tasks required of each worker, see R. E. Cole, *Work, Mobility and Participation: A Comparative Study of American and Japanese Industry* (Berkeley: University of California Press, 1979).

p. 243 Smith, *Wealth of Nations*, pp. 734–35. On the proportion of the U.S. workforce devoted to policing the work of others, see Bowles, Gordon, and Weisskopf, "Economic Strategy."

p. 244 Marglin, "What Do Bosses Do?" pp. 38–39.

p. 247 M. Mayer, *The Greatest Ever Bank Robbery: The Collapse of the Savings and Loan Industry* (New York: Scribners, 1990); S. Pizzo, M. Fricker, and P. Muolo, *Inside Job: The Looting of America's Savings and Loans* (New York: McGraw-Hill, 1991); R. Sherrill, "S & Ls, Big Banks, and Other Triumphs of Capitalism" *The Nation*, November 19, 1990, pp. 589–623.

p. 249 For a review of some evidence on how worker managed firms perform, see D. R. Fusfeld, "Labor-Managed and Participatory Firms: A Review Article," *Journal of Economic Issues* 17 (1983): 769–89.

p. 251 For an argument about the need for worker-manager cooperation to produce a viable American economic future, see I. Bluestone and B. Bluestone, *Negotiating the Future: A Labor Perspective on American Business* (New York: Basic, 1993). The quotation is from Bowles, Gordon, and Weisskopf, "Economic Strategy," p. 165.

CHAPTER 9: THE DEBASING OF EDUCATION: TURNING PLAY INTO WORK

p. 254 For a thorough, up-to-date discussion of the empirical evidence regarding the use of rewards in schools, see A. Kohn, *Punished by Rewards* (Boston: Houghton Mifflin, 1993). In this book, Kohn argues not only that the use of rewards has the kind of unfortunate side effects I will be describing in this chapter but also that rewards are not even especially effective in producing the effects for which they are intended.

p. 254 For the study with nursery school children, see M. R. Lepper, D.

Greene, and R. E. Nisbett, "Undermining Children's Intrinsic Interest with Extrinsic Rewards: A Test of the "Overjustification" Hypothesis," *Journal of Personality and Social Psychology* 28 (1973): 129–37.

p. 258 National Commission on Excellence in Education, *A Nation at Risk* (Washington, D.C.: Government Printing Office, 1984).

p. 261 E. B. Fiske, "America's Test Mania," *New York Times Educational Supplement*, September 10, 1989, pp. 16–20.

p. 263 L. Mitgang, "Teachers Boost Test Scores by Cheating, Report Says," *Philadelphia Inquirer*, September 9, 1989, p. A5.

p. 266 See Kohn, *Punished by Rewards.*

p. 267 See E. Deci, *Intrinsic Motivation* (New York: Plenum, 1975); M. R. Lepper and D. Greene, eds., *The Hidden Costs of Reward* (Hillsdale, N.J.: Erlbaum, 1978); and, for the rule-finding experiments, B. Schwartz, "Reinforcement-Induced Behavioral Stereotypy: How Not to Teach People to Discover Rules," *Journal of Experimental Psychology: General* 111 (1982): 23–59; and idem, "The Creation and Destruction of Value," *American Psychologist* 45 (1990): 7–15.

p. 272 C. S. Dweck and E. L. Leggett, "A Social-Cognitive Approach to Motivation and Personality," *Psychological Review* 95 (1988): 256–73.

p. 276 For an illuminating discussion and analysis of the recent explosion in college costs, see E. Negin, "Why College Tuitions Are So High," *The Atlantic*, March 1993, pp. 32–34, 43–44.

p. 277 For a discussion of the dramatic changes occurring in the course selections and career plans of students, see B. Ehrenreich, *Fear of Falling* (New York: Harper Perennial, 1990), pp. 209–14; and L. Menand, "What Are Universities For?" *Harper's*, December 1991, pp. 47–56.

p. 279 For reports on the growing frequency of cheating, see C. H. Deutsch, "Cheating: Alive and Flourishing," *New York Times Educational Supplement*, September 10, 1989, pp. 26–30; and G. Galles, "Psst Kid, Wanna Buy a Term Paper?" *Christian Science Monitor*, September 25, 1989, p. 19. And for an alarming case report of rampant cheating among the very best students at an elite high school in Pittsburgh, see G. Putka, "A Cheating Epidemic at a Top High School Teaches Sad Lessons," *Wall Street Journal*, June 29, 1992, pp. A1, A4–A5.

CHAPTER 10: THE SELLING OF DEMOCRACY:
PUBLIC LIFE AND PRIVATE INTERESTS

p. 286 J. K. Galbraith, *The New Industrial State* (New York: Signet, 1960), p. 404.

p. 288 F. Hirsch, *Social Limits to Growth* (Cambridge: Harvard University Press, 1976). Much of the argument in this chapter is derived from this extraordinary and prescient book.

p. 288 R. Reich, "Corporation and Nation," *The Atlantic*, May 1988, pp. 76–81.

p. 290 J. Schumpeter, *Capitalism, Socialism, and Democracy* (London: Unwin University Books, 1942). For a discussion of the contemporary consequences of this view of democracy, see D. C. Bennett and K. E. Sharpe, "Is There a Democracy 'Overload'?" *Dissent*, Summer 1984, pp. 319–26.

p. 292 P. M. Stern, *The Best Congress Money Can Buy* (New York: Pantheon, 1988).

p. 294 A. O. Hirschman, *The Passions and the Interests* (Princeton: Princeton University Press, 1977).

p. 295 R. Reich, "Secession of the Successful." *New York Times Magazine*, January 20, 1991, p. 42; for a more complete discussion, see his *The Work of Nations* (New York: Knopf, 1991). The data on public and private school attendance in Los Angeles come from H. Meyerson, "Falling Down," *New Republic*, May 3, 1993, pp. 12–14.

p. 296 J. D. Donahue, *The Privatization Decision* (New York: Basic, 1989).

p. 298 Ibid., pp. 108–9.

p. 300 J. E. Chubb and T. M. Moe, *Politics, Markets, and America's Schools* (Washington, D.C.: Brookings Institution, 1990).

p. 301 Donahue, *Privatization Decision*, p. 89.

p. 302 Ibid., p. 30.

p. 303 M. Walzer, *Spheres of Justice* (New York: Basic, 1983). For conclusions similar to Walzer's, based on somewhat different arguments, see Jane Jacobs, *Systems of Survival: A Dialogue on the Moral Foundations of Commerce and Politics* (New York: Random House, 1993).

p. 304 M. Kaus, *The End of Equality* (New York: Basic, 1992). The case of Pullman, Illinois, is discussed by Walzer in *Spheres of Justice*.

p. 307 R. A. Rankin, "Workers Losing Privacy, ACLU Says," *Philadelphia Inquirer*, December 19, 1990, p. 7A.

p. 312 G. Wood, *The Radicalism of the American Revolution* (New York: Knopf, 1992).

p. 313 R. Frost, "The Death of the Hired Man" (1914).

p. 313 R. N. Bellah, R. Madsen, W. M. Sullivan, A. Swidler, and S. M. Tipton, *Habits of the Heart* (Berkeley: University of California Press, 1985); A. de Tocqueville, *Democracy in America* (New York: Doubleday, 1969), p. 292.

p. 314 G. Blonston, "The American Dream," *Philadelphia Inquirer*, September 13, 1992, pp. C1, C3; R. S. Boyd, "A Widespread Unease on Nation's Future," ibid.

p. 315 For discussions of the social and political role of the black church in American history, see V. Harding, *Hope and History* (New York: Orbis Books, 1990); G. S. Wilmore, *Black Religion and Black Radicalism* (New York: Anchor Press, 1973); J. Winthrop, "A Model of Christian Charity" (1630); and J. Dewey, "Ethical Principles Underlying Education," in J. Dewey, *Early Works*, ed. J. A. Boydston, vol. 5 (Carbondale: Southern Illinois University Press, 1969), p. 62.

CHAPTER 11: FROM PROFITS TO PROPHETS

p. 317 G. Orwell, cited in A. Kazin, "Not One of Us," *New York Review of Books*, May 16, 1984, p. 15.

p. 320 See J. R. Washington, *Black Religion* (Boston: Beacon Press, 1964); G. Gutierrez, *A Theory of Liberation: History, Politics, and Salvation*, trans. C. Inda and J. Eagleson (Maryknoll, N.Y.: Orbis, 1973); and P. Lernoux, *People of God* (New York: Penguin, 1989).

p. 320 G. Tinder, "Can We Be Good without God?" *The Atlantic*, December 1989, p. 69; see also idem, *The Political Meaning of Christianity: An Interpretation* (New Orleans: Louisiana State University Press, 1989).

p. 324 The quotes from Dostoevsky are taken from Tinder, "Can We Be Good without God?"

p. 325 Ibid., p. 84.

p. 338 J. M. Cuddihy, *No Offense* (Boston: Beacon Press, 1978).

p. 342 M. Walzer, *Exodus and Revolution* (New York: Basic, 1984), p. 76.

p. 343 See Gutierrez, *Theory of Liberation*; and Lernoux, *People of God*. See also J. S. Croatto, *Exodus: A Hermeneutics of Freedom*, trans. S. Attanasio (Maryknoll, N.Y.: Orbis, 1981); and P. Berryman, *The Religious Roots of Rebellion* (Maryknoll, N.Y.: Orbis, 1984).

p. 346 Walzer, *Exodus and Revolution*, p. 149; Ahad Ha-Am, *Selected Essays of Ahad Ha-Am*, trans. L. Simon (New York: Atheneum, 1970), p. 320, cited ibid., p. 137.

CHAPTER 12: THE NAME OF THE GAME

p. 349 J. S. Duesenberry, "Comment on Becker's 'An Economic Analysis of Fertility,'" in *Demographic and Economic Change in Developed Countries* (a conference of the Universities–National Bureau Committee for Economic Research) (Princeton: Princeton University Press, 1960), p. 233.

p. 353 G. Wills, *Inventing America: Jefferson's Declaration of Independence* (New York: Doubleday, 1978).

p. 356 W. B. Yeats, "The Second Coming" (1919). The contradictory nature of modernity has been discussed by many writers, notable among them Daniel Bell, in *The Cultural Contradictions of Capitalism* (New York, Basic, 1975), Marshall Berman, in *All That Is Solid Melts into Air* (New York: Simon & Schuster, 1982), and Christopher Lasch, in *The True and Only Heaven* (New York: Norton, 1991). And the contradictoriness has been apparent for some time. Karl Marx, for example, at the same time that he celebrated a revolutionary consciousness that would break the bonds of feudalism, patriarchy, and exploitation and permit individual growth and self-realization, so that "in place of the old bourgeois society, with its classes and class antagonisms, we will have an association in which the free development of each will be the condition for the free development of all," also observed that it would produce "uninterrupted disturbance of all social relations, everlasting uncertainty and agitation," adding, "All fixed, fast-frozen relationships . . . are swept away, all new-formed ones become antiquated before they can ossify. All that is solid melts into air, all that is holy is profaned." K. Marx and F. Engels, *The Communist Manifesto* (1848), in *The Marx-Engels Reader*, cd. R. C. Tucker (New York: Norton, 1978), pp. 491, 476.

INDEX

,